Latino Politics *en Ciencia Política*

Latino Politics *en Ciencia Política*

The Search for Latino Identity and Racial Consciousness

Edited by Tony Affigne, Evelyn Hu-DeHart, and Marion Orr

NEW YORK UNIVERSITY PRESS
New York and London

NEW YORK UNIVERSITY PRESS
New York and London
www.nyupress.org

© 2014 by New York University
All rights reserved

References to Internet websites (URLs) were accurate at the time of writing.
Neither the author nor New York University Press is responsible for URLs
that may have expired or changed since the manuscript was prepared.

ISBN 978-0-8147-6379-7 (cl : alk paper)
ISBN 978-0-8147-6898-3 (pb : alk. paper)

For Library of Congress Cataloging-in-Publication data, please contact
the Library of Congress.

New York University Press books are printed on acid-free paper,
and their binding materials are chosen for strength and durability.
We strive to use environmentally responsible suppliers and materials
to the greatest extent possible in publishing our books.

Manufactured in the United States of America

c   10 9 8 7 6 5 4 3 2 1
p   10 9 8 7 6 5 4 3 2 1

Also available as an ebook

We dedicate this book to early pioneers of Latino political studies,
whose vision and perseverance made our own work possible

With our thanks

    Carlos H. Arce
    Rodolfo O. de la Garza
    Louis DeSipio
    Angelo Falcón
    F. Chris Garcia
    John A. García
    Ralph C. Guzmán
    Carol Hardy-Fanta
    Rodney E. Hero
    James Jennings
    Benjamin Márquez
    Carlos Muñoz, Jr.
    Harry P. Pachon
    Christine Marie Sierra
    Adaljiza Sosa-Riddell
    Maurilio Vigil
    Roberto E. Villarreal

Contents

Tables

Figures

Chapter Appendices

Foreword

Latino People, Politics, Communities, and Knowledge

JOHN A. GARCÍA

"How do you hold a moonbeam in your hand?" Although I am one who finds himself using musical metaphors far too often for others' tastes, the elusiveness and complexities involved in the examination of, and the directing of systematic queries and analyses about, political behavior in the Latino communities make it a daunting challenge, one that I have been pursuing for over forty years. Given my strong personal ties, I am privileged to have the opportunity to add a foreword to this collection of research pieces, based on the Latino National Survey and its New England spin-off. In this foreword, I will try to construct my comments and observations within the context of my personal and professional experiences, concentrating on the critical elements and dynamics integral to advancing our understanding of the Latino communities in the U.S. While building knowledge is central to more academically oriented endeavors, the knowledge generated is equally pertinent for its application in enhancing the well-being of Latinos.

The Social Sciences and Latinos

This volume's first chapter discusses the evolution of social science survey research, the inclusion of Latinos as respondents, and incorporating subject matter particular to Latino interests and concerns. While the contemporary social science community as well as broader media and advertising interests have directed more attention toward Latinos in recent years, Affigne's account of Latinos and social science research clearly indicates a very recent pattern of inclusion. The major social science surveys over the past thirty years were projects initiated by Latino scholars in the political science or other social science disciplines. The reporting of their findings is well documented in this book's first chapter, so I will not be commenting on that discussion.

An observation I would like to make is that the contemporary growth of surveys incorporating Latinos into the sampled respondents and/or as primary respondents continues to be influenced greatly by Latino social scientists. These recent surveys have some historical linkage with three major Latino political and social surveys (i.e., the National Chicano Survey, the Latino National Political Survey–LNPS, and the Latino National Survey–LNS), and it is clear that the absence of such collective efforts would have certainly delayed attention in this area. The rise of the Pew Hispanic Center (now known as the Hispanic Trends Project) had its origins with the partnership of the Kaiser Family Foundation, the *Washington Post*, and the Pew Foundation. At the same time, a small number of Latino social scientists met with Pew's sponsoring journalists and funders to discuss sampling challenges and substantive concerns, which must be considered in the conduct of survey research within Latino communities.

While my experience suggests strongly that the increased number and improved methodological training of Latino social scientists has been instrumental in creating Latino-inclusive surveys and interpreting their findings, a perennial debate continues to be about the comparative nature of survey design (i.e., whether a survey including Latinos must have a comparative sample of non-Latinos, or whether it is justifiable to have a survey of only Latinos). The edict of "compared to what" resonates among some scientists: that the significance of Latinos in American public life has real meaning when they are compared to other social groupings. For example, if one is studying minority group politics, is it necessary to design a survey which includes "majority" group members and other minority groups in addition to Latinos? In the case of the LNPS, comparing Latinos with non-Latinos (in the same communities from which the Latinos were selected) made possible within-group comparisons among people of Mexican, Cuban, and Puerto Rican origin as well as comparisons with non-Latinos living in proximity. Implicitly, acknowledging common political contexts in which different groups operate, while making visible any group-specific effects of such environments, was part of the LNPS design.

In contrast, planning for the LNS occurred against the backdrop of recent dramatic increases in the size, diversity, and complexity of the Latino population, sparking interest in a greater understanding of critical "internal" variations and commonalities within the "panethnic" group (i.e., national origin subgroups, nativity, language use, generational distance from the immigrant experience, established and new destination communities, etc.) and, thus, necessitating a Latino-specific sample. Clearly, the central objectives and organizing theoretical frameworks which guide any systematic study will determine the appropriate population from which survey respondents are selected. Recent, more extensive inclusion of Latino respondents signals recognition that Latino political behavior is being recognized as an important aspect of American political research.

Another recent example is the American National Election Study (ANES). While the ANES has been one of the longer-standing political surveys, its utility to examine the electoral behavior and attitudes of Latinos (and other minority communities) has been almost nonexistent until the 2008 study. For that year's study, a combination of growing interest by political science researchers, an open process for soliciting research foci and sample suggestions, and a team of principal co-investigators who study Latino and African American politics helped develop an expanded ANES (both in sufficient sample size of Latinos and African Americans and in question content applicable to these groups). In addition, the 2008 ANES instrument included a Spanish-language version for the first time. As I am one of the participants in this process, it is clear to me that our current ability to understand the Latino panethnic group, on the basis of social science survey endeavors, is attributable to the ever-present drive and persistent efforts, particularly by Latino scholars, to engage and promote systematic inclusion of Latino respondents and to expand the scope of content queries.

Are Latinos Distinctive, and If So, How?

An important underlying motivation to research Latino political behavior systematically, beyond the general imperatives of social science research, is to determine Latinos' distinctiveness. That is, are Latinos unique as a collective body in the American social fabric? Frequent characterization of Latinos as the fastest growing, and now largest, minority group intimates social changes and uncertain impacts on the sociocultural and political map of America. For example, with a fast rate of growth, Latinos are seen as perpetuating their "own" cultural traditions and practices (i.e., Spanish language persistence, more "traditional" familial values, residential concentrations, ties to home countries, etc.), which separate them from the American mainstream. All too often, being characterized as different evokes suspicion and fear that such perceived differences are dangerous and threatening.

Ironically, how well Latinos fit into American society is indicative of the complexity and variety within this panethnic aggregation. The concepts of race and ethnicity are intertwined so that meanings ascribed to national origin, culture, language, phenotypical traits, and minority group status are applied in complex ways, to persons from Latin America and the Iberian Peninsula. In trying to answer the question about the distinctiveness of Latinos, concepts such as community, commonalities, group status and identification, and social networks need to be measured and assessed. Even basic inquiries as to how persons ancestrally from Latin American nations, as well as individuals whose home has been the U.S. for multiple generations, see themselves, and who they identify themselves with, are essential. Basically, who are Latinos? And if they "exist" as a social category or grouping, what defines those group connections? This becomes the first order of business in trying to assess Latinos' distinctiveness in America.

This is not an easy task, since factors shaping the nature of any community presence, or limiting interactions within a community, must take into account such complexities as different historical presence and experiences in the U.S. (some groups were present even before this nation's formation), some degree of geographical separation, and relations with countries of origin. To some extent, assessing the depth of Latino distinctiveness may begin with intra- and intergroup examination among the national-origin groups that fall under the panethnic umbrella of *Latino*. Externally, one cannot overlook the role and impact of societal views and other groups in the U.S. and their perceptions, knowledge, stereotypes, and characterizations of Latinos. With this "external" dimension, an understanding of a sense of mutual community among Latinos can be both a function of the internal dynamics and how the "outside" world treats and views them.

So let us revisit the initial question posed in this section about determining Latinos as a distinctive group. One factor that can contribute to Latinos' distinctiveness is a sense of group affinity and affiliation. They share connections along a number of different dimensions such as language, cultural tradition and practices, social and economic status, and societal aggregation across national origin and generational "lines." It seems that for many observers, however, the distinctiveness query is directed primarily toward understanding collective views and actions that impact the sociopolitical system and its institutions. Do Latinos think similarly about pub-lic policies, political parties and candidates, and other forms of political behaviors? If Latinos are distinctive, what are the factors that create this "uniqueness," and to what degree are those factors necessary and sufficient? On the other hand, what if Latinos are *not* distinct from the broader American electorate? Does that then negate attention to, and discussion of, Latinos as a distinct political grouping? Obvi-ously, my short discussion points to a need for greater clarity in the way we think about, and describe, politically salient differences between Latinos and others. In fact, a growing body of research findings suggest that Latinos are distinctive in a number of ways but are less so in certain areas of policy. In addition, the context and/or situation Latinos finds themselves in affects how they respond. What are the sociopolitical triggers that guide their actions and attitudes? We have learned that whether Latinos appear as a distinctive group or not depends on which dimen-sions of group identity and behavior are examined, as well as individuals' degrees of engagement with public life, but in nearly all discussions, the extent of a Latino individual's community affinity and affiliation remains a central element.

Los Latinos and the American Character

One final point worth some discussion in this foreword lies with a prevalent charac-terization of Latinos in contemporary America. A significant contributor, to date, of Latinos' marked population growth has been international migration. I add the "to date" qualifier as it will be the native-born segment from which Latino growth will occur well into the future. Nevertheless, a popular characterization of Latinos is that of a primarily immigrant group. About two-fifths of all Latinos are foreign-born, and approximately one-third are naturalized citizens. In addition, of the estimated 8–10 million undocumented persons living in the U.S., about 70% are persons from Latin America. Clearly, this is a significant segment of the Latino community that is foreign-born, and the overall percentage of foreign-born persons in the U.S. from all over the world has reached record highs since the levels at the turn of the twen-tieth century.

As a result, concerns about the integration of newer populations, full assimila-tion into America's sociopolitical fabric, and allegiance to the American polity and all it stands for are the subject of much attention directed toward Latinos. Earlier research from the LNPS in the "Will the Real Americans Stand Up . . ." clearly indi-cates a strong congruence with foundational American values and beliefs among Latinos in 1989–1990. Subsequent research findings in more contemporary stud-ies indicate beliefs in opportunity, basic freedoms and rights, and civil liberties. Yet major suspicion and doubts have been posited by social scientists and organiza-tional leaders about the adequacy of "fit" of Latinos as loyal and "faithful" propo-nents of American democracy.

These "concerns" have been directed squarely at Latinos with a broad sweep that tends not to differentiate generational status in the U.S., extent of assimilation, English-language use and proficiency, and citizenship status. Resultant public poli-cies at the state and local level, under the rubric of public safety and law enforce-ment, have targeted undocumented persons, and Latinos specifically, concerning access to employment, housing, social services, public gatherings, legal rights and protections, and so on. Concomitantly, Latinos looking to the federal government for leadership and nonpunitive policies regarding immigration are finding very little responsiveness. Latinos have become the primary "target" of groups and political representatives in terms of policies and rhetoric. These more recent actions have added to the claims that Latinos are a distinctive group in the American polity.

In a post-9/11 America, issues of national identity and patriotism have produced a closing of the ranks with "We" and "They" categories. Ironically, at a time of twenty-first-century international dynamics, many nation-states are facing redefining notions of citizenship, nationality, and universal human rights. Developments like widespread international migration, dual citizenship, and transnationalism are producing new populations of "global" as well as national citizens. The significant growth of Latinos in the U.S. and increased globalization are providing major impetus to this reassessment of citizenship. Unfortunately, the major thrust of this reconsideration of citizenship and basic human rights and protections is directed toward more restrictive and punitive initiatives for a more limited notion of citizenship. Yet Latinos and others are providing the basis and dynamics to explore more productive and broader notions about citizenship in the twenty-first century. For example, at least nine Latin American nations allow expatriates to maintain their country-of-origin citizenship when they become U.S. citizens. In fact, the legislation that enables this situation results from expatriates' efforts to create such legislation in their home countries. Already, Latinos with dual citizenship can become engaged as civic and political participants in both political systems, as well as developing further skills to use in either context. This development illustrates the functioning of global citizens whereby there is congruence of one's interests and the political systems that affect the individual. When matters of national character and content are raised, the inclusion of Latinos as both affecting the meaning of such concepts and actively contributing to this discussion is essential.

Conclusion

As a longtime participant in social science research, and directing much of my attention and energy toward the understanding and analyses of Latinos in the U.S., I know that the availability of "good social science data" has been a real challenge of inclusion for Latino populations. As discussed by Affigne in chapter 1, the development of social science surveys began with sustained efforts to include Latinos as part of the "representative segment" of Americana, especially when trying to identify the thoughts, opinions, and behaviors of the general American populace. While it has been the case for more than a generation, there still remain some persistent issues relative to continued and consistent inclusion of Latinos in social science surveys. In addition, there is greater recognition of the utility of looking at the Latino community exclusively in light of the complexities and diversity within this broad panethnic aggregation.

The collection of research articles in this volume represents a diversity of trained research "eyes" utilizing two major contemporary social science surveys to explore a range of topics and questions that have a direct bearing on the condition, status, and dynamics of Latinos in the U.S. An added dimension is that the contributors represent the current generation of researchers who are building on the earlier efforts of a smaller and persistent cadre of Latino researchers. Thus, this cohort of scholars can provide additional theoretical formulations and calibrations, utilization of more powerful analytical techniques, and expansion of the scope of inquiry regarding Latinos and the American sociopolitical system. I would like to end this foreword with an important challenge to embrace the diversity and complexities associated with Latino communities and the realities that affect their lives. In doing so, researchers should not avoid the adversity and risks we sometimes face in conceptualizing, measuring, and analyzing, in a more complete and truthful manner, the sociopolitical phenomena that affect this community and the larger society.

Suggested Readings

Abrajano, Marisa A., and R. Michael Alvarez. *New Faces, New Voices: The Hispanic Electorate in America*. Princeton: Princeton University Press, 2010.

Beltrán, Cristina. *The Trouble with Unity: Latino Politics and the Creation of Identity*. New York: Oxford University Press, 2010.

Casellas, Jason. *Latino Representation in State Houses and Congress*. New York: Cambridge University Press, 2011.

Chavez, Leo. *The Latino Threat: Constructing Immigrants, Citizens, and the Nation*. Stanford: Stanford University Press, 2008.

Coll, Kathleen. *Remaking Citizenship: Latina Immigrants and New American Politics*. Stanford: Stanford University Press, 2010.

Espino, Rodolfo, David Leal, and Kenneth Meier. *Latino Politics: Identity, Mobilization, and Representation*. Charlottesville: University of Virginia Press, 2007.

Fraga, Luis, John A. García, Rodney Hero, Michael Jones-Correa, Valerie Martinez-Ebers, and Gary Segura. *Latino Lives in America: Making It Home*. Philadelphia: Temple University Press, 2010.

Garcia, F. Chris, and Gabriel R. Sanchez. *Hispanics and the U.S. Political System: Moving into the Mainstream*. Upper Saddle River, NJ: Prentice Hall, 2008.

García-Bedolla, Lisa. *Latino Politics*. Cambridge, UK: Polity, 2009.

Janoski, Thomas. *The Ironies of Citizenship: Naturalization and Integration in Industrialized Countries*. New York: Cambridge University Press, 2010.

Jimenez, Tomas. *Replenished Ethnicity: Mexican Americans, Immigration, and Identity*. Berkeley: University of California Press, 2009.

Lippard, Cameron D., and Charles A. Gallagher, eds. *Being Brown in Dixie: Race, Ethnicity, and Latino Immigration in the New South*. Boulder, CO: First Forum, 2010.

Ortiz, Vilma, and Edward Telles. *Generations of Exclusion: Mexican Americans, Assimilation, and Race*. New York: Russell Sage Foundation, 2009.

Pallares, Amalia, and Nilda Flores-Gonzalez, eds. *Marcha: Latino Chicago and the Immigrant Rights Movement*. Champaign: University of Illinois Press, 2010.

Acknowledgments

This book culminates a four-year collaborative effort, and we gratefully acknowledge all those people who have made its completion possible. Most importantly, we thank our seventeen authors, who have produced such richly empirical, thoroughly documented analyses of Latino political behavior. The findings they report in this book are from the Latino National Survey (LNS and LNS-NE, 2005–2008), the largest-ever survey of its kind, with 9,834 Latino respondents, sampled from Latino populations of twenty U.S. states and the District of Columbia. As you can imagine, the LNS data thus constituted an essential foundation for this entire volume.

Therefore we acknowledge a profound scholarly debt to Luis Fraga, John García, Gary Segura, Rodney Hero, Michael Jones Correa, and Valerie Martinez-Ebers—the LNS principal investigators. As soon as their research was complete, they made the entire dataset available to other researchers without cost or restrictions.[1] This open approach to data sharing reflects the best traditions of the political science discipline, and we thank the PIs for their generosity.

We also gratefully acknowledge the research grants we received from the Rhode Island Foundation (RIF) between 2007 and 2011, which provided crucial support for this edited volume, as well as for a national Latino political studies conference, precursor to this book, in 2009. In addition, the foundation's financial support allowed us to expand the original 2005–2006 LNS survey into New England, sending a second wave of LNS interviewers[2] into the field during 2007 and 2008, surveying large samples in Rhode Island,[3] Massachusetts, and Connecticut[4] (combined $n = 1,200$). With this New England supplement, the combined LNS sample ($n = 9,834$) constitutes one of the largest such datasets publicly available to scholars. For all of this, we gratefully acknowledge the leadership and grant-program staff at the Rhode Island Foundation, including Neil Steinberg, Anna Cano Morales, and Yvette Mendez.

The index for the book was compiled by Rosalind Fielder, reference and instruction librarian at Chicago State University. Professor Fielder is a specialist in political science, law, military science, and criminal justice, and we appreciate her skillful index design; it should help you find exactly what you need in our text.

Finally, we acknowledge excellent assistance by researchers Hongwei Xu, Flannery Patton, and Ulli Ryder at Brown University, and Johara Hall at Providence College. We drew inspiration and insights from other members of our LNS New England project team—José Itzigsohn, Matt García, Cynthia García Coll, and Jorge Elorza. And an effort like this one depends absolutely on efficient administrative support, provided in our case by Patricia Balsofiore and Andrea Casavant at Brown, and Emerald Lopes at Providence College. Their contributions were essential to this project. Many thanks to all.

Notes

1. Luis R. Fraga, John A. García, Rodney E. Hero, Michael Jones-Correa, Valerie Martinez-Ebers, and Gary Segura, *Latino National Survey (LNS), 2006* [Computer file], ICPSR20862-v4, Ann Arbor, MI: Inter-university Consortium for Political and Social Research [distributor], 2010-05-26, doi:10.3886/ICPSR20862.v4.

2. Evelyn Hu-DeHart, Matthew García, Cynthia García Coll, José Itzigsohn, Marion Orr, Tony Affigne, and Jorge Elorza, *Latino National Survey (LNS)—New England, 2006* [Computer file], ICPSR24502-v1, Ann Arbor, MI: Inter-university Consortium for Political and Social Research [distributor], 2009-06-04, doi:10.3886/ICPSR24502.v1.

3. See the report *Rhode Island Latinos—Debunking Myths and Uncovering Truths: Evidence from the New England Latino Survey*, by Evelyn Hu-DeHart, Matthew García, Cynthia García Coll, José Itzigsohn, Marion Orr, Tony Affigne, and Jorge Elorza, with Flannery Patton and Hongwei Xu (Providence, RI: Brown University, Center for the Study of Race and Ethnicity in America, 2009).

4. See the report *Connecticut Latinos: Evidence from the Connecticut Samples of the Latino National Survey—New England*, by Mark Abrahamson, Alexandra Alpert, Yazmin Garcia Trejo, Mark Overmyer-Velázquez, Werner Oyanadel, and Charles Robert Venator Santiago (Storrs: University of Connecticut, Roper Center for Public Opinion Research, 2010).

Introduction

TONY AFFIGNE, EVELYN HU-DEHART, AND MARION ORR

This book is a truly collaborative effort, allowing the final whole to be more than the sum of its initial parts. In a continuing spirit of cooperation, we now offer this book to scholars, students, policymakers, and community leaders, toward a better understanding of Latinos, in our nation's rapidly evolving plural society.

Our collection of original essays culminates the Latino National Survey–New England Extension project, which was generously funded by the Rhode Island Foundation. The book consists primarily of research papers first presented at our "National Conference on Latino Politics, Power, and Policy" held at Brown University in Providence, Rhode Island, during October 2009. These papers were then substantially revised and updated for publication. All of the conference presentations were original research using data from the Latino National Survey (2006), which, with a sample of 8,634 respondents, is the largest Latino-specific survey available to researchers and the general public. Six distinguished political scientists led the Latino National Survey project: Luis Fraga (University of Washington), John García (University of Michigan), Rodney Hero (University of California, Berkeley), Michael Jones-Correa (Cornell University), Valerie Martinez-Ebers (University of North Texas), and Gary Segura (Stanford University).

The New England project added 1,200 respondents surveyed in 2007 and 2008, from Latino populations in Rhode Island, Massachusetts, and Connecticut. Because the original LNS sampled from Latino populations of Washington, D.C., and seventeen states—Arizona, Arkansas, California, Colorado, Florida, Georgia, Illinois, Iowa, Nebraska, Nevada, New Jersey, New Mexico, New York, North Carolina, Texas, Virginia, and Washington—when the New England states were added, the cumulative sample of 9,834 had been drawn from a combined Latino population of nearly 40 million—a coverage area comprising 89.6% of all Latinos residing in the United States in 2006, including all of the states with the largest Latino populations (see table 1.2, "Sample Sizes—Latino National Survey/New England Extension, 2005–2008," in chapter 1).

The survey consisted of 165 question items, yielding 275 variables; some items were unique, while many others were adopted from widely used national surveys including the General Social Survey (GSS) and American National Election Study (ANES). The items addressed topics ranging from basic demographics to questions about local and national politics, religiosity, education, discrimination, race relations, level of integration and acculturation, and many more. The resulting data give us detailed and extensive insights into experiences, beliefs, and attitudes of Latinos across the nation, at a crucial moment in U.S. history and in the development of the national Latino political community. Respondents were offered the option of being interviewed in Spanish or English and were not queried directly about immigration status. For a detailed description of survey items, see appendix A, "The Latino National Survey Questionnaire," at the end of this book.

In addition to the LNS's broad national coverage and survey depth, it was also designed to facilitate comparison; at least 400 respondents were interviewed in each of eighteen subsamples, and for larger states, as many as 1,200—making possible a wide range of statistical comparisons across states and metropolitan areas, allowing researchers to identify contextualized variations in political attitudes, values, beliefs, and behaviors. It thus rectifies an important weakness of other national surveys, which have in effect oversampled more populous states and thus homogenized our picture of the Latino experience, as though Latino experiences in all states and regions were the same, making it harder for scholars to see important differences in state-level political cultures, opportunity structures, or social conditions. Additionally, the project's complex design captured a wide range of differences among Latinos' immigration histories, citizenship, national origins, gender, education, income, places of residence, population concentrations, and political affiliations, as well as state-level partisanship and institutional structures.

In sum, the Latino National Survey has provided a timely and much-needed empirical foundation for understanding a segment of the American population whose continued political incorporation is intimately tied to the future of the country, while also providing a substantially improved baseline for Latino attitudinal data, on which systematic policy analysis can rely and from which future scholars can build new theoretical understandings.

We in Rhode Island who led the New England extension of the national survey are grateful for the opportunity to add three distinctive states to the national dataset. Data for all twenty-one subsamples, and for both the national and New England surveys, are available to the public through the Resource Center for Minority Data (RCMD) of the Inter-university Consortium for Political and Social Research (ICPSR) at the University of Michigan. See appendix 1B, "Data Repositories and Datasets for Latino Political Studies (1979–2014)," in chapter 1, for links to datasets and documentation.

Plan of the Book

In chapter 1, Tony Affigne frames our authors' contributions, showing how today's scholars represent something of a third generation in the field, after earlier periods in formal political analysis (political science) which were characterized first by *exclusion* of Latino subjects before 1970. A second period from 1970 to 1998 represents a time of *emergence* for Latino political movements and for Latino political studies. And now, in the years since 1998, like the Latino political community itself, the study of Latino politics is experiencing a period of *empowerment*. The research chapters in this book, Affigne writes, reflect some of the best work from this new period, exploring questions about Latino identity (*latinidad*), the nature of Latino assimilation and community, racial identities, interminority relations, and more.

In chapter 2, Jessica Lavariega Monforti explores mechanisms for building a panethnic identity among Latinos. Once largely of Mexican and Puerto Rican descent, the Latino population in the U.S. is increasingly diverse. Latinos in the U.S. now have heritages from Cuba, Colombia, the Dominican Republic, Guatemala, and other Latin and Central American countries. Some earlier research suggested that the diversity among Latinos was one of the reasons why low levels of panethnicity existed among Latinos. Latinos living in the U.S. were more likely to identify with their nation of origin and/or ancestral home ("Mexican" or "Colombian") rather than embrace a panethnic identity. Results from the LNS show that this is changing, and more and more Latinos are now panethnic identifiers. In chapter 2, Lavariega Monforti systematically accounts for those factors that are critical in the process of Latinos developing a panethnic identity.

In chapter 3, Sarah Allen Gershon and Adrian Pantoja examine the controversial issue surrounding the relationship between transnational ties and Latino political incorporation in the U.S. Some critics of immigration argue that the ties that bind Latino immigrants to their home countries (e.g., visiting the home country, sending remittances, calling friends and relatives by telephone) inhibit the naturalization process and impede the incorporation of Latinos into American civic and political life. Utilizing a unique set of questions in the LNS about transnational activities, Gershon and Pantoja show that transnational ties influence Latino immigrants in different ways. For example, owning property in the home country decreases significantly the likelihood that a Latino immigrant will seek to become a U.S. citizen. However, Gershon and Pantoja's findings call into question the argument that transnational ties negatively influence the level of civic engagement in the U.S. In fact, Gershon and Pantoja's findings suggest that maintenance of transnational ties may positively influence the political incorporation process of Latino immigrants. Gershon and Pantoja show that immigrants from Latin America can maintain ties to their country of origin and simultaneously become incorporated into American political and civic life.

In chapter 4, Jessica Lavariega Monforti and Melissa Michelson provide a detailed empirical examination of political trust among Latinos. Political scientists have long argued that trust in government and government institutions is critical for functioning democracies. Since the 1970s, survey research has shown a considerable decline in the percentages of people who say that they have a high level of trust in government. Lavariega Monforti and Michelson report that recent surveys show that only about 5 percent of respondents in national surveys say that they trust the government "just about always." Latinos, however, are more trusting of government. Among respondents in the LNS, 12 percent reported that they could trust government "just about always." Lavariega Monforti and Michelson explore political trust among Latinos generally and within the various Latino subgroups. They show that increased trust in government is related to how Latinos are acculturated into a racialized subgroup and their level of linked fate with other Latinos. In other words, this research shows that for Latino immigrants, feelings of linked fate and a strong sense of community can serve as an antidote to political cynicism.

Before the LNS, we knew little about Latinos' stances on many of the key public policy issues facing the nation. In chapter 5, Regina Branton, Ana Franco, and Robert Wrinkle examine how acculturation and political knowledge influences

Latino attitudes across several public policy domains. Branton and her colleagues are able to provide these important insights because of the richness and range of the policy issues covered in the LNS. Their research shows important ways in which the level of political knowledge among Latinos mediates how acculturation influences Latino public opinion on education, abortion, same-sex marriage, immigration, and other policy matters. Branton, Franco, and Wrinkle's exploration of policy preferences among Latinos shows that acculturation matters. Their unique insight, however, is that political knowledge interacts with acculturation to influence Latino public opinion and the impact of the interaction varies across different policy domains.

In chapter 6, Heather Silber Mohamed explores the meaning of being an "American" to Latinos. The chapter examines differences in the boundaries of Americanism among individuals from distinct ancestral-origin subgroups, levels of integration, and regions of residence across the United States. Silber Mohamed measures how country of origin, place of resident, and acculturation into the U.S. shape whether or not Latinos perceive "American" to be an open category that they are able to be a part of. She finds, for example, that Latinos typically believe that speaking English is an important component of being American. Among the various Latino subgroups, Salvadorans have the most restrictive view of what it takes to be considered an American. This chapter provides researchers with a better understanding of the conditions under which Latino immigrants view "American" as an open or closed designation.

In chapter 7, Marion Orr, Domingo Morel, and Katrina Gamble make use of the New England extension of the LNS. They focus on the factors that predict whether or not Latinos in New England believe they have something in common with African Americans. A considerable amount of research focuses on competition between Blacks and Latinos. In this chapter, Orr, Morel, and Gamble, shift the focus from competition between Blacks and Latinos to political and economic commonality. Instead of analyzing potential hurdles to coalition building, this chapter helps us understand what contexts encourage coalition building. If Blacks and Latinos recognize that they are both politically and economically marginalized, they may decide to work together rather than fight over limited resources. Orr, Morel, and Gamble explore those factors that make Latinos more likely to believe they have something politically or economically in common with African Americans.

In chapter 8, Atiya Kai Stokes-Brown explores the ways in which racial identity influences Latino policy attitudes. Racial identity in the U.S. has typically been shaped along a Black-white paradigm. This racial paradigm is embedded in the nation's institutional structures. However, in the LNS, large majorities of Latinos responded that they consider themselves to be "some other race" than "Black" or "white." When asked to explain their "some other race" response, 75 percent identified "Latino" or "Hispanic" as their race. Stokes-Brown provides a broad overview of the controversial issues related to racial classification in the U.S. Using the responses from a unique set of questions in which LNS interviewers probed deeper into the respondents' self-identification, Stokes-Brown shows how racial identification shapes Latinos' opinions across of range of policy issues.

In chapter 9, Matt Barreto and Gabriel Sanchez expand the discussion of race by focusing on how variation in the state and local context influences Latinos' perceptions of group competition with African Americans. Barreto and Sanchez focus their analysis on Latinos in the South. As they note, the South has seen an explosion in the growth of the Latino population, creating new intergroup dynamics in a region in the country where group relations have largely been between Blacks and whites. Their work shows that nationally, Latinos tend to perceive that they are in competition more with other Latinos than with any other group. However, when the southern states are isolated, Latinos tend to perceive that Blacks are their nearest competitors. Barreto and Sanchez also note the significant role that having multiracial social networks plays in lowering Latinos' perceptions of group competition with African Americans and how Black population density influences Latinos' perceptions of group competition.

In chapter 10, Manny Avalos and Tony Affigne explore real-world lessons we should take from these research findings. Does it help us understand the 2012 elections, for example, to know how strongly, and for what reasons, individuals feel a sense of a panethnic (i.e., Latino or Hispanic) identity? Could the nation better navigate contentious immigration politics if it were widely understood that immigrants' home-country attachments have *countervailing* effects on their choice to pursue U.S. citizenship, with some transnational activities appearing to *promote* naturalization? Research questions like these, Avalos and Affigne argue, answered with empirical evidence and hypothesis testing, move students and scholars directly into the world of Latino communities, leaders, and political empowerment, armed with knowledge, separating political fact from fiction.

From one perspective, of course, that could be said to be the mission of the book itself: demonstrating the power of political analysis to inform our understanding of politics-in-the-world, showing how, when used properly, the rich LNS dataset —or any comparably robust social data—can educate as well as motivate, giving Latinos and others, but especially Latinos themselves, a clearer and more honest understanding of the Latino political condition, to better prepare ourselves and the nation for the challenging years ahead.

PART I

Latino Political Studies

The Latino Voice in Political Analysis, 1970–2014

From Exclusion to Empowerment

TONY AFFIGNE

During two decades of extraordinary growth—from 29 million Latinos in 1990, to more than 53 million today—the Latino population was frequently described as a "sleeping giant" in U.S. politics, with one observer after another hailing the imminent emergence of a powerful new voting bloc.[1] Until 2012, the moniker never really fit the facts, as Latino votes, while decisive in some states and metropolitan areas, never quite reached the point where they could be said to have determined the outcome in national elections. Now, however, pundits are not so sure. It may be that the giant has in fact awakened. In the elections of 2012, Latino communities expanded their share of the electorate and provided margins of victory for President Obama in the swing states of Ohio, Colorado, and Nevada, where more than 80% of Latinos voted for the president. Even before November 6, President Obama was crediting Latinos with his prospective victory. Nationally, 75% of Latino votes went to Obama (Barreto and Segura 2012). In addition to these national impacts, expanding populations have brought Latinos to a more powerful position in local, legislative, and statewide politics, across the country. Recent growth has been dramatic, as the Latino population grew by 43.9% between 2000 and 2010 and is expected to exceed 128 million by 2060 (U.S. Census Bureau 2012). Despite Latinos' long presence in U.S. society, and their importance in the nation's development, the political attitudes and behavior of Latinos have been of little interest to political science in the United States—until recently. None of the field's canonical work, for example, published between 1880 and 1980, gave any attention to Latinos at all, and only in 1970 did the first book devoted to Latino political affairs appear in print. In this chapter, lead editor Tony Affigne frames our contributors' work in the context of real-world Latino politics and within the political science subfield of Latino political studies.*

A New Role for Latinos in U.S. Politics

Just before winning reelection in 2012, President Barack Obama, the nation's first-ever African American president, told an Iowa newspaper that "a big reason" he expected to win a second term was his strong support among the nation's growing and politically energized Latino electorate.[2] As it turns out, President Obama was correct. With victories in key states that year (for example, in Colorado, New Mexico, Florida, and Nevada), Obama did owe his reelection, at least in part, to extraordinary support among Latino voters.

In fact, the Latino Decisions research group reported that an unprecedented 75% of Latino voters had cast ballots for Obama, leaving only 23% for Republican Mitt Romney—a dismal showing, especially when compared to George W. Bush's

* All chapter introductions are written by Tony Affigne.

reported 44% Latino vote share in 2004.[3] The 2012 Latino electorate's turnout for Obama ranked second only to African Americans (93% in exit polling)[4]—a lop-sided result explained in part by Latino voters' distaste for the Republican candidate, who famously suggested that harsh immigration policy could work by compelling immigrants (primarily Latinos) to "self-deport."[5] For his part, Romney apparently had seen the handwriting on the wall; he was recorded on a secret video six months before the election, telling wealthy Republican donors that "we're in trouble as a party" if Latinos become "as committed to the Democrats as the African American voting bloc has [been]."[6]

Romney's anxiety was well founded. We now know that in 2012 Latino voters in Colorado supported Obama by a margin of 87%–10%, approaching the very high levels of Democratic partisanship generally associated with the African American electorate.[7] Latino voters shaped the outcome of other major elections in 2012 as well, including the senatorial race in New Mexico, where Democrat Martin Heinrich, winning by just 5.6%, enjoyed a 77%–22% margin among Latino voters, a net advantage amounting to 21.8% of his total vote.[8] Thus, like Senators Harry Reid of Nevada and Michael Bennett of Colorado, whose 2010 victories were built on over-whelming support among Latinos, Heinrich owes a significant political debt to his state's Latino voters.[9] In 2011, Reid acknowledged to a Las Vegas audience, "I would not be the majority leader in the United States Senate today, but for the Hispanics in Nevada."[10]

Within days of the 2012 election, many Republicans had come to share Reid's assessment of the Latino electorate's growing power. Amid fierce criticism of Republicans' paltry Latino turnout, some party leaders dumped years of anti-immigrant rhetoric and signaled new openness to immigration reform. House Speaker John Boehner (R-OH) was among those with a newfound taste for Latino interests. In a widely reported account, under the headline "Obama's Big Hispanic Win Worries Republicans," Speaker Boehner told ABC News two days after the election that the immigration issue "has been around too long" and that a "comprehensive approach is long overdue."[11] Not surprisingly, newly elected Senator Heinrich quickly adopted his own proactive position on immigration reform, in his first month in Washington calling for a path to citizenship which is not "insurmountable" for currently undocumented immigrants.[12] Moreover, it is not just federal policy which is likely to change in coming years, as the Latino emergence continues apace. Beyond helping non-Latinos win office, Latino candidates themselves have been increasing their numbers, political influence, and seniority in state legislatures as well as in Congress. More than 5,900 Latinos/as currently serve in elected office, as do more than 10,500 African Americans and about 3,000 Asian Pacific Americans.[13] Because of coming demographic changes, these numbers are likely to or, more precisely, will *inevitably* grow.

Over the next three decades, in fact, Latino, Black, Asian American, and Native American electorates are all expected to increase dramatically in size. In late 2012, estimates from the Pew Hispanic Center were projecting a *doubling* of the Latino electorate by 2030.[14] A few weeks later, the Census Bureau released projections that the white population may peak in 2024 and then begin to fall, while by 2043 the steadily growing combined minority populations will surpass 50%, reaching an estimated 57% of the U.S. population by 2060.[15] It should not be surprising, then, that American popular culture, political pundits, candidates and parties, and—at long last—scholars of mainstream politics have turned their attention to the story of the nation's 53 million Hispanics.[16]

Will Latinos continue to assimilate into U.S. society, or will their growing numbers make preservation of a dualistic (Anglo/Latino) national culture possible? Are Latinos like other "minorities," or have Spanish-descent cultures, and immigration experiences, created distinct political goals and interests which are not shared with African Americans, Asian Pacific Americans, or Native Americans? In our nation's racially ordered politics, are Latinos likely to side with African Americans, Asians, and American Indians—or with whites? Since their forebears hail from twenty different national and colonial cultures, is it even possible for Latinos to think and behave as a single, cohesive community, or will they fracture into smaller groups, each with its own political interests, alliances, leadership, and strategies? In the chapters to follow, these and other questions will be explored. Before you examine those studies, however, it may be helpful to know some background about the field of Latino political studies—how the field developed and where we are right now— to better understand both the importance of the research reported in this book and how new work fits into the larger discipline of political science.

Today, research in Latino political studies can be classified into eight broad subfields. These include the areas of Latino *political behavior*; *racial consciousness, linked fate, and interminority relations*; *identity and social theory*; *gender and intersectionality*; *representation and leadership*; *media and political communication*; *immigration, citizenship, and transnationalism*; and *political history and social movements*. An estimated 139 books were published in these eight subfields between 1970 and 2014 —with at least 36 appearing in the five-year period 2010–2014 (see appendix 1A). While not large compared to the eight or nine *thousand* titles published since 1970 about all other aspects of American politics, this is nonetheless a substantial canon of work and a solid foundation for contemporary research.[17] You might be wondering, however, why I am using *1970* as a starting point for a count of Latino politics books. The answer is both simple and profoundly disturbing.

One Hundred Years of Exclusion

In short, the answer is this: it is impossible to count books that do not exist! Until recently, mainstream political scientists had little interest in studying Latinos; before 1970, there was no interest at all, and *not a single book* was published anywhere in the United States in which the political behavior, policy interests, or political leadership of the nation's Latino population were the subject. How can this be true? After all, we who practice the craft of political science generally assume that our efforts have value precisely because we make *objective*, *evidence-based*, and *relevant* insights available to the public, in hopes of improving the quality and wisdom of public discourse, the practice of democracy, and the direction of public policy. What then could be at all "scientific" about ignoring millions of citizens, when we analyze American national, state, or urban political life? After all, even in the early 1960s, when immigration policy still barred nearly all Mexican and other Latin

American immigrants, there were already more than 8 million Mexican Americans and Puerto Ricans living in the country, *as citizens or legal residents*.[18] Ideally, our discipline's professional standards encourage us to produce work as free as it can be of racial, ethnic, gender, partisan, ideological, or other biases, any of which would weaken our claim to objectivity. We aspire to systematic observation of the world *as it is*, by gathering evidence which we and others can evaluate for relevance and test for accuracy; by favoring facts over opinions; by using variables we can measure, more often than others which are intangible or imprecise; and, in the tradition of open, replicable scientific research, by making our evidence available for others to recalculate, evaluate, and critique. We favor logical arguments, tracing cause and effect as accurately and dispassionately as possible, so that fair-minded observers would agree, given the supporting evidence, that our conclusions are valid and, insofar as possible, a reflection of political reality. You will perhaps recognize this account of our method, and our ethics, as falling squarely within the broad tradition of positivist scientific method.

In that tradition, a political science researcher hopes to generate useful, valid, and "true" statements about the nature of political beliefs, institutions, and practices, by testing hypotheses with evidence and making claims which are justified in light of the evidence. Unfortunately, positivist political science has never been that simple, nor as successful as we might hope. In fact, the long history of positivism also parallels, to an unfortunate degree, the history of scientific racism and institutionalized bias. Scientists in every discipline, not just ours, have proven perfectly capable of poisoning scholarly work with ideological, cultural, and social prejudice. Most commonly in the social sciences, such biases manifest themselves in the researcher's choice of subject; anathema topics are simply ignored. At other times, the evidence cannot support claims and conclusions advanced by the practitioner. Instead, preconceptions about what is normal, and what is to be expected, encourage the reporting of findings which are not actually confirmed by the evidence. One reason this might happen is that data which could best answer the research question simply *do not exist*. At other times, the analysis stretches the limits of available data or is applied inappropriately. In short, our scientific method can fail—with predictably dire political consequences—because we have chosen a research question which misses the mark, tried to force conclusions from partial or nonexistent data, or allowed our presumptions about what we *should* find to color interpretations of what we *did* find. Is it possible that the systematic exclusion of Latino politics, comparable to what Hanes Walton called the "invisible politics" of African Americans, is the result of such failures in the application of science?[19] Or is the scientific method itself at fault?

Well, let us consider the history. The first political science department in the United States was at Columbia University in 1880, while the American Political Science Association was founded in 1903. Both were born at a time when Jim Crow racism was in full force. In this context, few (white) scholars devoted much thought to the politics of disenfranchised Black, Mexican, Puerto Rican, Chinese, or American Indian communities.[20] Eventually, however, the civil rights movements which jolted American society in the late twentieth century, overturning centuries of explicit white supremacy, led to profound changes in scholarly standards as well.

These changes were slow in coming, but by the late 1960s, they attracted new attention to our communities, making possible for the first time books like 1970's *The Mexican American People* and its successors—including the one in your hands—whose subjects have been the politics of the nation's "people of color," "minorities," or more precisely its African-, Latino-, Asian-, and Indigenous-descent people.[21]

After more than twenty years of introducing students to these questions, I have learned that for many of them, some common reactions, upon discovering the exclusion of minority subjects from scholarly narratives about U.S. politics, are to assume that the numbers of people involved were not large, or that their politics were underdeveloped, were adequately addressed in the general discussion of (white) politics, or were simply not significant for the life and development of the nation. A little reflection, however, makes clear that these assumptions are wrong, that there is in fact a puzzle to be solved here. Why have the political lives of millions of non-white people been so thoroughly marginalized within the formal study of American politics? How could it possibly be the case that political opinions of disenfranchised people would be identical to those who enjoy the full fruits of citizenship and social privilege? Could understanding the interests and behaviors of white Americans alone, despite the obvious contributions of other groups to the national project, truly be sufficient? After all, over 300 years and more, a large proportion of the African American population in the U.S. served as the primary agricultural and domestic labor force in the southern states, first as enslaved captives, then as indentured sharecroppers. Many Mexican Americans in the West and Southwest filled similar social and economic roles, a positioning for both groups which was characterized by extreme poverty and exclusion from full political and human rights.[22] Despite the centrality of the "Black question" (seen, for example, in struggles over slavery and the Civil War) and the "Mexican question" (in the development of southwestern and western land, industry, and agriculture), it took a very long time for political science to discover and begin to correct its own exclusionary traditions, in which epic political struggles by people of color were deemed unworthy of consideration.

In truth, Latinos—people who trace their lineage to, or are themselves immigrants from, the former colonies of the Spanish empire in the Americas—have been part of U.S. history since the very earliest Spanish settlers, beginning with the arrival of Cristóbal Colón (Christopher Columbus) himself. Contemporary political discourse in the U.S., especially around immigration policy and enforcement, reinforces the presumed *otherness* of Latinos, yet descendants of the Spanish colonial world in the Americas have not all been immigrants and outsiders. In reality, several hundred thousand Mexican citizens became citizens of the United States in 1848, with the end of the "Mexican-American War," when northern México was ceded to the U.S. in the Treaty of Guadalupe Hidalgo—delivering much of what are now modern-day California, Nevada, Arizona, New Mexico, Texas, Colorado, and Utah to the United States. Fifty years later in 1898, the Treaty of Paris settled accounts from the "Spanish-American War," obliging Spain to give the U.S. its colonies of Puerto Rico, Cuba, and the Philippines. While Cuba achieved self-rule shortly afterward, nearly one million Puerto Ricans found their nation permanently annexed to the United States and, since 1917, their citizenship securely annexed as well. By any honest reading of history, national development in the United States has been closely tied to the Caribbean, México, Central America, and South America, since the earliest days of European colonization. The region's linked fate can be seen throughout U.S. history, from the slaveholding plantation era, which gave rise to the Triangle Trade, through modern decades of banana dictatorship, *campesino* rebellion, and insurgency (including revolution in Cuba), to the present, in which U.S. Latinos' Latin American home countries represent powerful national interests in regional trade politics and in mass labor migration (i.e., "immigration"), two areas of perennial policy conflict in U.S. electoral competition, elsewhere in U.S. domestic politics, and in regional diplomacy. Despite this importance, the politics of Latinos in the U.S. have been poorly studied and poorly understood, for most of the life of the political science discipline.

The scholarly enterprise we call the *analysis* of political behavior—using principles of the scientific method to study politics—dates to the 1920s. For example, Charles Merriam and Harold Gosnell used survey methods to identify political behaviors and their correlates among social indicators, to explain the phenomenon of nonvoting in Chicago (in their 1924 book *Non-Voting*). Their work, and the research of V. O. Key, Jr., over the following three decades (reported in *Politics, Parties, and Pressure Groups*, 1942), did identify racial differences; in both analyses, Black ("Negro") voters were less likely to participate in elections, and less likely to feel attached to local political systems, than their white counterparts. Yet very shortly, other scholars, notably Seymour Martin Lipset in 1960 (in *Political Man*), found it possible to conduct major studies of political behavior without estimating any racial differences at all. In the path-breaking *The American Voter* (1960), based on national surveys during the 1952 and 1956 elections, Angus Campbell, Philip Converse, Warren Miller, and Donald Stokes did analyze electoral participation for "Negro" voters—and, like Key before them, were forthright about the impact of both legal and extralegal impediments to Black voting—but made no effort to include or explain the political behaviors of Latinos, even though the country's Mexican American population was already large and the Puerto Rican population, especially in New York City, was significant. A decade later, Sidney Verba, Norman Nie, and Jae-On Kim conducted a seven-nation study of political participation (*Participation and Political Equality*, published in 1978), and they also found it scientifically valid to analyze U.S. politics without *any* data whatsoever for the nation's millions of Latinos—despite the book's framing as a study of comparative political equality! When in 1960 E. E. Schattschneider published *The Semisovereign People*, as sharp a critique of U.S. democracy as mainstream political scientists had by then produced, he devoted no more than a handful of sentences to the peculiarly *un*democratic location of "Negroes" and "severely repressed minorities" but apparently saw no reason to expand on the nature of racially structured political exclusion, nor to give Mexicans and Puerto Ricans even passing mention.[23]

From examples like these, it would appear that from the 1930s to the 1970s, much of U.S. political analysis based on "large-*N*" behavioral datasets should be recognized for what it actually was: a massively detailed—but racially distorted—picture of the American polity. Where racial exclusion was most severe, and thus where social science might have had its greatest positive impact—in the segregated South—the forcible suppression of Black electorates meant candidates and policymakers had little reason to care about (or fear) attitudes of the region's Black voters. Researchers consequently had few reasons of their own to solicit difficult-to-obtain responses from Black southerners, and only began to do so routinely when the civil rights movement made continued "whites-only" analysis intellectually suspect.[24] Similarly, few social scientists of this period were Spanish-speaking, and even fewer were Latinos who might have crafted research models using personal understanding of the vernacular, the characteristics of Latino political cultures, and the pervasive sense of exclusion which characterized popular Latino political thought.[25] Doing so might have tapped distinctive patterns of belief and aspiration among Latino populations in large areas of the United States, especially in the old Southwest. It is hard not to conclude, then, that during the early decades of modern social analysis, the landmark voting behavior studies in political science that empirically tested some of the discipline's most important social science theories were, in effect, tabulating the *white* population's political and social beliefs, treating many millions of minority citizens either as uninteresting or as lacking in sufficient influence, both individually and collectively, to make their views central either for social science or in the national political discourse. In other words, social science datasets of the time mirrored precisely the social and political exclusion of the nation's Black, Latino, and other minority populations, which was typical of the era's real-world political conditions. This was, after all, the time of Jim Crow segregation, blackface entertainment, lynchings, and voter suppression; it was also the time of anti-Mexican vigilantism across the Southwest, the military suppression of Puerto Rico, and the creation of dense urban *barrios* in New York, Chicago, and Los Angeles.

In fact, it was not until 1980 that *any* of the discipline's leading (white) scholars published an analysis of political behavior which included Latinos; in *Who Votes?*, Raymond Wolfinger and Steven Rosenstone used the Census Bureau/Bureau of Labor Statistics' Current Population Surveys from 1972 and 1976, analyzing data for Black, Puerto Rican, Chicano, and white respondents, to explain patterns of electoral participation in the United States, establishing a demographic profile for both the active and inactive electorates. Among other findings, *Who Votes?* established that Chicanos and Puerto Ricans were "significantly underrepresented" in the active electorate, at rates which were one-third to one-half below their shares of the population. Beyond that, Wolfinger and Rosenstone had little to say about Latino participation, other than observing (somewhat implausibly) that the *ideological* and *partisan* characteristics of voters and nonvoters were not very different and thus, nonvoting did not seem to have any political impact. They did point out, however, that "little research has been done on the political behavior of Hispanic-Americans, of whom Chicanos and Puerto Ricans are the most numerous. These groups are represented by only a handful of respondents in the standard national survey sample. For example, the 1974 Michigan National Election Study reported turnout for just thirteen Chicanos and a lone Puerto Rican."[26]

Wolfinger and Rosenstone's recognition that small sample sizes for Latinos were problematic was an important observation, but it had little apparent impact on those who designed and conducted the major survey projects, including the American National Election Studies (ANES). By the 1980s, having refined survey techniques first used in the 1920s, political scientists were testing a wide range of propositions about mass preferences and behavior, by sampling the political beliefs and actions of individual respondents.[27] In the discipline's most important methodological approach, political scientists use the venerable technology of random-sample surveys, applying the mathematics of probability, creating aggregate profiles of a representative sample of *individuals*, to estimate *society*-wide distributions of opinions, underlying attitudes, and political behaviors. A vernacular variant of this technology, the "public opinion poll," has become a staple of electoral competition as well as governance, giving candidates, the media, government officials, and the general public snapshots of mass sentiment. As a consequence of the success of this mode of research, allowing researchers to visualize and analyze broad social patterns of interest and belief, the random-sample survey has become a powerful tool for social science, electoral politics, and even consumer marketing. Countless electoral campaigns, congressional policy debates, and bureaucratic procedures have been based on it. Over the years, academic and commercial survey researchers have become proficient at predicting the public's response to political events, identifying ideological and policy preferences, and forecasting the outcome of elections, with sometimes uncanny precision.

The technology, used correctly, is powerful. When a sample of individual respondents is truly chosen randomly, reflecting the broader population's demographic, socioeconomic, and political characteristics, the resulting collective profile will be remarkably similar, in its distribution of political sentiment, knowledge, and behavior, to the larger population that sample is selected to represent. However, the design of survey projects is crucial. If samples are unrepresentative, they can never truly reflect mass attitudes or opinion. If politically salient groups are excluded or undersampled, or if research questions are poorly phrased, the technique will generate distorted findings. Unfortunately, where America's minority populations are concerned, political science has been plagued by exactly these problems.

To fill the void left by mainstream researchers with little interest in minority politics, a small number of important new surveys were deployed after the early 1960s, designed specifically to measure African American political attitudes and to create baseline datasets on which future research could be built. These efforts began with the University of Michigan's *Negro Political Participation Study* in 1961–1962 (Donald Matthews and James Prothro). The work continued with the *Negro Political Attitudes* study of 1964 (Gary T. Marx), the *National Survey of Black Americans* in 1979–1980 (James S. Jackson and Gerald Gurin), the *National Black Election Panel Study* in 1984 and 1988 (James S. Jackson), the *National Black Politics Study* in 1993 (Michael Dawson, Ronald Brown, and James S. Jackson), and the *National Black Election Study* in 1996 (Katherine Tate).[28] These projects demonstrated the important potential of survey research in which minority subjects were centered, incorporating research questions (survey items) drawn from the lived experience of marginalized populations, as well as from conventional perspectives and existing mainstream research.

For the 1993 *National Black Politics Study*, for example, Michael Dawson, Ronald Brown, and James S. Jackson asked 1,206 Black respondents about economic conditions, policies to improve the lives of Black people, Black women and their role in the Black community, the role and extent of religion in Black politics, political self-identification, community and political involvement, and feelings toward various political leaders, political groups, and national policies. Its 223 variables provided a rich resource for scholars, and the survey is still being used as a baseline to track changes in Black attitudes and to recount the shape of Black politics at the beginning of the Clinton era.[29]

Katherine Tate's 1996 *National Black Election Study* (NBES) was an even more ambitious project, surveying a national sample of 1,216 Black Americans, identifying attitudes and political preferences of the Black electorate during the 1996 presidential election. The NBES included both pre- and postelection components. Tate's 395 survey items included variables for party identification, political interest, preferences for president, social and political values, perceptions of candidates and groups, opinions on public policies, participation in political life, race and gender issues, economic matters, quality of life, government spending, and religion. In addition, respondents were matched to congressional districts and asked to evaluate their House representatives. Tate's NBES data are also still in use, providing comparative evidence for recent analyses of Black mobilization in the 2008 presidential election.[30]

At the same time, several of the most important mainstream research projects, in the wake of the civil rights movement, took note of their weaknesses and began to survey larger samples of Black respondents more carefully and consistently. In the American National Election Studies (ANES) series, for example, Black respondents comprised between 10% and 13% of the overall respondent pool in each iteration of the survey between 1970 and 2008, closely tracking the Black share of the national population. Unfortunately, Hispanics did not fare as well, either with independent surveys or in the mainstream projects.

To illustrate the problem, consider that since 1948, the ANES has been one of the most important, and best designed, surveys in the discipline. For more than sixty years, ANES has gathered data on voter attitudes and preferences, conducting random-sample interviews before and after each presidential election and after most congressional elections. According to the project's description, it is "the oldest continuous series of survey data investigating electoral behavior and attitudes in the United States."[31] For most of its long history, however, the ANES sampled very few Hispanic respondents. Even as late as 2008, when ANES interviewed more than 2,300 respondents, and deliberately "oversampled" Latinos, Histpanic responses accounted for only 9% of the total—at a time when Latinos numbered nearly 47 million persons and were 15.5% of the population. As can be seen in table 1.1, the pattern of undersampling Hispanics was consistently a problem; in 1970, there were no Hispanic respondents at all, and in every survey through 2008 the Hispanic respondent share was lower than the Hispanic share of both the national population and eligible voters. The problem with these iterations of the ANES—and remember, this is one of the *best* mainstream surveys—is that few valid inferences about Latinos have been possible based on such small samples. Whatever its other merits, this long-running survey of political attitudes in the U.S.—sophisticated, well managed, and publicly available at no cost—was until recently of limited utility for anyone seeking detailed evidence about the political life and attitudes of America's

53 million Hispanics. To be fair, today's ANES investigators have become aware of its limitations with respect to Latino respondents, have reached out to Latino politics scholars and others seeking methodological advice, and have significantly improved the survey's sampling of Black and Hispanic respondents. The preliminary release of 2012 data, which took place just as this book was being finalized, represents a great improvement from past practice. As in 2008, the 2012 survey included large oversamples for both Black and Hispanic populations (American National Election Studies 2013).[32]

Nonetheless, despite years of development in technologies and practices of survey research, and despite the significant Latino presence in U.S. politics, conventional large-N political science research has typically had little to offer scholars of the Latino political experience, political behavior, and political interests. For that, we must turn to the very small number of Latino-centered survey projects which, despite immense organizational and financial challenges, managed to reach the field and find their way into the scholarly discourse.

Table 1.1: Racial Undersampling in the American National Election Studies (1970–2008)

	Respondent pool composition, by ANES survey year				
Racial group	1970	1980	1990	2000	2008
White, non-Hispanic					
Percentage in ANES sample	89.0%	83.0%	75.0%	74.0%	74.0%
Percentage in U.S. population	83.5%	79.6%	75.6%	69.1%	65.4%
White, non-Hispanic					
Oversample	5.5%	3.4%	−0.6%	4.9%	8.6%
Hispanic					
Hispanic population	9,600,000	14,000,000	22,300,000	35,300,000	46,800,000
Percentage in ANES sample	0%	3.0%	7.0%	7.0%	9.0%
Percentage in U.S. population	4.7%	6.4%	9.0%	12.5%	15.4%
Hispanic, all races					
Undersample	*N/A*	−3.4%	−2.0%	−5.5%	−6.4%
Black, non-Hispanic (U.S.)	11.1%	11.7%	12.1%	12.3%	12.8%
Percentage in ANES sample	10.0%	12.0%	13.0%	13.0%	12.0%
Asian, non-Hispanic (U.S.)	0.8%	1.5%	2.9%	4.2%	4.6%
Percentage in ANES sample	0%	1.0%	2.0%	3.0%	3.0%
Native, non-Hispanic (U.S.)	0.4%	0.6%	0.8%	1.5%	1.0%
Percentage in ANES sample	0%	2.0%	3.0%	3.0%	1.0%
N	1,507	1,612	1,979	1,767	2,313

Sources: The American National Election Studies, "Table 1A3. Race of the Respondent," *The ANES Guide to Public Opinion and Electoral Behavior* (Ann Arbor: University of Michigan, Center for Political Studies, 2010). Available online at http://electionstudies.org/nesguide/toptable/tab1a_3.htm; Campbell Gibson and Kay Jung, "Table F-1. Race and Hispanic Origin, for the United States and Historical Sections and Subsections of the United States: 1790 to 1990," in *Historical Census Statistics on Population Totals by Race, 1790 to 1990, and by Hispanic Origin, 1970 to 1990, for the United States, Regions, Divisions, and States* (Washington, DC: U.S. Census Bureau, Population Division, 2002); Census 2000 Population and Housing Tables (PHC-T Series), PHC-T-1. Population by Race and Hispanic or Latino Origin for the United States: 1990 and 2000, "Table 4. Difference in Population by Race and Hispanic or Latino Origin, for the United States: 1990 to 2000"; and "Table DP05—ACS Demographic and Housing Estimates: 2008," 2008 American Community Survey 1-Year Estimates (Washington, DC: U.S. Census Bureau); Population Division, U.S. Census Bureau, Table 3: Annual Estimates of the Resident Population by Sex, Race, and Hispanic Origin for the United States: April 1, 2000 to July 1, 2008 (NC-EST2008-03), release date: May 14, 2009.

Notes: For years between 1970 and 2000, population data are from the decennial Census. Definitions of the category for Hispanics have changed over time. In this table, for 1970, "Spanish Language (of any race)" and "White, not of Spanish Language" respondents were compared; for 1980, "White, Not of Spanish Origin" and "Spanish Origin (of any race)"; for 1990, "White, Not of Spanish Origin" and "Hispanic Origin (of any race)"; for 2000, "Hispanic or Latino (of any race)" and "Not Hispanic or Latino, White, Race Alone"; for the 2008 non-Census year, "White Alone, Not Hispanic or Latino" and "Hispanic or Latino (of any race)" data were reported in the 2008 American Community Survey.

The earliest of these was *Mexican Origin People in the United States: The 1979 Chicano Survey*, conducted by the Institute for Social Research at the University of Michigan, under the direction of Carlos H. Arce (see appendix 1B). This household (in-person) survey was conducted between February and September of 1979, interviewing persons of Mexican descent living in California, Arizona, New Mexico, Colorado, Texas, and Illinois. A total of 991 interviews were conducted, averaging three hours and twenty minutes in length, using a bilingual, 210-page questionnaire, yielding 1,792 variables. Survey questions addressed respondents' mental and physical health and use of health services, family background and composition, customs and values, language use and attitudes toward language, employment history, social identity, group consciousness, political opinions, and political participation. As the first of its kind, the 1979 Chicano Survey deliberately set high standards and worked to develop best practices, for similar surveys its investigators hoped would follow. As Arce wrote in the survey's codebook, "Because the survey involved use of a bilingual questionnaire, it was necessary for the project to recruit and train its own field staff of interviewers and in-house staff of coders. In these respects and many others, the project broke new ground and developed, *in medias res*, new survey methods appropriate for research on a minority population."[33] Unfortunately, no directly comparable surveys were subsequently deployed, and many of the Chicano Survey's practical lessons went unused for many years. In fact, it was ten years before another research team could field anything remotely comparable. In 1988, Rodolfo O. de la Garza, Angelo Falcón, F. Chris Garcia, and John A. García, with financial support from the University of Texas, developed the first-ever survey focused on Latinos in which all three of the nation's largest Hispanic populations were represented—the Latino National Political Survey (LNPS).

The LNPS included data from 3,415 personal interviews of Mexican Americans (n = 1,546), Puerto Ricans on the mainland (n = 589), Cuban Americans (n = 682), and non-Latinos (n = 598). Sixty percent of the Latino respondents were interviewed in Spanish, and the remainder in English. The survey was administered between July 1989 and March 1990. Among its 434 variables were respondents' family history, organizational memberships, political participation, voting practices, preferences on policy issues, views toward political parties and political candidates/ leaders, political behavior, sources of political information such as the media, feelings about political trust and efficacy, perceptions of the relationship between government and Latino groups, and degree of concern about international issues and social problems. The survey also included items for sex, age, ethnicity, skin color, marital status, education, education of parents and spouse, parental status, religious preference, employment status, occupation, home ownership, military service, country of origin, and citizenship. With so few large-N Latino surveys available to researchers, the LNPS's inherent strengths—large sample size, national scope, and comparison-friendly design—provided a data-rich foundation for more than fifty publications including books, journal articles, dissertations, theses, special reports, and conference proceedings, as well as numerous news articles.[34] In addition, unfortunately, researchers had few alternatives; by the time the Latino National Survey (LNS) was fielded in 2005–2006, more than fifteen years had passed and barely half a dozen publicly accessible Latino surveys had been completed.

Two of those, the Pew Hispanic Center's *National Survey of Latinos* in 2002 and follow-up *National Survey of Latinos—Politics and Civic Participation* in 2004, were comparable to the earlier surveys in their focus on political attitudes and political behavior. These were also reasonably large surveys, interviewing 2,929 Latinos in 2002 and 2,288 in 2004. In addition, the Pew surveys included Salvadoran, Dominican, Colombian, and Central and South American respondents, in addition to Mexican Americans, Puerto Ricans, and Cuban Americans. Two additional Pew surveys appeared in these years as well: one on education, the other on the news media. (Since the LNS, between 2006 and 2013, Pew released additional Latino survey datasets, including national Latino surveys in 2009 and 2010, pre- and post-election surveys in 2008, as well as two surveys on immigration and one each on health care and religion.)

Even so, Latino politics scholars have long been eager to improve on the Chicano Survey and the LNPS, applying the entire range of practical and methodological lessons learned in 1979 and 1989. To do this, six of our field's most skilled researchers set about an extensive planning and fund-raising effort, culminating in what was to become the largest and most richly textured survey of Latinos ever conducted in the United States—the Latino National Survey (LNS). Deployed in the field between November 2005 and August 2006, with a subsequent New England extension during late 2007 and early 2008, the LNS drew on both of the prior national Latino surveys and also incorporated items replicating portions of the General Social Survey (GSS) and the American National Election Study (ANES). With 8,634 completed interviews in the initial 2005–2006 survey, covering fifteen states and the District of Columbia metropolitan area, and an additional 1,200 in the 2007–2008 New England extension (Rhode Island, Connecticut, and Massachusetts), the Latino National Survey is more than three times the size of any previous survey. In addition, its design was specifically tailored to make inter- and intrastate analyses possible; thirteen of its state-level subsamples include at least 400 respondents each, while the five largest states, which also have the largest Latino populations, have even broader samples—Illinois has 600 respondents, New York, Florida, and Texas at least 800, and California, just over 1,200 (see table 1.2). The survey's combined 9,834 respondents represent twenty different Latino national-origin groups, including immigrants and descendants of immigrants, from Argentina, Bolivia, Chile, Colombia, Costa Rica, Cuba, Dominican Republic, Ecuador, El Salvador, Guatemala, Honduras, Mexico, Nicaragua, Panama, Paraguay, Peru, Puerto Rico, Spain, Uruguay, and Venezuela. These national origins are also represented in proportions closely matching their share of the national Latino population. And, because the states chosen for the survey were home to about 90% of all Latinos in the nation, the respondent pool could be drawn from a broadly representative population, reflecting virtually every conceivable local context and political culture.

The survey instrument contained approximately 165 items including demographic characteristics, political attitudes, and policy preferences, as well as a diverse social indicators and personal experiences, yielding 275 variables in the full dataset. Interviewers were bilingual and fluent in both English and Spanish (see appendix A and appendix B). Respondents were greeted in both languages and offered an opportunity to hear the questions and give their answers in either language. A con-

Table 1.2: Sample Sizes—Latino National Survey / New England Extension (2005–2008)

State	Subsample, number of respondents	State subsample's percentage of national sample	Latino population in state (2006)	State's percentage national Latino population
California	1,204	12.2%	13,074,156	29.5%
Texas	811	8.2%	8,385,139	18.9%
Florida	800	8.1%	3,646,499	8.2%
New York	800	8.1%	3,139,456	7.1%
Illinois	600	6.1%	1,886,933	4.3%
Arizona	400	4.1%	1,803,378	4.1%
New Jersey	403	4.1%	1,364,696	3.1%
Colorado	404	4.1%	934,413	2.1%
New Mexico	400	4.1%	860,688	1.9%
Georgia	400	4.1%	703,246	1.6%
Nevada	403	4.1%	610,052	1.4%
North Carolina	401	4.1%	593,896	1.3%
Washington	403	4.1%	581,357	1.3%
Massachusetts	400	4.1%	511,014	1.2%
Virginia	176	1.8%	470,871	1.1%
Connecticut	400	4.1%	391,935	0.9%
Maryland	166	1.7%	336,390	0.8%
Arkansas	401	4.1%	141,053	0.3%
Rhode Island	400	4.1%	117,701	0.3%
Iowa	400	4.1%	114,700	0.3%
District of Columbia	62	0.6%	47,774	0.1%
Total	9,834	100.0%	39,715,347	89.6%

Notes: New England states of Massachusetts, Connecticut, and Rhode Island were surveyed in 2007–2008, all others between November 2005 and August 2006.

Latino National Survey sample sizes are taken from Luis R. Fraga, John A. Garcia, Rodney Hero, Michael Jones-Correa, Valerie Martinez-Ebers, and Gary M. Segura, *Latino National Survey (LNS)*, *2006* [Computer file], ICPSR20862-v4, Ann Arbor, MI: Inter-university Consortium for Political and Social Research [distributor], 2010-05-26, doi:10.3886/ICPSR20862.v4; and New England data are from Evelyn Hu-Dehart, Matthew Garcia, Cynthia Garcia Coll, Jose Itzigsohn, Marion Orr, Tony Affigne, and Jorge Elorza, *Latino National Survey (LNS)—New England, 2006* [Computer file], ICPSR24502-v1, Ann Arbor, MI: Inter-university Consortium for Political and Social Research [distributor], 2009-06-04. doi:10.3886/ICPSR24502.v1.

Population data are from U.S. Census Bureau, Population Division, "Table 4: Annual Estimates of the Hispanic or Latino Population by Age and Sex for the United States: April 1, 2000 to July 1, 2006 (NC-EST2006-04-HISP)," release date: May 17, 2007. Available at http://www.census.gov/popest/data/national/asrh/2006/tables/NC-EST2006-04-HISP.xls.

sent script was also made available, allowing respondents to opt out of the survey altogether. To maximize analytical depth of the survey, each respondent was asked to provide information about his or her age, ancestry, birthplace, education level, ethnicity, marital status, military service, number of people in the household, number of children under the age of eighteen living in the household, political party affiliation, political ideology, religiosity, religious preference, race, skin color, and sex.

Finally, the survey itself was "in the field" just before and just after the unprecedented mass protests of spring 2006, when hundreds of thousands of immigrants' rights demonstrators—mostly Latino—thronged the streets of Los Angeles, Chicago, Columbus, Las Vegas, New York, Des Moines, Boston, Providence, Charleston, Oakland, Salt Lake City, San Jose, Dallas, San Diego, Miami, Birmingham, Boise, Denver, Phoenix, Milwaukee, Atlanta, Charlotte, Seattle, Reno, and dozens of other cities large and small. While that spring's protests including the April 10 "National Day of Action for Immigrant Justice" and the May 1 "Great American Boycott" failed to win the comprehensive immigration reform which proponents were seeking, the marches and rallies brought the faces and demands of the immigrant community to the fore, providing a mass movement backdrop to a national political debate in which Latinos were clearly central.[35] While it is impossible to know what impact this political context might have had on LNS respondents, we can at least be certain that many of them were aware of the way Latinos and their political interests had taken center stage in the national political discourse. In some ways, this coincidence was a striking reminder of 1970, when another transformational moment in political science was played out against the backdrop of a similarly powerful Latino political movement. In that year, moreover, federal Voting Rights Act extensions were approved which, among other provisions, outlawed for the first time the use of literacy tests in both California and Arizona and extended Section 5 preclearance requirements to eight additional counties in Arizona and two counties in California which were not covered under the Voting Rights Act of 1965.[36] In this context, it was in 1970 that the very first scholarly book devoted explicitly to Latino political life was published.

Latino Political Studies Were Born in 1970

A brief review touching on just a few of the books published since 1970 will show how the subfield has developed in these forty-odd years, growing in diversity, sophistication, and scope, and will help you locate the chapters to follow in the longer history of the field. The story begins in 1970 when Leo Grebler, Joan W. Moore, and Ralph C. Guzmán produced a dense, 777-page tome comparable in ambition to Gunnar Myrdal's *The American Dilemma: The Negro Problem and Modern Democracy* or E. Franklin Frazier's *The Negro in the United States.* Seven years in the making, *The Mexican American People: The Nation's Second Largest Minority* (1970) was ponderous, multidisciplinary, and by its very subject, an insurgent contribution to empirical social science in the 1970s. More than a century after northern Mexico *became* the United States, this was the first-ever in-depth, book-length scholarly study of Mexican Americans.[37] Grebler, Moore, and Guzmán applied multistate random-sample surveys in a sociopolitical model linking mass Chicano political behavior to patterns of educational and income inequality, poor living conditions, and residential segregation. Grebler was an urban land economist, Moore a sociologist, and Guzmán the first Mexican American, or for that matter the first Latino, to earn a doctorate in political science in the United States.

Their book drew heavily on ethnography, demography, and survey methods—yet was infused with a clear sense of Chicano history, grounding the analysis in the lived experience of the Mexican American population, from 1848 to the present. In their findings, Grebler, Moore, and Guzmán reported that extreme socioeconomic inequality was the primary reality shaping the Chicano minority's experience with the U.S. political system. Educational, economic, and social exclusion reinforced one another, creating structural barriers to Mexican Americans' full integration into American political communities at all levels of the U.S. polity, local, state, and federal. Despite years of struggle and participation in the life of the nation, Chicanos in the 1960s remained a virtual subcaste, separate, marginalized, and disempowered.

Published in 1970, at a crucial juncture in U.S. history and the Chicano civil rights movement, *The Mexican American People* appeared in the very year of the Los Angeles moratorium and high-school walkouts, the first California grape-growers' contract with César Chávez and the United Farm Workers—and the largest farm-workers' strike in U.S. history. In the broader world, 1970 was also an important year for the U.S. civil rights and anti–Vietnam War movements, when the U.S. military opened fire on unarmed protesters, killing students at both Kent State and Jackson State Universities. With such living history as backdrop, publication of *The Mexican American People* set a high standard for subsequent scholarly work, establishing scientific rigor and historical context, as well as relevance to contemporary politics, as benchmarks for later work in the field.

Yet even a book as ambitious and path-breaking as *The Mexican American People* can be limited by political and intellectual contexts in the era during which it is written. In this case, the authors labored at a time when there were *no* official estimates for the country's Mexican American population. Incredibly, from 1790 to 1980 the federal Census expended no effort at all to enumerate Mexican American or other Latino subgroups. Thus, during the years the book was researched and written (between 1963 and 1970), the most basic prerequisites of survey research, including selection of sampling units and respondents, could only be completed using labor-intensive estimates, from incomplete official data. Where, exactly, did Chicanos live? Without a reliable geography and demography for target populations, it is impossible to conduct random population sampling for group-specific social data. What to do? To solve this problem Grebler, Moore, and Guzmán interpolated Census data for "white persons of Spanish surname"—the bureau's only measure of Latino populations in 1970—while incorporating what they could learn about presumptive Mexican American neighborhoods from other sources, studying land-use patterns, urban plans, educational programs, and similar indirect measures. Even the study's most direct behavioral evidence, in the form of random-sample surveys, came primarily from two large urban areas, in just two states, California and Texas.

Despite these limitations, *The Mexican American People* remains a seminal masterwork in the field, both for the breadth of its analysis and for its position as the first such scholarly effort to focus exclusively on a Latino community, in this case the largest and oldest Hispanic population of all, Mexican Americans. A few years later, in *The Political Socialization of the Mexican-American People* (1976), Guzmán told the story of Mexican American socialization and empowerment by situating contemporary social data into historical context, incorporating for the first time an extensive household-level, random-sample survey of Latino respondents. With this method, he identified strong patterns linking experiences of social exclusion (poverty, poor housing, low wages, and unemployment) with respondents' attitudes and experiences of political exclusion and marginalization. The book's subject (Mexican Americans) and its findings (political attitudes shaped by poverty and social exclusion) challenged dominant narratives in political analysis and American politics, in which the only politics of significance were apparently those of Anglo (white) communities, leaders, organizations, parties, and interests. It is true that a handful of non-Latino political and social scientists had produced somewhat more inclusive research prior to 1970—Carey McWilliams, V. O. Key, Ralph Bunche, and Gunnar Myrdal come to mind—but with very few exceptions, the field of political science from the 1880s to 1970 was devoid of attention to what were already large and socially important minority communities.[38]

In *Chicano Politics* (1977), Maurilio Vigil opened a new direction, in which questions of leadership and political representation were central. His approach to the study of Chicano empowerment was to examine the nature and quality of Mexican American organizations and leaders. Organizational mobilization of Chicano voting, he believed, reflected a success of the Chicano political movement despite serious setbacks in other areas. *Puerto Rican Politics in New York City* (also 1977) represented a parallel effort by James Jennings to assess Puerto Rican leadership effectiveness, especially in comparison to the better established and better connected network of African American political power in New York City. The Puerto Rican community, he found, was beginning to flex its political muscles but still revolved around a small cadre of established leaders, especially Congressman Herman Badillo. Vigil then extended his earlier work, with publication of *Hispanics in American Politics* (1987), in which he expanded the frame to include other Latinos, in a study of ethnic and class differences among individual Hispanic subgroups: Mexican American, Puerto Rican, Cuban American, and other Hispanics (identified as the most recent immigrants to the U.S.). In what was to become a common thread in the field, Vigil concluded that where Latinos were concerned, the nation's political arena seemed not to reflect the pluralism said to be its hallmark. Yet he predicted continued growth in Latino political influence, driven largely by population growth, while pointing to a proliferation of empowering organizations.

While Guzmán and Vigil had begun to apply conventional opinion-research methods to Latino populations, the first major survey project in which Latinos were the primary subject did not appear in print until 1992, with publication of *Latino Voices: Mexican, Puerto Rican, and Cuban Perspectives on American Politics*, by Rodolfo O. de la Garza, Louis DeSipio, F. Chris Garcia, John García, and Angelo Falcón. Based on data from the Latino National Political Survey, *Latino Voices* represented the first systematic effort to describe Latino political attitudes in both depth and breadth, based on a national random sample of more than 3,000 Latino, Black, and white respondents. The same year saw publication of *Latinos and the U.S. Political System: Two-Tiered Pluralism* by Rodney Hero, the first major work using conventional methods, which evaluated the extent to which Latinos were, in fact, full participants in the nominally inclusive American polity, using the political science discipline's central paradigm of democratic *pluralism*. Hero's work built on the critical approach found in Guzmán and Roberto Villarreal (*Chicano Elites and Non-elites*, 1979), linking social inequality with political exclusion but extended that frame to include not just Mexican Americans but Cubans and Puerto Ricans as well. Hero found that for Latinos, pluralism seemed to be constrained, that there were in fact two tiers of political empowerment, separated by barriers of racial and ethnic exclusion, and that Latinos were, for the time being at least, relegated to the lower tier.

Another kind of two-tiered politics were revealed when Carol Hardy-Fanta studied community-level Latino mobilization and leadership in Boston, showing that differences in political ambition, connections to informal communication networks, and preference for shared or collective responsibility created very different political styles and political outcomes for female and male community and political leaders. In *Latina Politics, Latino Politics* (1993), she established the framework of a new approach to the study of gendered politics among Latinos by demonstrating that it was possible, using a deeply engaged blend of qualitative and quantitative analysis, to explicate real differences in the political experiences and preferences of Latinas and Latinos, without resorting to essentialism or folk mythologies about women, patriarchy, and community leadership. Careful and systematic analysis, she showed, could reveal underlying differences without imposing rigid roles and expectations on participants.

In a similar way, Harry Pachon and Louis DeSipio's *New Americans by Choice: Political Perspectives of Latino Immigrants* (1994) represented another thoughtful and systematic challenge to Latino stereotypes, in this case by exploring without preconception the attitudes of Latino immigrants. Pachon and DeSipio's findings about Latino immigrants' positive aspirations and commitments to the American dream remain relevant today. Like Grebler, Moore, and Guzmán in an earlier period, Pachon and DeSipio set a high standard for later work. Using the extensive ($n = 1,636$) National Latino Immigrant Survey, which included Mexican, Cuban, Dominican, Central American, and South American respondents, their findings upset conventional wisdom. Refuting common anti-immigrant and anti-Latino tropes of the day (even more common in today's hostile climate), they discovered that virtually all Latino immigrants at the time were planning to make the United States their permanent home; first-generation migrants were acculturating into U.S. society, albeit with difficulty; and those with five years or more of legal residence manifested high levels of labor-force participation, as well as household incomes measurably higher than for the Latino population as a whole.

In *Counting on the Latino Vote*, DeSipio (1996) went on to analyze impediments to social and political incorporation for the growing Latino population. He considered Latino voting patterns, political values and attitudes (ideology), partisanship, and policy concerns. Taking a close look at Latino impacts on statewide general elections and at increasing Latino political mobilization, he concluded that "with these increases, the opportunities for Latinos to influence electoral outcomes will also grow."[39] The overarching theme in *Counting on the Latino Vote* was that potential Latino influence in the realm of voting and political participation was likely to increase. He also considered the importance of naturalization and how decisions to naturalize (or not) would influence Latinos' group-based political incorporation, suggesting that strategic mobilization of new citizens, and the reinforcing effects of successful electoral involvement, could help Latino communities mobilize nonvoters and hence increase their potential influence.

By the end of this early period of emergence, several themes had become apparent. Scholars had successfully applied mainstream techniques to Latino subjects and, in doing so, had both challenged and illuminated earlier neglect. In fact, when scholars *looked* for political engagement, and took seriously the possibility that Latino interests may be *different* from non-Latinos', and when they incorporated common socioeconomic correlates into the analysis, the links between *social exclusion* and *political disengagement* were clear. Nowhere could this relationship be seen more clearly, as Pachon and DeSipio revealed, than in the marginalization and stereotyping of Latino immigrants.

A Redirection for Political Analysis—the Latino Challenge

Not long after DeSipio's 1996 *Counting on the Latino Vote*, the pace of scholarly work began to accelerate.[40] In retrospect, 1998 appears to be something of a major inflection point. In rapid succession, José Cruz told the story of political exclusion, empowerment, and strategic thinking for Puerto Ricans in Connecticut in *Identity and Power*. Frank Bonilla, Edwin Meléndez, Rebecca Morales, and Maria de los Angeles Torres assembled a team of scholars from several disciplines to show how Latino migration and transnational thought were creating new opportunities for political change on both sides of "The Border." Among other accomplishments in their *Borderless Borders*, they helped establish the collaborative, multidisciplinary edited volume as an important vehicle for innovative scholarship about Latino life and politics. In *Making Americans, Remaking America*, DeSipio and de la Garza went farther, suggesting that the political process for Latinos (especially immigrants) was recursive: just as processes of Latino migration were changing the migrants as people, they were also transforming underlying American political dynamics.

The same year, Michael Jones-Correa's *Between Two Nations: The Political Predicament of Latinos in New York City* explained how continuing immigration was challenging Latino communities and the broader political system, and how failure to incorporate new immigrants would be detrimental to the American polity at large. As it stood, Latino immigrants remained economically and thus politically disadvantaged, sometimes feeling as though they were not fully Americans but not fully of their home country either. Full incorporation of new citizens in the American political system, Jones-Correa showed, would require more than simply resettling immigrants in coethnic communities; it demands economic and political change as well and more opportunities for immigrants to feel both welcomed in the United States and connected to the home country in ways which are sustainable and real —including dual citizenship.

Then, just before the 2000 elections, when Latino voters were (yet again) thought to be potentially significant, twenty-one Latino politics authors came together and published a special symposium titled "Latino Politics in the United States," in *PS: Political Science and Politics*, a journal which reaches the entire membership of the American Political Science Association. In six collaborative articles, these Latino politics specialists outlined what was then known about Latino/a identity, immigration and citizenship, public policy, political behavior and officeholding, gender, and social movements. For the first time, a broad audience of political scientists—some of whom would soon appear as expert commentators on the 2000 elections—were exposed to key works in Latino political studies, to recent research findings, and to a framing for Latino involvement in 2000 which was based on empirical research and theory building, rather than on popular stereotypes or simplistic approaches. (See Affigne 2000; Hero et al. 2000; Márquez and Jennings 2000; Sierra et al. 2000; Schmidt et al. 2000; Montoya, Hardy-Fanta, and García 2000; Martinez-Ebers et al. 2000.)

The pace of scholarship in this mode accelerated again. To explore the question of Latino political leadership, David Rodriguez compared organizational strategies and management, in *Latino National Political Coalitions: Struggles and Challenges*

(2002). Like Guzmán before him, Rodriguez hypothesized that socioeconomic conditions were the most critical factors shaping political empowerment for Chicanos, Puerto Ricans, and Cubans, and he found that as a group, Latinos were much less educated, poorer, and more likely to be unemployed or concentrated in low-status, low-paying jobs than was the non-Latino white population. What impact, he wondered, were the national Hispanic advocacy coalitions having on this reality? Looking at the National Association of Latino Elected and Appointed Officials (NALEO), the National Council of La Raza (NCLR), the League of United Latin American Citizens (LULAC), and the Mexican American Legal Defense and Education Fund (MALDEF), Rodriguez concluded that such coalitions were essential to the political empowerment of the Latino community—but they all faced problems of leadership, funding, and communication and were largely powerless to directly improve socioeconomic conditions for Latinos. Four themes—the importance of leadership-driven electoral mobilization; the key, if sometimes problematic, role of established leaders, especially in Congress; the empowering activities and the organizational difficulties of national and local coalitions; and the disempowering effects of the population's generally low socioeconomic status—came to characterize much of the subsequent Latino leadership studies, including aspects of the most recent work in Michael D. Minta's *Oversight: Representing the Interests of Blacks and Latinos in Congress* (2011), Jason P. Casellas's *Latino Representation in State Houses and Congress* (2011), and Stella Rouse's *Latinos in the Legislative Process* (2013). Our communities may be only as empowered as our leaders, but our leaders are similarly dependent on the resources and political mobilization they can expect from our communities.

Kim Geron, in *Latino Political Power* (2005), and Lisa García Bedolla, in *Fluid Borders* (2005), moved the discourse in yet additional directions. Geron framed his work in terms of social as well as political inequality, tracing the development of Latino political power as a challenge of class as well as ethnic interests. His work showed how at numerous political moments, persistent inequality made cohesive action more difficult, and how very different political opportunity structures, in diverse local contexts, made steady progress toward empowerment unlikely. Whereas Geron told a story of differences in power across cities and regions, García Bedolla drew similar conclusions from a close look at two similarly situated, but differently resourced, Latino communities. In a qualitative comparison of East Los Angeles and Montebello, she showed how otherwise-similar ethnic communities might experience widely divergent levels of incorporation and empowerment, depending on the extent and the effectiveness of social capital available to community residents.

In New York City, Puerto Ricans have faced a similarly frustrating political environment, in which the broader polity sometimes appears to be responsive, with readily available coalition partners, and at other times seems not to care about Puerto Ricans at all. In *Boricua Power*, José Sánchez (2007) used the metaphor of the dance to suggest that one reason Puerto Rican political power rose and fell was because, like a dancer, at times Puerto Ricans focused in one direction, on building influence in the political realm, while at other times they turned away from the quest for power, to focus more on economic and cultural needs. Yet like other observers before him, Sánchez concluded that racial segregation, poverty, and lack of education have been key factors limiting Puerto Ricans' ability and desire to integrate into the larger American society. Despite a long history of political engagement and Puerto Rican political leaders who have achieved elected positions in city government, the state legislature, and Congress, the promise of effective empowerment remains unfulfilled.

In other areas of the country, empowerment has been an equally elusive goal, even where large Latino communities, more ethnically integrated political systems, and more inclusive political traditions are present. In Texas, for example, many Latino politicians have been able to build long-lasting careers, for themselves and for protégés. However, even there, where some resources for community empowerment have been abundant, leadership has often been exclusively male. Sonia García, Valerie Martinez-Ebers, Irasema Coronado, Sharon Navarro, and Patricia Jaramillo, in *Políticas* (2008), set out to discover when, and under what conditions, Latina women could rise to power. Their extensive interviews with successful Latina politicians revealed that there is no single route to empowerment, but in nearly every case, close connections to the community—as Hardy-Fanta found for Latinas in Boston—is both a more natural positioning for women leaders and a sine qua non for political success.

As García et al. looked closely at gender to see what characteristic patterns might be found, Atiya Stokes-Brown looked at the politics of racial identity, bias, and difference among Latinos. In *The Politics of Race in Latino Communities: Walking the Color Line* (2012), she asked whether their racial identities might play a role in Latinos' policy orientations and voting. She found that racial consciousness does have a powerful impact. For example, multiracial Latinos were more likely than other Latinos to oppose government intervention to reform health care. Differences were evident on other policy questions as well; Black Latinos were more likely to support same-sex marriage. White Latinos held divergent views with respect to government-sponsored health-care reform and support for the poor—they were less likely to support either policy. When comparing other-race Latinos, multiracial Latinos, and Black Latinos, she found that other-race Latinos were more likely to support liberal immigration policies, governmental income support for the poor, government invention to reform health care, and same-sex marriage. Like other research which is grounded in richly textured data, Stokes-Brown's analysis reveals the complexity of the subject and the nuanced approach which is most appropriate for the study of Latino politics. By disaggregating and then recategorizing respondents according to racial self-identification, she shows that skin-color differences, among presumptively similar individuals, have meaning. Such work reminds us that where "Latinos" are concerned, our expectations may be confounded by the data; our preconceptions may need to be abandoned; our quick assumptions about cause and effect may simply be wrong.

How to Use the Research in This Book

In the book you hold, seventeen contemporary scholars of Latino politics were invited to write research chapters based on data from the same rich dataset—the Latino National Surveys of 2006–2008. Because all of the studies use the same underlying survey instrument, once you become familiar with the variables and structure of the dataset—including its measures of Latinos' socioeconomic, attitudinal, and political characteristics—you will find it easier to understand each subsequent study. Although all use the same dataset, each chapter asks distinctive research questions and then, using appropriate statistical tests, determines the strength and direction of associations which might answer those questions. The authors offer analyses which are, in the best traditions of the formal discipline, grounded in evidence, attentive to alternative explanations, and carefully written to reduce misunderstanding and to encourage your thoughtful participation. Like any book, the editors have made judgments about what to include and what to leave out. As a result, you will not find studies from all eight of the subfields introduced earlier in this chapter. You will find work which fits into the broad rubric I have just outlined and, in some cases, directly engages earlier work in the field. These topics include Latino identity and panethnicity; immigration, transnationalism, and incorporation; social networks and linked fate; political knowledge and policy preferences; marginalization and exclusion; and racial attitudes and racial identity.

Although the chapters vary by subject, they have several common features which should help you make sense of the material and see how your own research might follow similar paths. Each begins with a list of research questions to be addressed. Findings from each analysis are clearly indicated and summarized for clarity. At the end of each chapter, you will find questions for study and review, a list of references, and an appendix listing the variables from the Latino National Survey which were used in that chapter's analysis. At the end of the book, you will find the complete LNS questionnaires in English and Spanish, so you can see what questions were asked and how they were phrased.

If all of this book's contributions are successful, you will learn a great deal about politics in the United States at a crucial moment in the nation's history, not just for Latinos but for the nation as a whole. You will be better prepared to understand profound changes now under way in the nature and direction of U.S. politics. And of course, after reading this book, you will surely understand more than you currently do about political ideas and experiences among the nation's large Latino population. What do Latinos believe and experience, and what political actions arise from those beliefs and from those experiences?

At the same time, as teachers, we all hope that when you read this book, you will *not* suspend your critical faculties but will evaluate the authors' strong claims about Latino political behavior, policy preferences, and attitudes. In fact, I want you to consider for a moment the underlying idea *behind* the book and ask whether the basic concept of *Latino politics* even makes sense. Ask the hard questions! Given the diversity of political interests arising from diverse national origins, cultures, ideologies, immigration experiences, educational and occupational statuses, racial identities, religious beliefs, gendered expectations, ages, local contexts, and more, *is there really such a thing as Latino politics*? In fact, is the underlying concept that Latinos constitute a single *panethnic* group, sharing common interests and demonstrating similar behaviors, valid or not? How *unified* can a Latino panethnic identity possibly be—if at all? How is a sense of "linked fate" among Latinos different from that felt between Latinos and African Americans? What ties do Latinos retain to their home cultures and politics, and how strong is residual attachment to nations of origin? More generally, how do Latinos see themselves and the political world around them? What are the key questions facing Latino political studies today? What methods can best address those questions? How can quantitative and qualitative projects each contribute to resolving them, using the comparative strengths of each research modality?

My hope is that this book will help you think about many such questions and others of your own mind. When you are ready to add your contributions to this body of knowledge, you can use the studies you find here to enrich your thinking and your research, as you consider how to replicate or improve the authors' research questions, analytical methods, and findings. Use this book like you would a rich vein of golden ore, mining for ideas, thinking about how the questions the LNS posed to its nearly 10,000 Latino respondents can reveal new knowledge about those respondents' values, life situations, and political engagement. Study the authors' methods to see what is possible, but use your own insights and skills, your own hypotheses and selection of variables, to bring something new into the world of Latino political knowledge!

And then, share what you discover. Remember, the rich LNS datasets have been made freely available to researchers anywhere, without cost. This is a very public resource, and I encourage you to honor that public- and community-spirited tradition. In the end, reader, if you do these things, you may well discover new ways to become a better student or teacher of Latino politics, as well as, perhaps, a better, more informed participant in the life of the nation, grounding your political opinions in *facts* about your fellow Latino citizens (and noncitizens) and not on the thinly disguised partisanship and self-interest which characterize so much of the nation's political discourse at the beginning of the twenty-first century. All of us who have contributed to this book have done so in the firm belief that political analysis, applied to Latino subjects with open-minded and open-hearted enthusiasm for *facts*, about Latino views on life, the nation, our identities as *Latinos*, and our engagement as political actors, can offer unprecedented depth of understanding of this unique American population—these *Latinos de los Estados Unidos*.

Appendix 1A: Recommended Books for the Study of Latino Politics (1970–2014)

Textbooks

García Bedolla, *Latino Politics*, 2nd ed.	2014
García, J., *Latino Politics in America*, 2nd ed.	2011
García Bedolla, *Latino Politics*	2009
Garcia, F. C., and Sanchez, *Hispanics and the U.S. Political System*	2008
Geron, *Latino Political Power*	2005
García, J., *Latino Politics in America*	2003

Political Behavior

Barreto, Segura, Manzano, Pantoja, and Sánchez, *Latino Voters in the Obama Era*	2014

Ramírez, *Mobilizing Opportunities*   2013
Fraga, García, Hero, Jones-Correa, Martinez-Ebers, and Segura,
   Latinos in the New Millennium   2012
Abrajano and Alvarez, *New Faces, New Voices*   2010
Barreto, *Ethnic Cues*   2010
de la Garza, DeSipio, and Leal (eds.), *Beyond the Barrio*   2010
Fraga, García, Hero, Jones-Correa, Martinez-Ebers, and Segura,
   Latino Lives in America   2010
Espino, Leal, and Meier (eds.), *Latino Politics*   2007
Torres (ed.), *Latinos in New England*   2006
de la Garza and DeSipio (eds.), *Muted Voices*   2005
García Bedolla, *Fluid Borders*   2005
Magaña, *Mexican Americans and the Politics of Diversity*   2005
Nelson and Lavariega Monforti (eds.), *Black and Latino/a Politics*   2005
Navarro and Mejia (eds.), *Latino Americans and Political Participation* 2004
Hardy-Fanta and Gerson (eds.), *Latino Politics in Massachusetts*   2002
de la Garza and DeSipio (eds.), *Awash in the Mainstream*   1999
Garcia, F. C. (ed.), *Pursuing Power*   1997
de la Garza and DeSipio (eds.), *Ethnic Ironies*   1996
DeSipio, *Counting on the Latino Vote*   1996
de la Garza, Menchaca, and DeSipio (eds.), *Barrio Ballots*   1994
de la Garza and DeSipio (eds.), *From Rhetoric to Reality*   1992
de la Garza, DeSipio, Garcia, García, and Falcón, *Latino Voices*   1992
Hero, *Latinos and the U.S. Political System*   1992
Garcia, F. C. (ed.), *Latinos and the Political System*   1988
de la Garza (ed.), *Ignored Voices*   1987
Vigil, *Hispanics in American Politics*   1987
Miyares, *Models of Political Participation of Hispanic-Americans*   1980
Guzmán, *The Political Socialization of the Mexican American People* 1976
Valdes y Tapia, *Hispanos and American Politics*   1976
Grebler, Moore, and Guzmán, *The Mexican-American People*   1970

Racial Consciousness, Linked Fate, and Interminority Relations

Hero and Preuhs, *Black-Latino Relations in U.S. National Politics* 2013
Bowler and Segura, *The Future Is Ours*   2012
Stokes-Brown, *The Politics of Race in Latino Communities*   2012
Chávez, *Everyday Injustice*   2011
Telles, Sawyer, and Rivera-Salgado (eds.), *Just Neighbors?*   2011
De Genova (ed.), *Racial Transformations*   2006
Dzidzienyo and Oboler (eds.), *Neither Enemies nor Friends*   2005
Segura and Bowler (eds.), *Diversity in Democracy*   2005
Alex-Assensoh and Hanks (eds.), *Black and Multiracial Politics in America* 2003
Browning, Marshall, and Tabb (eds.), *Racial Politics in American Cities*, 3rd ed. 2003
Betancur and Gills (eds.), *The Collaborative City*   2000
Schmidt, *Language Policy and Identity Politics in the United States* 2000
Cruz, *Identity and Power*   1998
Rich, *The Politics of Minority Coalitions*   1996
Jennings (ed.), *Blacks, Latinos, and Asians in Urban America*   1994
Browning, Marshall, and Tabb, *Protest Is Not Enough*   1984

Identity and Social Theory

Gender and Intersectionality

Representation and Leadership

Media and Political Communication

Immigration, Citizenship, and Transnationalism

Oboler (ed.), *Latinos and Citizenship*	2006
Wong, C., *Lobbying for Inclusion*	2006
Wong, J., *Democracy's Promise*	2006
Zuñiga and Hernández-Leon, *New Destinations*	2006
Ramakrishnan, *Democracy in Immigrant America*	2005
Smith, *Mexican New York*	2005
Johnson, *The "Huddled Masses" Myth*	2003
Magaña, *Straddling the Border: Immigration Policy and the INS*	2003
Massey, Durand, and Malone, *Beyond Smoke and Mirrors*	2003
Vélez-Ibáñez and Sampaio, *Transnational Latina/o Communities*	2002
de la Garza and Lowell (eds.), *Sending Money Home*	2002
Tichenor, *Dividing Lines*	2002
de la Garza and Pachon (eds.), *Latinos and U.S. Foreign Policy*	2000
Jaynes (ed.), *Immigration and Race*	2000
Menjívar, *Fragmented Ties*	2000
Bonilla, Meléndez, Morales, and de los Angeles Torres (eds.), *Borderless Borders*	1998
DeSipio and de la Garza, *Making Americans, Remaking America*	1998
Jones-Correa, *Between Two Nations*	1998
Gutiérrez, *Walls and Mirrors*	1995
Hondagneu-Sotelo, *Gendered Transitions*	1994
Pachon and DeSipio, *New Americans by Choice*	1994

Political History and Social Movements

Márquez, *Democratizing Texas Politics*	2013
Venator-Santiago, *Puerto Rico and the Origins of U.S. Global Empire*	2013
Gonzalez, *Harvest of Empire* (rev. ed.)	2011
Itzigsohn, *Encountering American Faultlines*	2009
Muñoz, *Youth, Identity, Power* (rev. ed.)	2007
Sánchez, *Boricua Power*	2007
Rodriguez, *Latino Politics in the United States*	2005
Melendez, *We Took the Streets*	2003
Gonzalez, *Harvest of Empire*	2000
Valle and Torres, *Latino Metropolis*	2000
de los Angeles Torres, *In the Land of Mirrors*	1999
Gutierrez, *The Making of a Chicano Militant*	1999
Montejano (ed.), *Chicano Politics and Society in the Late Twentieth Century*	1999
Torres and Katsiaficas (eds.), *Latino Social Movements*	1999
Torres and Velázquez (eds.), *The Puerto Rican Movement*	1998
Moore and Pinderhughes (eds.), *In the Barrios*	1993
Shorris, *Latinos*	1992
Gómez-Quiñones, *Chicano Politics*	1990
Muñoz, *Youth, Identity, Power*	1989
Márquez, *Power and Politics in a Chicano Barrio*	1985
Jennings and Rivera, *Puerto Rican Politics in Urban America*	1984
Barrera, *Race and Class in the Southwest*	1979
Villarreal, *Chicano Elites and Non-elites*	1979
Garcia, F. C., and de la Garza, *The Chicano Political Experience*	1977
Garcia, F. C. (ed.), *La Causa Política*	1974
Garcia, F. C. (ed.), *Chicano Politics*	1973

Note: For complete publication details, please see the References. No single listing could hope to include every relevant title, nor could any single classification system locate every book precisely; the reader is advised to consider this a starting point, not the final word, on the scope of work in Latino political studies. In general, titles were selected for inclusion because they utilize political science methodologies, were written by political scientists, or are widely used in political science classrooms. Naturally, most of us who study Latino politics have learned a great deal from scholars in other disciplines, especially sociology, history, and anthropology, as well as interdisciplinary fields including policy studies, Chicano studies, Puerto Rican and Caribbean studies, women's studies, and ethnic studies. Thus, many books which have influenced our work may not appear on this list. I welcome suggestions for additional titles which should be included in the future. The classification scheme is not rigid, and it should be noted that some titles fit multiple categories. Those which span multiple areas have for brevity's sake been assigned to a single category. For a broad bibliographic overview, see *Latino Politics: A Growing and Evolving Political Community* (*A Reference Guide*), compiled by García, Sanchez, and Peralta for the University of Arizona Libraries (2009).

Appendix 1B: Data Repositories and Datasets for Latino Political Studies (1979–2014)

Resource Center for Minority Data

Inter-university Consortium for Political and Social Research, University of Michigan (academic consortium); http://www.icpsr.umich.edu/icpsrweb/RCMD/index.jsp; User Support Staff: (734) 647-2200 / mailto:netmail@icpsr.umich.edu

Mexican Origin People in the United States: The 1979 Chicano Survey (*n* = 991)	1979
Persistent URL: http://doi.org/o/.7335/ICPSR/3175.v0	
Latino National Political Survey (*n* = 3,415)	1989
Persistent URL: http://doi.org/o/.7335/ICPSR/5310.v7	
Latino National Survey (*n* = 8,634)	2006
Persistent URL: http://doi.org/o/.7335/ICPSR./35..v1	
Latino National Survey—New England (*n* = 1,200)	
Persistent URL: http://doi.org/o/.7335/ICPSR.16/..v0	2008

Latino Decisions

Seattle, WA (private); http://www.latinodecisions.com/; Contact: (425) 271-2300

2012 Election Eve Poll—National Results (*November 6, 2012*)	2012
Download links: http://www.latinodecisions.com/recent-polls/	

Pew Research Center's Hispanic Trends Project

Washington, DC (private nonprofit); http://www.pewhispanic.org/category/datasets/; Hispanic Center Staff: (202) 419-3600 / mailto:info@pewhispanic.org

2010 National Survey of Latinos	2010
Field dates: August 17–September 19, 2010, Latino adults (*n* = 1,375)	
2009 National Survey of Latinos	2009
Field dates: August 5–September 16, 2009, Latinos 16 and older (*n* = 2,012)	
2008 Post-election National Survey of Latinos	2008
Field dates: November 11–30, 2008, Latino adults (*n* = 1,540)	
2008 National Survey of Latinos	2008
Field dates: June 9–July 13, 2008, Latino adults (*n* = 2,015)	

2006 National Survey of Latinos—The Immigration Debate 2006
  Field dates: June 5–July 3, 2006, Latino adults (*n* = 2,000)
2004 National Survey of Latinos—Politics and Civic Participation 2004
  Field dates: April 21–June 9, 2004, Latino adults (*n* = 2,288)
2002 National Survey of Latinos 2002
  Field dates: April 4–June 11, 2002, Latino adults (*n* = 2,929), non-Latinos (*n* = 1,284)

Roper Center for Public Opinion

University of Connecticut, Storrs; http://www.ropercenter.uconn.edu/data_access.html; Data Services Staff: (860) 486-4440 / mailto:dataservices-ropercenter@uconn.edu
NBC/MSNBC/Telemundo Poll: Immigration (United States) 2010
  Field dates: May 20–23, 2010, sample: Adults with Hispanic oversample (*n* = 918)
Time Magazine/SRBI Poll #2005-3575: Hispanic Poll (United States) 2005
  Field dates: July 28–August 3, 2005, sample: National Hispanic Adults (*n* = 503)

American National Election Studies

University of Michigan, Center for Political Studies; http://electionstudies.org; Inquiries: (734) 764-5494 / mailto: anes@electionstudies.org. *Note:* The ANES "Time Series" studies have been conducted since 1948, typically through in-person interviewing, during years of biennial national elections, with both pre- and postelection surveys. For the first time, ANES 2012 included face-to-face oversamples of 300 Hispanic and 300 African American respondents and an Internet sample of more than 3,500 respondents (of all backgrounds).
ANES 2012 Time Series Study (combined face-to-face and Internet, *n* = 5,916) 2012
  Field dates: September 8, 2012–January 24, 2013, sample: U.S. citizens 18 or older
  http://www.electionstudies.org/studypages/anes_timeseries_2012/anes_timeseries_
  2012.htm

Notes

1. In June 2013, the Census also reported that while the Latino population had surpassed 53 million in 2012, the Asian population was growing even more quickly, rising 2.9% in a single year, to 18.9 million (U.S. Census Bureau 2013). A few of the many scholars and activists who have talked about the Latino "sleeping giant" include Angelo Falcón (Maurice Carroll, "Hispanic-Voting Study Finds 'Sleeping Giant,'" *New York Times*, August 29, 1982), John Mollenkopf (Celia W. Dugger, "Immigrant Voters Reshape Politics," *New York Times*, March 10, 1996), and Michael Alvarez and Jonathan Nagler ("Is the Sleeping Giant Awakening? Latinos and California Politics in the 1990's," paper presented at the annual meeting of the Midwest Political Science Association, Chicago, April 1999).
2. Hector Becerra, "Obama Says Latinos Could Be 'Big Reason' He Wins Second Term," *Los Angeles Times*, October 26, 2012, http://articles.latimes.com/2012/oct/26/news/la-pn-obama-latinos-second-term-20121024.
3. The Latino Decisions Election Eve Poll found that among all Latinos, Obama's support was highest among Dominican (96%) and Puerto Rican voters (83%), followed by Mexican American (78%), Central American (76%), and South American (79%) heritage voters. The intra-Latino patterns for Obama support were especially important in Central and South Florida, where his Puerto Rican votes more than countered Romney's 54% support from the region's large Cuban American electorate, only 44% of whom voted for Obama. Details on Latino Election Eve Poll, including a methodology report, are available online: http://www.latinovote2012.com/app/.
4. This ranking is based on the Latino Decisions estimate of 75% Latino support for Obama.

If we instead use the CNN exit polls, Latinos' 71% for Obama would rank just behind Asian Pacific Americans at 73%. For comparison, Obama won just 39% of the white vote and could not have won the election at all without his extraordinary appeal among the nation's minority electorates. Full CNN exit poll data can be found online, along with state-by-state voting results: http://www.cnn.com/election/2012/results/race/president#exit-polls.

5. Benjy Sarlin, "Poll: Latino Vote Devastated GOP Even Worse than Exits Showed," *Talking Points Memo*, November 7, 2012, http://2012.talkingpointsmemo.com/2012/11/poll-latino-vote-devastated-gop-even-worse-than-exits-showed.php.

6. Reported in *Mother Jones*, in an article by David Corn, "Secret Video: Romney Tells Millionaire Donors What He REALLY Thinks of Obama Voters," September 17, 2012, http://www.motherjones.com/politics/2012/09/full-transcript-mitt-romney-secret-video.

7. Latino Decisions data, as reported by Victoria M. DeFrancesco Soto in "Obama's Re-election Sets Record for Support from Latino Voters," *Nation*, November 8, 2012, http://www.thenation.com/blog/171144/obamas-re-election-sets-record-support-latino-voters#.

8. Matt A. Barreto and Gary Segura, "2012 Latino Election Eve Poll," Seattle, WA: Impre-Media and Latino Decisions, November 7, 2012, http://www.latinodecisions.com/2012-election-eve-polls/.

9. To estimate Latino electoral influence on Barack Obama's first election, Matt A. Barreto, Loren Collingwood, and Sylvia Manzano devised a three-factor model, using Latino electorate size and growth, partisan attachment and competitiveness, and mobilization. Their findings suggested that *ceteris paribus*, Latino voters may have been decisive in "flipping" both Florida and Nevada to the Democrats (and candidate Obama) in 2008. See Barreto, Collingwood, and Manzano, "A New Measure of Group Influence in Presidential Elections: Assessing Latino Influence in 2008," *Political Research Quarterly* 63 (4) (2010): 908–921.

10. Laura Myers, "Reid: Hispanics Playing Bigger Political Role in Nevada, West," *Las Vegas Review-Journal*, October 16, 2011, http://www.lvrj.com/news/western-states-reject-extremism-reid-tells-democratic-summit-131950028.html.

11. Nicholas Riccardi, "Obama's Big Hispanic Win Worries Republicans," *Big Story*, Associated Press, November 8, 2012, http://bigstory.ap.org/article/obamas-big-hispanic-win-worries-gop.

12. Michael Coleman, "Bipartisan Immigration Compromise Unveiled," *Albuquerque Journal*, January 29, 2013, A1, http://www.abqjournal.com/main/2013/01/29/news/bipartisan-immigration-compromise-unveiled.html.

13. Data are from the National Association of Latino Elected and Appointed Officials (NALEO), unpublished database of 2012 elected officials, provided to the author. See also the NALEO *2011 Directory of Latino Elected Officials*; David A. Bositis, "Blacks and the 2012 Elections: A Preliminary Analysis," Joint Center for Political and Economic Studies (JCPES), December 2012, http://www.jointcenter.org/sites/default/files/upload/research/files/Bositis-Election%202012%20-%20merged.pdf; and Don Nakanishi and James Lai, *National Asian Pacific American Political Almanac*, 14th ed., UCLA Asian American Studies Center (AASC), December 2011.

14. Paul Taylor, Ana Gonzalez-Barrera, Jeffrey Passel, and Mark Hugo Lopez, "An Awakened Giant: The Hispanic Electorate Is Likely to Double by 2030," Washington, DC: Pew Hispanic Center, November 14, 2012, http://www.pewhispanic.org/files/2012/11/hispanic_vote_likely_to_double_by_2030_11-14-12.pdf. Presaging this forecast, the Census Bureau had already reported that more than half the nation's overall *population* growth between 2000 and 2010 had been Latinos. See the report by Jeffrey S. Passel, D'Vera Cohn, and Mark

Hugo Lopez: "Hispanics Account for More than Half of Nation's Growth in Past Decade," Washington, DC: Pew Hispanic Center, March 24, 2011.

15. U.S. Census Bureau, *2012 National Population Projections*, http://www.census.gov/population/projections/data/national/2012.html.

16. The most recent Census estimates available at the time this was written were the July 2012 data reporting monthly postcensal resident population, which can be located online: http://www.census.gov/popest/data/national/asrh/2011/2011-nat-res.html.

17. It would be difficult to make a precise count, but here is a simple way to generate a rough comparison: Using the Library of Congress online book-search feature, search for "Hispanic Americans—Politics and Government" and "United States—Politics and Government," limiting the search to years between 1970 and 1914. The results are startling. Just 137 books are cataloged in the Hispanic subject heading, compared to more than 10,000 in the general American politics listing. There are actually more titles than that, but the library's online catalog can only list the first 10,000!

18. See the discussion of minority population estimates in Ralph C. Guzmán, *The Political Socialization of the Mexican American People* (New York: Arno, 1976).

19. Hanes J. Walton, *Invisible Politics: Black Political Behavior* (Albany: SUNY Press, 1985).

20. For a brief history of political science, and its current profile, see Michael Brintnall, Tony Affigne, and Dianne Pinderhughes, "Political Science in the United States: Notes on the Discipline," paper presented at the International Political Science Association (IPSA), "Conference on International Political Science: New Theoretical and Regional Perspectives," Montreal, Quebec, Canada, April 30–May 2, 2008.

21. The limited interest in minority politics among mainstream political science scholars actually persisted well past 1970. In fact, an organized research subfield for race, ethnicity, and politics did not appear in the political science discipline until 1995. See Brintnall, Affigne, and Pinderhughes, "Political Science in the United States."

22. For more information about the Mexican experience in the U.S., see Mario Barrera, *Race and Class in the Southwest: A Theory of Inequality* (Notre Dame, IN: University of Notre Dame Press, 1979); Julian Samora and Patricia Vandel Simon, *A History of the Mexican-American People* (Notre Dame, IN: University of Notre Dame Press, 1993); and Rodolfo Acuña, *Occupied America: A History of Chicanos*, 7th ed. (New York: Longman, 2010).

23. Even his discussion of African Americans is embedded in a disquisition on conflict and social consensus and is not about enfranchisement at all. See E. E. Schattschneider, *The Semisovereign People* (New York: Harcourt Brace Jovanovich, 1960), 8.

24. See for example, Melissa Harris-Lacewell, "Political Science and the Study of African American Public Opinion," in *African American Perspectives on Political Science*, ed. Wilbur C. Rich, 107–129 (Philadelphia: Temple University Press, 2007). Harris-Lacewell writes, "The Voting Rights Act of 1965 and the urban riots of the late 1960s forced political scientists to consider the opinions of the masses of African Americans, both because Southern blacks entered the electorate and because urban blacks entered the American consciousness" (108).

25. Insightful discussions about Latino political cultures in this era can be found in Rodolfo Rosales, *The Illusion of Inclusion: The Untold Political Story of San Antonio* (Austin: University of Texas Press, 2000); and in Benjamin Márquez, *LULAC: The Evolution of a Mexican American Political Organization* (Austin: University of Texas Press, 1993).

26. Raymond Wolfinger and Steven Rosenstone, *Who Votes?* (New Haven: Yale University Press, 1980), 91.

27. One of the best eyewitness accounts of how political scientists envisioned and applied their craft, during early decades of the profession, can be found in Heinz Eulau, *Micro-Macro*

Dilemmas in Political Science: Personal Pathways through Complexity (Norman: University of Oklahoma Press, 1996).

28. Donald Matthews and James Prothro, *Negro Political Participation Study, 1961–1962* [Computer file], conducted by University of Michigan, Survey Research Center, ICPSR07255-v3, Ann Arbor, MI: Inter-university Consortium for Political and Social Research [producer], 1975, Ann Arbor, MI: Inter-university Consortium for Political and Social Research [distributor], 2006-08-15, doi:10.3886/ICPSR07255; Gary T. Marx, *Negro Political Attitudes, 1964* [Computer file], Berkeley, CA: Survey Research Center [producer], 1964; James S. Jackson and Gerald Gurin, *National Survey of Black Americans, 1979–1980* [Computer file], ICPSR08512-v1, Ann Arbor, MI: Inter-university Consortium for Political and Social Research [distributor], 1999, doi:10.3886/ICPSR08512; James S. Jackson, *National Black Election Panel Study, 1984 and 1988* [Computer file], ICPSR09954-v1, Ann Arbor, MI: Inter-university Consortium for Political and Social Research [distributor], 1997, doi:10.3886/ ICPSR09954.v1; Michael Dawson, Ronald Brown, and James S. Jackson, *National Black Politics Study, 1993* [Computer file], ICPSR02018-v2, Ann Arbor, MI: Inter-university Consortium for Political and Social Research [distributor], 2008-12-03, doi:10.3886/ICPSR02018; Katherine Tate, *National Black Election Study, 1996* [Computer file], ICPSR version, Columbus: Ohio State University [producer], 1997, Ann Arbor, MI: Inter-university Consortium for Political and Social Research [distributor], 2004, doi:10.3886/ICPSR02029.

29. As recently as 2011, Ray Block, Jr., used data from the *National Black Politics Study* to determine whether disillusionment with the pace of Black progress had moderated the influence of linked fate on individuals' support for Black nationalism. See Block, "What about Disillusionment? Exploring the Pathways to Black Nationalism," *Political Behavior* 33 (1) (March 2011): 27–51.

30. See Tasha S. Philpot, Daron R. Shaw, and Ernest B. McGowen, "Winning the Race: Black Voter Turnout in the 2008 Presidential Election," *Public Opinion Quarterly* 73 (5) (2009): 995–1022.

31. American National Election Studies (ANES), *American National Election Study, 2008: Pre- and Post-Election Survey*, ICPSR25383-v2, Ann Arbor, MI: Inter-university Consortium for Political and Social Research [distributor], 2012-08-30, doi:10.3886/ICPSR25383.v2.

32. Scholars of Asian Pacific American politics and Native American politics still face challenges, however. In the ANES of 2008, with 2,313 total respondents, only about 20 American Indians and 70 Asian Pacific Americans were surveyed. To help fill the void, Pei-te Lien conducted the *Pilot National Asian American Political Survey* (PNAAPS) in 2000–2001, the first multiethnic, multilingual, and multiregional political survey of Asian Americans. She surveyed 1,218 adults of Chinese, Korean, Vietnamese, Japanese, Filipino, and South Asian descent, generating 141 variables for ethnic identity, acculturation, homeland politics, voting and other types of political participation, political ideology, political partisanship, opinions on various social issues, social connectedness, racial integration, and group discrimination. For discussion based on the PNAAPS data, see Pei-te Lien, M. Margaret Conway, and Janelle Wong, *The Politics of Asian Americans: Diversity and Community* (New York: Routledge, 2004). More recent data for Asian Americans can be found in the National Asian American Surveys (2008 and 2012), conducted by Karthick Ramakrishnan, Taeku Lee, Jane Junn, and Janelle Wong, available online at http://www.naasurvey.com/. The 2008 survey data are available from ICPSR at the University of Michigan: Karthick Ramakrishnan, Jane Junn, Taeku Lee, and Janelle Wong, National Asian American Survey, 2008 [Computer file], ICPSR31481-v2, Ann Arbor, MI: Inter-university Consortium for Political and Social Research [distributor], 2012-07-19, doi:10.3886/ICPSR31481.v2 (http:// dx.doi.org/10.3886/ICPSR31481).

33. Carlos H. Arce, *Mexican Origin People in the United States: The 1979 Chicano Survey* [Computer file], ICPSR08436-v1, Ann Arbor, MI: Inter-university Consortium for Political and Social Research [distributor], 1997, doi:10.3886/ICPSR08436.

34. Rodolfo O. de la Garza, Angelo Falcón, F. Chris Garcia, and John A. García, *Latino National Political Survey, 1989–1990* [Computer file], ICPSR06841-v3, Ann Arbor, MI: Inter-university Consortium for Political and Social Research [distributor], 1998. doi:10.3886/ICPSR06841.

35. Sheryl Gay Stolberg, "After Immigration Protests, Goal Remains Elusive," *New York Times*, May 3, 2006.

36. U.S. Commission on Civil Rights, "The Voting Rights Act: Summary and Text," Clearinghouse Publication No. 32 (Washington, DC: Government Printing Office, September 1971).

37. Theirs was not the first such research, and in fact, the book's bibliography cataloged more than 1,500 older sources. However, most earlier studies were local and often rural in focus. Nothing written before this book had approached the national scope and rigor, for example, of Myrdal or Frazier.

38. Carey McWilliams, *North from Mexico: The Spanish-Speaking People of the United States* (Philadelphia: Lippincott, 1948); V. O. Key, *Southern Politics in State and Nation* (New York: Knopf, 1949); Myrdal, *American Dilemma*; Ralph J. Bunche, *The Political Status of the Negro in the Age of FDR*, ed. Dewey W. Grantham (1940; repr., Chicago: University of Chicago Press, 1973).

39. Louis DeSipio, *Counting on the Latino Vote: Latinos as a New Electorate* (Charlottesville: University Press of Virginia, 1996), 73.

40. Fifteen new books appeared in the four years between 1996 and 1999 (an average of 3.75 per year), nearly as many total entries as the relatively small coterie of political scientists studying Latino politics had produced in the prior *ten* years (between 1986 and 1995), when they wrote just nineteen new books (an average 1.9 per year). To date, this pace has continued to accelerate. In fact, scholars published ninety-one Latino politics books in the next fifteen years, between 2000 and 2014, at an average 6.1 per year, including thirty-six books in the past five years alone (7.2 per year). To put this new activity in the field in perspective, imagine that 7.2 books had been published *every* year since 1970, a period of forty-four years. In that event, instead of approximately 139 extant titles, we would today see more than 316 books in the field.

References

Abrajano, Marisa A. 2010. *Campaigning to the New American Electorate: Advertising to Latino Voters*. Stanford: Stanford University Press.

Abrajano, Marisa A., and R. Michael Alvarez. 2010. *New Faces, New Voices: The Hispanic Electorate in America*. Princeton: Princeton University Press.

Affigne, Tony. 2000. "Latino Politics in the United States." In "Symposium: Latino Politics in the United States." *PS: Political Science and Politics* 32 (3) (September): 523–527.

Alex-Assensoh, Yvette M., and Lawrence J. Hanks, eds. 2000. *Black and Multiracial Politics in America*. New York: NYU Press.

Alvarez, Michael, and Jonathan Nagler. 1999. "Is the Sleeping Giant Awakening? Latinos and California Politics in the 1990's." Paper presented at the annual meeting of the Midwest Political Science Association, Chicago, April.

American National Election Studies. 2013. "User's Guide and Codebook for the Preliminary Release of the ANES 2012 Time Series Study." August 28. http://www.electionstudies.org/studypages/anes_timeseries_2012/anes_timeseries_2012_userguidecodebook.pdf.

Arce, Carlos H. 1997. *Mexican Origin People in the United States: The 1979 Chicano Survey*. Computer file. ICPSR08436-v1. Ann Arbor, MI: Inter-university Consortium for Political and Social Research [distributor]. doi:10.3886/ICPSR08436.

Arnold, Kathleen R. 2011. *American Immigration after 1996: The Shifting Ground of Political Inclusion*. University Park: Penn State University Press.

Barrera, Mario. 1979. *Race and Class in the Southwest: A Theory of Racial Inequality*. Notre Dame, IN: University of Notre Dame Press.

Barreto, Matt A. 2010. *Ethnic Cues: The Role of Shared Ethnicity in Latino Political Participation*. Ann Arbor: University of Michigan Press.

Barreto, Matt A., Loren Collingwood, and Sylvia Manzano. 2010. "A New Measure of Group Influence in Presidential Elections: Assessing Latino Influence in 2008." *Political Research Quarterly* 63 (4): 908–921.

Barreto, Matt A., and Gary Segura. 2012. "2012 Latino Election Eve Poll." Seattle: ImpreMedia/Latino Decisions. http://www.latinodecisions.com/2012-election-eve-polls/.

Barreto, Matt A., Gary Segura, Sylvia Manzano, Adrian Pantoja, and Gabriel Sanchez. 2014. *Latino Voters in the Obama Era*. New York: PublicAffairs.

Barvosa, Edwina. 2008. *Wealth of Selves: Multiple Identities, Mestiza Consciousness, and the Subject of Politics*. College Station: Texas A&M University Press.

Bejarano, Christina. 2013. *The Latina Advantage: Gender, Race, and Political Success*. Austin: University of Texas Press.

Beltrán, Cristina. 2010. *The Trouble with Unity: Latino Politics and the Creation of Identity*. New York: Oxford University Press.

Betancur, John J., and Douglas C. Gills, eds. 2000. *The Collaborative City: Opportunities and Struggles for Blacks and Latinos in U.S. Cities*. New York: Garland.

Bonilla, Frank, Edwin Meléndez, Rebecca Morales, and María de los Angeles Torres, eds. 1998. *Borderless Borders: U.S. Latinos, Latin Americans, and the Paradox of Interdependence*. Philadelphia: Temple University Press.

Bowler, Shaun, and Gary Segura. 2012. *The Future Is Ours*. Thousand Oaks, CA: CQ/Sage.

Brintnall, Michael, Tony Affigne, and Dianne Pinderhughes. 2008. "Political Science in the United States: Notes on the Discipline." Paper presented at the International Political Science Association (IPSA), "Conference on International Political Science: New Theoretical and Regional Perspectives," Montreal, Quebec, Canada, April 30–May 2, 2008.

Browning, Rufus P., Dale Rogers Marshall, and David H. Tabb. 1984. *Protest Is Not Enough: The Struggle of Blacks and Hispanics for Equality in Urban Politics*. Berkeley: University of California Press.

Browning, Rufus P., Dale Rogers Marshall, and David H. Tabb, eds. 2003. *Racial Politics in American Cities*. 3rd ed. New York: Longman.

Bunche, Ralph J. (1940) 1973. *The Political Status of the Negro in the Age of FDR*. Edited by Dewey W. Grantham. Chicago: University of Chicago Press.

Campbell, Angus, Philip E. Converse, Warren E. Miller, and Donald E. Stokes. 1960. *The American Voter*. New York: Wiley.

Carroll, Maurice. 1982. "Hispanic-Voting Study Finds 'Sleeping Giant.'" *New York Times*, August 29. http://www.nytimes.com/1982/08/29/nyregion/hispanic-voting-study-finds-sleeping-giant.html.

Casellas, Jason P. 2011. *Latino Representation in State Houses and Congress*. New York: Cambridge University Press.

Chávez, Maria. 2011. *Everyday Injustice: Latino Professionals and Racism*. Lanham, MD: Rowman and Littlefield.

Chávez, Maria, Jessica Lavariega Monforti, and Melissa Michelson. 2014. *Living the Dream: America's Abandoned Latino Youth*. Boulder, CO: Paradigm.

Connaughton, Stacey L. 2005. *Inviting Latino Voters: Party Messages and Latino Party Identification*. New York: Routledge.

Cruz, José E. 1998. *Identity and Power: Puerto Rican Politics and the Challenge of Ethnicity*. Philadelphia: Temple University Press.

Dávila, Arlene. 2008. *Latino Spin: Public Image and the Whitewashing of Race*. New York: NYU Press.

Dawson, Michael, Ronald Brown, and James S. Jackson. 2008. *National Black Politics Study, 1993*. Computer file. ICPSR02018-v2. Ann Arbor, MI: Inter-university Consortium for Political and Social Research [distributor], 2008-12-03. doi:10.3886/ICPSR02018.

De Genova, Nicholas, ed. 2006. *Racial Transformations: Latinos and Asians Remaking the United States*. Durham: Duke University Press.

de la Garza, Rodolfo O., ed. 1987. *Ignored Voices: Public Opinion Polls and the Latino Community*. Austin: Center for Mexican American Studies, University of Texas at Austin.

de la Garza, Rodolfo O., and Louis DeSipio, eds. 1992. *From Rhetoric to Reality: Latino Politics in the 1988 Elections*. Boulder, CO: Westview.

de la Garza, Rodolfo O., and Louis DeSipio, eds. 1996. *Ethnic Ironies: Latino Politics in the 1992 Elections*. Boulder, CO: Westview.

de la Garza, Rodolfo O., and Louis DeSipio, eds. 1999. *Awash in the Mainstream: Latino Politics in the 1996 Elections*. Boulder, CO: Westview.

de la Garza, Rodolfo O., and Louis DeSipio. 2005. *Muted Voices: Latinos and the 2000 Elections*. Lanham, MD: Rowman and Littlefield.

de la Garza, Rodolfo O., Louis DeSipio, F. Chris Garcia, John García, and Angelo Falcón. 1992. *Latino Voices: Mexican, Puerto Rican, and Cuban Perspectives on American Politics*. Boulder, CO: Westview.

de la Garza, Rodolfo O., Louis DeSipio, and David L. Leal, eds. 2010. *Beyond the Barrio: Latinos in the 2004 Election*. Notre Dame, IN: University of Notre Dame Press.

de la Garza, Rodolfo O., Angelo Falcón, F. Chris Garcia, and John A. García. 1998. *Latino National Political Survey, 1989–1990*. Computer file. ICPSR06841-v3. Ann Arbor, MI: Inter-university Consortium for Political and Social Research [distributor]. doi:10.3886/ICPSR06841.

de la Garza, Rodolfo O., and Brian Lindsay Lowell, eds. 2002. *Sending Money Home: Hispanic Remittances and Community Development*. Lanham, MD: Rowman and Littlefield.

de la Garza, Rodolfo O., Martha Menchaca, and Louis DeSipio, eds. 1994. *Barrio Ballots: Latino Politics in the 1990 Elections*. Boulder, CO: Westview.

de la Garza, Rodolfo O., and Harry P. Pachon, eds. 2000. *Latinos and U.S. Foreign Policy: Representing the "Homeland"?* Lanham, MD: Rowman and Littlefield.

de los Angeles Torres, María. 1999. *In the Land of Mirrors: Cuban Exile Politics in the United States*. Ann Arbor: University of Michigan Press.

de los Angeles Torres, María, ed. 2003. *By Heart / De Memoria: Cuban Women's Journeys in and out of Exile*. Philadelphia: Temple University Press.

DeSipio, Louis. 1996. *Counting on the Latino Vote: Latinos as a New Electorate*. Charlottesville: University of Virginia Press.

DeSipio, Louis, and Rodolfo O. de la Garza. 1998. *Making Americans, Remaking America: Immigration and Immigrant Policy*. Boulder, CO: Westview.

Dugger, Celia W. 1996. "Immigrant Voters Reshape Politics." *New York Times*, March 10, 1996. http://www.nytimes.com/1996/03/10/nyregion/immigrant-voters-reshape-politics.html?pagewanted=all&src=pm.

Dzidzienyo, Anani, and Suzanne Oboler, eds. 2005. *Neither Enemies nor Friends: Latinos, Blacks, Afro-Latinos*. New York: Palgrave Macmillan.

Espino, Rodolfo, David L. Leal, and Kenneth J. Meier, eds. 2007. *Latino Politics: Identity, Mobilization, and Representation*. Charlottesville: University of Virginia Press.

Flores, Henry. 2003. *The Evolution of the Liberal Democratic State with a Case Study of Latinos in San Antonio, Texas*. New York: Edwin Mellen.

Fraga, Luis R., John A. García, Rodney E. Hero, Michael Jones-Correa, Valerie Martinez-Ebers, and Gary Segura. 2010. *Latino Lives in America: Making It Home*. Philadelphia: Temple University Press.

Fraga, Luis R., John A. García, Rodney E. Hero, Michael Jones-Correa, Valerie Martinez-Ebers, and Gary Segura. 2012. *Latinos in the New Millennium: An Almanac of Opinion, Behavior, and Policy Preferences*. New York: Cambridge University Press.

Frazier, E. Franklin. 1949. *The Negro in the United States*. New York: Macmillan.

Garcia, F. Chris, ed. 1973. *Chicano Politics: Readings*. New York: MSS Information.

Garcia, F. Chris, ed. 1974. *La Causa Política: A Chicano Politics Reader*. Notre Dame, IN: University of Notre Dame Press.

Garcia, F. Chris, ed. 1988. *Latinos and the Political System*. Notre Dame, IN: University of Notre Dame Press.

Garcia, F. Chris, ed. 1997. *Pursuing Power: Latinos and the Political System*. Notre Dame, IN: University of Notre Dame Press.

Garcia, F. Chris, and Rudolph O. de la Garza. 1977. *The Chicano Political Experience: Three Perspectives*. North Scituate, MA: Duxbury.

Garcia, F. Chris, and Gabriel R. Sanchez. 2008. *Hispanics and the U.S. Political System: Moving into the Mainstream*. Upper Saddle River, NJ: Prentice Hall.

García, John A. 2003. *Latino Politics in America: Community, Culture, and Interests*. Lanham, MD: Rowman and Littlefield.

García, John A. 2011. *Latino Politics in America: Community, Culture, and Interests*. 2nd ed. Lanham, MD: Rowman and Littlefield.

García, John A., Gabriel R. Sanchez, and J. Salvador Peralta. 2009. *Latino Politics: A Growing and Evolving Political Community (A Reference Guide)*. Ebook available online at http://uair .arizona.edu/system/files/latinopolitics/Latino_Politics_Full_eBook.pdf.

García, Sonia R., Valerie Martinez-Ebers, Irasema Coronado, Sharon A. Navarro, and Patricia A. Jaramillo. 2008. *Políticas: Latina Public Officials in Texas*. Austin: University of Texas Press.

García Bedolla, Lisa. 2005. *Fluid Borders: Latino Power, Identity, and Politics in Los Angeles*. Berkeley: University of California Press.

García Bedolla, Lisa. 2009. *Latino Politics*. Cambridge, UK: Polity.

García Bedolla, Lisa. 2014. *Latino Politics*. 2nd ed. Cambridge, UK: Polity.

Geron, Kim. 2005. *Latino Political Power*. Boulder, CO: Lynne Rienner.

Gibson, Campbell, and Kay Jung. 2002. *Historical Census Statistics on Population Totals by Race, 1790 to 1990, and by Hispanic Origin, 1970 to 1990, for the United States, Regions, Divisions, and States*. Washington, DC: U.S. Census Bureau, Population Division.

Gómez-Quiñones, Juan. 1990. *Chicano Politics: Reality and Promise, 1940–1990*. Albuquerque: University of New Mexico Press.

Gonzales, Alfonso. 2013. *Reform without Justice: Latino Migrant Politics and the Homeland Security State*. New York: Oxford University Press.

Gonzalez, Juan. 2000. *Harvest of Empire: A History of Latinos in America*. New York: Viking.

Gonzalez, Juan. 2011. *Harvest of Empire: A History of Latinos in America*. Rev. ed. New York: Penguin.

Grebler, Leo, Joan W. Moore, and Ralph C. Guzmán. 1970. *The Mexican-American People: The Nation's Second Largest Minority*. New York: Free Press.

Gutierrez, Jose Angel. 1999. *The Making of a Chicano Militant: Lessons from Cristal*. Madison: University of Wisconsin Press.

Gutiérrez, David. 1995. *Walls and Mirrors: Mexican Americans, Mexican Immigrants, and the Politics of Ethnicity*. Berkeley: University of California Press.

Guzmán, Ralph C. 1976. *The Political Socialization of the Mexican American People*. New York: Arno.

Hardy-Fanta, Carol. 1993. *Latina Politics, Latino Politics: Gender, Culture, and Political Participation in Boston*. Philadelphia: Temple University Press.

Hardy-Fanta, Carol, ed. 2007. *Intersectionality and Politics: Recent Research on Gender, Race, and Political Representation in the United States*. New York: Haworth.

Hardy-Fanta, Carol, and Jeffrey Gerson, eds. 2002. *Latino Politics in Massachusetts: Struggles, Strategies and Prospects*. New York: Routledge.

Hattam, Victoria. 2007. *In the Shadow of Race: Jews, Latinos, and Immigrant Politics in the United States*. Chicago: University of Chicago Press.

Hero, Rodney E. 1992. *Latinos and the U.S. Political System: Two-Tiered Pluralism*. Philadelphia: Temple University Press.

Hero, Rodney E., F. Chris Garcia, John García, and Harry Pachon. 2000. "Latino Participation, Partisanship, and Office Holding." In "Symposium: Latino Politics in the United States." *PS: Political Science and Politics* 32 (3) (September): 529–534.

Hero, Rodney E., and Robert R. Preuhs. 2013. *Black-Latino Relations in U.S. National Politics: Beyond Conflict or Cooperation*. New York: Cambridge University Press.

Hondagneu-Sotelo, Pierrette. 1994. *Gendered Transitions: Mexican Experiences of Immigration*. Berkeley: University of California Press.

Itzigsohn, José. 2009. *Encountering American Faultlines: Race, Class, and the Dominican Experience in Providence*. New York: Russell Sage Foundation.

Jackson, James S. 1997. *National Black Election Panel Study, 1984 and 1988*. Computer file. ICPSR09954-v1. Ann Arbor, MI: Inter-university Consortium for Political and Social Research [distributor]. doi:10.3886/ICPSR09954.v1.

Jackson, James S., and Gerald Gurin. 1999. *National Survey of Black Americans, 1979–1980*. Computer file. ICPSR08512-v1. Ann Arbor, MI: Inter-university Consortium for Political and Social Research [distributor]. doi:10.3886/ICPSR08512.

Jaynes, Gerald D., ed. 2000. *Immigration and Race: New Challenges for American Democracy*. New Haven: Yale University Press.

Jennings, James. 1977. *Puerto Rican Politics in New York City*. Washington, DC: University Press of America.

Jennings, James, ed. 1994. *Blacks, Latinos, and Asians in Urban America: Status and Prospects for Politics and Activism*. Westport, CT: Praeger.

Jennings, James, and Monte Rivera. 1984. *Puerto Rican Politics in Urban America*. Westport, CT: Greenwood.

Jiménez, Miriam. 2013. *Inventive Politicians and Ethnic Ascent in American Politics: The Uphill Elections of Italians and Mexicans to the U.S. Congress*. New York: Routledge.

Johnson, Kevin R. 2003. *The "Huddled Masses" Myth: Immigration and Civil Rights*. Philadelphia: Temple University Press.

Jones-Correa, Michael. 1998. *Between Two Nations: The Political Predicament of Latinos in New York City*. Ithaca: Cornell University Press.

Junn, Jane, and Kerry L. Haynie, eds. 2008. *New Race Politics in America: Understanding Minority and Immigrant Politics*. New York: Cambridge University Press.

Key, V. O., Jr. 1942. *Politics, Parties, and Pressure Groups*. New York: Thomas Y. Crowell.

Key, V. O., Jr. 1949. *Southern Politics in State and Nation*. New York: Knopf.

Leal, David L., and José E. Limón, eds. 2013. *Immigration and the Border: Politics and Policy in the New Latino Century*. South Bend, IN: University of Notre Dame Press.

Leal, David L., and Kenneth J. Meier, eds. 2011. *The Politics of Latino Education*. New York: Teachers College Press.

Lee, Taeku, S. Karthick Ramakrishnan, and Ricardo Ramirez. 2006. *Transforming Politics,*

Transforming America: The Political and Civic Incorporation of Immigrants in the United States. Charlottesville: University of Virginia Press.

Lipset, Seymour Martin. 1960. *Political Man*. London: Heinemann.

Magaña, Lisa. 2003. *Straddling the Border: Immigration Policy and the INS*. Austin: University of Texas Press.

Magaña, Lisa. 2005. *Mexican Americans and the Politics of Diversity: Querer Es Poder!* Tucson: University of Arizona Press.

Magaña, Lisa, and Erik Lee. 2013. *Latino Politics and Arizona's Immigration Law SB 1070*. New York: Springer.

Marquardt, Marie, Tim Steigenga, Philip Williams, and Manuel Vásquez. 2011. *Living Illegal: The Human Face of Unauthorized Immigration*. New York: New Press.

Márquez, Benjamin. 1985. *Power and Politics in a Chicano Barrio: A Study of Mobilization Efforts and Community Power in El Paso*. Lanham, MD: University Press of America.

Márquez, Benjamin. 1993. *LULAC: The Evolution of a Mexican American Political Organization*. Austin: University of Texas Press.

Márquez, Benjamin. 2003. *Constructing Identities in Mexican-American Political Organizations: Choosing Issues, Taking Sides*. Austin: University of Texas Press.

Márquez, Benjamin. 2013. *Democratizing Texas Politics: Race and Party Politics, 1945–2002*. Austin: University of Texas Press.

Márquez, Benjamin, and James Jennings. 2000. "Representation by Other Means: Mexican American and Puerto Rican Social Movement Organizations." In "Symposium: Latino Politics in the United States." *PS: Political Science and Politics* 32 (3) (September): 541–546.

Martinez-Ebers, Valerie, Luis Fraga, Linda Lopez, and Arturo Vega. 2000. "Latino Interests in Education, Health, and Criminal Justice Policy." In "Symposium: Latino Politics in the United States." *PS: Political Science and Politics* 32 (3) (September): 547–554.

Marx, Gary T. 1964. *Negro Political Attitudes, 1964*. Computer file. Berkeley, CA: Survey Research Center [producer].

Massey, Douglas, Jorge Durand, and Nolan Malone. 2003. *Beyond Smoke and Mirrors: Mexican Immigration in an Era of Economic Integration*. New York: Russell Sage Foundation.

Matthews, Donald, and James Prothro. 1975. *Negro Political Participation Study, 1961–1962*. Computer file. Conducted by University of Michigan, Survey Research Center. ICPSR07255-v3. Ann Arbor, MI: Inter-university Consortium for Political and Social Research [producer]. Ann Arbor, MI: Inter-university Consortium for Political and Social Research [distributor], 2006-08-15. doi:10.3886/ICPSR07255.

McWilliams, Carey. 1948. *North from Mexico: The Spanish-Speaking People of the United States*. Philadelphia: Lippincott.

Melendez, Mickey. 2003. *We Took the Streets: Fighting for Latino Rights with the Young Lords*. New York: St. Martin's.

Menjívar, Cecilia. 2000. *Fragmented Ties: Salvadoran Immigrant Networks in America*. Berkeley: University of California Press.

Merriam, Charles, and Harold Gosnell. 1924. *Non-Voting: Causes and Methods of Control*. Chicago: University of Chicago Press.

Minta, Michael D. 2011. *Oversight: Representing the Interests of Blacks and Latinos in Congress*. Princeton: Princeton University Press.

Miyares, Marcelino. 1980. *Models of Political Participation of Hispanic-Americans*. New York: Arno.

Montejano, David, ed. 1999. *Chicano Politics and Society in the Late Twentieth Century*. Austin: University of Texas Press.

Montoya, Lisa J., Carol Hardy-Fanta, and Sonia García. 2000. "Latina Politics: Gender,

Participation, and Leadership." In "Symposium: Latino Politics in the United States." *PS: Political Science and Politics* 32 (3) (September): 555–561.

Moore, Joan, and Raquel Pinderhughes, eds. 1993. *In the Barrios: Latinos and the Underclass Debate*. New York: Russell Sage Foundation.

Muñoz, Carlos, Jr. 1989. *Youth, Identity, Power: The Chicano Movement*. New York: Verso.

Muñoz, Carlos, Jr. 2007. *Youth, Identity, Power: The Chicano Movement*. Rev. and exp. ed. New York: Verso.

Myrdal, Gunnar. 1944. *An American Dilemma: The Negro Problem and Modern Democracy*. New York: Harper.

Navarro, Sharon A., and Armando Xavier Mejia, eds. 2004. *Latino Americans and Political Participation: A Reference Handbook*. Santa Barbara, CA: ABC-CLIO.

Navarro, Sharon A., and Rodolfo Rosales. 2013. *The Roots of Latino Urban Agency*. Denton: University of North Texas Press.

Nelson, William E., Jr., and Jessica Lavariega Monforti, eds. 2005. *Black and Latino/a Politics: Issues in Political Development in the United States*. Miami, FL: Barnhardt and Ashe.

Newton, Lina. 2008. *Illegal, Alien, or Immigrant: The Politics of Immigration Reform*. New York: NYU Press.

Oboler, Suzanne, ed. 2006. *Latinos and Citizenship: The Dilemma of Belonging*. New York: Palgrave Macmillan.

Olivas, Michael A., ed. 2013. *In Defense of My People: Alonso S. Perales and the Development of Mexican-American Public Intellectuals*. Houston: Arte Público.

Pachon, Harry, and Louis DeSipio. 1994. *New Americans by Choice: Political Perspectives of Latino Immigrants*. Boulder, CO: Westview.

Passel, Jeffrey S., D'Vera Cohn, and Mark Hugo Lopez. 2011. "Hispanics Account for More than Half of Nation's Growth in Past Decade." Washington, DC: Pew Hispanic Center, March 24.

Ramakrishnan, S. Karthick. 2005. *Democracy in Immigrant America: Changing Demographics and Political Participation*. Stanford: Stanford University Press.

Ramírez, Ricardo. 2013. *Mobilizing Opportunities: The Evolving Latino Electorate and the Future of American Politics*. Charlottesville: University of Virginia Press.

Rich, Wilbur C. 1996. *The Politics of Minority Coalitions: Race, Ethnicity, and Shared Uncertainties*. Westport, CT: Praeger.

Rodriguez, David. 2002. *Latino National Political Coalitions: Struggles and Challenges*. New York: Routledge.

Rodriguez, Victor M. 2005. *Latino Politics in the United States: Race, Ethnicity, Class, and Gender in the Mexican American and Puerto Rican Experience*. Dubuque, IA: Kendall/Hunt.

Rosales, Rodolfo. 2000. *The Illusion of Inclusion: The Untold Political Story of San Antonio*. Austin: University of Texas Press.

Rouse, Stella M. 2013. *Latinos in the Legislative Process: Interests and Influence*. New York: Cambridge University Press.

Sánchez, José Ramón. 2007. *Boricua Power: A Political History of Puerto Ricans in the United States*. New York: NYU Press.

Schattschneider, E. E. 1960. *The Semisovereign People*. New York: Harcourt Brace Jovanovich.

Schmidt, Ronald, Sr. 2000. *Language Policy and Identity Politics in the United States*. Philadelphia: Temple University Press.

Schmidt, Ronald, Sr., Yvette Alex-Assensoh, Andrew Aoki, and Rodney E. Hero. 2010. *Newcomers, Outsiders, and Insiders: Immigrants and American Racial Politics in the Early Twenty-First Century*. Ann Arbor: University of Michigan Press.

Schmidt, Ronald, Sr., Edwina Barvosa-Carter, and Rodolfo D. Torres. 2000. "Latina/o Identities:

Social Diversity and U.S. Politics." In "Symposium: Latino Politics in the United States." *PS: Political Science and Politics* 32 (3) (September): 563–567.

Segura, Gary M., and Shaun Bowler, eds. 2005. *Diversity in Democracy: Minority Representation in the United States*. Charlottesville: University of Virginia Press.

Shorris, Earl. 1992. *Latinos: A Biography of the People*. New York: Norton.

Sierra, Christine Marie, Teresa Carrillo, Louis DeSipio, and Michael Jones-Correa. 2000. "Latino Immigration and Citizenship." In "Symposium: Latino Politics in the United States." *PS: Political Science and Politics* 32 (3) (September): 535–540.

Smith, Robert. 2005. *Mexican New York: Transnational Lives of Immigrants*. Berkeley: University of California Press.

Stokes-Brown, Atiya Kai. 2012. *The Politics of Race in Latino Communities: Walking the Color Line*. New York: Routledge.

Subervi-Vélez, Federico A., ed. 2008. *The Mass Media and Latino Politics: Studies of U.S. Media Content, Campaign Strategies and Survey Research, 1984–2004*. New York: Routledge.

Tate, Katherine. 1997. *National Black Election Study, 1996*. Computer file. ICPSR version. Columbus: Ohio State University [producer]. Ann Arbor, MI: Inter-university Consortium for Political and Social Research [distributor], 2004. doi:10.3886/ICPSR02029.

Telles, Edward, Mark Sawyer, and Gaspar Rivera-Salgado, eds. 2011. *Just Neighbors? Research on African American and Latino Relations in the United States*. New York: Russell Sage Foundation.

Tichenor, Daniel. 2002. *Dividing Lines: The Politics of Immigration Control in America*. Princeton: Princeton University Press.

Torres, Andrés, ed. 2006. *Latinos in New England*. Philadelphia: Temple University Press.

Torres, Andrés, and José E. Velázquez, eds. 1998. *The Puerto Rican Movement: Voices from the Diaspora*. Philadelphia: Temple University Press.

Torres, Rodolfo D., and George Katsiaficas, eds. 1999. *Latino Social Movements: Historical and Theoretical Perspectives: A New Political Science Reader*. New York: Routledge.

U.S. Census Bureau, Population Division. 2012. *Table 4. Projections of the Population by Sex, Race, and Hispanic Origin for the United States: 2015–2060*. Table NP2012-T4. http://www.census.gov/population/projections/data/national/2012.html.

U.S. Census Bureau, Population Division. 2013. "Asians Fastest-Growing Race or Ethnic Group in 2012, Census Bureau Reports." http://www.census.gov/newsroom/releases/archives/population/cb13-112.html.

Valdes y Tapia, Daniel. 1976. *Hispanos and American Politics*. New York: Arno.

Valle, Victor M., and Rodolfo D. Torres. 2000. *Latino Metropolis*. Minneapolis: University of Minnesota Press.

Varsanyi, Monica, ed. 2010. *Taking Local Control: Immigration Policy and Activism in U.S. Cities and States*. Stanford: Stanford University Press.

Vélez-Ibáñez, Carlos G., and Anna Sampaio, eds.. 2002. *Transnational Latina/o Communities: Politics, Processes, and Cultures*. Lanham, MD: Rowman and Littlefield.

Venator-Santiago, Charles R. 2013. *Puerto Rico and the Origins of U.S. Global Empire: The Disembodied Shade*. New York: Routledge.

Verba, Sidney, Norman Nie, and Jae-On Kim. 1978. *Participation and Political Equality: A Seven-Nation Comparison*. New York: Cambridge University Press.

Vigil, Maurilio E. 1977. *Chicano Politics*. Washington, DC: University Press of America.

Vigil, Maurilio E. 1987. *Hispanics in American Politics: The Search for Political Power*. Lanham, MD: University Press of America.

Vigil, Maurilio E. 1996. *Hispanics in Congress: A Historical and Political Survey*. Lanham, MD: University Press of America.

Villarreal, Roberto E. 1979. *Chicano Elites and Non-elites: An Inquiry into Social and Political Change*. Palo Alto, CA: R&E Research.

Villarreal, Roberto E., and Norma G. Hernandez, eds. 1991. *Latinos and Political Coalitions: Political Empowerment for the 1990s*. Westport, CT: Praeger.

Villarreal, Roberto E., Norma G. Hernandez, and Howard D. Neighbor, eds. 1988. *Latino Empowerment: Progress, Problems, and Prospects*. Westport, CT: Greenwood.

Wolfinger, Raymond E., and Steven J. Rosenstone. 1980. *Who Votes?* New Haven: Yale University Press.

Wong, Carolyn. 2006. *Lobbying for Inclusion*. Stanford: Stanford University Press.

Wong, Janelle S. 2006. *Democracy's Promise: Immigrants and American Civic Institutions*. Ann Arbor: University of Michigan Press.

Zuñiga, Victor, and Rubén Hernández-Leon. 2006. *New Destinations: Mexican Immigration in the United States*. New York: Russell Sage Foundation.

PART II

Latinidad

The Question of "Latino" Identity

2

Identity Revisited

Latinos(as) and Panethnicity

JESSICA LAVARIEGA MONFORTI

The wide availability of Hispanic-centered social data is a relatively recent development in the social sciences. Consider this: although Mexican, Indigenous, and other Spanish colonial migrants had resided, been conquered, and migrated to the U.S. for nearly 200 years, it was not until 1970 that the decennial census included a way for respondents to group themselves by Latino self-identification. At about the same time, Latino social movements made clear that demographers, political scientists, and policymakers should not assume homogeneity among "Latinos"—in the era of nationalist Chicano and Puerto Rican social movements and the Cuban American emergence in South Florida, "Hispanic" identity was subject to multiple definitions. On the other hand, Latinos themselves frequently articulated a pan-Latino political agenda and identity. These are more than theoretical questions; early in 2013, the Census Bureau announced it would again reconsider options for Hispanic self-classification, perhaps recasting the category as a *race*—which would, of course, mean adopting the ultimate "pan-ethnic" identity, with connotations of biological and cultural commonality.[1] In this chapter, Jessica Lavariega Monforti returns to the fundamental question, using the Latino National Survey to ask whether there is any such a thing as Latino panethnicity and, if so, to measure its dimensions and limitations.

Understanding Panethnic Identity

Scholars have defined panethnic identity as a collective-generated identity that transcends the boundaries of the individual identities of different Spanish-speaking populations and represents a distinct, separate group identification and consciousness (Padilla 1985).[2] Panethnic Latino identity emerged as the set of Spanish speaking and origin populations grew in size, became closer in residential proximity, and had shared interests (García 2003). The goal of the proposed study is to determine the processes involved in the development of panethnic Latino identities today and to compare these results to a baseline that was set using the Latino National Political Survey (LNPS; 1989–90).

In Louis DeSipio's (1996) theory of panethnic identity, he points to characteristics that are mutually reinforcing in the process of forming the foundation for panethnicity Latino identity: (1) common cultural characteristics; (2) mandated common ethnicity and statutory recognition of Latino- rather than national-origin-based ethnicity; (3) the role of Latino elites in shaping a common identity; (4) the common public policy needs and concerns of Latino communities; and (5) increasing contact among Latino populations with various ancestries. My previous research tested DeSipio's theories using the data from the 1989–90 LNPS (de la Garza et al. 1992), and concluded that panethnic identifiers are distinctive on some of these

---

Research Questions

- Do panethnic Latino identifiers constitute a politically, socially distinctive subgroup within the Latino population?
- What specific characteristics or variables set them apart?

---

measures, such as language preference, age at immigration, reasons for immigrating to the U.S., contact with diverse Latino populations, and perceptions of discrimination (Lavariega Monforti 2007). At that time, the data revealed mixed support for DeSipio's theory; it is essential to update these analyses with more recent data.[3]

In 1990, the LNPS reported that approximately one-third of Latino respondents self-identified using panethnic terms such as "Latino" and/or "Hispanic" (de la Garza et al. 1989–1990). Of the respondents in the 2006 LNS (Fraga et al. 2006), just over 87% indicated that they "somewhat" or "strongly" identify with these same panethnic terms about a decade and a half later; preference for panethnicity was more than double what was found in the LNPS. Changes in the level of panethnicity may seriously impact both intra- and intergroup relations. The way Latinos work, play, and socialize with other Latinos may be impacted—translating into an interesting exchange of intragroup politics.

The analysis here again examines the variables outlined in DeSipio's theory of panethnic identification and includes the following questions: Do these identifiers constitute a politically, socially distinctive subgroup within the Latino population? What specific characteristics or variables set them apart? Before delving into an examination of these research questions, one must provide a historical context regarding Latino populations in the United States as well as a conceptual framework for Latino panethnicity.

[handwritten margin note: what is she studying?]

Latinos in the United States: A Brief Historical Review of These Populations since 1980

In 1980, the Latino population constituted only 6% of the U.S. population. However, according to a report from the U.S. Census Bureau titled "The Hispanic Population in the United States: March 2002," there were 37.4 million Latinos in the civilian noninstitutional population in that year, when more than one in eight people in the United States were of Hispanic origin (Ramirez and de la Cruz 2003). Between 1980 and 2000, the rate of growth among Hispanics was nearly four times that of the general population. By 2010, the Latino population had grown to 50.5 million, 16.3% of the total, after increasing by 43% in the prior decade.

Not only has the population increased in size over time, but its internal composition has also shifted. While the Hispanic population has grown as a whole, certain segments such as Puerto Ricans and Cuban Americans are now relatively smaller, while others such as people of Mexican origin and "other Hispanics" have grown substantially.[4] Further, newer immigrants from diverse countries of origin have

Table 2.1: Hispanic Population of the United States by
National Origin Group, 1980 and 2010

	1980	2010
Total Hispanic population	14.6 million	50.5 million
% of U.S. population	6.4%	16.3%
Mexican American	59.8	63.0
Puerto Rican	14.0	9.2
Cuban American	5.5	3.5
Other Hispanic	20.7	24.3

Sources: U.S. Census Bureau 1983; and U.S. Census Bureau, 2010 Census,
Summary File 1, Table PCT 11.

settled in areas previously dominated by established Latino populations, while these more established groups have continued to settle these areas as well as move into new regions (see table 2.1).[5]

As Latino populations have grown and transformed internally, a panethnic Latino identity has emerged as a part of the process of intergroup relations and communication between these assorted Spanish-speaking groups. An example comes from Felix Padilla's study of Puerto Rican and Mexican American efforts to come together politically as Latinos in the urban U.S. (Padilla 1985). Padilla's research on the development of Latino consciousness discusses how previously disunited Latino subgroups made conscientious efforts to transcend traditional national-origin boundaries to form a broader configuration in Chicago as the two populations grew in size. In this case, demands and political activism were structured to advance Latino interests and panethnic associations rather than country-of-origin concerns. Thus, panethnic Latino identity emerged as the set of Spanish-speaking and Latino populations grew in size and became closer in residential proximity (García 2003). The goal of this study, using the most recent data, is to determine the processes involved in the development of Latino panethnicity, known as *latinidad*.

Panethnicity and the Potential Building Blocks of *Latinidad*

One scholar who shaped the panethnicity literature is Yen Le Espiritu, who writes, "Ethnic groups are created and altered in encounters among groups, and to interact meaningfully with those in the larger society, individuals have to identify themselves in terms intelligible to outsiders" (1992, 10). How and through what processes individuals choose panethnic identities is the focus of this research. "Panethnicity" is the generalization of solidarity among ethnic subgroups or nationalities, and in this study, it refers to the use of "Hispanic" or "Latino," rather than identities based on national origin or other cultural factors. Many scholars have highlighted the obstacles to panethnicity. Berta Hernández-Truyol states,

> Latinas/os are a diverse community, whose identity components—race, sex, ethnicity, language, and sexuality to name a few of the pertinent ones—are indivisible yet diverse and varied. Such diversity, to date, has not allowed for a cohesive Latina/o theoretical model to be articulated. Rather, it has been the basis of skepticism as to whether such a model could exist. . . . In the context of the majority culture in the

U.S., such diversity has resulted in a fragmenting of identities within each individual depending on external social/political contexts.[6]

Nevertheless, scholars have not thoroughly examined panethnicity as a concept relating to the U.S. Latino community in terms of its component parts and potential impact on political opinion and behavior.[7] The study of panethnicity is important because it directs research and theoretical debate toward those conditions under which identities can be a mobilizing political force—"political participation on the basis of ethnicity provides a rationale for, and indeed demands, the mobilization of political participation along ethnic lines" (Espiritu 1992, 9–10).

DeSipio (1996) points to five mutually reinforcing characteristics in the process of *latinidad* foundation formation: (1) common set of cultural traditions; (2) mandated common ethnicity and statutory recognition of Latino- based ethnicity; (3) the role of community-based elites in shaping a common identity; (4) the common public policy needs and concerns of Latino communities; and (5) increasing contact across Latino national-origin populations. One must provide a comprehensive discussion about these variables because scholars can use them to examine theories of identity building.

Cultural Commonalities

DeSipio (1996) singles out language as one of the most important of common cultural characteristics because English and Spanish are the dominant languages spoken in Latino communities. One must account for two perspectives when speaking about language: the experience of immigrants and the experience of native-born U.S. Latinos. Among immigrants, Spanish is overwhelmingly the dominant language, while for most second-generation and beyond Latinos, English is dominant (de la Garza et al. 1992; Pérez-Monforti 2001). However, the part of the Latino experience that binds these two groups together is that their exclusion from the dominant society has been centered on their use or their ancestors' use of Spanish (DeSipio 1996). Thus, the claim is that Latinos who are native English speakers continue to be sensitive to the needs of the Spanish-speaking segment of the population because of family ties (Pérez-Monforti 2001). In other words, language serves as a cultural and symbolic link to the larger Latino community (Schmidt 1997; Pérez-Monforti 2001).

The second common cultural factor is ethnic-racial mixture. Historically, throughout Latin America, there has been a continuous influx and intermingling of people of various ancestral lineages. The populations of and from this region therefore have become hybrid—there are traces and combinations of Indigenous, Spanish, Asian, African, and other European descent; therefore, Latinos challenge the dominant U.S. society's simplistic and dichotomized understanding of race in terms of just white and black. This ethnic-racial mixture challenge has directed the U.S. Bureau of the Census to classify Latinos in both racial and ethnic terms, which has led to the popularization of the term "Hispanic."[8] This effort among some Latinos to distinguish themselves from the dominant society's bifurcated notion of race offers a potential unifying factor and perhaps a building block for a national panethnic Latino identity.

The third common cultural characteristic is political socialization in Latin America. People socialized in Latin America over the past several generations have had experiences that include a widespread experience with totalitarian corporatist governments and highly unarticulated class systems as opposed to the "liberal" individualist values of the U.S. system. Some critics have argued that Latinos have failed to take advantage of the liberal political system and instead have accepted some form of machine or boss rule (Anders 1979). DeSipio (1996) states the there is some evidence to support this claim in that Latino respondents to the LNPS (de la Garza et al. 1989–1990) reported a preference for larger governments, which are involved in a wider range of policy areas. However, he also points out that an alternative explanation is the socioeconomic status of Latinos,[9] and thus one should interpret the legacy of socialization in Latin America with caution.

An experience with or a direct connection to immigration is the final common cultural experience. Latino immigration currently constitutes the largest portion of contemporary immigration experience, and most Hispanics in the U.S. are linked to that experience.[10] While most Latinos can trace their roots to an immigration experience, this fact does not imply that the content of their immigration experiences are the same. On the contrary, Mexican American immigration experiences differ significantly from those of Puerto Ricans, who are U.S. citizens by birth, and Cubans, many of whom are escaping communism.[11] However, the continuous nature of immigration allows Latino communities to maintain linkages with the immigration experience, thus providing another potential building block for *latinidad*.

Identity as Mandate

The second set of variables considered as potential building blocks for *latinidad* includes a mandated common ethnicity and statutory recognition of panethnic rather than national-origin-based ethnicity. For the purposes of federal programs, such as the Voting Rights Act of 1975, the concept of the Spanish-origin population may offer an inducement for ethnic-group leaders to identify as Latinos rather than as Chicanos, Puerto Ricans, and Cubanos because their respective fates are linked through this type of legislation. Therefore, the third variable that could build *latinidad* is the role of Latino elites in shaping a common identity (Skerry 1997). Organizations attempting to speak for Latino communities, such as the Congressional Hispanic Caucus (CHC), the National Association of Latino Elected Officials (NALEO), and the National Hispanic Chamber of Commerce, developed in the 1970s alongside the panethnic notion of *latinidad*. Additionally, organizations with a more specific group focus, such as the Mexican American Legal Defense and Education Fund (MALDEF) and La Raza Unida, have broadened their advocacy and research foci to be more inclusive (DeSipio 1996). For example, in November 2005, the Institute for Puerto Rican Policy changed its name to the National Institute for Latino Policy to more accurately reflect the national scope and pan-Latino nature of its work. However, DeSipio also points out, "The efforts to create an organizational infrastructure to support a pan-ethnic identity have met with mixed success" (1996, 185).

In support of some of DeSipio's theory, José Calderón (1992) states that categorization of Chicano, Puerto Rican, Cuban, and other Latin American groups under the term "Hispanic" may have arisen from external forces such as the use of the term by the media, the U.S. Census Bureau, and other government agencies and politicians on the federal level, rather than from any cohesion of the groups themselves. Angharad Valdivia (2010) provides further support in her examination of the relatively recent boom in English-language Latino media. She concludes, "Latinidad is included in the media" (188). An argument can be made that the Spanish-language media, such as Univision, TV Azteca, and Telemundo, speak to the growth, diversity, and increased external pressure to support *latinidad* (see Rodriguez 1999).

Policy Needs and Community Leadership

The next potential panethnic identification builder is the common public policy needs and concerns of Latino communities (Fraga 1992). According to DeSipio (1996), these needs would include political empowerment, naturalization and immigration settlement assistance, primary and secondary education, access to higher education, job training, social service delivery, child poverty, housing, and crime prevention.[12] These issues transcend national-origin-based needs, offer the foundation for a Latino political agenda, and set the issues of concern for Latinos apart from those of African Americans, Anglos, and others (for a broader discussion, see Tolbert and Hero 1996; Hood, Morris, and Shirkey 1997; Kinder and Winter 2001).

Cross-Ethnic Contact

Finally, the last variable that DeSipio (1996) discusses is the increasing contact between Latino populations with various ancestries due to geographic overlap. Thirty years ago, it would have been reasonable to state that Mexican Americans lived in the Southwest, Puerto Ricans lived on the island and in the tristate area of New York–New Jersey–Connecticut, and Cubans and Cuban Americans lived in Florida. As immigration from Latin America has grown and diversified, the picture of Latino communities has become more geographically, and thus more socially, complicated. For example, New York is now home to Dominicans, Colombians, and Mexicans; Los Angeles has added Salvadorans and Guatemalans to the preexisting Mexican American population; and sizeable Cuban American populations live in New Jersey and Texas. One should note that Latino communities are extending themselves to states, such as Georgia and North Carolina, in which, historically, Latinos have not been a major presence. This geographical overlap has increased the amount and perhaps the intensity of contact between these national-origin groups, thereby providing an additional possibility for unity among them. One can analyze DeSipio's theory to determine whether the variables he outlines are predictors of panethnic identification.

Theory and Data

The LNS (Fraga et al. 2006) is a significant study that provides the most recent set of comprehensive data with a large number of respondents from various Latino populations. Given the timing, depth, and scope of this survey instrument, these data can provide scholars with a major data source. The LNS measured the political attitudes and behaviors of a variety of specific Latino groups in the United States:

Mexican Americans, Puerto Ricans, Cuban Americans, Dominicans, and Salvador-ans. With a few exceptions, demographic characteristics of the sample mirror those of the populations as a whole.[13]

The models examined here include the five sets of independent variables that test DeSipio's (1996) potential building blocks for *latinidad*, outlined in the preceding section. The goal is to discover whether panethnic Latino identifiers constitute a politically, socially distinctive subgroup within Latino populations on the basis of DeSipio's theory of *latinidad*. The dependent variable in each of the multivariate models was created to distinguish panethnic identifiers from non-panethnic identifiers. Therefore, a new variable was created from the LNS so that respondents who chose "Either Hispanic or Latino" when asked their ethnic identity preference would be thereafter defined as panethnic identifiers. This variable then would reflect a respondent's predilection to choose either panethnic identity rather than not.[14] The question asked, "The most frequently used terms to describe persons of Latin American descent living in the United States are 'Hispanic and 'Latino.' Of the two, which do you prefer, or do you not care about this terminology?"

The first model measures the concept of common cultural characteristics as a potential building block for *latinidad*. The common cultural characteristics that were examined included *language, ethnic diversity, political socialization in Latin America, immigration, experiences with employment and police discrimination,* and *socioeconomic class.* Language is based on the language of the interview. I used data that asked about the place of grandparents' birth as the measure of ethnic diversity.[15]

Political socialization in Latin America and *age at the time of immigration* were measured by the respondents' age at the time of immigration and then collapsed into categories based on the political socialization literature. Those respondents born in the United States received a zero on this measure. The next category includes those who immigrated to the United States between the ages of one and five. These respondents were preschool aged at the time of immigration; their political development included only the knowledge that authority figures were good, and the agents of socialization during this period were their parents (Easton and Dennis 1965; Beck and Jennings 1975; Renshon 1975).

The second category included those who immigrated during early childhood, between the ages of six and nine. During this time period, political party identification forms without any specific knowledge of what this identification means. The agents of socialization here are parents and schools (Langton 1967; Langton and Jennings 1968). The next category encompasses those who immigrated during late childhood, between ten and thirteen years of age, as they began to recognize the meaning of party identification and some political issues (Campbell 1980). The agents here are parents, schools, and at age thirteen, peers. The category that follows includes those who immigrated during adolescence, between fourteen and eighteen years of age. Adolescents develop more complexity in views and ideas, and the agents remain the same, with peers having the most influence. Those who immigrated during early adulthood, between the ages of nineteen and twenty-six, form the next category. The agents during this period are peers, the college experience, and events such as a traumatic economic state or war (Conway et al. 1981; Sears and Valentino 1997). According to the political socialization literature, political views do not change dramatically after the age of twenty-six without the occurrence of traumatic events, so the remaining respondents were coded into categories in ten-year increments through the age of sixty-five. Those in the sixty-five and over age category constitute their own group.

To capture geographically based socialization processes, I created dichotomous variables for respondents in California and Texas; I also created dichotomous variables for Mexican- and Caribbean-origin respondents to capture identification preferences by country-of-origin groups. Discrimination is measured by two questions that asked whether respondents have experienced discrimination personally at work and by police. Socioeconomic status is measured by yearly income[16] and educational attainment. Further, I also included measures that specify the reason that respondents immigrated to the United States, such as to join family, for economic reasons, or because they were escaping a dangerous situation in their country of origin. Gender and age variables serve as controls. In previous research using the LNPS data, *age at immigration, income, being brought to the U.S. by family, income,* and *citizenship status* were statistically significant predictors in the model for all panethnic identifiers. I expect to find similar results in the LNS analyses.

The next model measures the impact of *mandated common ethnicity and statutory recognition* of a panethnic identity. This model is the only one that examined respondents' answers regarding the meaning of identifiers such as "Hispanic" and "Latino." The question asked respondents if they feel that the group they identified with (Latino, Hispanic, Neither, or Either) "make up a distinct racial group in America." If panethnic identifiers' answers indicated that panethnicity is not a distinct group, then we can infer that respondents might identify with panethnicity as a result of mandated common ethnicity and/or statutory recognition. In previous research that employed the LNPS, a very small percentage of panethnic identifiers, less than 1%, defined *latinidad* in terms of a mandated ethnic identity or statutes. In this study, I expect similar results from the LNS analyses.

The third model examines the role of Mexican American, Cuban American, Puerto Rican, and other Latino elites in shaping a common identity. This model also considers whether organizational membership and activity are predictors of panethnic identification, along with measures of the common public policy needs and concerns of Latino communities, based on respondents' answers to a list of policy questions; this model includes an analysis of responses to questions regarding the most important issue in the nation and for Latinos in general. It is important to note that the policy concerns of the Latino community have shifted since the LNPS. In 1989–1990, the top national policy concern was *drugs, drug abuse, and alcoholism,* while the top ethnic-community concern was *lack of education and English skills.* In 2006, the LNS respondents indicated that their top national concern was Iraq and foreign policy, while their top community concern was immigration. In the LNPS analyses, four variables were significant for panethnic identifiers: *ideology* and the *issue of drug and alcohol abuse* and, at the ethnic-group level, *education* and *citizenship.* I expect to find similar results in the LNS analyses, such that national and ethnic-community policy concerns will be significant, along with ideology, education, and citizenship.

The final model in this series measures whether increasing contact with members of Latino populations increases the chance of panethnic identification. Here we created a variable that tallies the frequency of contact that Latinos have with other Latinos, reported for each respondent in the workplace and with friends. I also included a variable that indicates whether the respondent's spouse is Latino/a, along with control variables. In the LNPS analyses, *citizenship* and *income* were significant predictors; however, *contact with other Latinos/Hispanics* clearly drove the model. Therefore, it is expected that respondents who have a more diverse ethnic ancestry, have more contact with Latinos outside their national-origin group, and married a spouse from a different country-of-origin group will be more likely to choose *latinidad*.

Expectations and Analyses

Logistic regression was employed as the method of analysis for all of the multivariate models because the dependent variable, *panethnic identification*, is dichotomous.[17] The first model attempts to measure the concept of common cultural characteristics as a potential building block for *latinidad*. The common cultural characteristics to be examined include language, ethnic diversity, political socialization in Latin America, immigration, discrimination in employment and by police, geographic and cultural socialization, and socioeconomic class. In this first model, we expect to find that respondents who (1) speak English more often, (2) immigrated for economic reasons, family reasons, and to escape a poor political situation, (3) avoided experiences with employment discrimination, (4) were not of Caribbean origin, and (5) are California residents are more likely to identify with *latinidad* (see table 2.2).

For all panethnic identifiers, language, ethnic diversity, immigrated for/with family, experience of police discrimination, and educational attainment are statistically significant. I was also able to run simulations to determine the predicted probabilities of the significant variables.[18] As we move from an interview in English to one in Spanish, there is a .08 increase in the probability of choosing *latinidad*, holding all other variables constant. As a hypothetical respondent moves from having all grandparents born in the U.S. to having all grandparents born outside the U.S., he or she is .13 less likely to choose *latinidad*. Those panethnic identifiers brought to the United States for economic reasons or for family reasons, rather than for other reasons, were .06 more likely to choose *latinidad*. As we move from having experience with police discrimination to not, respondents are .06 more likely to choose *latinidad*. Further, as we move from low to high levels of education, there is a .04 increase in the probability of choosing *latinidad* when all other variables hold constant; however, including the construction of the dependent variable assumes that no differences exist between Hispanic and Latino identifiers. To avoid making this assumption, one must analyze Latino-specific identifiers and Hispanic-specific identifiers separately for each of the models.

For Hispanic identifiers, six of the seventeen variables are statistically significant: *language*, *ethnic diversity*, *employment discrimination*, *gender*, and *California*. It is notable that the panethnic and Hispanic models share two statistically significant variables in common but that four variables are found to be important in the latter and not in the former. The magnitude of change for language in the Hispanic model

Table 2.2: Multivariate Logistic Regression: Common Cultural Characteristics as Building Blocks of Latinidad

	All panethnic identifiers		Hispanic identifiers		Latino identifiers	
	Coefficient (SE)	Predicted probabilities	Coefficient (SE)	Predicted probabilities	Coefficient (SE)	Predicted probabilities
Language	.32***	.08	.26**	.06	.18	
	(.09)		(.09)		(.12)	
Ethnic diversity	−.13***	.13	−.17***	.16	.06*	.02
	(.02)		(.02)		(.03)	
Immigrated for economic reasons	.10		.17		.10	
	(.09)		(.11)		(.13)	
Immigrated for family reasons	.24*	.06	.17		.17	
	(.10)		(.11)		(.14)	
Immigrated to flee situation	−.00		.07		−.13	
	(.16)		(.18)		(.24)	
Age at immigration (cohort)	−.02		−.02		.00	
	(.02)		(.03)		(.03)	
Discrimination in employment	−.11		−.23*	.05	.15	
	(.09)		(.09)		(.11)	
Discrimination by police	.22*	.06	−.01		.40*	.05
	(.10)		(.11)		(.12)	
Yearly income	−.01		.00		−.01	
	(.04)		(.05)		(.06)	
Educational attainment	.04*	.04	.02		.04⁺	.02
	(.02)		(.02)		(.03)	
Gender	.04		.15*	.03	−.18	.02
	(.06)		(.06)		(.09)	
Citizenship	.03		.03		.00	
	(.08)		(.09)		(.11)	
Mexican	−.02		.09		−.19⁺	.02
	(.08)		(.08)		(.11)	
Caribbean	−.20		−.18		−.08	
	(.13)		(.14)		(.18)	
California	−.02		−.20*	.04	.29⁺	.04
	(.08)		(.08)		(.10)	
Texas	.05		.14		−.18	
	(.10)		(.10)		(.16)	
Age	.00		.00		.00	
	(.00)		(.00)		(.00)	
Constant	−.35		−.92**		−2.04	
	(.26)		(.28)		(.37)	
N	4755		4755		4755	

⁺ p < .10, * p < .05, ** p < .001, *** p < .000

is .06, smaller than in the panethnic model; for ethnic diversity, the magnitude of change is .16 in the Hispanic model, larger than in the panethnic model. Further, as we move from having experience with employment discrimination to not, respondents are .05 more likely to choose *Hispanic identity*. Females were .03 more likely to choose Hispanic identity than were males, and non-California residents were more likely to choose Hispanic identity than were California residents.

In the Latino model, six variables are statistically significant: *ethnic diversity, discrimination by police, educational attainment, gender, Mexican origin,* and *California.* In this model, the sign of variable coefficient for ethnic diversity switches from negative in the panethnic and Hispanic model to positive in the Latino model. Therefore, as a respondent moves from no ethnic diversity to more ethnic diversity, he or she is .02 more likely to choose Latino identity. Experience with police discrimination increases a respondent's likelihood of choosing Latino identity .05; higher levels of education led to a .02 increased chance of Latino identity; and women were .02 more likely than men to choose Latino identity. Finally, respondents of Mexican origin were .02 less likely to choose Latino identity, while California residents were .04 more likely to do so. Clearly, based on the predicted probabilities, ethnic diversity is the biggest driver of both the panethnic and Hispanic models, while police discrimination and geographical location drive the Latino model. As we can see, the significant predictors vary from population to population, which may indicate separate identities that are not interchangeable. This finding contradicts the conventional wisdom in the field.

The next model measures the impact of mandated common ethnicity and statutory recognition of a panethnic Latino identity. This impact is measured through an examination of respondents' answers to the question about whether the group they identify with, "Either Latino or Hispanic," "Hispanic," or "Latino," makes up a distinctive racial group in America. If panethnic identifiers' answers are largely negative, then this may point to support for the idea of a mandated common ethnicity and statutory recognition in their definition of *latinidad* (see table 2.3). The data in table 2.3 demonstrate that there is little difference between Hispanic and Latino identifiers: for both, about 56% say yes, about 3% say maybe, and about 40% say no. "Either Latino or Hispanic" identifiers were more evenly divided, with about 50% saying yes and 47% saying no. Most interestingly, the respondents who indicated that they "don't care" about this kind of identification responded yes at the highest rate, with 63% indicating that Latinos make up a distinctive race and only 33% saying no. These data, therefore, do not necessarily support mandated common ethnicity and statutory recognition as a building block of *latinidad*, as 50% or more of the respondents across all identification categories answered in the affirmative.[19]

The third model examines the role of elites and public policy in shaping a common identity. Almost three-fourths of respondents said that it was important for a candidate to be Latino, and 83% said it was important for a candidate to speak Spanish. This finding demonstrates that candidates, as community leaders, may influence a sense of *latinidad*. Further, about 20% of panethnic identifiers indicated that they were members of at least one organization, thus increasing the chance of elite influence. In terms of policy concerns, the survey asked respondents to indicate the most important problem facing the nation and their ethnic group.

Table 2.3: Mandated Common Ethnicity

Identity response categories	Do you feel that _____ make up a distinctive racial group in America?		
	Yes	Maybe	No
Hispanic	56.3%	3.5%	40.1%
	(1759)	(110)	(1252)
Latino	56.7	2.8%	41.5
	(698)	(35)	(498)
Either	49.6	4.2	46.2
	(1531)	(131)	(1427)
Don't care	64.3	3.5	32.2
	(1048)	(57)	(525)

Pearson's R = .14; Sig.000 (two-tailed)

Table 2.4 provides an evaluation of the most important issues at the national and ethnic-group level for all respondents, as well as for panethnic, Latino, Hispanic, and non-panethnic identifiers. One could conclude that panethnic identifiers are unique if their opinion regarding the most important issue at each of these levels differs from that of all respondents or non-panethnic identifiers. At the national level, each of the groups specified the same top-three policy concerns: (1) the war in Iraq and national security; (2) the economy combined with unemployment and the increase in the cost of living; and (3) immigration, illegal immigration, and border-control issues. Therefore, one could say that panethnic identifiers are not particularly unique in this area of concern; however, it is important to point out that non-panethnic identifiers offered immigration as a top national issue less often the panethnic and Hispanic identifiers did. Just as was done for the national level, an additive issue index was created at the ethnic-group level. The ethnic-group-level issue index includes policy preferences on the following top issues of concern for all groups of respondents: *immigration, the economy*, and *lack of education*. However, 37% of panethnic identifiers as opposed to 25.5% of non-panethnic identifiers chose ethnic-group issue index. Alternatively, about 13% of non-panethnic identifiers said lack of education was the biggest ethnic-group issue, in comparison to only 8% of panethnic identifiers. Given this information, we may expect that those respondents who have higher levels of exposure to elite influence and who hold these common policy concerns will be more likely to identify with *latinidad* (see table 2.4).

In table 2.5, six variables are significant for panethnic identifiers: *ethnic-organization membership, ethnic-group issue index, conservative ideology, centrist ideology, do not think ideologically*, and *education*. All of the coefficients are in the expected direction. Ethnic-organization members are .06 more likely to choose panethnicity. As we move from no on the ethnic policy index to yes, the probability of choosing a panethnic identity increases .04. There is a .07 drop for respondents with a conservative ideology, and a .08 drop for respondents with a centrist ideology. There is a .07 increase in the probability of *latinidad* for respondents who do not think in

Table 2.4: Policy Concerns of Panethnic Identifiers

	Either ethnic identifier N = 3347	Hispanic N = 3332	Latino N = 1297	Non-panethnic identifiers N = 5205	All respondents N = 9834
National-Level Concerns					
Iraq / foreign folicy and international relations / national defense	36% (1195)	32% (1076)	37% (475)	35% (1829)	34% (3380)
Economy / unemployment / rising cost of living / inflation / taxes	19% (625)	19% (633)	21% (261)	19% (971)	19% (1895)
Immigration / illegal immigration / border control	12% (413)	10% (343)	9% (113)	11% (580)	11% (1036)
Ethnic-Group-Level Concerns					
Immigration / illegal immigration / border control	6% (1191)	27% (915)	278% (366)	31% (1631)	30% (2912)
Economy / unemployment / cost of living / inflation / taxes	18% (615)	20% (678)	19% (251)	19% (963)	19% (1892)
Lack of education	8% (259)	9% (310)	11% (141)	9% (489)	10% (940)

Table 2.5: Multivariate Logistic Regression: Elite Leadership and Public Policy Influences on Latinidad

	All panethnic identifiers		Hispanic identifiers		Latino identifiers	
	Coefficient (SE)	Predicted probabilities	Coefficient (SE)	Predicted probabilities	Coefficient (SE)	Predicted probabilities
Ethnic-group organization membership	.23⁺ (.12)	−.06	.07 (.13)		.29⁺ (.16)	.04
Economy, national issue	−.02 (.07)		−.13* (.07)	.02	.18* (.09)	−.02
Immigration, national issue	−.04 (.09)		.04 (.09)		−.17 (.14)	
National security, national issue	.09 (.08)		.02 (.08)		.15 (.12)	
Ethnic-group issue index: immigration/ economy/education	−.15*** (.06)	.04	−.10⁺ (.06)	.02	−.13 (.08)	
Conservative	−.29**** (.08)	.07	−.44**** (.08)	.09	.24* (.11)	−.03
Middle	−.34**** (.08)	.08	−.57**** (.09)	.12	.33** (.12)	−.04
Don't think ideologically	−.27**** (.07)	.07	−.36**** (.07)	.08	.13 (.10)	
No ideology	.09 (.07)		.15* (.07)	−.03	−.10 (.10)	
Yearly income	−.03 (.04)		−.04 (.04)		.01 (.06)	
Educational attainment	.04* (.02)	−.03	.02 (.02)		.04* (.02)	−.02
Gender	.04 (.05)		.17** (.06)	−.04	−.22** (.08)	.03
Citizenship	−.05 (.06)		.03 (.07)		−.15⁺ (.09)	.02
Constant	.07 (.13)		−.56**** (.14)		−1.7***** (.19)	
N = 5,653						

⁺ < .10, * p < .05, ** p < .01, *** p < .001, **** p < .000

ideological terms. Finally, as respondents' level of education increases, they were .03 more likely to choose *latinidad*. The data in this table indicate that there is some support for the theory that a common policy is important for *latinidad*, particularly for the idea that elites influence identity, as membership in organizations with mostly Latinos is statistically significant. Again, it is necessary to examine Hispanic and Latino identifiers separately.

To some extent, the findings for Hispanics mimic the results for all panethnic identifiers in that ethnic-group issue index and the ideology measures are significant and in the same direction. The major departures here are that (1) ethnic-organization membership is not significant, while Iraq as a top national-level issue is, (2) not having an ideology is significant, and (3) gender becomes a statistically significant predictor. In both of these models, the ideology measures are the most impactful.

The model for Latino identifiers is a mixed bag, with seven significant variables. As with panethnic and Hispanic identifiers, conservative and centrist ideologies are significant. Like panethnic identifiers, ethnic-organization membership and education are significant, and like Hispanic identifiers, Iraq as a policy concern and gender are significant. However, for Latino identifiers, citizenship is also significant, with noncitizens .02 more likely to chose Latino identity than citizens. While the magnitudes of change across all of the variables in this model are relatively small, ethnic-organization membership and having a centrist ideology drive Latino identity.

The fourth and final model examining DeSipio's theory measured whether increasing contact within Latino populations increases the chance of being a panethnic identifier. It is expected that respondents who have a more diverse ethnic ancestry (i.e., four foreign-born grandparents), have more contact with Latinos, and married a Latino or Latina will be more likely to choose *latinidad* (see table 2.6). Diverse contact is measured by *Latino friends* and *Latino co-workers*; both are statistically significant predictors of panethnic identity. Ethnic diversity is negatively and significantly associated with panethnicity, along with education (which is positively associated). The ethnic-diversity measure provides the largest magnitude of change, as less ethnic diversity in one's family tree leads to a .12 increase in the likelihood of choosing *latinidad*. The data in table 2.6 demonstrate that as respondents' contact with members of Latino populations increases, so does the likelihood of identifying with *latinidad*. These findings support the diverse-contact portion of DeSipio's theory of potential building blocks.

When focusing solely on Hispanics, *contact with Latino friends* and *co-workers*, *Latino/a spouse*, *ethnic diversity*, and *gender* are significant predictors. Again, ethnic diversity drives the likelihood of choosing Hispanic identity. For Latinos, having a Latino/a spouse, ethnic diversity, gender, and education are significant. Interestingly, the spouse variable switches signs here and is negative such that respondents without a Latino/a spouse are .03 more likely to choose Latino identity. Ethnic

Table 2.6: Multivariate Logistic Regression of Diverse Contact and Latinidad

	All panethnic identifiers		Hispanic identifiers		Latino identifiers	
	Coefficient (SE)	Predicted probabilities	Coefficient (SE)	Predicted probabilities	Coefficient (SE)	Predicted probabilities
Latino friends	.16**	−.04	.14*	−.03	.08	
	(.06)		(.06)		(.09)	
Latino co-workers	.20**	−.05	.17*	−.04	.10	
	(.06)		(.07)		(.09)	
Latino/a spouse	−.08		.13*	−.03	−.34**	.03
	(.06)		(.06)		(.08)	
Ethnic diversity	−.12****	.12	−.16****	.15	.07*	−.03
	(.02)		(.02)		(.03)	
Gender	.05		.16****	−.04	−.19*	.02
	(.06)		(.06)		(.08)	
Citizenship	−.02		.03		−.08	
	(.06)		(.07)		(.09)	
Educational attainment	.03*	−.03	.01		.04+	−.02
	(.02)		(.02)		(.02)	
Yearly income	.02		.00		.03	
	(.04)		(.04)		(.06)	
Constant	−.00		−.61****		−1.9****	
	(.14)		(.15)		(.21)	
N = 5,519						

+ < .10, * p < .05, ** p < .001, *** p < .001, **** p < .000

Table 2.7: Multivariate Logistic Regression of All Variables from DeSipio's Theory

	All panethnic identifiers		Hispanic identifiers		Latino identifiers	
	Coefficient (SE)	Predicted probabilities	Coefficient (SE)	Predicted probabilities	Coefficient (SE)	Predicted probabilities
Language	.31** (9.09)	−.08	.26** (.10)	−.06		
Ethnic mix	−.13**** (.02)	.13	−.15**** (.02)	.14		
Immigrated for/with family	.24* (.10)	−.06				
Discrimination in employment			−.25* (.09)	.05		
Discrimination by police	.23* (.10)	−.06	(.13)		.40*	−.02
Immigration, national issue	−.23 (.10)	.06	−.20* (.11)	.04		
National security, national issue	−.18* (.07)	.04	.34**** (.08)	.08	.25* (.10)	−.03
Ethnic-group issue index: immigration/ economy/education	−.19* (.06)	.05	−.11⁺ (.07)	.02	−.17* (.09)	.02
Latino friends	.17* (.07)	−.04	.13⁺ (.07)	−.03		
Latino co-workers	.21* (.07)	−.05	.21* (.07)	−.05		
Latino/a spouse			.16* (.07)	−.03	−.21* (.09)	.02
Conservative	−.29** (.09)	.07	−.46**** (.09)	.10	.25* (.12)	−.03
Middle	−.29* (.09)	.07	−.58**** (.10)	.12	.42** (.13)	−.05
Don't think ideologically	−.19* (.08)	.05	−.30**** (.08)	.07	.20⁺ (.11)	−.02
Gender		(.07)	.14*	−.03		
California			−.26* (.09)	.06	.28** (.11)	−.04
Education	.05* (.02)	−.08	.04* (.02)	−.04		
Constant	−.20 (.27)		−.64* (.29)		−2.3**** (.39)	
N = 4,755						

⁺ $p < .10$, * $p < .05$, ** $p < .01$, *** $p < .001$, **** $p < .0000$

diversity is positively correlated here such that as the diversity in respondents' family trees increases, the likelihood of choosing Latino identity drops .03. Men are .02 more likely to choose Latino identity than women are in this model. Finally, as respondents' level of education increases, their likelihood of choosing Latino identity drops by .02. One can see that predictors for Hispanic and Latino identification are somewhat different, which bolsters the idea that these are separate phenomena.

Now that the building blocks of DeSipio's theory have been analyzed, a comprehensive examination of all twenty-nine variables is required (see table 2.7). In the comprehensive model for all panethnic identifiers, thirteen variables are statistically significant: *language, ethnic diversity, immigrated for/with family, police discrimination, immigration as a national policy concern, national security/Iraq as a national policy concern, ethnic-group issue index, contact with Latino friends and co-workers, conservative ideology, centrist ideology, no thinking in ideological terms, and education.* All of the coefficients are in the expected direction, except the policy variables, and the largest magnitude of change can be found in the *ethnic diversity* variable (.13). In the Hispanic model, we find that *language, ethnic diversity* (the largest impact), *employment discrimination* (negatively correlated), *immigration as a top national issue* (negatively correlated), *national security/Iraq as a top national issue, ethnic-group issue index* (negatively correlated), *contact with Latino friends and co-workers, Latino/a spouse, conservative ideology, centrist ideology, no thinking in ideological terms, gender, California,* and *education* are statistically significant, whereas fewer predictors are significant for Latino identifiers. For Latinos, *police discrimination, national security/Iraq as a policy concern, ethnic-group issue index, contact with Latino friends and co-workers, Latino/a spouse, conservative ideology, centrist ideology* (largest impact), *no thinking in ideological terms,* and *California* are significant. Therefore, we find mixed support for DeSipio's theory across the models. DeSipio's theory seems to fit the case of Hispanics the best.

Conclusion and Discussion

This endeavor began by asking whether panethnic identifiers constitute a politically, socially distinctive subgroup within the Latino population. If so, what specific characteristics or variables set them apart? It was also the goal to compare the findings of the LNS with those of the LNPS. The previous findings of the LNPS concluded that panethnic identifiers were distinctive on some of the measures and models. For example, only two of the substantive (as opposed to control) variables were statistically significant on the common cultural characteristics for all panethnic identifiers (age at immigration and immigration for family reasons); in the LNS, we find more statistically significant variables (language, ethnic diversity, family reasons for immigration, police discrimination, and education).

There are similar results across the two surveys in the area of elite leadership and public policy influences, but the LNS findings provide more support for DeSipio's theory because ethnic-organization membership is a significant predictor of panethnic and Latino identity. Further, the LNS findings are more supportive of DeSipio's theory than those of the LNPS in terms of diverse contact as well because contact with Latino friends and co-workers and having a Latino/a spouse are significant predictors in the LNS. Therefore, between our two data-collection points, having a Latino/a spouse has become important for Hispanic and Latino identity. In the comprehensive model, LNPS data from 1989–1990 resulted in only four significant predictors: language, immigration for family reasons, age at immigration, and contact with Latinos. There is much broader support for DeSipio's theory in 2006, as borne out in the LNS findings. Here we find that there are thirteen significant variables, representing all of the variable building blocks DeSipio (1996) discussed.

However, perhaps more importantly, it was demonstrated by the LNPS that distinct factors drive Hispanic and Latino identity and that evidence suggested that scholars should not view them as interchangeable categories. The LNPS findings demonstrated, in the case of Hispanics, that common cultural characteristics and

Key Findings

- The previous findings concluded that panethnic identifiers were distinctive on some of the measures and models; in the LNS, we find an increased number of statistically significant variables. In the comprehensive model, there is much broader support for DeSipio's theory in 2006: thirteen significant variables, representing all of the building blocks of the theory being examined.

- It was demonstrated by the LNPS, in 1989, that distinct factors drive Hispanic and Latino identity and that evidence suggested that scholars should not view them as interchangeable categories. The findings of the LNS demonstrate this same theme. While there are some similarities in each set of models across panethnic, Hispanic, and Latino identifiers, it is clear that differences exist.

- In the end, panethnic, Latino, and Hispanic identities may not be merely rhetorical but also socially and politically important concepts.

- These findings are important because perceptions about group identity have real-world consequences in a larger sociopolitical context. Just a few areas that are clearly impacted by perceptions of identity include coalition building, funding and resource allocation, public policy, urban development, and education. The potential for future research in these areas will be very rich if trends continue on their current paths.

diverse contact were key—there was no support for models involving mandated common ethnicity, the role of elites, or shared public policy concerns. Alternatively, for Latinos, only diverse contact remained significant in the comprehensive model. The findings of the LNS demonstrate this same theme. While there are some similarities in each set of models across panethnic, Hispanic, and Latino identifiers, it is clear that differences exist.

Therefore, this study finds higher levels of support for DeSipio's theory as compared to previous research. It is important to understand the theoretical framework underpinning Latino panethnic identity because it reflects what processes are taking place beneath the surface of this large, rapidly growing population, as its internal dynamics become increasingly diverse in terms of national origin. In the long run, given this trend of identity formation, Latinos could become a major ethnic voting bloc. Some scholars have argued that this pattern began with the 2008 presidential election. In the end, panethnic Latino and Hispanic identities may not be merely rhetorical but also socially and politically important concepts. However, even if Latinos do not become a major ethnic voting bloc, these findings are important because perceptions about group identity have real-world consequences in a larger sociopolitical context. Just a few areas that are clearly impacted by perceptions of identity include coalition building, funding and resource allocation, public policy, urban development, and education. The potential for future research in these areas will be very rich if trends continue on their current paths.

Study Questions

1. Why is it important to understand panethnic identity?

2. Which variables from the LNS are predictors of panethnic identity, for the entire sample? What are the notable subgroup differences?

3. Are the categories of "Hispanic" and "Latino" interchangeable? Why or why not?

4. How do demographic factors such as gender impact identity?

Appendix 2A: Question Wording and Variable Coding for *Panethnicity*

Dependent Variable

PANETHNICITY	Question asked: "The most frequently used terms to describe persons of Latin American descent living in the United States are 'Hispanic' and 'Latino.' Of the two, which do you prefer, or do you not care about this terminology?"

Independent Variables

LANGUAGE	Language of the interview (1 = English, 2 = Spanish)
ETHNIC DIVERSITY	Recoded granborn (0 = all grandparents born in U.S., 4 = all grandparents foreign-born)
IMMECON	Immigrated for economic reasons (0 = no, 1 = yes)
FAMILY	Immigrated for family reasons (0 = no, 1 = yes)
FLEE	Immigrated to escape (0 = no, 1 = yes)
CAGEIMM	Age at immigration by cohort (0 = U.S. born, 10 = 65+ years)
DFIRED	Unfairly fired or denied a job or promotion (0 = no, 1 = yes)
DBADPOL	Unfairly treated by the police (0 = no, 1 = yes)
YRINCOME	Collapsed categories with imputed missing data (1 = low income, 3 = high income)
REDU	Educational attainment (1 = none, 7 = graduate/professional degree)
GENDER	Male = 1, female = 2
CITIZEN	Citizenship (includes both U.S. born and naturalized; 0 = no, 1 = yes)
MEXICAN	Mexican origin (0 = no, 1 = yes)
CARIBBEAN	Caribbean origin (includes Puerto Ricans and Dominicans; 0 = no, 1 = yes)
CALIFORNIA	California residents (0 = no, 1 = yes)
TEXAS	Texas residents (0 = no, 1 = yes)
AGE	Age in years (18–97 years)
IRAQNATL	Iraq, national security, war as top national issue (0 = no, 1 = yes)
ECONATL	Economy, rising cost of living as top national issue (0 = no, 1 = yes)
IMMNATL	Immigration/border control as top national issue (0 = no, 1 = yes)

ETHNICIINDEX	Index of immigration, economy, and lack of education as top ethnic-group issues (0 = no, 1 = yes)
ETHNICORG	Member of an organization with mostly Latino members (0 = no, 1 = yes)
Ideology dummies (deleted group = LIBERAL)	
CONSERVATIVE	(0 = no, 1 = yes)
MIDDLE	(0 = no, 1 = yes)
NO THINK IDEO	(0 = no, 1 = yes)
NO IDEOLOGY	(0 = no, 1 = yes)
FRIEND2	Dichotomized race/ethnicity of friends (0 = other, 1 = mostly Latino)
COWORK2	Dichotomized race/ethnicity of co-workers (0 = other, 1 = mostly Latino)
RSPOURACE	Dichotomized race/ethnicity of spouse (0 = not Latino/a, 1 = Latino/a)

Notes

1. See the official announcement from August 8, 2012, "Census Bureau Releases Results from the 2010 Census Race and Hispanic Origin Alternative Questionnaire Research," suggesting that a single *race or origin* category might be used in 2020, instead of 2010's two-part question structure, asking first for "*person's Hispanic, Latino or Spanish origin*," followed by "*person's race*." Using experimental responses from the 2010 Census, the bureau discovered that "a higher number of individuals were more likely to respond to a combined race and Hispanic origin question than to separate questions." See also Hayat El Nasser's article in *USA Today*, "Census Rethinks Hispanic on Questionnaire," January 3, 2013, http://www.usatoday.com/story/news/nation/2013/01/03/hispanics-may-be-added-to-census-race-category/1808087/.

2. My thanks to Rodolfo de la Garza, Angelo Falcón, F. Chris Garcia, and John A. García for the use of their 1989 data, and Luis Fraga, John A. García, Rodney Hero, Michael Jones-Correa, Valerie Martinez-Ebers, and Gary Segura for the use of their LNS data. The author gratefully acknowledges help from Regina Branton, Simon Jackman, Gary Segura, and James Wenzel. All errors, of course, are my own.

3. In the case of Hispanic identifiers, common cultural characteristics and diverse contact are key factors—there is no support for models involving mandated common ethnicity, the role of elites, or shared public policy concerns. Alternatively, for Latino identifiers, the majority of DeSipio's theory is not borne out. Only diverse contact is significant in a comprehensive model. In light of these findings, I believe that distinct factors drive Hispanic and Latino identity, and recommend that scholars should not view them as interchangeable categories.

4. "Other Hispanics" was broken down further in 2000. Central Americans constituted 4.8%, Dominicans 2.2%, South Americans 3.8%, Spaniards 0.3%, and all other Hispanics 17.3%.

5. Latinos are concentrated in the following states: California, Texas, Florida, New York, Illinois, Arizona, New Jersey, Colorado, New Mexico, and Nevada—in each of these states, the Latino population exceeds 15% of the population and includes more than 500,000 persons (Passel, Cohn, and Lopez 2011).

6. Berta Hernández-Truyol, in "Panel: Latina/o Identity and Pan-ethnicity: Toward LatCrit Subjectivities," *Harvard Latino Law Review* 2 (1997), available online at http://biblioteca

.uprrp.edu/LatCritCD/Publications/PublishedSymposium/LCIHarvardLat(1997)/
LCIBerta.pdf.

7. Exceptions include Michael Jones-Correa and David Leal's 1996 work titled "Becoming Hispanic: Secondary Panethnic Identification among Latin American–Origin Populations in the United States," *Hispanic Journal of Behavioral Science* 18 (2) (1996): 214–254; and John A. García, "Pan Ethnicity: Politically Relevant for Latino/a Political Engagement?," in *Black and Latino/a Politics: Issues in Political Development in the United States*, ed. William Nelson, Jr., and Jessica Lavariega Monforti, 12–20 (Miami, FL: Barnhardt and Ashe, 2006).

8. "Throughout U.S. history, this ongoing effort to limit the conception of race to a white and black dichotomy has led to the classification of Mexican Americans and then other Latinos as white" (In re Rodriguez, District Court, Western District of Texas, 3 May 1897; Mendez vs. Westminster School District, 161 F. 2d. 774, 1947); also see DeSipio's article "More than the Sum of Its Parts: The Building Blocks of a Pan-ethnic Latino Identity," in *The Politics of Minority Coalitions: Race, Ethnicity, and Shared Uncertainties*, ed. Wilbur C. Rich Westport, CT: Praeger, 1996), 180.

9. According to DeSipio, "Overall, Latinos earn less, have less formal education, and have lower prestige jobs than do non-Hispanic whites (Anglos); their family incomes are, on average, seven to eight thousand dollars less per year than those of Anglo families" (1996, 182).

10. Not all Latinos trace their ancestry to immigrants to the United States. At the time of the ratification of the Treaty of Guadalupe Hidalgo, approximately 100,000 former Mexican subjects resided in the United States. These Latinos with a territorial connection to what is today the southwestern United States are an exception (DeSipio 1996; Schmidt, Barvosa-Carter, and Torres 2000). Further, some scholars continue to argue that the U.S. colonized Puerto Rico. In fact, the majority of island Puerto Ricans view Puerto Rico as a colony under its current status, even if they want to maintain some kind of relationship with the United States. However, given the combination of colonialism and U.S. citizenship found in this case, Puerto Ricans fall outside the "official" technical definition of an immigrant.

11. While many Cubans immigrated to escape communism during the early post–Cuban Revolution waves, research by Silvia Pedraza (1985) has shown that many recent Cuban immigrants (especially after the 1980s Mariel Boatlift) have left for economic reasons.

12. While it is important to note that Puerto Ricans are U.S. citizens by birth and therefore do not need to deal directly with naturalization, the political influence of this group is linked to the settlement and naturalization of other Latinos in the area they reside, such as, for instance, Dominicans in New York.

13. For this reason, all analyses in this chapter are conducted using the national weights.

14. It is also important to point out that we are not necessarily interested in whether respondents chose one panethnic identifier or another; therefore this new variable was created to reflect the appropriate focus.

15. In previous research, this variable was created by scoring respondents' ethnic composition based on their responses about the ethnic/racial origins of their parents and grandparents; this produced an additive index. For example, a respondent who indicated that both parents and both paternal and maternal grandparents were born in Mexico would receive a score of zero. Alternatively, a respondent who indicated that all relatives except one were born in Cuba or Puerto Rico would receive a score of one, and so on. However, this method could not be replicated here because respondents were directed to choose only one country-of-origin for their family members.

16. Because a significant portion (21.6%) of LNS respondents declined to answer the household-income question, missing values are imputed based on other variables, including

media consumption, household size, nativity, education, parents' education, home owner-ship, language of interview, employment status, financial situation, and gender. In order to reduce the amount of error from these imputed values, income is then recoded into low (under $25K), medium ($25–45K), and high (over $45K). Details of how the missing val-ues were imputed are available from the authors on request.

17. All logit models were run using Stata software. Logistic regression (sometimes called the logistic model or logit model) is used for prediction of the probability of occurrence of an event by fitting data to a logit function logistic curve; it is most commonly used when the dependent variable in analysis is binary. Logistic regression has several advantages: it is more robust; the independent variables do not have to be normally distributed or have equal variance in each group; it does not assume a linear relationship between the IV and DV; it may handle nonlinear effects; explicit interaction and power terms can be added; the DV need not be normally distributed; there is no homogeneity of variance assumption; normally distributed error terms are not assumed; it does not require that the indepen-dents be interval; and it does not require that the independents be unbounded. However, logistic regression requires much more data to achieve stable, meaningful results. For logistic regression, at least fifty data points per predictor are necessary to achieve stable results (Dufty 2007). For more information about logistic regression, see Tim Futing Lao, *Interpreting Probability Models: Logit, Probit, and Other Generalized Linear Models* (Thousand Oaks, CA: Sage, 1994). Also see Timothy M. Hagle and Glenn E. Mitchell II, "Goodness-of-Fit Measures for Probit and Logit," *American Journal of Political Science* 36 (3) (1992): 762–784.

18. I have set all of the independent variables at their mean; Spost was used to calculate all predicted probabilities. All variables move from their minimum to their maximum value, except age and education, which went from one standard deviation below the mean to one standard deviation above the mean, to calculate their magnitude of change.

19. While it would be ideal to have multiple measures of this concept, no additional variables exist in the data that could directly or indirectly measure it.

References

Anders, Evan. 1979. *Boss Rule in South Texas: The Progressive Era*. Austin: University of Texas Press.

Beck, Paul Allen, and M. Kent Jennings. 1975. "Parents as 'Middlepersons' in Political Socializa-tion." *Journal of Politics* 37 (1): 83–107.

Calderón, José. 1992. "'Hispanic' and 'Latino': The Viability of Categories for Panethnic Unity." *Latin American Perspectives* 19 (4): 37–44.

Campbell, Bruce A. 1980. "A Theoretical Approach to Peer Influence in Adolescent Socialization." *American Journal of Political Science* 24 (2): 324–344.

Conway, M. Margaret, Mike L. Wyckoff, Eleanor Feldbaum, and David Ahern. 1981. "The News Media in Children's Political Socialization." *Public Opinion Quarterly* 45 (2): 164–178.

de la Garza, Rodolfo O., Louis DeSipio, F. Chris Garcia, John A. García, and Angelo Falcón. 1992. *Latino Voices: Mexican, Puerto Rican, and Cuban Perspectives on American Politics*. Boulder, CO: Westview.

de la Garza, Rodolfo O., Angelo Falcón, F. Chris Garcia, and John A. García. 1989–1990. *Latino National Political Survey, 1989–1990* [Computer file]. ICPSR06841-v3. Ann Arbor, MI: Inter-university Consortium for Political and Social Research [distributor].

DeSipio, Louis. 1996. "More than the Sum of Its Parts: The Building Blocks of a Pan-ethnic Latino Identity." In *The Politics of Minority Coalitions: Race, Ethnicity, and Shared Uncertain-ties*, ed. Wilbur C. Rich, 177–189. Westport, CT: Praeger.

Dufty, David. 2007. "What Is Logistic Regression?" StatGun Statistics Consulting, 2007. http://www.statgun.com/tutorials/logistic-regression.html (accessed October 8, 2010).

Easton, David, and Jack Dennis. 1965. "The Child's Image of Government." In "Political Socialization: Its Role in the Political Process," *Annals of the American Academy of Political and Social Science* 361:40–57.

Espiritu, Yen Le. 1992. *Asian American Panethnicity: Bridging Institutions and Identities*. Philadelphia: Temple University Press.

Fraga, Luis R. 1992. "Self-Determination, Cultural Pluralism, and Politics." *National Political Science Review* 3:132–136.

Fraga, Luis R., John A. García, Rodney Hero, Michael Jones-Correa, Valerie Martinez-Ebers, and Gary M. Segura. 2006. *Latino National Survey (LNS), 2006* [Computer file]. ICPSR20862-v4. Ann Arbor, MI: Inter-university Consortium for Political and Social Research [distributor], 2010-05-26.

García, John A. 2003. *Latino Politics: Community, Culture, and Interests*. Lanham, MD: Rowman and Littlefield.

García, John A. 2006. "Pan Ethnicity: Politically Relevant for Latino/a Political Engagement?" In *Black and Latino/a Politics: Issues in Political Development in the United States*, ed. William E. Nelson Jr. and Jessica Lavariega Monforti, 12–20. Miami, FL: Barnhardt and Ashe.

Hood, M. V., III, Irwin L. Morris, and Kurt A. Shirkey. 1997. "'¡Quedate o Vente!': Uncovering the Determinants of Hispanic Public Opinion toward Immigration." *Political Research Quarterly* 50 (3): 627–647.

Kinder, Donald R., and Nicholas Winter. 2001. "Exploring the Racial Divide: Blacks, Whites, and Opinion on National Policy." *American Journal of Political Science* 45 (2): 439–456.

Langton, Kenneth P. 1967. "Peer Group and School and the Political Socialization Process." *American Political Science Review* 61 (3): 751–758.

Langton, Kenneth P., and M. Kent Jennings. 1968. "Political Socialization and the High School Civics Curriculum in the United States." *American Political Science Review* 62 (3): 852–867.

Lavariega Monforti, Jessica. 2007. "Rhetoric or Meaningful Identifiers? Latinos(as) and Panethnicity." *Latino(a) Research Review* 6 (1–2): 7–32.

Padilla, Felix. 1985. *Latino Ethnic Consciousness: The Case of Mexicans Americans and Puerto Ricans in Chicago*. Notre Dame, IN: University of Notre Dame Press.

Passel, Jeffrey S., D'Vera Cohn, and Mark Hugo Lopez. 2011. "Hispanics Account for More than Half of Nation's Growth in Past Decade." Washington, DC: Pew Hispanic Center, March 24.

Pedraza, Silvia. 1985. *Political and Economic Migrants in America: Cubans and Mexicans*. Austin: University of Texas Press.

Pérez-Monforti, Jessica. 2001. "A Model of Minority: The Paradox of Cuban American Political Participation Regarding Official Language Policy in Miami-Dade County, Florida." Ph.D. dissertation, The Ohio State University.

Ramirez, Roberto R., and G. Patricia de la Cruz. 2003. *The Hispanic Population in the United States: March 2002*. Washington, DC: U.S. Census Bureau, June.

Renshon, Stanley Allen. 1975. "Personality and Family Dynamics in the Political Socialization Process." *American Journal of Political Science* 19 (1): 63–80.

Rodriguez, America. 1999. *Making Latino News: Race, Language, and Class*. Thousand Oaks, CA: Sage.

Schmidt, Ronald, Sr. 1997. "Latinos and Language Policy." In *Pursuing Power: Latinos and the Political System*, ed. F. Chris Garcia, 343–367. Notre Dame, IN: University of Notre Dame Press.

Schmidt, Ronald, Sr., Edwina Barvosa-Carter, and Rodolfo D. Torres. 2000. "Latino/a Identities: Social Diversity and U.S. Politics." *PS: Political Science* 33 (3): 563–567.

Sears, David, and Nicholas A. Valentino. 1997. "Politics Matters: Political Events as Catalysts for Preadult Socialization." *American Political Science Review* 91 (1): 45–65.

Skerry, Peter. 1997. "E Pluribus Hispanic?" In *Pursuing Power: Latinos and the Political System*, ed. F. Chris Garcia, 16–30. Notre Dame, IN: University of Notre Dame Press.

Tolbert Caroline J., and Rodney E. Hero. 1996. "Race/Ethnicity and Direct Democracy: An Analysis of California's Illegal Immigration Initiative." *Journal of Politics* 58 (3): 806–818.

U.S. Census Bureau. 1983. *Census of Population and Housing, 1980: Public-Use Microdata Sample.* Machine-readable data file. Washington, DC: Bureau of the Census.

Valdivia, Angharad N. 2010. *Latina/as and the Media.* Cambridge, UK: Polity.

3

Latino Immigrant Transnational Ties

Who Has Them, and Why Do They Matter?

SARAH ALLEN GERSHON AND ADRIAN D. PANTOJA

After years of contentious debate, the seismic shift of the 2012 election and prospects for continued electoral uncertainty as 50,000 new Hispanic voters come of age each month may have been responsible for giving the federal government—especially recalcitrant Republicans in Congress—an incentive to reform the nation's immigration policies. Still, questions will probably always remain about how completely the immigrant population is assimilating. One concern has been that continued interest and involvement in the affairs of the home country—or transnational ties—will delay incorporation and discourage immigrants from fully attaching, emotionally, politically, and culturally, to their new homes in the United States. In this chapter, Gershon and Pantoja test this proposition. They ask which Latinos are most prone to continued transnational engagement and whether such ties have any impact on incorporation.

Transnationalism and Immigrant Political Incorporation

The surge in immigration to the United States since the 1965 Immigration Act has heightened interest and research exploring the factors fostering and/or impeding immigrant political incorporation, with much of it focusing on Latinos, the largest group making up the contemporary immigration wave. Increasingly, statistically oriented researchers are examining the consequences of transnational ties on immigrant political incorporation (e.g., Staton, Jackson, and Canache 2007; Cain and Doherty 2006; Pantoja 2005). In this study, we add to this growing literature by examining *who* has transnational ties among contemporary Latino immigrants and *why* they matter, through the use of survey data from the 2006 Latino National Survey (LNS).

We begin our study by uncovering patters of transnational ties across different Latino national-origin groups and varying sociodemographic levels in an effort to identify the characteristics of the transnationally active. Next, we examine the impact of a wide range of transnational activities in shaping Latinos' political incorporation, via the acquisition of U.S. citizenship and civic participation. We focus on these two indicators of political incorporation for a few reasons. First, naturalization is a critical step in the incorporation process, since it confers on immigrants the right to vote and hold elective office, allowing them to participate fully in the American political system. Second, civic engagement is an agent for immigrant political socialization and empowerment which may occur *prior* to naturalization and is therefore critical to understanding the incorporation of immigrants (both citizen and noncitizen).

What Are Transnational Ties, and Who Has Them?

Transnational ties are a murky concept, which may be defined as "the process by which immigrants forge and sustain simultaneous multi-stranded social relations that link together their societies of origin and settlement" (Basch, Schiller, and Blanc 1994, 7). Although ties to the country of ancestry are not unique to Latino immigrants and are not a new phenomenon (Foner 2001), it is argued that advances in technology facilitating communication and travel, increased economic and political ties between the U.S. and immigrant-sending countries, intense outreach efforts by home countries to their diasporas, the rise in multiculturalism, and dual citizenship have enabled immigrants to create and maintain transnational links to a greater degree than immigrants from previous waves (Foner 2001).

Transnational ties vary widely by type and intensity (Itzigsohn and Saucedo 2002; Itzigsohn and Villacrés 2008). Some ties require little effort, such as following sports teams from the home country on television or calling relatives by telephone. Others take more time, effort, and resources, such as traveling to the home country or voting aboard. Despite the existence of these varied transnational activities, most quantitative works limit transnational measures to one or two activities (e.g., dual citizenship and the sending of remittances) (Staton, Jackson, Canache 2007; Cain and Doherty 2006). Others rely on multiple indicators but do not often assess the degree to which individuals are simultaneously active across the different transnational activities or assess the impact of dense versus weak transnational networks (DeSipio 2006; Pantoja 2005; DeSipio and Pantoja 2007). Since it is likely that many immigrants who remain connected with their home country engage in more than one transnational activity, it is appropriate to examine the extent and diversity of immigrants' transnational ties. We are fortunate that the LNS includes questions capturing a variety of transnational activities, of which we examine six: (1) contact with friends and family in the home country, (2) visiting the home country, (3) sending remittances, (4) participating in home-country associations, (5) interest in home-country politics, and (6) owning property or business in the nation of origin (see appendix 3A for complete coding procedures).

Table 3.1 shows Latino immigrant involvement across the six transnational activities. First, we observe that the most common transnational activity is contacting friends and family (89%), and the least common is participation in home-country

---

Research Questions

- What are transnational ties?
- How can transnational ties be measured?
- What are the reasons for the rise in transnational ties among contemporary immigrants?
- Which groups within the Latino community are the most transnationally engaged?
- How do these transnational ties shape political incorporation for Latino immigrants?

Table 3.1: Proportion of Respondents Participating in Transnational Activities

| Transnational activity | Number of respondents participating in activity (percentage of total sample) | |
	All immigrants	Immigrants eligible for citizenship*
Contacts friends and family	5,657 (89.1%)	5,099 (88.4%)
Visits home country	4,127 (65.0%)	3,951 (68.5%)
Sends remittances	3,905 (61.5%)	3,484 (60.4%)
Participates in home-country associations	334 (5.3%)	300 (5.2%)
Follows home-country politics	3,830 (60.3%)	3,430 (59.5%)
Is home-country property or business owner	2,079 (32.7%)	1,826 (31.7%)
N	6,350	5,767

* Immigrants eligible for citizenship have been in the U.S. for at least five years.

associations (5.3%). Participation in the other activities fall between these two extremes: visiting one's home country (65%), sending remittances (61%), owning property and businesses in the home country (33%), and maintaining an interest in home-country politics (60%). Clearly, some transnational activities such as maintaining contact with friends and family back home are common, perhaps because they require little effort, while other transborder ties are more difficult to sustain and therefore less common. In our sample, approximately 1.5% of respondents participated in all six activities, while about 3% of respondents participated in none. Combining the six transnational activities reveals that, on average, most Latino immigrants participate in approximately three transnational activities (mean = 3.13).

Next, we examine variation in transnational ties among Latino immigrants by nativity and sociodemographic characteristics, relying on difference of means tests to assess statistical significance. As shown in figure 3.1, a comparison of transnational ties across the three largest groups interviewed by the LNS—Cuban, Mexican, and Dominican immigrants—reveals that Dominicans are the most transnationally engaged while Cubans are the least engaged abroad. No doubt, decades of hostilities between Cuba and the diaspora in Miami, as well as the ongoing embargo, have adversely impacted Cuban American transnational ties with the island (Eckstein and Barberia 2002). On the other hand, the Dominican Republic, presumably due in large part to its growing dependency on remittances, has gone out of its way to promote and sustain ties with its diaspora (Pantoja 2005; DeSipio and Pantoja 2007). Mexican American transnational ties fall in between these populations. The differences across the three groups are statistically significant (F = 101.15 p < .000).

In addition to nativity, there is reason to expect that transnational ties will vary among immigrants depending on the resources, skills, and experiences they possess. Research by Guarnizo, Portes, and Haller finds that transnational ties vary significantly by select sociodemographic characteristics of immigrants. Specifically, transnational ties were strongest among immigrant males with high levels of education and income, leading the researchers to conclude that "transnationalism is not a refuge for the marginal and downtrodden, but a practice associated with greater stability and resources brought from the home country" (2003, 1232). Our analysis of LNS data (figures 3.1 and 3.2) reveals a similar pattern with regard to education. Immigrants with a high school education were more transnationally engaged than those without a high school diploma. In contrast, the effects of income are constant. The absence of a positive linear pattern between income and transnational networks may be due to the use of a single scale measuring all transnational ties (possibly masking variance in activity by income groups). To test this possibility, we examined the correlation between income and the six measures of transnational ties individually. This analysis revealed that income is positively and significantly correlated with frequency of visits, belonging to a hometown association, and having an interest in home-country politics. Conversely, contact with the home country and sending remittances occur with greater frequency among immigrants in

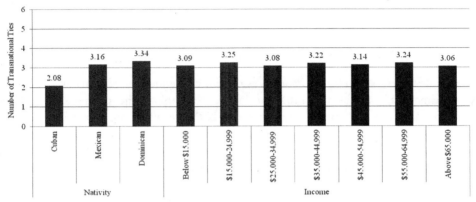

Fig. 3.1. Average number of transnational ties by immigrants' nation of origin and income level. *Note*: Nativity includes 355 Cubans, 3,965 Mexicans, and 464 Dominicans. Mean differences are statistically significant (F = 130.51, p < .000). Income includes 1,124 making less than $15,000, 1,369 earning $15,000–$24,999, 1,569 earning $25,000–$34,999, 1,069 earning $35,000–$44,999, 544 earning $45,000–$54,999, 247 earning $55,000–$64,999, and 427 earning more than $65,000. Mean differences are statistically significant (F = 3.16, p < .004).

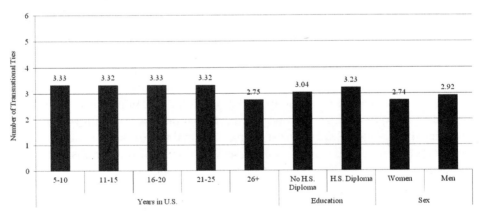

Fig. 3.2. Average number of transnational ties by immigrants' years in the U.S., education, and sex. *Note*: Years in U.S. includes 1,473 five- to ten-year residents, 843 eleven- to fifteen-year residents, 950 sixteen- to twenty-year residents, 582 twenty-one- to twenty-five-year residents, and 1,452 twenty-six-plus-year residents. Mean differences are statistically significant (F = 56.08, p < .000). Education includes 3,125 with less than a high school diploma, 3,225 with at least a high school diploma. Mean differences are statistically significant (F = 33.70, p < .000). Sex includes 3,493 women, 2,857 men. Mean differences are statistically significant (F = 45.68, p < .000).

the lower income brackets. The data also show that men are more transnationally engaged (mean = 2.92) than are women (mean = 2.74) and that transnational ties decrease with years spent in the United States.

Clearly not all Latino immigrants are equally engaged abroad. Transnational ties vary by ancestry group and across select sociodemographic characteristics, with ties abroad being strongest among Dominicans, men, and immigrants who possess greater resources (e.g., education). Further, transnational ties decrease as years of residency in the U.S. increase, and the effects of income are mixed. While these descriptive differences in transnational ties are key to understanding the immigrant experience, equally critical is our next task: identifying the consequences of transnational ties for Latino immigrant political incorporation in the United States.

Do Transnational Ties Matter? Previous Research and Expectations

There are three competing perspectives on the consequences of transnational ties for immigrant political incorporation. For some scholars, the slowness by which Latino immigrants are politically integrated is the result of the transnational ties they maintain with their ancestral homelands (Staton, Jackson, and Canache 2007; Cain and Doherty 2006; Huntington 2004; Torres-Saillant 1989). Some of these scholars consider transnational networks to be incompatible with incorporation (particularly naturalization), arguing that they may foster divided loyalties among immigrants (Huntington 2004). Others contend that transnational ties impede immigrant political incorporation because of the costs associated with participating politically and socially in both the U.S. and the country of origin (Cain and Doherty 2006). For example, Staton, Jackson, and Canache (2007) found that immigrant dual citizens (proxy for transnational ties) are less likely to be civically engaged or have positive civic orientations toward the United States, while others have found that dual citizenship depresses voter registration, electoral participation, and naturalization (Cain and Doherty 2006; Yang 1994).

In contrast to the foregoing works, several scholars argue that transnational ties spur political integration among Latino immigrants, many of whom wish to stay connected to their homeland while forging new ties in the U.S. (Pantoja 2005; Guarnizo, Portes, and Haller 2003; Jones-Correa 1998, 2001). These studies generally find that immigrants from countries that are supportive of transnational ties are more likely to pursue naturalization and participation in U.S. politics since these latter activities will not lead to the severing of formal ties to the homeland (Jones-Correa 1998, 2001; Escobar 2004). Conversely, immigrants from nations which discourage transnational ties will be less inclined to pursue activities in the U.S. that may threaten their connections to their native country. For example, Jones-Correa (2001) found that Latin American immigrants from countries that recognize dual nationality averaged higher naturalization rates than those from countries that do not. Pantoja (2005) found that certain transnational ties fostered U.S. civic engagement among Dominicans.

Finally, some scholars contend that transnational ties are unrelated to immigrant political integration and that traditional socioeconomic, demographic, and psychological factors are the key determinants driving naturalization and political engagement, suggesting that the alleged deleterious effects of immigrant transnational ties are overstated (DeSipio 2006; Barreto and Muñoz 2003).

Although there are three broad perspectives regarding the impact of transnational ties on immigrant political incorporation, we contend that resource-rich immigrants possess qualities and skills necessary to sustain transnational linkages *and* the pursuit of U.S. civic incorporation. In fact, both pursuits are complementary and driven by similar social forces. Guarnizo, Portes, and Haller's (2003) study reveals that resource-poor immigrants typically have weak transnational ties relative to resource-rich immigrants, or those with higher levels of education, income, and other sociodemographic and cognitive resources necessary for such engagement. These select characteristics are also predictive of naturalization and participation in U.S. politics. So it is the transnationally *disengaged* who are *less likely* to be politically incorporated in the United States because they generally lack the resources necessary for such incorporation.

Resource-poor immigrants are not only on the margins of U.S. politics but also on the margins of the politics and society of their ancestral homelands. Furthermore, when seeking U.S. citizenship, immigrants must have the competence and confidence to negotiate the bureaucratic hurdles of the United States Customs and Immigration Services, formerly known as the Immigration and Naturalization Service (DeSipio 1996; North 1987; Pachon 1987). It is likely that immigrants who regularly travel abroad or send remittances have developed some of that competence and confidence through their interactions with consulates, state departments, and U.S. financial institutions. This experience and confidence no doubt enables such immigrants to seek out naturalization at higher rates. Thus, we believe that, rather than acting as an impediment to incorporation, engagement in the home country's social, economic, and political life promotes immigrant incorporation in the United States. Based on this research, we anticipate that the transnational measures identified in table 3.1 will have a positive effect on Latino immigrant political incorporation.

Methods and Data

As noted before, we use two well-accepted measures of immigrant incorporation: naturalization and civic engagement. *Naturalization*, a step necessary for complete political and legal participation in the American system, is measured relying on a scale indicating whether respondents are naturalized, are in the process of naturalization, have plans to apply for citizenship, or have no plans to apply for citizenship (no plans to apply = 0 to naturalized citizen = 3).

While citizenship is a critical indicator of immigrant incorporation, the naturalization process is lengthy, and Latino immigrants often spend years in the U.S. before acquiring citizenship and the legal right to vote. Although unable to formally participate in elections, immigrants may still impact local and national politics by working with community leaders, groups, and elected officials to solve problems. Our dependent variable measuring *civic engagement* is a scale based on responses to three questions asking respondents about (1) participation in social and/or political groups, (2) working with others in a group and/or informally to solve problems, and

(3) contacting public officials (high civic engagement = 5, no civic engagement = 0). We expect *transnational ties* to positively and significantly impact immigrant incorporation via naturalization and civic engagement.

The primary focus of this analysis is to determine whether *transnational ties* positively or negatively impact Latino immigrants' incorporation into the American system via naturalization and civic engagement. The six transnational activities are (1) contact with friends and family, (2) visiting the nation of origin, (3) sending remittances to the home country, (4) participating in home-country organizations, (5) interest in home-country politics, and (6) owning property or business in the nation of origin (see appendix 3A for coding).

We anticipate that, beyond transnational ties, several behavioral, attitudinal, and demographic variables may account for variation in immigrants' pursuit of citizenship and civic engagement. First, the attitudes and orientations immigrants have toward the United States are expected to be significant predictors of incorporation. Immigrants who are positively oriented toward the U.S. are expected to pursue incorporation (via naturalization and participation) at a higher rate than others (Gershon and Pantoja 2007; Leal 2002). We include a measure of interest in politics to capture the impact of positive orientations on immigrant incorporation. *Political interest* is based on a question asking respondents, "How interested are you in politics and public affairs?" (0 = not interested, 2 = very interested).

The next set of variables thought to influence incorporation generally relate to social interactions and experiences in the United States. It is expected that contextual factors in the U.S., so-called destination characteristics, will influence immigrants' choice to naturalize and become engaged socially and politically in the United States. Contextual factors in the United States include sustained contact with Anglos, residing in an urban context, and the presence of a spouse, children, or extended kin in the U.S. (Aguirre and Saenz 2002; DeSipio 1996; Yang 1994; Portes and Curtis 1987). We attempt to account for many of these variables in our models. First, we measure interaction with other racial or ethnic groups, expecting that sustained contact with other racial and ethnic groups (besides Latinos) may influence the choice to participate in civic activities and to become a citizen. Relying on two questions asking respondents to describe the racial and ethnic composition of (1) their friends and (2) their co-workers, we create a variable—*ethnic isolation*—based on a three-point scale (0 = socialize and work primarily with non-Latinos, 1 = socialize *or* work primarily with Latinos, 2 = socialize *and* work primarily with Latinos). We also measure experiences with discrimination using responses to questions asking about discrimination experiences in the workplace, in restaurants, in housing, and from the police. The variable, *discrimination*, is a scale (0 = no experiences with discrimination, 4 = high levels of discrimination experienced).

The attitudes and orientations immigrants have toward the United States are expected to be significant predictors of political incorporation. The acquisition of U.S. citizenship is often regarded as an outcome of attachments to the values and political institutions of the United States (Alvarez 1987). Symbolically, the final step to becoming a U.S. citizen is taking the Oath of Allegiance, renouncing all foreign allegiances while declaring allegiance to the United States and a willingness to support and defend its Constitution and laws.[1] Researchers find that immigrants who have affective attachments to the United States, an American identity, and positive civic orientations incorporate into the U.S. more quickly than do individuals lacking these qualities (e.g., DeSipio 1996; Pantoja and Gershon 2006; Yang 1994; Portes and Curtis 1987; García 1981). We attempt to account for these factors in our analyses. We include two variables to tap respondents' identities, *American identity* and *nation of origin identity*. These variables are based on questions asking respondents, "In general, how strongly do you think of yourself as (American / nation of origin)?" (very strongly = 3, somewhat strongly = 2, not very strongly = 1, not at all = 0). We expect that stronger identification as an American will increase immigrants' likelihood of incorporating, while strong identification with one's nation of origin may negatively affect the decision to naturalize and engage in civic activities in the U.S.

Broadly, scholars have found that the decision to naturalize and participate in the American system is strongly influenced by macro- and micro-level factors in the country of origin. For example, research by Portes and Mozo (1985) and Aguirre and Saenz (2002) indicate that immigrants who left for political reasons (e.g., Cubans) have significantly higher rates of naturalization than do immigrants who migrated for economic reasons. Likewise, those who migrate for political reasons (and likely will not return to their nation of origin) may more quickly engage in their new homeland, compared with migrants who came to the U.S. for other reasons. In this analysis, we account for respondents' reason for migration, relying on three binary variables which identify whether immigrants came to the U.S. for *economic*, *family*, or *political* reasons. We also include a binary variable for immigrants who were brought to the U.S. as children (*child*). Finally, we include binary variables for *Dominican*, *Mexican*, and *Cuban* respondents.

The naturalization and participation literature identifies a host of sociodemographic determinants responsible for shaping political incorporation. One of the most consistent findings in this regard is that length of residency is a powerful predictor of incorporation; with immigrants who have resided in the country for longer periods more likely to naturalize and engage than those who have been in the country for a shorter period of time (DeSipio 1987). In our models, we account for this important variable with a continuous measure of immigrants' tenure in America, *years in U.S.*

Beyond length of residency, the sociodemographic characteristics of immigrants are also found to yield consistent and significant effects on naturalization and civic engagement. Immigrants who possess greater resources in the form of higher incomes, home ownership, education, and greater knowledge of the English language (often used as a proxy for acculturation) are more likely to become incorporated than are immigrants lacking these resources (Gershon and Pantoja 2007). Again, we account for many of these critical demographic variables in our model. To identify respondents' familiarity with the English language, we include a binary variable, *English survey*, identifying the language the respondent took the survey in (English = 1, Spanish = 0). Our measure of income is an ordinal scale, ranging from those earning below $15,000 to those earning above $65,000 per year. Immigrants' level of education is based on the question "What is your highest year of formal education completed?" (graduate or professional degree = 7, four-year college = 6, some college = 5, high school graduate = 4, GED = 3, some high school = 2, eighth grade or below = 1, none = 0).

Other sociodemographic predictors include age, professional status or occupation, marital status, and gender (DeSipio 2006; Pantoja and Gershon 2006; Pachon 1987; Grebler 1966). In this analysis, we control for whether a respondent is *female* (1 = female, 0 = male), which has been found in previous research to positively influence naturalization rates and nonelectoral participation (Gershon and Pantoja 2007). We also include a continuous variable measuring *age*, which is expected to positively impact immigrants' likelihood of naturalizing and becoming civically engaged (DeSipio 1987).

Results

The 2006 LNS included approximately 6,350 immigrant respondents. To examine the role transnational ties play in Latino immigrants' choice to pursue citizenship and civic engagement, we rely on ordered logistic regression.[2] The impact of transnational ties on immigrants' political incorporation is examined in table 3.2. Model 1 examines immigrants' pursuit of citizenship, while Model II examines civic engagement. In the model examining pursuit of citizenship, we removed the immigrants who had not been in the United States for at least five years (and were therefore ineligible for citizenship), leaving an initial sample of 5,767 respondents. The models in table 3.2 present two sets of results: (1) the ordered logistic coefficients with robust standard errors and (2) the average unit change in the dependent variable, given a fixed change in the independent variable from its minimum to its maximum value, holding all others constant at their mean (Long 1997).

The results presented in table 3.2 concerning the impact of transnational ties on political incorporation largely confirm expectations with regard to civic engagement (Model II) and are mixed with regard to naturalization (Model I). Although we anticipated that transnational ties would largely spur political incorporation, in Model I (predicting progress toward citizenship), two of the six transnational ties exert a significant and negative impact on the dependent variable. Specifically, owning property or a business in the country of origin and higher levels of contact with friends and family back home both decrease respondents' likelihood of naturalizing. Nonetheless, the remaining transnational measures did not depress naturalization, and one of them, visiting one's nation of origin, exerts a positive and significant impact on the choice to pursue citizenship. The negative impact of two transnational measures in our model is consistent with findings by Cain and Dohert (2006) and Pantoja (2005), who found certain measures of transnationalism to be negatively association with the pursuit of U.S. citizenship. Nonetheless, the results in this chapter also find transnationalism (Model II) to have a significant and positive impact on civic engagement (mirroring the findings of Pantoja 2005). Specifically, the findings in Model II show that contacting friends and family, sending remittances, participating in home-country associations, and remaining informed about home-country politics all positively and significantly influence immigrants'

Table 3.2: Ordered Logistic Regression Predicting Immigrant Political Incorporation

	Model I: Naturalization		Model II: Civic Engagement	
	Coefficients (S.E.)	Min.–Max.	Coefficients (S.E.)	Min.–Max.
Transnational Ties				
Contact	−.095 (.038)*	.0351	.115 (.038)**	.0268
Visits	.155 (.017)**	.0941	−.004 (.016)	.0017
Remittances	−.028 (.018)	.0171	.036 (.017)*	.0144
H.C. associations	.101 (.126)	.0124	.810 (.130)**	.0665
Following H.C. politics	.009 (.027)	.0036	.090 (.026)**	.0215
Property or business owner	−.241 (.063)**	.0291	.088 (.060)	.0070
Control Variables				
Political interest	.170 (.042)**	.0415	.541 (.043)**	.0853
American identity	.248 (.028)**	.0894	.108 (.027)**	.0255
Home-country identity	−.043 (.036)	.0161	.047 (.036)	.0111
Discrimination	.043 (.035)	.0217	.203 (.037)**	.0666
Economic migration	−.048 (.090)	.0059	−.258 (.089)**	.0205
Family migration	−.158 (.126)	.0191	−.164 (.121)	.0128
Political migration	.384 (.148)**	.0476	−.428 (.158)**	.0321
Child migration	.401 (.124)**	.0495	−.291 (.122)*	.0224
Ethnic isolation	−.113 (.038)**	.0274	−.094 (.035)**	.0148
Female	.155 (.061)*	.0177	.219 (.058)**	.0173
English survey	.747 (.083)**	.0921	−.165 (.099)	.0129
Mexican	−.203 (.076)**	.0248	.148 (.072)*	.0116
Cuban	.922 (.166)**	.1131	−.055 (.174)	.0043
Dominican	.825 (.12)**	.1017	.224 (.124)	.0180
Years in U.S.	.062 (.004)**	.3900	.024 (.003)**	.1501
Income	.220 (.043)**	.0538	.105 (.019)**	.0326
Age	.001 (.003)	.0049	−.011 (.003)**	.0654
Education	.147 (.017)**	.1239	.155 (.016)**	.0846
Cutpoint 1	1.581		.3441	
Cutpoint 2	3.080		2.594	
Cutpoint 3	3.409		4.267	
Cutpoint 4	—		5.627	
Cutpoint 5	—		7.970	
N	4,876		4,628	
Chi-square	1398.43**		727.39**	

* Two tailed tests, significance levels: * p < .05, ** p < .01

level of civic engagement in the U.S. The remaining measures of transnational ties —visiting and owning property in the nation of origin—do not significantly influence the dependent variable.

Taken together, the results presented in Model II indicate that those migrants who maintain strong connections with their country of origin are the same immigrants who engage socially, culturally, and politically in their new homeland. These results largely support those of previous scholars (e.g., Jones-Correa 2001; Escobar 2004; Pantoja 2005), who argued that transnational ties may encourage immigrant incorporation in the United States. We believe (like many of these scholars) that transnational ties encourage immigrant incorporation, especially in nonelectoral political and civic activities, in large part because fostering transnational connections requires the same resources, experiences, and skills which also enable immigrants to engage socially and politically in the United States.

While research by some scholars (e.g., Cain and Doherty 2006; Staton, Jackson, and Canache 2007; Yang 1994) indicates that immigrants cannot maintain ties to their country of origin and simultaneously forge new bonds in America, the results of our analysis suggest that is precisely what is occurring. These findings may have important implications for policymakers and interest groups desiring to increase Latino naturalization and civic engagement. On the one hand, some transnational ties appear to be an impediment to naturalization, while most spur civic engagement. Rather than attempting to sever immigrants' connection to their home country, policymakers and interest groups should encourage immigrants to maintain these ties, particularly those which clearly aid in the process of political incorporation.

In addition to transnational ties, several of our predictors significantly influence immigrants' likelihood of incorporating in the U.S. and merit some discussion. First, the results suggest that incorporation into the American system is positively influenced by interest in politics. Immigrants who are interested in politics may translate their interest into action by participating in nonelectoral political and community activities and pursuing citizenship (a necessary step for formal participation in the American political system).

Immigrants' reason for migration, as well as the nation they migrated from, impacts the pursuit of citizenship. Presumably because those who were brought to the United States as children have lived the majority of their lives in the U.S., they are more likely to pursue citizenship, compared with their counterparts who migrated for economic, family, or other reasons. On the other hand, these immigrants are less likely to be civically or politically engaged than their peers are. Similarly, those who migrated for political reasons appear to move toward citizenship at a swifter pace than others do, supporting research by Aguirre and Saenz (2002) and others who have found that immigrants who come to the U.S. to escape political repression often naturalize at higher rates. Experiences in the U.S. appear to drive incorporation to some extent, with those immigrants who have been the victims of discrimination being significantly more likely than others to engage civically and politically in their new homeland.

Our national-origin controls also exert a significant influence on naturalization rates. The impact of being Dominican or Cuban is positive and significant for immigrants' pursuit of citizenship. However, as found by previous research (Aguirre and Saenz 2002; Portes and Mozo 1985), the average unit change in naturalization (holding all other variables constant at their means) indicates that immigrants from Cuba pursue citizenship at a greater rate than other Latinos do. Other the other hand, immigrants from Mexico are less likely to pursue citizenship. Additionally, compared with other Latino immigrants, Dominicans and Mexicans are more likely to be civically engaged in the U.S. The lower levels of nonelectoral participation among Cubans relative to other Latinos are consistent with previous research (e.g., Wrinkle et al. 1996).

The results further reveal that identities shape the decision to become a U.S. citizen among Latino immigrants. Specifically, identifying strongly as an American significantly and positively impacts respondents' likelihood of becoming incorporated in the U.S. through naturalization and engagement, confirming earlier findings (e.g., García 1981). On the other hand, identities connected with one's homeland exert no significant influence on the decision to pursue or forgo incorporation, perhaps indicating that American and country-of-origin identities are not mutually exclusive (Fraga et al. 2010).

Finally, many of our sociodemographic variables confirm earlier findings (e.g., DeSipio 2006; Gershon and Pantoja 2007; Pachon 1987, Grebler 1966). Controlling for other influences on incorporation, women are significantly more likely than men to pursue naturalization and become civically engaged. Those immigrants who have remained ethnically isolated (working and socializing exclusively with other Latinos) are significantly less likely to pursue incorporation (through civic participation) than are their peers who interact with a more diverse group. As anticipated, English proficiency and tenure in the U.S. are both positively and significantly related to naturalization, and a greater number of years in the U.S. also improves civic participation. Income exerts a positive and significant influence on both dependent variables, indicating that, all else equal, those who have greater financial resources are more likely to pursue citizenship and become civically engaged. The variable measuring age indicates that younger immigrants have significantly higher levels of civic engagement than their older peers do. Finally, those with more education—perhaps better equipped to manage the naturalization process and participate in community and political activities—are more likely to become incorporated in the U.S.

Conclusion

The terms "incorporation" and "transnationalism" as applied to immigrants are contested ideas. Thus, the degree to which immigrants are incorporated in the *destination country* or transnationally connected with the *source country* is largely dependent on how one operationalizes and measures these concepts. Often limited by available data, scholars typically employ a single indicator of incorporation and a single measure of transnationalism, on the basis of which they conclude that the

---

Key Findings

- The level and intensity of transnational ties are varied; with some ties being more common than others, and certain groups such as Dominicans manifesting them at higher rates than other Latino groups.

- Transnational ties also vary by education, gender, and years spent in the U.S.

- Transnational ties influence political incorporation among Latino immigrants in different ways:

  - Contacting friends and family, sending remittances, participating in home-country associations, and remaining informed about home-country politics all positively and significantly influence immigrants' level of civic engagement in the U.S.

  - Two of the six transnational ties examined, owning property or a business in the country of origin and higher levels of contact with friends and family back home, decrease respondents' likelihood of naturalizing.

---

effects of transnational ties are either positive (beneficial), negative (detrimental), or null (inconsequential). However, conclusions drawn from such studies may be limited by relatively narrow indicators of incorporation or transnationalism, as well as examinations of a single or a few immigrant groups. In this chapter, we expand this research by employing the 2006 Latino National Survey, a dataset which allows us to develop multiple indicators of incorporation and transnationalism as well as to consider their relationship across several Latino immigrant groups.

Contrary to prior research, which finds that transnational ties have either a limited or negative impact on immigrant incorporation (e.g., Cain and Doherty 2006; Pantoja 2005; Jones-Correa 2001; Yang 1994; DeSipio 2006; Barreto and Muñoz 2003), our analysis (based on this expansive dataset) presents a more optimistic scenario, at least when it comes to civic engagement. The results indicate that immigrants' ties to their home country encourage and perhaps facilitate political engagement. However, we also find evidence that certain measures of transnationalism negatively impact naturalization. Overall, these results present a more nuanced understanding of the effects of varied indicators of transnational ties.

The results, like those of previous scholars (e.g., Pantoja 2005; Escobar 2004; Jones-Correa 2001), indicate that immigrant political incorporation should not be thought of as occurring in a vacuum. Immigration is not necessarily a process of casting aside one's existing identity and ties, replacing them with new ones. Rather, many immigrants seem to maintain for a time period connections with the homeland, while simultaneously developing new attachments to the United States (Escobar 2004). Although some scholars (and politicians) have suggested that transnational ties may be a threat to national unity, slowing down the integration process by fostering transient mentalities or divided loyalties among immigrants, we find the opposite to be generally true. The task for academics, policymakers, and community activists is to identify why certain types of transnational ties quicken political incorporation while others seem to stall the process. In addition, it will be useful to consider this dynamic within different subsets of the Latino population and across other immigrant groups. We suspect that the pathways to incorporation will be as diverse as these immigrant groups are.

Study Questions

1. Is the role of transnational ties in immigrant incorporation politically controversial? Why or why not?

2. Do transnational ties help or hurt incorporation? More broadly, are transnational ties a normatively good or bad thing for immigrants? For the health of democracy in the U.S.?

3. What are the policy implications of this research? Should policymakers encourage or discourage transnational ties? What are the ways they might implement these changes?

Appendix 3A: Question Wording and Variable Coding for *Transnationalism* and *Incorporation*

Dependent Variables

NATURALIZATION   "Are you a U.S. citizen, currently applying for citizenship, planning to apply to citizenship, not planning on becoming a citizen?" (0 = no plans to apply, 1 = planning to apply, 2 = currently applying for citizenship, 3 = naturalized citizen)

CIVIC PARTICIPATION   Based on responses to three questions: "Do you participate in the activities of one social, cultural, civic, or political group, more than one such group, or do you not participate in the activities of any such groups?" (more than one group = 2, one group = 1, none/other = 0); "When an issue or problem needs to be addressed, would you work through existing groups or organizations to bring people together, would you get together informally, or would you do nothing to deal with this matter?" (both work through existing groups and get together informally = 2, get together informally or work through existing groups = 1, do nothing/other = 0); "Have you ever tried to get government officials to pay attention to something that concerned you, either by calling, writing a letter, or going to a meeting?" (yes = 1, no/other = 0); responses summed to create a 0–5 scale (0 indicates no participation, 5 indicates participation in all activities mentioned)

Independent Variables

TRANSNATIONAL TIES   Based on responses to six questions: "How often do you visit [nation of origin]?" (0 = never, 1 = more than five years ago, 2 = one in the past five years, 3 = once in the past three years, 4 = once a year, 5 = more than once a year); "How often do you have contact with friends and family in [nation of origin]?" (0 = never, 1 = once every several months, 2 = once a month or so, 3 = once a week or more); "How often do you send money [home]?" (0 = never, 1 = less than once a year, 2 = once a year, 3 = once every few months, 4 = once a month, 5 = more than once a month); "Do you participate in the activities of a club, association, or federation connected to the town or province your family came from in [nation of origin]?" (1 = yes, 0 = no); "How much attention would you say you pay to politics in [nation of origin]?" (0 = none, 1 = a little, 2 = some, 3 = a lot); "Are you the owner of land, a house, or a business in [nation of origin]?" (1 = yes, 0 = no)

POLITICAL INTEREST   "How interested are you in politics and public affairs?" (very interested = 2, somewhat interested = 1, not interested = 0)

REASONS FOR MIGRATION   "What would you say is the main reason you came to live in the United States?" (responses were used to create several binary variables for family, political, and economic reasons,

	as well as a variable indicating if the respondent was brought to the U.S. as a child)
ETHNIC ISOLATION	Based on responses to two questions: "How would you describe your friends? Are they mostly [Latino], mostly white, mixed [Latino] and white, mostly black, mixed [Latino] and black?" (1 = mostly Latinos, 0 = other); "How would you describe your co-workers? Are they mostly [Latino], mostly white, mixed [Latino] and white, mostly black, mixed [Latino] and black?" (1 = mostly Latinos, 0 = other); used to create a three-point scale (0 = socialize and work primarily with non-Latinos, 1 = socialize or work mostly with Latinos, 2 = socialize and work mostly with Latinos)
DISCRIMINATION	"In the following questions we are interested in your beliefs about the way other people have treated you in the U.S. Have you ever . . . Been unfairly fired or denied a job or promotion? Been unfairly treated by the police? Been unfairly prevented from moving into a neighborhood (*vecindario o barrio*) because the landlord or a realtor refused to sell or rent you a house or apartment? Been treated unfairly or badly at restaurants or stores? (each response is coded as 1 = yes, 0 = no); responses were summed to create a scale (0 = no experiences with discrimination, 4 = multiple experiences with discrimination)
AMERICAN IDENTITY	"[In general,] how strongly or not do you think of yourself as American?" (0 = not at all, 1 = not very strongly, 2 = somewhat strongly, 3 = very strongly)
HOME COUNTRY IDENTITY	"[In general,] how strongly or not do you think of yourself as [nation of origin descriptor]?" (0 = not at all, 1 = not very strongly, 2 = somewhat strongly, 3 = very strongly)
FEMALE	"Are you male or female?" (1 = female, 0 = male)
ENGLISH PROFICIENCY	Did the respondent take the survey in English or Spanish? (English survey = 1, Spanish survey = 0)
NATION OF ORIGIN	"Where were you born?" (responses used to create binary variables for Mexicans, Cubans, Dominicans, and Central Americans; the Central American category includes immigrants from Costa Rica, El Salvador, Guatemala, Honduras, Nicaragua, and Panama)
YEARS IN U.S.	"When did you first arrive in the U.S?" (year of arrival subtracted from 2006)
INCOME	"Which of the following best describes the total income earned by all members of your household during 2004?" (1 = below $15,000, 2 = $15,000–24,999, 3 = $25,000–34,999, 4 = $35,000–44,999, 5 = $45,000–54,999, 6 = $55,000–64,999, 7 = above $65,000). *Note*: A sizable portion of respondents refused to identify their income level. Income levels for those who declined to answer this question were estimated using a host of demographic characteristics, including sex, home ownership, birthplace, language proficiency, media usage, employment, and education.

AGE   "What year were you born?"

EDUCATION   "What is your highest level of formal education completed?"
                              (graduate or professional degree = 7, four-year college = 6,
                              some college = 5, high school graduate = 4, GED = 3, some
                              high school = 2, eighth grade or below = 1, none = 0)

Notes

1. The Oath of Allegiance is, "I hereby declare, on oath, that I absolutely and entirely
   renounce and abjure all allegiance and fidelity to any foreign prince, potentate, state, or
   sovereignty of whom or which I have heretofore been a subject or citizen; that I will support and defend the Constitution and laws of the United States of America against all
   enemies, foreign and domestic; that I will bear true faith and allegiance to the same; that I
   will bear arms on behalf of the United States when required by the law; that I will perform
   noncombatant service in the Armed Forces of the United States when required by the law;
   that I will perform work of national importance under civilian direction when required by
   the law; and that I take this obligation freely without any mental reservation or purpose of
   evasion; so help me God."

2. To examine the impact of transnational ties on political incorporation (via naturalization
   and civic engagement), controlling for alternative explanations, we relied on a multivariate
   analysis. While there are a number of different methods which researchers use to examine
   the relationship between multiple variables, we chose to rely on ordered logistic regression
   in this chapter because of the nature of our dependent variables. Both of our dependent
   variables are ordinal, meaning that the variables have ordered (but not necessarily equally
   spaced) categories. Essentially, the ordered logistic regression estimates the impact the
   independent variables have on the likelihood of observations being in the next highest category of the dependent variable (in this case, progress toward naturalization). See Borooah
   2002 and Long and Freese 2006 for a deeper discussion of the methods used here.

References

Aguirre, Benigno E., and Rogelio Saenz. 2002. "Testing the Effects of Collectively Expected
   Durations of Migration: The Naturalization of Mexicans and Cubans." *International Migration
   Review* 36:103–124.

Alvarez, Robert R. 1987. "A Profile of the Citizenship Process among Hispanics in the United
   States." *International Migration Review* 21:327–251.

Barreto, Matt A., and Jose A. Muñoz. 2003. "Reexamining the 'Politics of In-Between': Political
   Participation among Mexican Immigrants in the United States." *Hispanic Journal of Behavioral Sciences*. 25:427–447.

Basch, Linda, Nina Glick Schiller, and Cristina Szanton Blanc. 1994. *Nations Unbound: Transnational Projects, Postcolonial Predicaments, and the Deterritorialized Nation-State*. Amsterdam:
   Gordon and Breach.

Borooah, Vani K. 2002. *Logit and Probit: Ordered and Multinomial Models*. Thousand Oaks, CA:
   Sage.

Cain, Bruce, and Brendan Doherty. 2006. "The Impact of Dual Nationality on Political Participation." In *Transforming Politics, Transforming America: The Political and Civic Incorporation
   of Immigrants in the United States*, ed. Taeku Lee, S. Karthick Ramakrishnan, and Ricardo
   Ramirez, 89–105. Virginia: University of Virginia Press.

DeSipio, Louis. 1987. "Social Science Literature and the Naturalization Process." *International
   Migration Review* 21:390–405.

DeSipio, Louis. 1996. *Counting on the Latino Vote: Latinos as a New Electorate*. Charlottesville: University of Virginia Press.

DeSipio, Louis. 2006. "Transnational Political and Civic Engagement: Do Home-Country Political Ties Limit Latino Immigrant Pursuit of U.S. Civic Engagement and Citizenship?" In *Transforming Politics, Transforming America: The Political and Civic Incorporation of Immigrants in the United States*, ed. Taeku Lee, S. Karthick Ramakrishnan, and Ricardo Ramirez, 106–126. Charlottesville: University of Virginia Press.

DeSipio, Louis, and Adrian D. Pantoja. 2007. "Puerto Rican Exceptionalism? A Comparative Analysis of Puerto Rican, Mexican, Salvadoran, and Dominican Transnational Civic and Political Ties." In *Latino Politics, Identity, Mobilization, and Representation*, ed. Rodolfo Espino, David L. Leal, and Kenneth J. Meier, 104–120. Charlottesville: University of Virginia Press.

Eckstein, Susan, and Lorena Barberia. 2002. "Grounding Immigrant Generations in History: Cuban Americans and Their Transnational Ties." *International Migration Review* 36:799–837.

Escobar, Cristina. 2004. "Dual Citizenship and Political Participation: Migrants in the Interplay of United States and Colombian Politics." *Latino Studies* 2 (1): 45–69.

Foner, Nancy. 2001. "Transnationalism Then and Now: New York Immigrants Today and at the Turn of the Twentieth Century." In *Migration, Transnationalization, and Race in a Changing New York*, ed. Héctor R. Cordero-Guzmán, Robert C. Smith, and Ramón Grosfoguel, 35–57. Philadelphia: Temple University Press.

Fraga, Luis, John A. García, Rodney Hero, Michael Jones-Correa, Valerie Martinez-Ebers, and Gary Segura. 2010. *Latino Lives in America: Making It Home*. Philadelphia: Temple University Press.

García, John. 1981. "Political Integration of Mexican Immigrants: Explorations into the Naturalization Process." *International Migration Review* 15:608–625.

Gershon, Sarah Allen, and Adrian D. Pantoja. 2007. "Political Orientations and Latino Immigrant Incorporation." In *Latinas/os in the United States: Changing the Face of América*, ed. Havidán Rodríguez, Rogelio Saenz, and Cecilia Menjívar. New York: Springer.

Grebler, Leo. 1966. "The Naturalization of Mexican Immigrants in the United States." *International Migration Review* 1:17–32.

Guarnizo, Luis Eduardo, Alejandro Portes, and William Haller. 2003. "Assimilation and Transnationalism: Determinants of Transnational Political Action among Contemporary Migrants." *American Journal of Sociology* 108:1211–1248.

Huntington, Samuel P. 2004. *Who Are We? The Challenges to America's National Identity*. New York: Simon and Schuster.

Itzigsohn, José, and Silvia Giorguli Saucedo. 2002. "Immigrant Incorporation and Sociocultural Transnationalism." *International Migration Review* 36 (3): 766–798.

Itzigsohn, José, and Daniela Villacrés. 2008. "Migrant Political Transnationalism and the Practice of Democracy: Dominican External Voting Rights and Salvadoran Home Town Associations." *Ethnic and Racial Studies* 31 (4): 664–686.

Jones-Correa, Michael. 1998. *Between Two Nations: The Political Predicament of Latinos in New York City*. Ithaca: Cornell University Press.

Jones-Correa, Michael. 2001. "Under Two Flags: Dual Nationality in Latin America and Its Consequences for Naturalization in the United States." *International Migration Review* 35:997–1029.

Leal, David L. 2002. "Political Participation by Latino Non-citizens in the United States." *British Journal of Political Science* 32:353–370.

Long, Jay Scott. 1997. "Regression Models for Categorical and Limited Dependent Variables." In *Advanced Quantitative Techniques in the Social Sciences*. Vol. 7. Thousand Oaks, CA: Sage.

Long, Jay Scott, and Jeremy Freese, eds. 2006. *Regression Models for Categorical Dependent Variables Using Stata*. College Station, TX: Stata.

North, David S. 1987. "The Long Grey Welcome: A Study of the American Naturalization Program." *International Migration Review* 21:311–326.

Pachon, Harry P. 1987. "An Overview of Citizenship in the Hispanic Community." *International Migration Review* 21:299–310.

Pantoja, Adrian. 2005. "Transnational Ties and Immigrant Political Incorporation: The Case of Dominicans in Washington Heights, New York." *International Migration* 43:123–146.

Pantoja, Adrian D., and Sarah Allen Gershon. 2006. "Political Orientations and Naturalization among Latino and Latina Immigrants." *Social Science Quarterly* 87 (5) 1171–1187.

Portes, Alejandro, and John W. Curtis. 1987. "Changing Flags: Naturalization and Its Determinants among Mexican Immigrants." *International Migration Review* 21:352–371.

Portes, Alejandro, and Rafael Mozo. 1985. "The Political Adaptation Process of Cubans and Other Ethnic Minorities in the United States: A Preliminary Analysis." *International Migration Review* 19:35–63.

Staton, Jeffrey K., Robert A. Jackson, and Damarys Canache. 2007. "Dual Nationality among Latinos: What Are the Implications for Political Connectedness?" *Journal of Politics* 69:470–482.

Torres-Saillant, Silvio. 1989. "Dominicans as a New York Community: A Social Appraisal." *Punto 7 Review: A Journal of Marginal Discourse* 2 (1): 7–25.

Wrinkle, Robert D., Jerry L. Polinard, Kenneth J. Meier, and John R. Arvizu. 1996. "Ethnicity and Nonelectoral Political Participation." *Hispanic Journal of Behavioral Sciences* 18:142–153.

Yang, Philip Q. 1994. "Explaining Immigrant Naturalization." *International Migration Review* 28:449–477.

4

Multiple Paths to Cynicism

Social Networks, Identity, and Linked Fate among Latinos

JESSICA LAVARIEGA MONFORTI AND MELISSA R. MICHELSON

If citizens (or noncitizens, for that matter) lose trust in government, how are democratic politics affected? Will participation suffer? Will it become more difficult for leaders to govern? In particular, what would it mean if a loss of trust were tied to immigration status or assimilation or ethnicity? In this chapter, Lavariega Monforti and Michelson ask whether we can predict the loss of trust among Latinos or identify the kinds of individual or collective experiences that enhance or diminish that trust.

The Political Implications of Latinos' Trust in Government

Scholars and students have wondered for some time about causes and consequences of Americans' trust in government, generally understood as "a basic evaluative orientation toward the government founded on how well the government is operating according to people's normative expectations" (Hetherington 1998, 791).[1] In survey research, we measure the prevalence of this attitude—*political trust*—by asking population samples, "How much of the time do you trust the government to do what is right—just about always, most of the time, some of the time, or never?" Using this concept, we have learned that calculating levels of trust in government can help explain individual political behavior as well as government effectiveness, and gauge the vitality of civil society. Although a "healthy skepticism of citizens is a prerequisite of democracy" (Levi 1998, 96), an excess of distrust has notable negative consequences, including decreased capacity of the state to govern and increased citizen noncompliance with government regulations, laws, and judicial decisions. At extreme levels, distrust can lead to widespread antagonism to government policy and even active resistance (Levi 1998; Scholtz and Lubell 1998; Tyler 1998).

For years, scholars have noted with concern the increasing political cynicism of the U.S. public. More recently, research has shown that the presence or absence of public trust in government has important repercussions, impacting both government effectiveness and individual political behavior. Marc Hetherington found that trust translates into warmer feelings for elected officials and political institutions, which "provides leaders more leeway to govern effectively," while distrust creates an environment in which it is difficult for those in government to succeed (1998, 803). Virginia Chanley, Thomas Rudolph, and Wendy Rahn find that "declining trust in government in turn leads to less positive evaluations of Congress and reduced support for government action to address a range of domestic policy concerns" (2001, 239). While earlier research found no link between feelings of trust and individual political behavior (W. Miller 1980; Muller, Jukam, and Seligson 1982; Pierce and

---

Research Questions

- What attitudinal and demographic variables predict Latino trust in government, both generally and within national-origin subgroups?
- Are acculturation and social incorporation correlated with political trust?
- Is political trust linked to experiences with or perceptions of discrimination?

Converse 1989), more recent work finds that cynical voters are less likely to choose major-party candidates and more likely to vote for third-party candidates (Southwell and Everest 1998; Peterson and Wrighton 1998; Hetherington 1999). Recent debates about social capital inspired by the work of Robert Putnam (1995) indicate that public cynicism may also be a measure of the health of civil society. While the social capital literature focuses on social trust rather than political trust, other work shows that the two concepts are closely related (Lane 1959; Levi 1996; Brehm and Rahn 1997).

Existing research clearly establishes the importance of political trust, although debate continues over just what the standard survey questions are measuring. While some scholars claim that the trust questions measure support for specific government outputs and individuals (Citrin 1974; Citrin and Green 1986; Lipset and Schneider 1983), others find that they measure diffuse support for the political regime (A. Miller 1974a, 1974b; Miller, Goldenberg, and Erbring 1979; Miller and Listhaug 1990). Regardless of which of these views is correct (if not both; see Erber and Lau 1990), the persistence of distrust is significant because of the impact of feelings of trust on government effectiveness and on individual political behavior. This raises questions about what determines political trust and why it continues to decline.

Anglo (non-Latino white) trust in government has declined dramatically since the late 1960s, and members of the U.S. public are, in general, quite cynical about politics. Conventional wisdom holds that the decades-long trend of increasing cynicism is due to the series of political tragedies and scandals which have plagued the nation since the 1960s, including the Vietnam War, Watergate, and the Iran-Contra affair. As low as Anglos score on surveys of political trust, African Americans score even lower. These differences have been investigated by a number of scholars. Suggested explanations include socioeconomic factors (Matthews and Prothro 1966), the notion of black consciousness (Gamson 1968, 1971; Gurin, Gurin, and Beattie 1969; Gurin and Epps 1975; Shingles 1981), compensatory theory (Orum 1966), ethnic community (Gutterbock and London 1983), and black political power, also known as political reality theory (Abramson 1983; Howell and Fagan 1988; Bobo and Gilliam 1990; Emig, Hesse, and Fisher 1996).

While many researchers have documented and examined the decades-long trend of increasing cynicism among whites and blacks, political trust among Latinos is less well understood. While several studies have shown that Latinos are more trusting of government than are Anglos (Guzmán 1970; Garcia 1973; de la Garza et al. 1992; Putnam 2001), Latinos are also quite cynical about government. Various theories have been advanced to explain Latino distrust and variations in levels of trust within the Latino community. According to Putnam (2000), one contributing factor is feelings of interpersonal trust—in other words, individuals who are more trusting of other individuals are also more likely to trust the government, and vice versa. Anne Schneider and Helen Ingram's (1993) work on the social construction of target populations suggests that Latino trust in government is in part a reflection of the stereotypes about Latinos that are communicated through various state and local government policies. Another possible source of feelings of trust in government is conditions in the sending country: Sergio Wals (2011) finds that Mexican immigrants with higher levels of trust in the Mexican government are more likely to be trusting of the U.S. government. Studies of Mexican American youth have found that youths become increasingly distrustful as they reach adolescence (Garcia 1973), that those who identify as Chicano are more cynical than those who identify as Mexican American (Gutierrez and Hirsch 1973), and that those living in cities with more Mexican American political influence are more trusting (Buzan 1980). More recent work finds that Mexican American citizens are more cynical than are noncitizens of Mexican descent (Michelson 2001), that Puerto Ricans born in the mainland United States are less trusting than are Puerto Ricans born on the island of Puerto Rico (de la Garza 1995; Michelson 2003a), and that Mexican American adults who are more acculturated or see more discrimination against those of Mexican descent are more cynical than are those who are less acculturated or see less discrimination (Michelson 2003b).

Yet that those who are more acculturated or more concerned about discrimination are less trusting does not paint a complete picture of cynicism among Latinos. Those who are more acculturated may be more aware of discrimination, as they are more likely to have encountered "harsh reality" (Garcia 1973), or they may simply be disillusioned by the same sorts of government misbehavior as are other Americans. In other words, it is not clear whether Latino immigrants are cynical because they have been acculturated into the mainstream or because they believe that the government is racist/ethnocentric and/or anti-immigrant.

Generally, political incorporation is understood to include political empowerment, or political voice (Pérez-Monforti 2001). Latino immigrants, citizens or not, live and work in U.S. society, send their children to U.S. schools, and are exposed to U.S. culture. Even if they do not become politically empowered, they are a part of U.S. society and this is their home. As a result, their attitudes about government may change to more closely reflect opinions held by most Americans, such as distrust in government. In other words, they may as part of their cultural assimilation become more cynical of government. Yet social incorporation may mean the kind of cultural learning that is associated with group membership and minority identity. Rather than adopting the political attitudes of mainstream (Anglo) Americans, they may instead adopt the political attitudes of the majority of members of their shared national-origin group (e.g., Mexicans or Puerto Ricans) or of their larger panethnic group (Latinos), much as they learn political partisanship (see Alvarez and García Bedolla 2003; Lavariega Monforti 2007).

This dichotomized view of the acculturation process, while intellectually useful, does not completely reflect the myriad ways in which Latino immigrants incorporate into U.S. society. Alejandro Portes and Rubén Rumbaut (2006) describe the process of segmented assimilation, in which a variety of modes of acculturation are available that depend on the degree to which parents (first generation) and children (second generation) learn U.S. culture and language and are a part of an ethnic community, the degree of discrimination encountered, and the availability of family and community resources. A similar point is made by Luis Fraga et al. in their discussion of a series of focus groups:

> Latino immigrants identify themselves as "American" and see themselves as remaining in this country. However, there is also some ambivalence, particularly among first-generation immigrants, about their sense of belonging—made to choose among their identification with the United States and their country of origin their American identity is not their first preference; this is not translated, however, into a desire to return. (2010, 143–144)[2]

In other words, the absence of a sense of belonging, or even the presence of feelings of not being wanted, does not necessarily mean that immigrants will fail to socially incorporate into U.S. society. This point is illustrated by the tendency of Latino immigrants, in the wake of the anti-Latino atmosphere of the mid-1990s, to become citizens and to vote (Wong 2006). Even as the host society was making them feel unwelcome and working to bar them from receiving government services, Latinos did not choose retreat (e.g., return to the country of origin) but instead chose to further become involved in the U.S. political system (Michelson and Pallares 2001).

Lisa García Bedolla notes that crossing the physical border to the United States, and becoming an immigrant, is just one way in which Latino immigrants become Americans. Multiple boundaries, both physical and psychological, are involved in their politicization:

> In terms of geography, migrants clearly have chosen to cross a line dividing nation-states. After arriving in the United States, they encounter additional physical boundaries as they settle in places that provide differential access to transportation, jobs, services, and housing. These boundaries affect their everyday lives and chances for socioeconomic mobility. In terms of psychological borders, immigrants leave their home countries with a certain understanding of self and nation, but this will evolve with time as they experience life in the United States. . . . Because they are members of a marginal group in the United States, Latino immigrants and their children confront multiple boundaries that affect their socialization into the U.S. political system —boundaries that they are not always empowered to cross. (2005, 2)

According to García Bedolla, Latinos determine their sense of place in the U.S. political system based on the interaction of two spheres: individual feelings of personal agency (psychological capital) and contextual capital, including membership in community organizations, the local political institutional environment, and the racial composition and politicization of individual social networks. Feminist Chicana theorists Gloria Anzaldúa and Emma Pérez offer additional caveats. Anzaldúa writes that Chicanos "straddle the borderlands" (1987, 84)—they are neither Anglos nor Mexicans. Pérez (1999) argues that Mexican immigrants never fully assimilate into U.S. culture but instead always retain a degree of Mexican culture.

Existing theory, then, is inconclusive as to whether Latino immigrants in the United States are likely to acculturate in ways that include adoption of mainstream feelings about the government or whether their multiple identities and retained country-of-origin culture will lead them to adopt very different, or differently based, attitudes. In order to develop a fuller theoretical and empirical understanding of what drives Latino political trust, this chapter examines responses to the 2006 Latino National Survey (LNS), a random-digit dialing (RDD) sample of 9,834 self-identified Latino/Hispanic residents of the U.S. conducted from November 17, 2005, through August 4, 2006. Measures of acculturation, attitudes toward acculturation, measures of political identity and linked fate, and experiences of discrimination are explored as possible explanatory factors. As has been demonstrated by previous research, Latinos are not a monolithic group (García Bedolla, Lavariega Monforti, and Pantoja 2006; Lavariega Monforti 2007). Thus, the analysis of patterns of political trust is also conducted for available Latino national-origin subgroups, including Mexicans, Puerto Ricans, Cubans, Dominicans, and Salvadorans. Predictors of trust determined by previous research, including partisanship, political ideology, and approval of the U.S. president, are also included.

Hypotheses

The following four hypotheses, derived from findings from previous research on Latino trust in government, are tested in this chapter:

H_1: Latinos who prefer to identify as American will be more trusting than will Latinos who prefer to identify as Latino/Hispanic or as a member of a Latino national-origin group.

H_2: Latinos whose friends and co-workers are majority-Latino will be less trusting than will Latinos whose friends and co-workers include individuals from a variety of races/ethnicities.

H_3: Latinos with stronger feelings of linked fate with the Latino community will be more trusting than will Latinos with weaker feelings of linked fate.

H_4: Latinos who support "blending in" to the host culture of the U.S. will be more trusting than will those who are less supportive of acculturation.

In addition, based on previous research, more acculturated Latinos are expected to be more trusting, measured here using nativity and English-language fluency. The latter is measured using both self-reported language ability and a variable constructed using the language in which respondents chose to complete the interview. This includes not only the language they chose at the beginning at the interview but also whether they switched languages at some point.

Other research shows that more conservative and more Republican (or Republican-leaning) Latinos tend to be more trusting, as are those who approve of the current U.S. president (then-president George W. Bush). Significant portions of the LNS sample declined to answer the ideology, partisanship, and presidential-approval survey items (47.1 percent, 35.9 percent, and 30.3 percent, respectively). Dropping individuals for whom this information is missing would create a truncated sample biased to include only more politically sophisticated respondents. Thus, the models used here split partisanship and ideology into dummy variables, leaving out as controls those who are Democrats or who identify as liberal. Responses to the survey item inquiring about whether the respondent approved of President Bush are recoded into a trichotomous variable with those declining to give an opinion designated as neutral. Finally, the models include standard socioeconomic controls of age, education, and income.[3]

Results

Consistent with previous survey research, Latinos are quite trusting of the government, particularly when compared to national surveys of the general population. The LNS question wording mirrors that used in surveys since 1958. Respondents were asked, "How much of the time do you trust the government to do what is right —just about always, most of the time, some of the time, or never?" In the 2008 American National Election Study (ANES), only 5 percent of respondents said they trust the government "just about always." In fact, not since 1966 have more than 9 percent of ANES respondents to this question given the most trusting response. In contrast, 12 percent of respondents to the LNS said that they trust the government "just about always." In addition, 19.3 percent said they trust the government most of the time, 49.8 percent trust the government some of the time, and 18.9 percent never trust the government.

In line with H_1, responses to the trust-in-government question are correlated with feelings of political identity. The LNS asked respondents four identity questions, including the degree to which they considered themselves American, Hispanic/Latino, and a member of their national-origin group and then which of the above they most preferred. Respondents who identify more strongly as American tend to be more trusting; individuals who identify more strongly as Latino or Hispanic or as a member of a national-origin group tend to be less trusting. When asked to give a preference among the three political identities, Latinos who prefer to identify as American are the least likely to say they trust the government "just about always" but also much more likely to say they trust the government most of the time and the least likely to say that they never trust the government. In sum, these results point to a positive relationship between an "American" political identity and increased trust in government. In the multivariate regression that follows, we include the original variable indicating strength of "American" identity and a dichotomized version of the final question, recoded to indicate whether the individual prefers "American" over the other two identities.

Survey items that asked respondents to identify the racial/ethnic composition of their friends and co-workers are used to explore H_2. The original LNS wording includes a variety of possible responses to these questions, but the theory explored here hinges on the degree to which individuals are experiencing a racialized acculturation process. Thus, these items are recoded to note simply whether an individual's social networks are majority Latino or not. Individuals whose social networks include mostly coethnics tend to be less trusting of government; this is most clearly shown in the proportion of respondents saying that they "never" trust the government to do the right thing. These variables are included in the multivariate models that follow.

Michael Dawson's (1994) theory of linked fate posits that individuals who share a strong group identity believe that their personal fate is tied to that of the collective—in other words, that the success of individuals and the group are tied together. Subsequent research has found linked fate to also be relevant to Latinos (García Bedolla 2005). While a number of scholars have recently investigated predictors of linked fate (e.g., Sanchez 2008; Jimeno and Espino 2009), this chapter is more concerned with linked fate as an exogenous variable predicting feelings of trust in government. As stated in H_3, individuals with stronger feelings of linked fate are hypothesized to be more trusting because they have a base of social capital that increases their feelings of interpersonal trust, which as noted earlier is closely related to feelings of trust in government.

The LNS includes two linked fate variables, one that measures the degree to which respondents feel that their national-origin group's "doing well" depends on whether other Latinos are doing well (LATFATE) and another that measures linked fate with others from their shared national-origin group (RGFATE). The questions are highly correlated, with a Cronbach's Alpha of .55 and loading on a single factor; thus, they are combined here to create a single measure. This linked fate index shows a relatively linear relationship to feelings of trust in government, with those who score low on linked fate the most likely to say they never trust the government and with those who score highest on linked fate the most likely to say they trust the government "just about always."

The final hypothesis examined here relates to two LNS survey items that asked respondents the degree to which they felt it important to blend into U.S. culture or to retain the culture of their Latino/Hispanic heritage. The relationship is extremely linear, particularly for the BLEND variable. Individuals who think it is more important to blend into U.S. society are more trusting of government.

All of these variables were combined into a more rigorous, multivariate analysis of trust in government. The model also includes variables for gender, political interest, nativity, English-language fluency, and experiences of discrimination, as these have been shown by previous research to be important predictors of feelings of trust in government (Lawless 2004; Cook and Gronke 2005; Michelson 2003b, 2007). Because the endogenous variable (TRUST) is ordinal, data is explored using ordered logit.[4] The model is weighted to be representative of the total U.S. adult Latino population, using the LNS national weight variable. The impact of coefficient estimates for major independent variables is further explored using predicted probabilities. The magnitude of change is largest across all categories of trust for linked fate and "Like Bush."

The question wording for the dependent variable was "How much of the time do you trust the government to do what is right—just about always, most of the time, some of the time, or never?" Because the dependent variable includes an ordered list of four possible answers, ordered logit was used to model responses; the "cut"

Table 4.1: Predictors of Trust in Government among LNS Respondents (Ordered Logit Regression Model)

Independent variable	Ordered logit coefficient estimate	S.E.	Never	Some of the time	Most of the time	Just about always
				Change in predicted probabilities		
American identity	.09**	.03	−.03	−.02	.03	.02
National-origin group identity	−.05	.03				
Latino identity	−.01	.04				
Prefer American identity	.14^	.04	−.02	−.01	.02	.01
Mostly Latino friends	.06	.06				
Mostly Latino co-workers	.02	.06				
Linked fate index	.25**	.04	−.11	−.04	.09	.07
Support blending into U.S. culture	.13**	.04	−.04	−.02	.03	.02
Support maintaining distinct culture	.03	.05				
Political interest	.15**	.04	−.06	−.03	.05	.04
Discrimination: fired	.36**	.07	.05	.02	−.04	−.03
Discrimination: bad police	.26**	.07	.04	.02	−.03	−.02
Discrimination: housing	.05	.11				
Discrimination: restaurant/store	.02	.07				
Native-born	−.08	.07				
English fluency	.07*	.03	−.04	−.02	.03	.02
Language of interview	.08^	.05	−.02	−.01	.02	.02
Gender	−.11*	.05	.01	.01	−.01	−.01
Age	−.01**	.002	.03	.02	−.02	−.02
Education	−.02	.02				
Income	−.01	.03				
Republican	.23**	.08	−.03	−.02	.03	.02
Independent party ID	−.09	.07				
Don't care about party ID	−.28**	.08	.04	.02	−.03	−.02
Other party ID	−.13^	.08	.02	.01	−.02	−.01
Conservative ideology	.06	.08				
Middle ideology	−.07	.08				
Don't think about ideology	−.07	.08				
No ideology	−.16	.10				
Like Bush	.44**	.03	−.11	−.07	.10	.08
/cut1	2.08**	.40				
/cut2	4.57**	.40				
/cut3	5.91**	.40				
N	6,296					

^ p ≤ .10, * p ≤ .05, ** p ≤ .01, two-tailed

Note: Question wording for the dependent variable (*trust in government*) was "How much of the time do you trust the government to do what is right—just about always, most of the time, some of the time, or never?" Language of interview is coded from 1 = all English to 4 = all Spanish; Gender is coded 1 = male, 2 = female. Deleted groups for dummy variable sets are Democrat (Party Identification) and Liberal (Ideology).

coefficient estimates indicate the degree to which the different answers are distinct from one another. Changes in the predicted probabilities were calculated as the predicted change in the likelihood of each of the four responses when moving from the minimum to the maximum value of each independent variable, while holding all other independent variables constant at their means. There were two exceptions to this method: predicted probability estimates for age and education reflect the change in the predicted probabilities of holding each attitude for an increase from one standard deviation below the mean to one standard deviation above the mean, while holding all other independent variables constant at their means. Estimates for the discrimination variables reflect the change in the predicted probabilities of holding each attitude as we move from a no response to a yes response, while holding all other independent variables constant at their means.

Three of the four hypotheses presented earlier find significant support in the model, with statistically significant coefficient estimates for the variables "American Identity," "Linked Fate Index" and "Support Blend into US Culture." In other words, Latinos who more strongly identify as American are more trusting of the government (H_1). Latinos with stronger feelings of linked fate are more trusting of the government (H_3), and Latinos who feel it is more important to blend into the larger American society are also more trusting (H_4). At the same time, no significant relationship is found between trust and support for retention of a distinct Latino/Hispanic culture ("Support Maintaining Distinct Culture") or for the ethnic composition of respondents' friends or co-workers (H_2).

That only two of the survey items about discrimination are statistically significant ("Discrimination: Fired" and "Discrimination: Police") may reflect the different environments in which such incidents occurred. In other words, discrimination in a housing situation ("Discrimination: Housing") or at a store or restaurant ("Discrimination: Restaurant/Store") might be more likely blamed on the individual restaurant server or store employee, while discrimination by the police might be more likely blamed on widespread racism within the criminal justice system and thus on the government. Regardless, that experiences of discrimination are linked to decreased trust in government supports findings from previous scholarship, as does the statistically significant coefficient estimate for political interest. As expected, Republicans are more trusting than Democrats (the excluded category of partisanship dummy variables), as are respondents who are more supportive of then-president Bush. Latinos with higher incomes or who are more fluent in English are also more trusting. Trust declines slightly as age increases, and women are less trusting than are men.

Subgroup Analysis

Increasingly, the study of Latino politics in the United States has turned from monolithic treatments to more nuanced studies that recognize the important differences between national-origin groups within the Latino community. As García Bedolla notes, "Latino national-origin groups have had very different experiences in the United States. They arrived at different points in American history, migrated for very different reasons, settled in different geographic settings, and have been treated in disparate ways by the United States government" (2009, 4). What does this mean for trust in government?

For the Mexican-descent subsample, the findings were expected to generally reflect the original four hypotheses presented earlier. This is due to two factors. First, most previous scholarship in Latino politics has focused either on exclusively Mexican-descent samples or on samples that are heavily dominated by Mexicans. In other words, the theories explored in this chapter are derived from scholarship on respondents of Mexican descent and thus should find their strongest support in that subsample of the LNS dataset. Second, as with that previous scholarship, Mexican-descent respondents constitute the vast majority of LNS respondents.

One of the major strengths of the LNS is the diversity of Latino national-origin

Table 4.2: Trust in Government, LNS National-Origin Subgroups

	Just about always	Most of the time	Some of the time	Never
Mexicans (N = 5,903)	11.9	19.3	49.8	19.0
Cubans (N = 522)	16.3	20.5	46.2	17.1
Dominicans (N = 413)	15.5	14.5	47.7	22.3
Puerto Ricans (N = 848)	8.6	21.1	52.2	18.0
Salvadorans (N = 477)	16.1	15.3	47.0	21.6
Total (N = 9,833)	12.0	19.0	49.6	19.4

Note: Question wording for the dependent variable (*trust in government*) was "How much of the time to you trust the government to do what is right—just about always, most of the time, some of the time, or never?"

groups represented in large enough numbers to allow for subgroup analyses and testing of hypotheses. This includes substantial numbers of Mexicans, Cubans, Dominicans, Puerto Ricans, and Salvadorans. As shown in table 4.2, there are significant differences in feelings of trust in government among the various Latino subgroups in the LNS. Puerto Ricans are the least likely to trust the government "just about always"; Cubans are the most likely to say that they trust the government "just about always." Dominicans are most likely to say they never trust the government.

These observed different levels of trust in government among the Latino national-origin subsamples are hypothesized to be due to their different political histories and demographic characteristics. For Cubans, this reflects their experiences as an ethnic enclave in the Miami area, as well as their unique history with the Republican Party and the exile (rather than immigrant) experience. Historically, the community has focused on cultural maintenance, in anticipation of their return to Cuba (García Bedolla 2009, 134). Early waves of Cuban exiles have received unparalleled access to and aid from the U.S. government, including direct economic assistance and refugee support. Experiences related to home-country politics, as well as local politics in South Florida, have encouraged a strong affiliation with the GOP, in sharp contrast to the preference for the Democratic Party displayed by non-Cuban Latinos. Thus, for Cubans, we expect a very different model of political trust, with higher trust expected among Republicans and a reversed relationship between assimilation and trust, with those more supportive of maintaining a distinct Cuban culture, rather than those supporting blending in, hypothesized to be more trusting.

Puerto Ricans and Dominicans (as well as Cubans) are distinct in that these populations tend to be more racially diverse than Mexican-descent Latinos, with larger proportions identifying as Black or having darker skin tone. This is hypothesized to affect the model of trust in several ways. First, individuals in these subgroups are expected to be more sensitive to experiences of discrimination. Second, the power of linked fate is expected to be weaker, as some Puerto Ricans and Dominicans may feel a sense of linked fate with Blacks either instead of or in addition to feelings of linked fate with other Latinos. Finally, having exclusively Latino friends and co-workers is expected to be less important for these individuals, as they are more likely to be acculturating into multiracial social networks.

Finally, for Salvadorans, a unique model of trust is expected to result due to the history of ideological civil war in the home country (1980–1992), including support for the Salvadoran government from the Reagan administration and denial of refugee status for those fleeing the repression and violence. This led exiles in the United States to work to raise awareness of the situation in their home country and to pressure changes to U.S. government foreign policy and policies affecting Salvadoran immigrants and refugees (García Bedolla 2009). In terms of modeling trust, partisanship and political ideology are thus expected to have strong impacts.

Results from the subgroup analyses are shown in table 4.3. For clarity, only statistically significant coefficients are shown, but all models were estimated with all of the variables used in the general model from table 4.1. Due to the smaller sample sizes, these tables also include coefficient estimates that approach statistical significance ($p \leq .10$). These results should be interpreted with caution, as they do not reach standard $p \leq .05$ levels of statistical significance.

Table 4.3: Trust in Government among LNS National-Origin Subgroups (Ordered Logit Regression Models and Predicted Probabilities)

Variable	Ordered logit coefficient estimate	S.E.	Change in predicted probabilities			
			Never	Some of the time	Most of the time	Just about always
Mexicans (N = 4,450)						
American identity	.10**	.03	−.04	−.02	.04	.03
National-origin group identity	−.07^	.04	.02	.02	−.02	−.02
Mostly Latino friends	.14*	.07	−.02	.01	.02	.01
Linked fate index	.27**	.05	−.12	−.05	.09	.07
Support blending into U.S. culture	.15**	.04	−.04	−.02	.04	.03
Political interest	.13**	.05	−.05	−.03	.05	.04
Discrimination: fired	.36**	.08	.05	.02	−.04	.03
Discrimination: police	.40**	.09	.06	.02	−.05	−.03
English fluency	.08*	.04	−.04	−.03	.04	.03
Gender	−.10^	.06	.01	.01	−.01	−.01
Don't care about party ID	−.33**	.10	.05	.02	−.04	−.03
Conservative ideology	.17^	.10	−.02	−.02	.02	.02
Like Bush	.48**	.04	−.12	−.08	.11	.09
Age	−.01**	.002	.03	.02	−.03	−.02
Education	.03^	.02	−.02	−.01	.02	.01
Puerto Ricans (N = 503)						
Mostly Latino friends	−.54*	.25	.08	.02	−.07	−.03
Linked fate index	.24^	.14	−.10	−.04	.10	.04
Support blending into U.S. culture	−.23^	.12	.05	.04	−.07	−.03
Support maintaining distinct culture	.36^	.21	−.11	−.02	.10	.03
Discrimination: fired	.43^	.26	.06	.02	−.06	−.02
Discrimination: police	−.45^	.25	−.05	−.05	.07	.03
Discrimination: restaurant/store	.63*	.25	.09	.03	−.08	−.03
Language of interview	.30^	.18	−.07	−.06	.09	.04
Independent party ID	−.46^	.26	.06	.02	−.06	−.02
Like Bush	.37**	.12	−.09	−.06	.11	.04
Cubans (N = 213)						
Mostly Latino co-workers	−.76^	.44	.07	.10	−.11	−.06
Support maintaining distinct culture	1.01**	.31	−.24	−.08	.22	.10
Discrimination: housing	1.72^	.89	.22	.05	−.19	−.08
Native-born	.74^	.39	−.04	−.14	.11	.08
Gender	−.76^	.30	.05	.12	−.10	−.06
Republican	1.17**	.40	−.07	−.21	.16	.12
Independent party ID	−.96**	.45	.09	.11	−.13	−.07
Like Bush	.43*	.19	−.06	−.13	.12	.07

Table 4.3 (continued)

Variable	Ordered logit coefficient estimate	S.E.	Change in predicted probabilities			
			Never	Some of the time	Most of the time	Just about always
Dominicans (N = 222)						
National-origin group identity	−.49*	.21	.15	.18	−.11	−.22
Prefer American identity	1.57**	.57	−.16	−.21	.12	.26
Political interest	.65**	.22	−.35	.01	.16	.17
Native-born	−1.08*	.43	.20	−.02	−.09	−.08
Independent party ID	−.85ˆ	.46	.16	−.01	−.08	−.07
Like Bush	.57**	.20	−.17	−.07	.11	.13
Salvadorans (N = 284)						
American identity	.43**	.13	−.15	−.11	.11	.14
Linked fate index	.43*	.20	−.16	−.07	.11	.12
Support blend into U.S. culture	.61**	.22	−.17	−.04	.10	.11
Political interest	.38ˆ	.21	−.13	−.10	.10	.12
Discrimination: police	1.04*	.42	.04	.03	−.03	−.03
Native-born	.85ˆ	.47	−.07	−.13	.07	.12
Independent party ID	−.71*	.35	.09	.05	−.07	−.07
Middle ideology	−1.09*	.53	.15	.04	−.10	.41
Don't think about ideology	−1.11*	.45	.14	.07	−.10	.45
Like Bush	.73**	.17	−.16	−.12	.12	.16

ˆ p ≤ .10, * p ≤ .05, ** p ≤ .01, two-tailed

Note: Question wording for the dependent variable (*trust in government*) was "How much of the time do you trust the government to do what is right—just about always, most of the time, some of the time, or never?" Language of interview is coded from 1 = all English to 4 = all Spanish; gender is coded 1 = male, 2 = female. Deleted groups for dummy variable sets are Democrat (Party Identification) and Liberal (Ideology). Coefficient estimates and predicted probabilities are only shown for independent variables that reach or approach standard levels of statistical significance; a full list of included variables is shown in table 4-1. Changes in the predicted probabilities were calculated as the predicted change in the likelihood of each of the four responses when moving from the minimum to the maximum value of each independent variable, while holding all other independent variables constant at their means. Exceptions: age and education reflect the change in the predicted probabilities of holding each attitude for an increase from one standard deviation below the mean to one standard deviation above the mean, while holding all other independent variables constant at their means.

Testament to the importance of being attentive to subgroup differences, none of the variables aside from evaluations of Bush are statistically significant for all of the five national-origin groups. Some of this may be due to the relatively small sample sizes that result once all variables of interest are included. For example, while there are 848 Puerto Ricans in the LNS dataset, the model includes only 503 once cases are dropped due to missing values. For Cubans, the number of cases drops from 522 to 213. Thus, despite the relatively large national-origin group samples in the LNS, the models are underpowered. Still, these are more detailed results than have been available based on previous survey research, and they provide important advances in our understanding of trust in government among Latinos.

Among Mexican-descent respondents, all four of the hypotheses listed earlier are supported, with statistically significant coefficient estimates for "American Identity," "Mostly Latino Friends," "Linked Fate Index," and "Support Blend into US Culture." The Mexican subsample model mirrors findings from table 4.1 in other aspects as well; Mexicans who have experienced discrimination in the workplace or at the hands of police officers are less trusting, as are those who are more fluent in English and those who are not partisans. Trust also declines slightly with age and is lower among women. Trust is higher among Mexican-descent respondents who supported President Bush. The predicted probabilities in this subsample also basically mirror the findings from table 4.1. As noted earlier, that the four hypotheses are more consistently supported in the Mexican-only subsample is likely due to the emphasis in prior research on samples dominated by Mexican-origin respondents.

For Puerto Ricans, none of the original four hypotheses are supported, and the coefficient estimate for "Mostly Latino Friends" is statistically significant but of the opposite sign. In other words, those who have more exclusively Latino friends are less trusting rather than more trusting. Puerto Ricans are the only subgroup for whom discrimination in restaurants and stores is a predictor of decreased trust; as noted earlier, this is likely due to the racial diversity within the Puerto Rican community. Further research that incorporates attention to race is needed to better understand how race and ethnicity interact to affect individual acculturation and political incorporation.

Among Cuban-descent respondents, unique predictors of political trust are support for maintaining a distinct Cuban culture, as well as gender—Cuban women are less trusting than are Cuban men. Cubans were also less trusting if they had experienced discrimination in housing or if they are U.S.-born. Other predictors of increased trust for Cubans include identification with the Republican Party and support for Bush; those who identify as politically independent are less trusting. The findings related to maintaining a distinct culture and to affiliation with the GOP are consistent with the hypotheses presented earlier regarding the history of the Cuban community in the United States.

Dominican respondents present yet another unique model of political trust. Trust is higher among those who prefer an American identity, while trust is lower for those who have a strong Dominican identity. Trust is higher among those who have more political interest, have higher incomes, and like President Bush and lower among those who were born in the United States and those who do not identify with either major political party.

For Salvadorans, increased trust is found among those who identify strongly as American, have stronger feelings of linked fate, support blending into mainstream U.S. culture, have higher political interest, have been discriminated against by the police, and support President Bush. In addition, Salvadorans are unique for the role of political ideology, with statistically significant coefficient estimates for several of the dummy variables in this category; this is consistent with the expectations presented earlier about the Salvadoran community's politicization during the bloody civil war in their home country.

Further research with larger subgroups is necessary to better understand trust among non-Mexican Latino subgroups. The distinct model generated for Cubans is consistent with previous research, in that Cubans are consistently more conservative and more strongly Republican than are other Latinos. For all other groups, the findings are quite the opposite, in that those who feel more strongly American or who prefer an American identity and those who believe more strongly in blending into U.S. culture are more trusting. The somewhat scattered findings for partisanship and ideology are mostly consistent with expectations. Future research should be attentive to the tendency of Latino respondents to decline to answer these questions and should probe further for leanings toward a particular party or ideological label in order to help reduce measurement error and uncertainty regarding these relationships.

Conclusions

The LNS data allow for a more nuanced look at Latino trust in government than was possible with previous data, due to the variety of relevant survey questions that were included and the size and diversity of the sample. This research adds to the increasing body of scholarship in this area with an investigation of four distinct hypotheses about how various aspects of Latino acculturation impact feelings of political trust, aimed at exploring the broader question of which path to cynicism is a more accurate reflection of the Latino experience in the United States. The results lend significant support for the conclusion that acculturation into the mainstream is not driving cynicism. Rather, those who more strongly identify as American and who support blending into U.S. culture (H_1 and H_4) are more trusting of government than are those who do not. The path to cynicism is thus more likely one of acculturation into a racialized subgroup. While many non-Latino Americans are cynical about the U.S. government, trust is not a function of feelings of belonging to the polity. As stated in H_2, social networks were hypothesized to serve as another measure of the degree and nature of acculturation by Latinos, with those who acculturate into minority subcultures (and thus with more exclusively Latino social networks) less likely to trust the government. This hypothesis is supported by results from the Mexican-descent subsample.

Latinos with stronger feelings that their fate and the fate of their national-origin group are linked to the fate of Latinos in general are more trusting of the government. That those with stronger feelings of linked fate are more trusting suggests that cynicism can be inoculated against if individuals have a strong sense of belonging and community. Linked fate suggests a feeling that one is a member of a subgroup, rather than part of the mainstream U.S. population. Thus, the positives of linked fate may mitigate the usual corrosive effect on trust in government, reflecting perceived reserves of social capital, interpersonal trust, or a sense of power as a subgroup (particularly given that the LNS was in the field concurrent with the immigration

---

Key Findings

- Latinos who more strongly identify as "American" or who have stronger feelings of linked fate or who feel it is more important to blend into the larger American society are more trusting of government.

- Latinos who had experienced discrimination, in their interactions with police or on the job, are less trusting of the government.

- Acculturation into the mainstream is not driving cynicism among Latinos. Cynicism is a result of a lack of a feeling of belonging, combined with acculturation into a racialized subgroup, more than into the dominant culture.

- In contrast, Cubans who maintain a strong sense of identity and pride in their culture trust the government more, because a strong subgroup culture mitigates the sometimes identity-corrosive effect of acculturation.

---

marches of 2006). Put another way, Latinos who acculturate into a racialized sub-group and also have strong feelings of linked fate have a group in which they feel that they belong, and thus their feelings of trust in government are relatively posi-tive. Latinos acculturating into a racialized subgroup but lacking feelings of linked fate feel more isolated and thus less trusting. As for those who acculturate into the mainstream, again these individuals will have a sense of group belonging and inter-personal trust and thus will be relatively trusting of the government (despite the mainstream U.S. political culture of cynicism). Cynicism is not only a result of a particular path of acculturation but more basically a result of a lack of a feeling of belonging.

Also interesting are the contrary results found for Cuban-descent respondents, whose trust is linked to support for maintenance of a distinct Cuban culture. As demonstrated by previous scholarship, Cubans are often quite distinctive in their patterns of political attitudes and behaviors. In addition, these findings further sup-port the conclusion that feelings of belonging and community are more powerful determinants of trust than is any particular type of acculturation. In other words, Cubans with a strong sense of identity and pride in their culture trust the govern-ment because they have a strong subgroup culture that has a mitigating effect on the usual corrosive effect of acculturation. Min Zhou (2004) discusses the positive impact of ethnic enclaves on assimilation. Similarly, Cubans not assimilating into the mainstream are able to maintain political trust.

Trust is not a function of support for U.S. culture or American identity. Cynicism is not just a result of being exposed to the "harsh reality" of racism and discrimina-tion in this country or to the political attacks on immigrants, such as those experi-enced by the Latino community in 2006. Rather, cynicism (or trust) is a reflection of a sense of belonging and community, of social capital and interpersonal trust. Low and generally declining levels of trust in government among the U.S. popula-tion belie a simplistic assumption that those who are more acculturated will also be less trusting, as acculturation has been found in previous research to be corro-sive of trust in government. In fact, these results speak to the inadequacies of such an explanation, as nativity is not consistently linked to feelings of political trust. Instead, cynicism is caused by acculturation into a racialized subculture combined with the absence of a sense of belonging. Those who reject an "American" identity and reject blending into U.S. culture but also reject the concept of linked fate are least likely to trust the government. If individuals feel that they belong to the main-stream culture, as evidenced by support for an American identity and U.S. culture, they tend to be more trusting. Likewise, if they reject mainstream culture but report a sense of linked fate, and thus belonging, with a Latino or national-origin-group subculture, they are inoculated against the usual corrosive effect of exposure to the harsh realities of U.S. racism and discrimination and are more trusting than would otherwise be expected.

These results serve as a reminder that how members of racial/ethnic minority groups are treated, and the degree to which members of those groups feel that they belong to the broader polity, will affect their method and degree of acculturation. Acculturation is a function of not only the degree to which individuals want to acculturate but also the degree to which the host society welcomes them (LeMay

2005). Trust is a reflection of political identity and a sense of belonging to a broader community, either a community of coethnics, of Latinos, or of Americans more generally. Increasing trust among Latinos and increasing the political integration of Latinos into mainstream political parties and political action does not necessarily mean that Latinos must be acculturated into mainstream American culture. Instead, it requires support for community and culture more broadly defined and ideally an end to culture wars that attack Latino ethnic enclaves and subcultures, such as those recently witnessed in Arizona.

Study Questions

1. Why is it important to know whether or not Latinos trust the government?

2. What variables from the LNS are predictors of trust in government for the entire sample? What are the notable subgroup (national-origin) differences?

3. Is cynicism among Latinos related to acculturation into the U.S. mainstream or into a minority subculture? How do the unique findings for Cubans help us understand this aspect of Latino trust in government?

4. How does the racial diversity of some Latino national-origin groups likely affect their experiences and feelings of political trust?

Appendix 4A: Question Wording and Variable Coding for *Political Trust*

Dependent Variable

POLITICAL TRUST	"How much of the time to you trust the government to do what is right—just about always, most of the time, some of the time, or never?"

Independent Variables

AMERICAN IDENTITY	Degree of "American" political identity (1 = low, 4 = high)
NATIONAL-ORIGIN GROUP IDENTITY	Degree of national-origin group identity (1 = low, 4 = high)
LATINO IDENTITY	Degree of Latino/Hispanic group identity (1 = low, 4 = high)
PREFER AMERICAN IDENTITY	Prefer American identity (0 = no, 1 = yes)
LINKED FATE INDEX	Linked fate index (1 = low, 4 = high)
MOSTLY LATINO FRIENDS	Dichotomized race/ethnicity of friends (0 = other, 1 = mostly Latino)
MOSTLY LATINO COWORKERS	Dichotomized race/ethnicity of co-workers (0 = other, 1 = mostly Latino)
SUPPORT BLENDING INTO US CULTURE	Support for blending into U.S. culture (1 = low, 3 = high)
SUPPORT MAINTAINING DISTINCT CULTURE	Support for maintaining distinct Latino/Hispanic culture (1 = low, 3 = high)

POLITICAL INTEREST	Degree of political interest (0 = low, 2 = high)
DISCRIMINATION: FIRED	Unfairly fired or denied a job or promotion (0 = no, 1 = yes)
DISCRIMINATION: BADPOLICE	Unfairly treated by the police (0 = no, 1 = yes)
DISCRIMINATION HOUSING	Unfairly prevented from moving into a neighborhood (0 = no, 1 = yes)
DISCRIMINATION: RESTAURANT/STORE	Unfairly or badly treated at restaurants or stores (0 = no, 1 = yes)
NATIVE-BORN	Born in the mainland U.S. or not (0 = no, 1 = yes)
ENGLISH FLUENCY	Degree of English fluency (1 = low, 5 = high)
LANGUAGE OF INTERVIEW	Degree of use of English in interview (1 = all English, 2 = claimed to prefer English but switched to Spanish, 3 = claimed to prefer Spanish but switched to English, 4 = all Spanish)
GENDER	Male = 1, Female = 2

Party ID dummies
   (deleted group = DEMOCRAT)
   REPUBLICAN
   INDEPENDENT
   NO CARE PARTY   Don't care about political parties
   OTHER PARTY
Ideology dummies
   (deleted group = LIBERAL)
   CONSERVATIVE
   MIDDLE IDEOLOGY
   NO THINK IDEOLOGY

DON'T THINK IDEOLOGY	Don't think in terms of ideology
LIKE BUSH	1 = dislike, 2 = neutral, 3 = like
EDUCATION	0 = none to 7 = graduate/professional degree
INCOME	1 = less than $25K, 2 = $25K–less than $45K, 3 = $45K or more

Notes

1. The authors gratefully acknowledge help from Simon Jackman, Gary Segura, and James Wenzel, as well as constructive comments from the authors and contributors to this volume. All errors, of course, are our own.

2. Latino immigrants almost all reject the notion that they are only in the United States temporarily. Although they may still have significant ties to their country of origin and may remit large sums of money to their family members or to hometown associations, most immigrants are here to stay (Jones-Correa 2004).

3. Because a significant portion (21.6%) of LNS respondents declined to answer the household-income question, missing values are imputed based on other variables, including media consumption, household size, nativity, education, parents' education, home ownership, language of interview, employment status, financial situation, and gender. In order to reduce the amount of error from these imputed values, income is then recoded into low (under $25K) medium ($25K–45K) and high (over $45K). Details of how the missing values were imputed are available from the authors on request.

4. One of the standard regression assumptions is that a dependent variable is continuous. When the dependent variable instead consists of two or more outcome categories, logit or probit models (for dichotomous dependent variables) or ordered logit or probit models

(for ordinal-level dependent variables) generally are more efficient. (See Vani K. Borooah, *Logit and Probit: Ordered and Multinomial Models*, Quantitative Applications in the Social Sciences 138 [Thousand Oaks, CA: Sage, 2002].)

References

Abramson, Paul R. 1983. *Political Attitudes in America: Formation and Change*. San Francisco: W. H. Freeman.

Alvarez, R. Michael, and Lisa García Bedolla. 2003. "The Foundations of Latino Voter Partisanship: Evidence from the 2000 Election." *Journal of Politics* 65 (1): 31–49.

Anzaldúa, Gloria. 1987. *Borderlands/La Frontera: The New Mestiza*. San Francisco: Spinsters/Aunt Lute.

Bobo, Lawrence, and Franklin D. Gilliam, Jr. 1990. "Race, Sociopolitical Participation, and Black Empowerment." *American Political Science Review* 84 (2) (June): 377–393.

Brehm, John, and Wendy Rahn. 1997. "Individual-Level Evidence for the Causes and Consequences of Social Capital." *American Journal of Political Science* 41 (3) (July): 999–1023.

Buzan, Bert C. 1980. "Chicano Community Control, Political Cynicism and the Validity of Political Trust Measures." *Western Political Quarterly* 33 (1): 108–120.

Chanley, Virginia A., Thomas J. Rudolph, and Wendy M. Rahn. 2001. "The Origins and Consequences of Public Trust in Government: A Time Series Analysis." *Public Opinion Quarterly* 64 (3) (Fall): 239–256.

Citrin, Jack. 1974. "Comment: The Political Relevance of Trust in Government." *American Political Science Review* 68: 973–988.

Citrin, Jack, and Donald Philip Green. 1986. "Presidential Leadership and the Resurgence of Trust in Government." *British Journal of Political Science* 16 (October): 431–453.

Cook, Timothy E., and Paul Gronke. 2005. "The Skeptical American: Revisiting the Meanings of Trust in Government and Confidence in Institutions." *Journal of Politics* 67 (3) (August): 784–803.

Dawson, Michael C. 1994. *Behind the Mule: Race and Class in African-American Politics*. Princeton: Princeton University Press.

de la Garza, Rodolfo O. 1995. "The Effects of Ethnicity on Political Culture." In *Classifying by Race*, ed. Paul E. Peterson, 333–353. Princeton: Princeton University Press.

de la Garza, Rodolfo O., Louis DeSipio, F. Chris Garcia, John García, and Angelo Falcón. 1992. *Latino Voices: Mexican, Puerto Rican, and Cuban Perspectives on American Politics*. Boulder, CO: Westview.

Emig, Arthur G., Michael B. Hesse, and Samuel H. Fisher III. 1996. "Black-White Differences in Political Efficacy, Trust, and Sociopolitical Participation: A Critique of the Empowerment Hypothesis." *Urban Affairs Review* 32 (2) (November): 264–276.

Erber, Ralph, and Richard R. Lau. 1990. "Political Cynicism Revisited: An Information-Processing Reconciliation of Policy-Based and Incumbency-Based Interpretations of Changes in Trust in Government." *American Journal of Political Science* 34 (1): 236–253.

Fraga, Luis, John A. García, Rodney Hero, Michael Jones-Correa, Valerie Martinez-Ebers, and Gary M. Segura. 2010. *Latino Lives in America: Making It Home*. Philadelphia: Temple University Press.

Gamson, William A. 1968. *Power and Discontent*. Homewood, IL: Dorsey.

Gamson, William A. 1971. "Political Trust and Its Ramifications." In *Social Psychology and Political Behavior*, ed. Gilbert Abcarian and John W. Soule, 41–55. New York: Charles E. Merrill.

Garcia, F. Chris. 1973. *Political Socialization of Chicano Children: A Comparative Study with Anglos in California Schools*. New York: Praeger.

García Bedolla, Lisa. 2005. *Fluid Borders: Latino Power, Identity, and Politics in Los Angeles.* Berkeley: University of California Press.

García Bedolla, Lisa. 2009. *Latino Politics.* Cambridge, UK: Polity.

García Bedolla, Lisa, Jessica Lavariega Monforti, and Adrian Pantoja. 2006. "A Second Look: The Latina/o Gap." *Journal of Women, Politics, & Policy* 28 (3–4): 147–171.

Gurin, Patricia, and Edgar Epps. 1975. *Black Consciousness, Identity and Achievement.* New York: Wiley.

Gurin, Patricia, Gerald Gurin, and Leo M. Beattie. 1969. "Internal-External Control in the Motivational Dynamics of Negroes." *Journal of Social Issues* 25 (3) (Summer): 29–53.

Gutierrez, Armando, and Herbert Hirsch. 1973. "The Militant Challenge to the American Ethos: 'Chicanos' and 'Mexican Americans.'" *Social Science Quarterly* 53 (1): 830–849.

Gutterbock, Thomas M., and Bruce London. 1983. "Race, Political Orientation, and Participation: An Empirical Test of Four Competing Theories." *American Sociological Review* 48:439–453.

Guzmán, Ralph. 1970. "The Political Socialization of the Mexican American People." Ph.D. dissertation, University of California, Los Angeles.

Hetherington, Marc. 1998. "The Political Relevance of Political Trust." *American Political Science Review* 92 (4) (December): 791–808.

Hetherington, Marc. 1999. "The Effect of Political Trust on the Presidential Vote, 1968–96." *American Political Science Review* 93 (2) (June): 311–326.

Howell, Susan E., and Deborah Fagan. 1988. "Race and Trust in Government: Testing the Political Reality Model." *Public Opinion Quarterly* 52 (3) (Fall): 343–350.

Jimeno, Rafael, and Rodolfo Espino. 2009. "Latino Linked Fate and Complex Causality." Paper presented at the thirteenth meeting of the Politics of Race, Immigration, and Ethnicity Consortium (PRIEC), Riverside, CA, January 30.

Jones-Correa, Michael. 2004. "Transnationalism and Dual Loyalties." In *The Hispanic Challenge? What We Know about Latino Immigration,* ed. Philippa Strum and Andrew Selee, 18–23. Washington DC: Woodrow Wilson International Center for Scholars.

Lane, Robert E. 1959. *Political Life: Why and How People Get Involved in Politics.* New York: Free Press.

Lavariega Monforti, Jessica. 2007. "Rhetoric or Meaningful Identifiers? Latinos(as) and Panethnicity." *Latino(a) Research Review* 6 (1–2): 7–32.

Lawless, Jennifer. 2004. "Politics of Presence? Congresswomen and Symbolic Representation." *Political Research Quarterly* 57 (1) (March): 81–99.

LeMay, Michael. 2005. *The Perennial Struggle: Race, Ethnicity, and Minority Group Relations in the United States.* 2nd ed. Upper Saddle River, NJ: Prentice Hall.

Levi, Margaret. 1996. "Social and Unsocial Capital: A Review Essay of Robert Putnam's *Making Democracy Work.*" *Politics & Society* 24:45–55.

Levi, Margaret. 1998. "A State of Trust." In *Trust and Governance,* ed. Valerie Braithwaite and Margaret Levi, 77–101. New York: Russell Sage Foundation.

Lipset, Seymour Martin, and William Schneider. 1983. *The Confidence Gap: Business, Labor, and Government in the Public Mind.* New York: Free Press.

Matthews, Donald R., and James W. Prothro. 1966. *Negroes and the New Southern Politics.* New York: Harcourt, Brace.

Michelson, Melissa R. 2001. "Political Trust among Chicago Latinos." *Journal of Urban Affairs* 23:323–334.

Michelson, Melissa R. 2003a. "Boricua in the Barrio: Political Trust among Puerto Ricans." *Centro: Journal of the Center for Puerto Rican Studies* 15 (1): 138–151.

Michelson, Melissa R. 2003b. "The Corrosive Effect of Assimilation: How Mexican-Americans Lose Political Trust." *Social Science Quarterly* 84 (4): 918–933.

Michelson, Melissa R. 2007. "All Roads Lead to Rust: How Acculturation Erodes Latino Immigrant Trust in Government." *Aztlán: A Journal of Chicano Studies* 32 (2) (Fall): 21–46.

Michelson, Melissa R., and Amalia Pallares. 2001. "The Politicization of Mexican-Americans: Naturalization, the Vote, and Perceptions of Discrimination." *Aztlán: A Journal of Chicano Studies* 26 (2): 63–85.

Miller, Arthur H. 1974a. "Political Issues and Trust in Government, 1964–1970." *American Political Science Review* 68 (3) (September): 951–972.

Miller, Arthur H. 1974b. "Rejoinder to 'Comment' by Jack Citrin: Political Discontent or Ritualism?" *American Political Science Review* 68 (3): 989–1001.

Miller, Arthur H., Edie Goldenberg, and Lutz Erbring. 1979. "Typeset Politics: Impact of Newspapers on Public Confidence." *American Political Science Review* 73 (March): 67–84.

Miller, Arthur H., and Ola Listhaug. 1990. "Political Parties and Confidence in Government: A Comparison of Norway, Sweden and the United States." *British Journal of Political Science* 20 (July): 357–386.

Miller, Warren E. 1980. "Disinterest, Disaffection, and Participation in Presidential Politics." *Political Behavior* 2 (1): 7–32.

Muller, Edward N., Thomas O. Jukam, and Mitchell A. Seligson. 1982. "Diffuse Political Support and Antisystem Political Behavior: A Comparative Analysis." *American Journal of Political Science* 26 (2) (May): 240–264.

Orum, Anthony M. 1966. "A Reappraisal of the Social and Political Participation of Negroes." *American Journal of Sociology* 72 (1) (July): 32–46.

Pérez, Emma. 1999. *The Decolonial Imaginary: Writing Chicanas into History*. Bloomington: Indiana University Press.

Pérez-Monforti, Jessica. 2001. "A Model of Minority: The Paradox of Cuban American Political Participation Regarding Official Language Policy in Miami-Dade County, Florida." Ph.D. dissertation, The Ohio State University.

Peterson, Geoff, and J. Mark Wrighton. 1998. "Expressions of Distrust: Third Party Voting and Cynicism in Government." *Political Behavior* 20 (1) (March): 17–34.

Pierce, Roy, and Philip E. Converse. 1989. "Attitudinal Roots of Popular Protest: The French Upheaval of May 1968." *International Journal of Public Opinion Research* 1 (3) (Autumn): 221–241.

Portes, Alejandro, and Rubén G. Rumbaut. 2006. *Immigrant America: A Portrait*. 3rd ed. Berkeley: University of California Press.

Putnam, Robert D. 1995. "Bowling Alone: America's Declining Social Capital." *Journal of Democracy* 6 (1) (January): 65–78.

Putnam, Robert D. 2000. *Bowling Alone: The Collapse and Revival of American Community*. New York: Simon and Schuster.

Putnam, Robert D., principal investigator. 2001. *The Social Capital Community Benchmark Survey*. Cambridge: Harvard University, John F. Kennedy School of Government, Saguaro Seminar. http://www.ropercenter.uconn.edu/data_access/data/datasets/social_capital_community_survey.html#.Ty64hF34QVA.

Sanchez, Gabriel R. 2008. "Latino Group Consciousness and Perceptions of Commonality with African Americans." *Social Science Quarterly* 89 (2): 428–444.

Schneider, Anne, and Helen Ingram. 1993. "Social Construction of Target Populations: Implications for Politics and Policy." *American Political Science Review* 87 (2): 334–347.

Scholtz, John T., and Mark Lubell. 1998. "Trust and Taxpaying: Testing the Heuristic Approach to Collective Action." *American Journal of Political Science* 42: 398–417.

Shingles, Richard D. 1981. "Black Consciousness and Political Participation: The Missing Link." *American Political Science Review* 75 (1): 76–91.

Southwell, Priscilla Lewis, and Marcy Jean Everest. 1998. "The Electoral Consequences of Alienation: Nonvoting and Protest Voting in the 1992 Presidential Race." *Social Science Journal* 35 (1): 43–51.

Tyler, Tom R. 1998. "Trust and Democratic Governance." In *Trust and Governance*, ed. Valerie Braithwaite and Margaret Levi, 269–294. New York: Russell Sage Foundation.

Wals, Sergio C. 2011. "Does What Happens in Los Mochis Stay in Los Mochis? Explaining Postmigration Political Behavior." *Political Research Quarterly* 64 (3): 600–611.

Wong, Janelle S. 2006. *Democracy's Promise: Immigrants and American Civic Institutions*. Ann Arbor: University of Michigan Press.

Zhou, Min. 2004. "Assimilation, the Asian Way." In *Reinventing the Melting Pot: The New Immigrants and What It Means to Be American*, ed. Tamar Jacoby, 139–154. New York: Perseus.

PART III

Acculturation, Differentiation, and Political Community

5

¿Quién Apoya Qué?

The Influence of Acculturation and
Political Knowledge on Latino
Policy Attitudes

REGINA BRANTON, ANA FRANCO,
AND ROBERT WRINKLE

Latinos, like other Americans, are concerned about a wide range of public policy questions, including economic policy, taxes, education, social policy, and more. Yet the public discourse frequently seems to portray Latinos as only being concerned with "Latino-centric" or "minority" issues, including immigration, affirmative action, bilingual education, and the like. But beyond the popular (and often mistaken) conventional wisdom, what do we actually know about how Latinos, especially those who are becoming more acculturated, form their policy preferences? In this chapter, Branton, Franco, and Wrinkle take a closer look at Latino attitudes toward several different policy domains—not just "Latino" issues—and ask whether higher levels of political knowledge, as well as acculturation, may be shaping policy preferences.

Attitudinal Foundations for Latino Policy Preferences

Latinos are the largest and fastest-growing minority group in the nation. This dramatic change in the demographic makeup of the United States underscores the need to understand the political attitudes and behavior of the Latino community. The potential impact of Latinos on U.S. politics depends on the existence of unified attitudes. However, there is a great deal of variation among Latinos in terms of nativity, acculturation, and national origin. These variations lead to differences in attitudes toward public policies.

Latino public opinion research has largely focused on immigration or ethnic-related issues. Determining both common and distinctive predictors of Latino preferences across a wider range of policy areas has received relatively little consideration. This chapter attempts to address this gap by examining Latino attitudes toward different policy domains. This study also extends the literature by considering the relationship between acculturation and Latino policy preferences conditioned on political knowledge.

Using data from the 2006 Latino National Survey (LNS), we examine Latino attitudes toward Latino-centric, social welfare, and moralistic public policies. The findings indicate that acculturation is associated with attitudes across a range of policy issues. Additionally, the relationship between acculturation and Latino policy attitudes is conditioned on political knowledge.

Research Questions

- Do unique and/or common determinants of Latino attitudes exist across different public policy domains?
- Is the influence of acculturation on Latino attitudes moderated by political knowledge?

Latino Attitudes toward Various Policy Domains

As noted, the main line of inquiry in Latino public opinion research has been immigration-related issues. A considerably smaller body of work examines Latino attitudes on nonimmigration policies, such as abortion (Bolks et al. 2000; Ellison, Echevarría, and Smith 2005), education (Sanchez 2006), the death penalty (Sanchez 2006), and government spending (Branton 2007). Relatively little attention has been given to the determinants of Latino attitudes toward distinct policy domains. The lack of research and the importance of gaining a better understanding of Latino policy preferences motivate us to examine Latino attitudes toward different areas of public policy.

We rely on extant research regarding the role of acculturation and ethnic identity in conceptualizing our policy domains of interest. Evidence suggests both common and unique determinants of Latino attitudes in separate areas of public policy. Research finds that while ethnic identity is not associated with Latino attitudes toward abortion, it is associated with attitudes toward immigration and other salient "ethnic" issues (Sanchez 2006; Leal 2004; Masuoka 2006; Vega 2005). Further, Regina Branton (2007) suggests that the impact of acculturation extends beyond immigration to other areas of public policy, such as education and policies benefiting minorities.

Thus, we focus on the following policy areas: Latino-centric, social welfare, and moralistic public policies. The Latino-centric dimension examines attitudes toward matrícula consular identification[1] and immigration policy. The social welfare policy domain focuses on attitudes regarding school vouchers, equal funding for schools, and guaranteed income. Finally, the "moral" policy dimension focuses on abortion and same-sex marriage.

Latino Policy Attitudes

A growing body of research examines the role of acculturation in shaping Latino attitudes toward immigration policy (Branton 2007; Hood, Morris, and Shirkey 1997; Binder, Polinard, and Wrinkle 1997; de la Garza et al. 1991, 1993). This research indicates that more acculturated Latinos are more likely to support restrictive immigration policies than are less acculturated Latinos (Hood, Morris, and Shirkey 1997; Binder, Polinard, and Wrinkle 1997; de la Garza et al. 1993). Additionally, less acculturated Latinos are more likely to support policies that benefit immigrants (Miller, Polinard, and Wrinkle 1984; Polinard, Wrinkle, and de la Garza

1984; Branton 2007). This research implicitly suggests that Latino immigrants and their descendants begin to lose their native cultural attachments over time, replacing them with U.S. cultural traits. Given these findings, we expect higher levels of acculturation to be associated with less support of policies beneficial to immigrants. Specifically, we predict,

> H_1: Less acculturated Latinos are more likely to support policies beneficial to immigrants than are more acculturated Latinos.

Extant research also suggests that acculturation is associated with a host of other Latino political attitudes and behaviors, including political trust (Michelson 2001; Wenzel 2006), health care behaviors (Mainous, Diaz, and Geesey 2008), party identification (Fraga, Valenzuela, and Harlan 2009), and attitudes toward other policy areas (Branton 2007). Together, these works suggest that the influence of acculturation may extend to nonimmigration policies. We pursue this line of inquiry by examining the role of acculturation in shaping Latino attitudes toward social welfare policies and "moral" policies.

The social welfare domain includes policies that are potentially beneficial to minorities in general rather than to Latinos specifically. Branton (2007) finds that less acculturated Latinos are more supportive of policies that benefit minorities, such as government provision of services for the needy, affirmative action, and the No Child Left Behind Act, than are their more acculturated coethnics. It is plausible that social welfare issues are more salient to less acculturated Latinos, perhaps due to socioeconomic factors and immigrant experiences. Thus, it is also reasonable to expect them to exhibit greater levels of support for related policies. Accordingly, we predict,

> H_2: Less acculturated Latinos are more likely to support social welfare policies than are more acculturated Latinos.

The role of acculturation in predicting Latino public opinion on "moralistic" policy issues remains relatively unexplored. Gabriel Sanchez (2006) finds that foreign-born Latinos express higher support for abortion, while opposition to abortion increases with time spent in the United States. Other research finds that acculturation is positively associated with support for abortion. For instance, Christopher Ellison et al. (2005) find that foreign-born Latinos are more likely to favor restrictive abortion policies than are native-born Latinos. Additionally, Robert Wrinkle et al. (2009) find a strong positive relationship between acculturation and support for abortion rights among Latinos.

The effect of acculturation on Latino support for same-sex marriage is less clear. According to Arturo Vega (2005), Latinos overwhelmingly disapprove of homosexuality (approximately 70%). Anglo attitudes are disapproving but slightly more approving than Latinos. Thus, we expect increased that levels of acculturation will lead to Latinos having views more consistent with Anglos on the subject of same-sex marriage. Further, there is survey evidence of differences in attitudes on moral public policies among Latinos as a function of acculturation. Notably, the Pew/Kaiser 2002 National Survey of Latinos finds that less acculturated Latinos are more likely to oppose homosexuality and abortion than are more acculturated Latinos (Suro et al. 2002). Thus, we predict,

> H₃: Less acculturated Latinos are more likely to oppose abortion and same-sex marriage than are more acculturated Latinos.

Assessing the Interaction between Acculturation and Political Knowledge

Extant research finds that political knowledge is associated with political attitudes and behavior. Michael Delli Carpini and Scott Keeter argue that increased political knowledge leads to increased tolerance, political participation, and more "stable, consistent opinions"; additionally, heightened political knowledge helps individuals "identify their true interests" and align their political attitudes and behavior accordingly (1996, 219). For example, Kristy Michaud et al. (2009) find that individuals with greater political knowledge are more likely to exhibit ideological coherence than are their less informed counterparts (see also Sniderman, Brody, and Tetlock 1991; Zaller 1992). Moreover, political knowledge is commonly found to be a moderating variable with regard to attitudes and behavior (e.g., Brewer 2003; Pantoja and Segura 2003; Nicholson, Pantoja, and Segura 2006; Michaud, Carlisle, and Smith 2009). For example, Stephen Nicholson et al. (2006) find that Latino policy preferences influence electoral choices, conditioned on political knowledge. Latinos with greater political knowledge are more likely to rely on issue positions when judging the candidates in an election, while Latinos with low political knowledge are more likely to rely on symbolism and partisanship.

In our previous hypotheses, we outline our expectations regarding differences in policy attitudes as a function of acculturation. However, this discussion does not consider whether the relationship between acculturation and attitudes may differ among politically informed and uninformed individuals. As noted, the extant public opinion research demonstrates differences in public opinion as a function of political knowledge. It is plausible that the relationship between acculturation and Latino policy attitudes may differ among politically informed and uninformed individuals.

Thus, we propose that political knowledge serves to moderate the effect of acculturation on policy attitudes. Specifically, we propose that the difference in policy preferences between less and more acculturated Latinos who are politically uninformed may be greater than the difference in preferences between less and more acculturated Latinos who are politically informed. We propose this narrowing divide in attitudes between less and more acculturated Latinos due to heightened political knowledge on the basis of the rationale that more politically informed Latinos have more uniform political preferences regardless of their level of acculturation. It is plausible that more knowledgeable Latinos are more aware of policy positions that benefit themselves and/or Latinos more generally than are less informed Latinos.

H₄: The effect of acculturation on Latino attitudes is conditioned on political knowledge.

Data and Methods

To examine the proposed relationship between acculturation and policy preferences conditioned on political knowledge, we use the 2006 Latino National Survey (LNS). The dependent variables of interest consist of seven significant policy issues falling under the three identified policy domains.[2] The Latino-centric policy items are matrícula consular ID and immigration policy. Social/welfare policy items include guaranteed income, school equality, and school vouchers. The moral policy domain includes same-sex marriage and abortion.

Dependent Variables

The *immigration policy* item queried respondents about their preferred policy on undocumented or illegal immigration: immediate legalization of undocumented immigrants, a guest-worker program leading to legalization, a guest-worker program that permits immigrants to be in the country, or an effort to seal the border to stop illegal immigration.[3] The *matrícula consular ID* item asked the level of support/opposition for matrícula consular IDs as an acceptable form of identification for immigrants in the U.S. The *guaranteed income* question asked the level of support/opposition for the government providing income to those who try to provide for themselves but cannot adequately do so. The *school equality* question asked the level of support/opposition for equal spending per student in public schools. The *school voucher* item asked the level of support/opposition for school vouchers. The *abortion* question asked whether abortion should be legal in all circumstances, legal in most circumstances, legal only when necessary to save the life of the woman or in cases of rape or incest, or illegal in all circumstances. The *same-sex marriage* item asked whether same-sex couples should be allowed to legally marry, enter into civil unions, or receive no legal recognition.

Independent Variables

The independent variables of interest are acculturation and political knowledge. *Acculturation* is measured using an additive scale based on the following items: generational status, language preference, and one's ability to carry on a conversation in the nondominant language (see Branton 2007 and Marin et al. 1987). The measure is anchored by "1," representing the lowest level of acculturation, and "6," reflecting the highest level of acculturation. Political knowledge (*PolKnow*) is an additive scale based on responses to three survey items. Respondents were asked to identify which political party had a majority in the U.S. House of Representatives, what presidential candidate won the 2004 election in their state, and which political party is more conservative than the other at the national level. Responses were coded "1" if a response was correct and "0" otherwise. Scores range from 0 to 3, with higher scores indicating a higher degree of political knowledge. As noted, we propose that the relationship between acculturation and policy preferences is conditioned on political knowledge. Thus, the models include an interaction between political knowledge and acculturation (Brambor, Clark, and Golder 2006; Kam and Franzese 2007).[4]

In addition to the variables of interest, the models include several other independent variables. Extant literature finds that in-group affect is associated with Latino public opinion. For instance, several works find that linked fate, or the notion that one's interests and future are inextricably linked to the experience of one's ethnic group, has a significant impact on Latino attitudes (McClain et al. 2006; Sanchez 2006; Masuoka 2006). This literature finds that in-group affect is associated with attitudes toward Latino-centric policies; however, it is not associated with attitudes on non-immigration-related policies such as abortion (Sanchez 2006; Vega 2005). We include three variables in the models that tap into the concept of in-group affect: linked fated, commonality, and discrimination. We measure *Linked fate* using the following question: "How much does your 'doing well' depend on other [Latinos/Hispanics] doing well?" We measure Latino group commonality (*Common*) using a question asking the respondent how much he or she shared in common with other Latinos/Hispanics in terms of "job opportunities, education, and income." Both questions are a four-point ordered scale ranging from "nothing" to "a lot." We measure discrimination using a series of questions concerning perceived discrimination in a variety of contexts. *Discrimination* is coded "0" if a respondent answered negatively to all questions (no perceived discrimination) and "1" if at least one affirmative answer was given. Based on the previous research, it is reasonable to expect that factors such as group commonality, linked fate, and perceived discrimination are associated with issues salient to Latinos yet not significantly related to attitudes toward nonsalient issues. As such, these predictors likely are associated with Latino attitudes on Latino-centric and social welfare policies but not related to attitudes on "moral" policies.

Existing literature also finds that various individual-level demographic characteristics are associated with Latino policy preferences (e.g., Bolks et al. 2000; Ellison, Echevarría, and Smith 2005; Hardy-Fanta 2000; Kelly and Morgan 2008). As such, our models account for a respondent's age, gender, education, ethnic identity, partisanship, ideology, and religiosity. *Age* is measured in years. Gender is a dichotomous variable (*Female*) coded "1" if female, "0" if male. Education is measured by two binary indicators: *No high school* for respondents with less than a high school education and *College grad* for respondents with a college degree or more. We also use a series of binary indicators to control for ethnic identity (*Mexican, Puerto Rican, Cuban,* and *Hispanic*), partisan affiliation (*Democrat* and *Independent*), and ideology (*Liberal* and *Moderate*). Religiosity is measured using two binary variables: *Church attendance,* coded "1" if attending church and "0" otherwise; and *Catholic,* coded "1" if Catholic and "0" otherwise.

Statistical Models

The dependent variables are categorical ordinal variables; thus, a model appropriate for ordered data is required. Typically, ordered logit—or some cumulative link model—is utilized with an ordered dependent variable. One of the key assumptions of ordered logit is proportional odds, which requires that the effects of the independent variables are constant across categories of the dependent variable. To evaluate the proportional odds assumption, we estimated an ordered logit model followed by the Brant test of proportionality (Brant 1990). In each model, one or more of the independent variables exhibited nonproportionality, violating the proportional odds assumption. As such, we employ a partial proportional odds model (Peterson and Harrell 1990; Williams 2006), which is similar to the proportional odds model. It estimates two sets of coefficients: β and ζ. β represents the estimates for those variables that meet the proportional odds assumption, and ζ are the estimates for the variables that violate the proportional odds assumption.

For example, the *matrícula consular* measure has four categories: 1 = oppose strongly, 2 = oppose, 3 = support, and 4 = strongly support. For those variables with proportional odds, β, there is a single parameter estimate. For variables violating the proportional odds assumption, ζ, there are three sets of logit estimates. The first set of logit estimates gives the log odds of a respondent answering above the first cut point (i.e., category = 2, 3, 4) versus below the first cut point (i.e., category = 1). The second set of logit estimates gives the log odds of a respondent answering above the second cut point (i.e., category = 3, 4) versus below the second cut point (i.e., category = 1, 2). The third set of logit estimates give the log odds of a respondent answering above the third cut point (i.e., category = 4) versus below the third cut point (i.e., category = 1, 2, 3). Each set of estimates is interpreted as a "stand-alone" logit, with the outcome representing the log odds of placement above or below a certain cut point. The analysis includes seven dependent variables. As such, the results presented in the tables refer only to the cut points of interest—for instance, the log odds of supporting versus opposing a policy.

Our principal argument is that the relationship between acculturation and Latino policy preferences is conditioned on political knowledge. Thus, the main covariates of interest are acculturation, political knowledge, and the interaction between acculturation and political knowledge.[5] To demonstrate the nature of the conditional relationship, we present predicted probabilities (and corresponding 95% confidence intervals) in table 5.1.[6] The first two rows reflect the probabilities for the Latino-centric items; the next three rows present the probabilities for the social welfare items; and the final two rows present the probabilities for the moral policy items.

Table 5.1: Latino Attitudes across Three Domains of Public Policies: Predicted Probabilities

	Low political knowledge		High political knowledge	
	Low acculturation	High acculturation	Low acculturation	High acculturation
Latino-centric				
Matrícula consular ID	.86 [.82, .90]	.54 [.39, .69]	.83 [.78, .89]	.60 [.49, .71]
Immigration	.87 [.85, .89]	.54 [.44, .64]	.85 [.82, .88]	.72 [.65, .79]
Social welfare				
Guaranteed income	.87 [.85, .90]	.76 [.66, .85]	.85 [.81, .89]	.95 [.91, .98]
School equality	.94 [.93, .96]	.84 [.76, .91]	.94 [.92, .96]	.91 [.87, .94]
School vouchers	.75 [.70, .79]	.17 [.08, .25]	.55 [.48, .62]	.32 [.23, .41]
Moral				
Same-sex marriage	.33 [.27, .38]	.35 [.20, .50]	.16 [.11, .21]	.39 [.28, .50]
Abortion	.10 [.08, .13]	.31 [.20, .42]	.15 [.11, .19]	.60 [51, .69]

Note: The estimates are predicted probabilities. The probabilities were calculated using the Delta method. The 95% confidence intervals are presented in brackets. The probabilities were calculated using the "nlcom" command in STATA 11.

For each policy item, the relationship between acculturation and policy preferences is conditioned on two levels of political knowledge: low and high. Further, probabilities are presented for two levels of acculturation: least and most.[7] These levels were selected to illustrate the nature and direction of the relationship.

Results

First, we begin by discussing the Latino-centric items. The predicted probabilities demonstrate that—regardless of one's level of political knowledge—as acculturation increases, support for Latino-centric policies decreases, which supports H_1. Additionally, the findings reveal the conditioning effect of political knowledge, which supports H_4. For instance, conditioning on low political knowledge, we find that as acculturation increases from low to high, the probability of supporting matrícula consular IDs decreases from .86 to .54. For those with high political knowledge, as acculturation increases, the probability of supporting matrícula consular IDs decreases from .83 to .60. Substantively, this suggests that as the level of acculturation increases, the difference in support between those with high and low political knowledge decreases. The probability estimates for the immigration policy item reveal the same conditional relationship. For Latinos with low political knowledge, as acculturation increases, the probability of supporting an immigration policy with a path to legalization decreases by .33 from .87 to .54. The gap among those with high political knowledge is considerably smaller. Among Latinos with high political knowledge, as acculturation increases, the probability of supporting this policy position decreases by .13 from .85 to .72. Together, the results suggest that more acculturated Latinos are less supportive of these Latino-centric policy items than are less acculturated Latinos; however, as political knowledge increases, the difference in support between least and most acculturated Latinos decreases.

Next, we examine Latino attitudes on social welfare policies. The predicted probabilities demonstrate that—regardless of one's level of political knowledge—as acculturation increases, support for school equality and school vouchers decreases, which supports H_2. Additionally, the probabilities illustrate the conditioning effect of political knowledge, which supports H_4.

The results for the guaranteed income item indicate that the conditioning effect of political knowledge renders an interesting outcome. For Latinos with low political knowledge, as acculturation increases from low to high, the probability of supporting guaranteed income decreases from .87 to .76. Yet for Latinos with high political knowledge, as acculturation increases, the probability of supporting guaranteed income increases from .85 to .95. Among those with low levels of political knowledge, increased acculturation leads to less support for this policy, yet for those with high levels of political knowledge, increased acculturation leads to heightened support for the policy. Obviously, this pattern does not completely align with our expectations outlined in H_2. Our expectations hold that for Latinos with low political knowledge, as acculturation increases, support for this social welfare policy decreases. However, among those with higher political knowledge, increased acculturation leads to heightened support for this policy item.

Next, the predicted probabilities indicate that there is a significant difference in attitudes regarding school equality between less and more acculturated Latinos with a low level of political knowledge. The probability of a less acculturated Latino with low political knowledge supporting school equality is .94, while the probability for a highly acculturated Latino with low political knowledge is .84. Although both demonstrate overwhelming support, less acculturated Latinos are significantly more likely to support school equality. Yet among Latinos with high political knowledge, there is no difference in support for this policy position as a function of acculturation. This suggests that heightened political knowledge eliminates the difference in support for school equality as a function of how acculturated a Latino is into U.S. society, which supports H_4.

Finally, the probabilities for the school voucher item also indicate that political knowledge has a significant conditioning effect on the relationship between acculturation and support for vouchers. Again, the difference in support among those with low levels of political knowledge is much larger than among those with high levels of political knowledge. Indeed, among those with low levels of political knowledge, the gap in support between those with low acculturation and high acculturation is .58. The probability of a less acculturated Latino with low political knowledge supporting vouchers is .75, while the probability for a highly acculturated Latino with low political knowledge is .17. Among Latinos with high political knowledge, the gap in support for vouchers between lowly and highly acculturated Latinos is .23. The probability of a Latino with high political knowledge and low acculturation supporting vouchers is .55, while the probability for a Latino with high political knowledge and high acculturation is .32. This suggests that as political knowledge increases, the difference in support as a function of acculturation —although sizeable and significant—is diminished.

Taken together, the findings generally indicate that less acculturated Latinos are more likely to support social welfare policies than are more acculturated Latinos. However, as political knowledge increases, the gap in support between less and more acculturated Latinos begins to decrease (and in some instances to disappear).

Finally, we turn attention to Latino attitudes on two moralistic public policies: abortion and same-sex marriage. The predicted probabilities (and corresponding 95% confidence intervals) demonstrate that there is no significant difference in attitudes regarding same-sex marriage among Latinos with low political knowledge. However, as political knowledge increases, there is evidence of significant differences in attitudes regarding same-sex marriage as a function of acculturation. For instance, for Latinos with high political knowledge, as acculturation increases from low to high, the probability of supporting same-sex marriage increases from .16 to .39. The findings lend support for the conditional relationship outlined in H_4, although the nature of the relationship is not as expected.

As for Latino attitudes regarding abortion rights, regardless of political knowledge, as acculturation increases, the probability of supporting abortion rights increases. This finding is consistent with the findings offered by Ellison et al. (2005) and Wrinkle et al. (2009) and lends support for H_3. Further, the results indicate that the conditioning effect of political knowledge is considerable. Among Latinos with low political knowledge, the probability of supporting abortion rights increases by .21—from .10 to .31—as acculturation increases from low to high. The findings also indicate that the gap in support is even larger among those with high levels of political knowledge. The probability of support among those least acculturated and with high political knowledge is .15, while the probability of supporting abortion rights among the most acculturated is .60. For Latinos with high levels of political knowledge, as acculturation increases from low to high, the difference in probability of supporting abortion is .45.

Obviously, these findings stand in stark contrast to the findings regarding Latino attitudes on Latino-centric and social welfare policies. As acculturation increases, Latinos are more likely to express liberal views on moralistic public policies. Alternatively, as acculturation increases, Latinos are less likely to support Latino-centric and social welfare policies. Further, when considering the conditioning effect of political knowledge, the difference in support for moralistic policies among less and more acculturated Latinos increases as political knowledge increases. Alternatively, the difference in support for Latino-centric and social welfare policies among less and more acculturated Latinos decreases as political knowledge increases. Together, the results suggest that the largest conditioning effect of political knowledge on social welfare and Latino-centric policies exists among less acculturated Latinos, while on moralistic issues the largest conditioning effect of political knowledge occurs among more acculturated Latinos. These data show how acculturation has a differential effect on policy attitudes due to one's level of political knowledge. However, it is clear from our data that the combined effect of political knowledge and acculturation can vary in direction and magnitude depending on the specific policy domain.

Before moving to a discussion of the results, we would like to address some of the other covariates included in the models. The results regarding Latino in-group affect indicate that linked fate is associated with attitudes across the three policy domains. Latinos who feel that their own chances in life are tied to other Latinos doing well are more likely to support Latino-centric and social welfare policies and less likely to support moralistic policies than are Latinos who do not feel their well-being is tied to other Latinos. For example, as linked fate increases from the minimum to maximum value, the probability of supporting the use of matrícula consular IDs increases by .11. Further, as linked fate increases from minimum to maximum, the probability of supporting immigration with some form of legalization increases by .07. For the school voucher policy, as linked fate increases, the probability of a Latino supporting this policy increases from .49 to .59. Additionally, the results indicate that as linked fate increases from the minimum to maximum value, the probability of a Latino supporting abortion rights decreases from .21 to .16. These findings suggest that this form of in-group affect is significantly associated with Latino attitudes on a range of policy issues.

The results likewise indicate that ethnic identity is associated with attitudes on Latino-centric and moral public policies; however, it is not associated with attitudes toward social welfare policies.[8] Latinos who identify themselves as Mexican are significantly more likely to support matrícula consular IDs than are Latinos of any other ethnic identity. Puerto Ricans are .13 less likely to support an immigration policy with a path to legalization than are Mexican respondents. In terms of Latino attitudes on moral public policies, the results indicate that Cuban Americans are more likely to support legal marriage for same-sex couples than are Central/South Americans. Additionally, Cubans are more likely to support abortion in most or all circumstances than are Latinos of any other ethnic identity. Together these findings indicate that ethnic identity is associated with attitudes when considering Latino-centric or moral issues, yet the nature of the relationship varies with respect to the specific public policy and ethnic identity.

Additionally, the results indicate that education is consistently associated with attitudes on Latino-centric and moralistic public policies. Latinos with a college degree are less likely to support Latino-centric policies and more likely to support moralistic policies than are Latinos without a college degree. For example, the probability of a college-educated Latino supporting abortion is .23, while the probability of a Latino with less than a high school degree supporting abortion is .15. Additionally, age is negatively related to Latino attitudes regarding Latino-centric and moral public policies. Substantively, the results suggest that younger Latinos are more supportive of Latino-centric and moral policies than are older Latinos. For example, as age increases from eighteen to sixty-five, the probability of supporting the use of matrícula consular IDs decreases by .10; likewise, as age increases from eighteen to sixty-five, the probability of supporting abortion decreases from .20 to .14.

The findings indicate that religiosity, partisanship, and ideology are associated with attitudes regarding moral issues. A Catholic Latino has a .14 higher probability of supporting same-sex marriage when compared to non-Catholic Latinos, while a Catholic has a .05 higher probability of supporting abortion rights than that of a non-Catholic. Latinos who attend church have a .14 lower probability of supporting same-sex marriage when compared to Latinos who do not attend church and have a .09 lower probability of supporting abortion rights. Further, the findings indicate

---

Key Findings

- We found that within the Latino population, levels of acculturation (measured by generational status and English language ability) *were* associated with political attitudes, for a wide range of social welfare, moralistic, and Latino-centric policy issues—but the associations varied and were mediated by respondents' levels of political knowledge (as measured by correct responses about political parties and electoral politics).

- Among less acculturated Latinos, we found links between political knowledge and attitudes on social welfare (income and education equality) and Latino-centric issues (tolerant immigration policy, including matrícula consular ID).

- Among more acculturated Latinos, the largest effect for political knowledge was on attitudes about moralistic policies (same-sex marriage, abortion rights).

- Our findings stand in stark contrast to previous findings regarding Latino attitudes on Latino-centric and social welfare policies. Our analysis suggests that as acculturation increases, Latinos are more likely to express liberal views on moralistic public policies. Alternatively, as acculturation increases, Latinos are less likely to support Latino-centric and social welfare policies.

---

that liberal and moderate Latinos are more likely to support same-sex marriage and abortion than are those identifying themselves as conservative. On the issue of abortion, Democrats and independents are more likely to support some form of abortion rights than are Republicans.

Finally, the results reveal limited evidence of gender differences across the three policy domains. Here we find no gender differences in attitudes toward each of the social welfare items, Mexican consular IDs, and abortion. These findings are consistent with extant research (i.e., Montoya 1996; Abrajano, Nagler, and Alvarez 2002). Our findings also indicate that there are gender differences regarding immigration policy and same-sex marriage. Substantively, the results suggest that Latinas are more likely to support an immigration policy with some form of legalization and same-sex marriage than are Latinos. Gender differences in attitudes toward immigration contrasts with the extant research (Binder, Polinard, and Wrinkle 1997; Branton 2007; Hood, Morris, and Shirkey 1997). However, prior research considers attitudes toward immigration levels, while the measure included in this study deals with various types of immigration policy.

Together, these findings demonstrate that there are many factors associated with Latino policy attitudes. That said, we feel the findings regarding the impact of acculturation on attitudes conditioned on political knowledge offer clear and strong empirical evidence that these factors are substantial contributors to attitudinal differences among Latinos.

Conclusion

In general, the literature on Latino policy attitudes reveals a set of influences that differ among various public policy issues. As noted, the influence of acculturation on Latino policy attitudes is well documented. Our chapter complements these studies by finding common and distinctive determinants across diverse policy domains.

However, almost absent from the literature is any consideration of the impact of political knowledge. We argue that a broader examination of Latino policy attitudes is a needed development. In this study, we examine the effect of acculturation and political knowledge on Latino policy attitudes. We find that the effect of acculturation on Latino policy attitudes is moderated by a respondent's level of political knowledge.

Our data highlight complex differences in policy attitudes among Latinos: the magnitude and direction of the conditioning effect of political knowledge varies across different policy domains. Acculturation, moderated by political knowledge, has a differential effect on policy attitudes. Consistent with the existing literature on Latino attitudes toward immigration policy, we find that support for Latino-centric policies decreases dramatically as acculturation increases. Yet, in the same domain, political knowledge attenuates this effect of acculturation. In contrast, political knowledge intensifies the effect of acculturation in our moralistic policy domain.

Indeed, the conditional relationship between acculturation and political knowledge can even yield counterintuitive results. Acculturation has a liberalizing effect on Latino attitudes toward moralistic policies yet has the opposite effect on Latino-centric and social welfare policies. When political knowledge is taken into consideration, more acculturated, politically knowledgeable Latinos are more likely to support liberal immigration or social welfare policies and twice as likely to express support for abortion rights than are less knowledgeable but equally acculturated Latinos.

The contemporary discussion of Latino policy attitudes has considered acculturation to have a one-dimensional effect. However, as powerful as acculturation is, it does not lead down the same road in all policy domains. Clearly, Latino policy attitudes are a complex set of relationships. This chapter contributes to the literature on Latino policy attitudes by illustrating this point. We should no longer consider the effect of acculturation on Latino policy attitudes as a simple, direct force. Rather, the nature of the relationship of acculturation to policy attitudes is clearly dependent on the type of policy being examined and other attributes of the individuals, including, especially, political knowledge.

Study Questions

1. Historically, what role has acculturation played in Latino attitudes?

2. How does acculturation influence Latino attitudes across different policy domains?

3. Consider and explain the relationship between political knowledge and acculturation.

4. When and how does political knowledge moderate the impact of acculturation?

5. Explain the impact of acculturation for different policy domains.

6. Explain and discuss the role of linked fate on Latino political attitudes.

Appendix 5A: Item Wording and Variable Coding for *Acculturation* and *Political Knowledge*

Dependent Variables

MATRÍCULA CONSULAR	1 = "strongly oppose," 2 = "oppose," 3 = "support," 4 = "strongly support"
IMMIGRATION	1 = "an effort to seal or close off the border to stop illegal immigration," 2 = "a guest-worker program that permits immigrants to be in the country, but only temporarily," 3 = "a guest-worker program leading to legalization eventually," and 4 = "immediate legalization of current undocumented immigrants"
GUARANTEED INCOME	1 = "strongly oppose," 2 = "oppose," 3 = "support," 4 = "strongly support"
SCHOOL EQUALITY	1 = "strongly oppose," 2 = "oppose," 3 = "support," 4 = "strongly support"
VOUCHERS	1 = "strongly oppose," 2 = "oppose," 3 = "support," 4 = "strongly support"
SAME-SEX MARRIAGE	1 = "no legal recognition," 2 = "civil unions," 3 = "legal marriage"

ABORTION	1 = "illegal in all circumstances," 2 = "legal only when necessary to save the life of the woman or in cases of rape or incest," 3 = "legal in most circumstances," and 4 = "legal in all circumstances"

Independent Variables

ACCULTURATION	Additive scale of generational status, language preference, and one's ability to carry on a conversation in the nondominant language. The scale ranges from 1 to 6, with a mean of 2.26 and a median of 2. A score of "1" indicates that a respondent is foreign-born, is Spanish dominant, and speaks little or no English. A score of "2" could indicate that a respondent is foreign-born, is Spanish dominant, and speaks English very well. Likewise, a score of "2" could indicate that a respondent is foreign-born, is Spanish dominant, and speaks little or no English. A score of "6" indicates that a respondent is third-plus generation, is English dominant, and speaks little or no Spanish. In sum, respondents are awarded points on the basis of their response to these three items.
POLITICAL KNOWLEDGE	Based on response to three questions: "Which political party, Democrat or Republican, has a majority in the United House of Representatives?"; "Which one of the political parties is more conservative than the other at the national level, the Democrats or the Republicans?"; and "In the United States, presidential elections are decided state-by-state. Can you tell me, in the election of 2004, which candidate, Bush or Kerry, won the most votes in [the state the respondent resides]?" The value is the number of correct responses and ranges from 0 to 3.
LINKED FATE	1 = "nothing," 2 = "little," 3 = "some," and 4 = "lot"
DISCRIMINATION	0 = "no" and 1 = "yes"
COMMON	1 = "nothing," 2 = "little," 3 = "some," and 4 = "lot"
DEMOCRAT	1 if a Democrat, 0 otherwise
INDEPENDENT	1 if an independent, 0 otherwise
LIBERAL	1 if a liberal, 0 otherwise
MODERATE	1 if a moderate, 0 otherwise
AGE	A continuous variable ranging from eighteen to ninety-seven
FEMALE	1 if female, 0 otherwise
MEXICAN	1 if Mexican origin or background, 0 otherwise
PUERTO RICAN	1 if Puerto Rican origin or background, 0 otherwise
CUBAN	1 if Cuban origin or background, 0 otherwise
HISPANIC	1 if Hispanic origin or background, 0 otherwise
LESS THAN HIGH SCHOOL	1 if less than a high school degree, 0 otherwise
COLLEGE DEGREE	1 if college degree or greater, 0 otherwise
CATHOLIC	1 if Catholic, 0 otherwise
ATTEND CHURCH	1 if attend church, 0 otherwise

Appendix 5B: Latino Attitudes across Three Domains of Public Policies

	Latino-centric		Social welfare			Moral	
	Matrícula consular ID	Immigration policy	Guaranteed income	School equality	School vouchers	Same-sex marriage	Abortion rights
Acculturation	−.33 (.06)**	−.35 (.05)**	−.15 (.06)**	−.22 (.07)**	−.54 (.07)**	.02 (.08)	.27 (.07)**
Know	−.10 (.09)	−.14 (.07)*	−.18 (.08)*	−.05 (.08)	−.41 (.09)**	−.38 (.11)**	.09 (.10)
Accult*Know	.03 (.03)^c	.07 (.02)^c	.12 (.03)^c	.04 (.03)^c	.12 (.03)^c	.07 (.04)^c	.05 (.03)^c
Linked Fate	.21 (.05)**	.17 (.03)**	.08 (.05)	.04 (.04)	.13 (.04)**	−.01 (.05)	−.09 (.04)*
Discrimination	−.03 (.10)	−.03 (.07)	.02 (.10)	.14 (.10)	−.29 (.10)**	.12 (.12)	.17 (.10)
Common	−.01 (.06)	.21 (.05)**	.05 (.06)	.09 (.05)	.01 (.05)	.09 (.07)	−.05 (.06)
Democrat	.06 (.11)	.18 (.08)*	.01 (.11)	.21 (.10)*	−.06 (.10)	.18 (.13)	.23 (.11)*
Independent	−.25 (.13)	.18 (.09)*	.16 (.12)	−.28 (.21)	.02 (.13)	.42 (.17)*	.40 (.14)**
Liberal	−.08 (.14)	−.01 (.07)	.12 (.15)	.07 (.15)	−.35 (.14)*	1.07 (.18)**	.76 (.17)**
Moderate	−.04 (.10)	−.03 (.07)	−.19 (.10)	−.08 (.09)	−.31 (.10)*	.47 (.13)**	.39 (.11)**
Age	−.01 (.00)**	−.01 (.00)**	.00 (.00)	.01 (.00)*	.00 (.00)	−.03 (.00)**	−.01 (.00)*
Female	.07 (.09)	.30 (.07)**	.13 (.09)	−.01 (.09)	−.09 (.09)	.32 (.12)**	.05 (.10)
Mexican	.39 (.14)**	.08 (.12)	.03 (.14)	−.00 (.14)	−.31 (.13)*	.23 (.21)	−.17 (.20)
Puerto Rican	−.18 (.20)	−.23 (.14)	.60 (.29)**	.05 (.19)	−.24 (.19)	.55 (.27)*	.22 (.25)
Cuban	−.13 (.23)	.04 (.20)	.14 (.21)	−.09 (.26)	−.39 (.22)	.88 (.28)**	.59 (.25)*
Hispanic	−.09 (.21)	−.12 (.16)	−.36 (.20)	−.20 (.21)	−.35 (.21)	.54 (.26)*	.40 (.22)
No High School	.34 (.11)**	−.04 (.11)	.25 (.11)*	−.12 (.10)	.20 (.11)	−.02 (.15)	−.25 (.12)*
College Grad	−.13 (.13)	−.18 (.09)*	−.06 (.13)	−.07 (.13)	.13 (.12)	.32 (.15)*	.29 (.13)*
Catholic	−.17 (.10)	.06 (.07)	.33 (.15)*	−.04 (.10)	.02 (.10)	.75 (.13)**	.34 (.11)**
Church Attend	.20 (.15)	−.07 (.10)	−.03 (.14)	−.09 (.15)	.25 (.14)	−.66 (.17)**	−.54 (.17)**
Constant	1.62 (.35)**	1.21 (.27)**	1.13 (.36)**	2.45 (.37)**	1.33 (.33)**	−.65 (.43)	−1.98 (.36)**
Wald χ²	260.51**	737.92**	86.88**	51.16**	261.88**	212.24**	317.02**
N cases	2,850	6,057	3,016	3,402	2,917	2,061	2,925

* p < .05 ** p < .01

^{c} Significant conditional standard errors

Note: Coefficients for this model are partial proportional odds with robust standard errors.. The sample sizes differ across the policy items due to split-sample survey items. The models were estimated in STATA 11 using the "gologit2" command.

Notes

1. *Matrícula consular* is a form of identification issued by Mexican consulate offices to Mexican nationals residing in the U.S.

2. The policy items used in the analyses were included due to the topic areas and the saliency of the issues to the Latino community.

3. With the exception of the immigration item and the "moral" policies, the dependent variables have a four-point Likert-type scale ranging from "strongly support" to "strongly oppose" as a response set. Appendix 5A offers a description of each dependent and independent variable.

4. Political knowledge and acculturation are correlated at only .35.

5. Thomas Brambor et al. note that it is possible for a conditional relationship between two independent variables to exist even when the coefficient on the interaction term is non-significant. Therefore, one cannot determine if an interaction is significant simply based on the p-value on the interaction term (2006, 74). As such, we calculated the marginal effect (and standard errors) of acculturation on Latino attitudes on each policy item, conditioned on political knowledge (Brambor, Clark, and Golder 2006; Kam and Franzese 2007). The results indicate that for all the dependent variables, the relationship between acculturation and Latino policy attitudes is statistically significant across the range of the political knowledge measure.

6. The parameter estimates and standard errors are presented in appendix 5B.
7. A score of 0 on the political knowledge measure denotes "low political knowledge," and a score of 3 denotes "high political knowledge." A score of 1 on acculturation denotes "least acculturated," and a score of 6 denotes "most acculturated."
8. Ethnic identity is measured using dummy variables, where Central/South American serves as the baseline category. We used t-tests to examine differences between the groups.

References

Abrajano, Marisa, Jonathan Nagler, and R. Michael Alvarez. 2002. "Is Abortion a Wedge Issue for Latino Voters?" Paper presented at the annual meeting of the American Political Science Association, Boston, MA, August 29–September 1.

Binder, Norman, J. L. Polinard, and Robert Wrinkle. 1997. "Mexican American and Anglo Attitudes toward Immigration Reform: A View from the Border." *Social Science Quarterly* 78:324–337.

Bolks, Sean M., Diana Evans, J. L. Polinard, and Robert D. Wrinkle. 2000. "Core Beliefs and Abortion Attitudes: A Look at Latinos." *Social Science Quarterly* 81 (1): 253–260.

Brambor, Thomas, William R. Clark, and Matt Golder. 2006. "Understanding Interaction Models: Improving Empirical Analyses." *Political Analysis* 14:63–82.

Brant, R. 1990. "Assessing Proportionality in the Proportional Odds Model for Ordinal Logistic Regression." *Biometrics* 46:1171–1178.

Branton, Regina. 2007. "Latino Attitudes toward Various Areas of Public Policy: The Importance of Acculturation." *Political Research Quarterly* 60:293–303.

Brewer, Paul. 2003. "Values, Political Knowledge, and Public Opinion about Gay Rights." *Public Opinion Quarterly* 67:173–201.

de la Garza, Rodolfo, Angelo Falcón, F. Chris Garcia, and John García. 1993. "Attitudes toward U.S. Immigration Policy." *Migration World Magazine* 21:13–16.

de la Garza, Rodolfo, Jerry L. Polinard, Robert Wrinkle, and Tomás Longoria, Jr. 1991. "Understanding Intra-Ethnic Attitude Variations: Mexican Origin Population Views of Immigration." *Social Science Quarterly* 72:379–387.

Delli Carpini, Michael, and Scott Keeter. 1996. *What Americans Know about Politics and Why It Matters*. New Haven: Yale University Press.

Ellison, Christopher G., Samuel Echevarría, and Brad Smith. 2005. "Religion and Abortion Attitudes among US. Hispanics: Findings from the 1990 Latino National Political Survey. *Social Science Quarterly* 86 (1): 192–208.

Fraga, Luis Ricardo, Ali Adam Valenzuela, and Danielle Harlan. 2009. "Patterns of Latino Partisanship: Foundations and the Prospects for Change." Paper presented at the annual meeting of the Western Political Science Association, Vancouver, BC, Canada, March 19–21.

Hardy-Fanta, Carol. 2000. "A Latino Gender Gap? Evidence from the 1996 Election." *Milenio* 2 (February). Notre Dame, IN: Inter-university Program for Latino Research.

Hood, M.V., III, Irwin L. Morris, and Kurt A. Shirkey. 1997. " '¡Quedate o Vente!': Uncovering the Determinants of Hispanic Public Opinion toward Immigration." *Political Research Quarterly* 50 (3): 627–647.

Kam, Cindy, and Robert Franzese. 2007. *Modeling and Interpreting Interactive Hypotheses in Regression Analysis*. Ann Arbor: University of Michigan Press.

Kelly, Nathan, and Jana Morgan. 2008. "Religious Traditionalism and Latino Politics in the United States." *American Politics Research* 36:236–263.

Leal, David L. 2004. "Latinos and School Vouchers: Testing the 'Minority Support' Hypothesis." *Social Science Quarterly* 85:1227–1237.

Mainous, Arch, III, Vanessa Diaz, and Mark Geesey. 2008. "Acculturation and Healthy Lifestyle among Latinos with Diabetes." *Annals of Family Medicine* 6:131–137.

Marin, Gerardo, Fabio Sabogal, Barbara Vanoss Marin, Regina Otero-Sabogal, and Eliseo Perez-Stable. 1987. "Development of a Short Acculturation Scale for Hispanics." *Hispanic Journal of Behavioral Sciences* 9:183–205.

Masuoka, Natalie. 2006. "Together They Become One: Examining the Predictors of Panethnic Group Consciousness among Asian Americans and Latinos." *Social Science Quarterly* 87 (5): 993–1101.

McClain, Paula D., Niambi M. Carter, Victoria M. DeFrancesco Soto, Monique L. Lyle, Jeffrey D. Grynaviski, Shayla C. Nunnally, Thomas J. Scotto, J. Alan Kendrick, Gerald F. Lackey, and Kendra Davenport Cotton. 2006. "Racial Distancing in a Southern City: Latino Immigrants' Views of Black Americans." *Journal of Politics* 68 (3): 571–584.

Michaud, Kristy, Juliet Carlisle, and Eric Smith. 2009. "The Relationship between Cultural Values and Political Ideology, and the Role of Political Knowledge." *Political Psychology* 30:27–42.

Michelson, Melissa R. 2001. "Political Trust among Chicago Latinos." *Journal of Urban Affairs* 23:323–334.

Miller, Lawrence, Jerry Polinard, and Robert Wrinkle. 1984. "Attitudes toward Undocumented Workers: The Mexican American Perspective." *Social Science Quarterly* 65:482–494.

Montoya, Lisa J. 1996. "Latino Gender Differences in Public Opinion: Results from the Latino National Political Survey." *Hispanic Journal of Behavioral Sciences* 18 (2): 255–276.

Nicholson, Stephen, Adrian Pantoja, and Gary Segura. 2006. "Political Knowledge and Issue Voting among the Latino Electorate." *Political Research Quarterly* 59:259–271.

Pantoja, Adrian, and Gary Segura. 2003. "Fear and Loathing in California: Contextual Threat and Political Sophistication among Latino Voters." *Political Behavior* 25:265–286.

Peterson, Bercedis, and Frank Harrell. 1990. "Partial Proportional Odds Models for Ordinal Response Variables." *Applied Statistics* 39:205–217.

Polinard, Jerry, Robert D. Wrinkle, and Rodolfo de la Garza. 1984. "Attitudes of Mexican Americans toward Irregular Mexican Immigration." *International Migration Review* 18:782–799.

Sanchez, Gabriel R. 2006. "The Role of Group Consciousness in Latino Public Opinion." *Political Research Quarterly* 59:435–446.

Sniderman, Paul M., Richard A. Brody, and Phillip E. Tetlock. 1991. *Reasoning and Choice: Explorations in Political Psychology.* New York: Cambridge University Press.

Suro, Roberto, Mollyann Brodie, Annie Steffenson, Jaime Valdez, and Rebecca Levin. 2002. *2002 National Survey of Latinos: Summary of Findings.* Menlo Park, CA / Washington, DC: Henry J. Kaiser Family Foundation / Pew Hispanic Center.

Vega, Arturo. 2005. "'Americanizing?' Attitudes and Perceptions of U.S. Latinos." *Harvard Journal of Hispanic Policy* 18:39–57.

Wenzel, James. 2006. "Acculturation Effects on Trust in National and Local Government among Mexican Americans." *Social Science Quarterly* 87:1073–1087.

Williams, Richard. 2006. "Generalized Ordered Logit/Partial Proportional Odds Models for Ordinal Dependent Variables." *Stata Journal* 6 (1): 58–82.

Wrinkle, Robert, Joseph Stewart, Jr., James Wenzel, Jerry L. Polinard, and Victoria Ibañez. 2009. "Determinants of Latino Attitudes toward Abortion: Examining Acculturation and Religiosity." Paper presented at the annual meeting of the Western Political Science Association, Vancouver, BC, Canada, March 19–21.

Zaller, John R. 1992. *The Nature and Origins of Mass Opinion.* Cambridge: Cambridge University Press.

6

The Boundaries of Americanness

Perceived Barriers among Latino Subgroups

HEATHER SILBER MOHAMED

Shortly after the 2012 elections, the Census Bureau reported that the nation's non-Hispanic white population was projected to peak by 2024 and decline steadily afterward. The bureau reported that "the U.S. is projected to become a majority-minority nation for the first time in 2043," when the Hispanic population's 100 million persons would constitute 27% of the total.[1] This coming transformation has profound implications for the nation's economic and social life, as our labor markets, school systems, tax revenues, entrepreneurial activity, cultural and artistic production, and health care, for example, will be shaped more than ever by attitudes and behaviors of Latinos, especially their understanding of what it means to be an "American"—and, crucially, whether they feel it is possible for them to share in the benefits of this core identity. In this chapter, Heather Silber Mohamed uses LNS data to measure whether, and with what reservations, Latinos actually feel themselves to be full members, or potential members, of the national community.

Becoming American: Boundaries of Language, Birthplace, Race, and Religion

From the Founding Fathers to the present day, the meaning of "American" is frequently conceptualized around ideology. Discussions of liberalism (Hartz 1950), the American "dream" (Hochschild 1995), and the American creed (Huntington 1981; Myrdal 1944) emphasize the centrality of ideological pursuits such as individualism and democracy to the character of the United States.

Yet, throughout history, more ascriptive, limited definitions of what it means to be American have also persisted. Particularly during periods of demographic and other change, "nativists" have frequently sought to redefine what it means to be American on the basis of religious, racial, and other restrictive grounds (Higham 1988; Citrin, Reingold, and Green 1990). Referring to such descriptors as "ethnocultural Americanism," Rogers Smith (1988) argues that throughout time, these factors have been more decisive in shaping U.S. immigration and citizenship policy than have liberal ideas. In a provocative article and subsequent book, Samuel Huntington (2004a, 2004b) exemplifies this emphasis on ethnocultural attributes. He asserts that early settlers initially defined America with their own ascriptive characteristics: primarily white, English speaking, and Christian. In what he terms "the Hispanic Challenge," Huntington argues that the modern-day influx of Latino immigrants threatens such key aspects of American society and culture. He points to the persistence of Spanish rather than English and the potential departure from an "Anglo" society as particular threats posed by the burgeoning Latino population.

Research Questions

- How do individuals' experiences shape their definitions of what it means to be "American"?

- Specifically, do country of origin, level of integration in the United States, and region of residence impact the extent to which Latinos view "American" as an ascriptive category, which may be closed to them simply by virtue of their Latino origins, or an open category, which they may join?

Yet how do Latinos understand what it means to be American? The perception of "American" as an open, ideological category to which newcomers might seek admission, versus a closed, ascriptive category from which they are excluded, has clear implications for immigrants seeking to incorporate into U.S. society. However, extant literature contains few studies that explore the views of minority groups regarding what it means to be American. In part, this gap in the literature may be a consequence of limited data; the General Social Survey, for instance, did not begin to target large numbers of Spanish speakers until 2006. One notable exception, by Jack Citrin, Cara Wong, and Brian Duff (2001), uses data from the 1994 and 1995 Los Angeles County Social Surveys to study perceptions held by Asians and Latinos in the LA metropolitan area about what it means to be American. More recently, Deborah Schildkraut (2011) explores the perceptions of Latinos, African Americans, Asians, and whites about what it means to be American across a number of dimensions. But her limited sample of Latinos (n = 441) does not allow for a wide range of comparisons within this broadly defined group.

Fortunately, the large sample size of the 2006 Latino National Survey and the diversity of respondents in terms of generational status, country of origin or ancestry, and geographic place of residence in the United States facilitates a broader examination of what it means to be American for different subsets of the Latino population. Specifically, questions in the survey regarding the importance of certain ascriptive characteristics enable an assessment of Latino perceptions regarding the boundaries of American society.

Depending on one's ancestral origin group, Latino immigrants are likely to have had vastly different historical experiences prior to arrival in the U.S. Further, some subgroups have since developed distinct legal and political relationships with the U.S. government, guided largely by federal immigration policy. Regional differences upon arrival in the United States are also likely to yield divergent experiences for some Latinos. Moreover, since the 1990s, an increasing number of states and communities have initiated their own immigration-related provisions (Newton and Adams 2009). As a consequence of these varied experiences, as well as individuals' levels of integration into U.S. society, I hypothesize that different subsets of the Latino population are likely to have distinct perspectives on what it means to be American. Through multivariate analysis, I explore how these factors contribute to the ways in which Latinos conceptualize group membership. Specifically, this chapter focuses on four ascriptive features commonly associated with being American: race, religion, language, and birthplace.

In studies that focus primarily on the majority (non-Hispanic white) population, existing research demonstrates that perceptions of "American" as an open or closed group are closely connected to positions on public policy (Citrin, Reingold, and Green 1990; Citrin, Wong, and Duff 2001; Schildkraut 2005) as well as political knowledge and participation (Huddy and Khatib 2007). For Latinos, whether individuals perceive "American" as a broad, open category may impact not only public opinion and political behavior but also an individual's very sense of belonging and inclusion in the U.S. By better understanding the different ways in which Latinos interpret what it means to be American, this line of research has important implications regarding political learning and socialization, immigrant incorporation, and the acquisition of new identities in a host society.

Identities, Political Learning, and Political Socialization

Much of the existing political science literature on identities draws on psychology's social identity theory, which emphasizes the process by which individuals distinguish their own in-group from a larger out-group (Brewer 2003; Tajfel 1970). According to this theory, in cases where groups are assigned or group membership is assumed, individuals tend to favor their own in-group. This postulate holds true even under minimal conditions of similarity, such as when respondents are assigned into specific groups for role-playing exercises (see, for instance, Zimbardo, Maslach, and Haney 2000).

Social identity theory provides tremendous insight in cases where identities may be "primordial," assigned, or otherwise clearly established. Yet, as Leonie Huddy (2001) points out, the theory is less successful in explaining the acquisition of *new* identities. Developing a better understanding of the process by which individuals assume new identities is essential for refining our knowledge of immigrant integration into host societies.

As McClain et al. (2009) explain, group membership can refer both to how one describes oneself as well as to ascriptive characteristics that shape the way others might categorize people. Scholars of self-categorization emphasize the importance of a "prototype" group member, real or imagined, who exhibits a range of attributes or characteristics common to the group. An individual's perceived proximity to this prototypical person helps to determine whether one self-categorizes as a member of that group (Lakoff 1987; Turner et al. 1987). An extension of this theory suggests that the more immigrants think "American" is defined by ascriptive features that they may not share, the less likely they are to see this category as one to which they might ultimately gain admission. In other words, the perceived strength of group boundaries can play an important role in determining one's own self-identification and sense of belonging in society. Indeed, Tanya Golash-Boza (2006) argues that foreignness associated with Latinos can prevent them from developing an identity as American. Likewise, John García (1981) finds that among Mexican immigrants, an American identity is the most significant factor in determining whether or not an individual chooses to naturalize. This research suggests that the perceived fluidity of group boundaries influences an individual's perceptions about whether it is possible to incorporate into a societal group.

Yet existing scholarship does not explain the factors that lead to varied perceptions regarding the boundaries of group membership in the first place. In this chapter, I seek to contribute to this gap in the literature with a focus on the Latino population. Drawing on existing research regarding political socialization and political learning, I hypothesize that three key variables—country of origin / ancestry, place of residence in the U.S., and level of integration into U.S. society—influence whether certain Latinos perceive "American" to be an open category that they are able to join or a closed one, defined in terms of less malleable characteristics such as birthplace and skin color, from which they are more likely to be excluded.

Hypotheses

Using data from the LNS, this chapter focuses on the five largest Latino-origin subgroups in the United States: Cubans, Dominicans, Salvadorans, Mexicans, and Puerto Ricans. These groups constitute over 80% of the Latino population currently living in the United States (Ennis, Rios-Vargas, and Albert 2011). I test three hypotheses to explore variation in the ways in which Latinos define "American."

The first hypothesis draws on literature regarding political socialization, which emphasizes the ways in which citizenship, party membership, and political participation develop. Scholars in this tradition emphasize that children acquire political ideas at a young age from their parents (see Sapiro 2004 for a full review of this literature). For immigrant populations, this literature is also beginning to study behavior in one's home country as an independent variable, focusing on transnational activities and, to the extent possible, political behavior prior to arrival in the U.S. (Jones-Correa 1998a; Ramakrishnan 2005). This line of research suggests that for immigrants, prior political experiences in one's country of origin can be instrumental in shaping political behavior and attitudes long after arrival in the U.S.

Similarly, scholarship on political learning argues that an individual's experience with the government shapes his or her perspective on both governance and citizenship. From welfare recipients in the United States (Soss 1999) to peasants in India (Corbridge et al. 2005), researchers in this tradition emphasize that one's interactions and experiences with state institutions contribute to an individual's most fundamental understanding of citizenship. More recently, Vesla Weaver and Amy Lerman (2010) find that punitive interactions with the criminal justice system have significant negative consequences for individual feelings of belonging as well as political participation.

Drawing on this research, I suggest that the varied experiences of Latino immigrants and their families upon arrival in the U.S. may influence their opinions about what it means to be American. Using country of origin or ancestry as a proxy for these experiences, the *political learning hypothesis* anticipates that variance in U.S. policy toward an individual's country of origin or ancestry is likely to correlate with distinct perceptions of one's sense of citizenship or belonging. Those subgroups whose members have been treated more favorably by U.S. policy, and are more likely to have had positive interactions with the U.S. government, are also likely to have a more open perception of what it means to be American. In contrast, members of subgroups that have faced more adversity, and have had more negative experiences with the government, are likely to see "American" as a restrictive and potentially inaccessible category.

The second hypothesis explores the role played by Latinos' level of incorporation. Chapter 5 in this volume, by Regina Branton, Ana Franco and Robert Wrinkle, demonstrates the impact that acculturation can have on Latino policy attitudes. Likewise, existing literature finds that later generations of immigrants, those who speak English, and those who have lived in the United States for a significant period of time are more likely to distance themselves from other Latinos and incorporate into broader U.S. society (García Bedolla 2005; Lavariega Monforti and Sanchez 2010). Accordingly, I propose the *integration hypothesis*, which suggests that across subgroups, immigrants who are more incorporated in the United States are more likely to view American as an accessible category and less likely to define it in ascriptive terms. In contrast, I anticipate that respondents who are less integrated, and are more likely to see their fate as closely linked to that of other Latinos, will have a more restricted understanding of what it means to be American.

The final hypothesis explores the importance of where an individual lives in the U.S. This hypothesis follows a tradition of scholarship emphasizing the importance of geography on political behavior (Huckfeldt 1996; Tam Cho, Gimpel, and Dyck 2006). Looking at the general population in the U.S., Joel Lieske (1993) advances the idea of regional subcultures, using demographic, economic, and structural indicators to explain variation in social and political behavior. Historically, Mexicans in the U.S. have settled in the Southwest, with Cubans in Florida and Puerto Ricans and Dominicans in the Northeast. These patterns, as well as more recent Latino settlement trends, contribute to distinct incorporation experiences, which are also influenced by the characteristics of one's receiving community (Segura and Rodrigues 2006). Likewise, chapter 9 in this volume, by Gabriel Sanchez and Matt Barreto, emphasizes the importance of various contextual factors in shaping Latino attitudes toward government. Building on this range of literature, I develop the *regional hypothesis*, which suggests that factors specific to one's area of residence may also result in varied understandings of what it means to be American.

Divergent Paths, Convergent Presents?

A significant body of literature focuses on the conditions under which Latinos adopt panethnic (Latino/Hispanic) identities. In chapter 2, Lavariega Monforti documents a large increase in receptivity toward these categories, with nearly 90% of LNS respondents indicating they "strongly" or "very strongly" identify with a Latino/Hispanic identifier. As reflected in figure 6-1, however, considerable variation exists in the extent to which members of different ancestral origin groups describe themselves as American. I suggest that this variation better underscores divisions within the Hispanic community regarding its standing in the U.S. and may ultimately help to explain differences in Latino political participation and behavior.

While a full discussion of the historical experience of each Latino subgroup is beyond the scope of this chapter, a brief overview is important to better understand

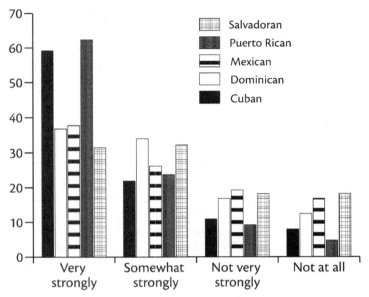

Fig. 6.1. Percentage of respondents who self-identify as American, by country of origin. Using raw data from the 2006 LNS, this graph illustrates the degree to which respondents self-identify as American, on a scale from 1 (not at all) to 4 (very strongly).

the underlying hypothesis regarding varied group experiences (for a more complete description, see García Bedolla 2009). This section presents a short discussion of U.S. immigration policy and history with respect to the countries of ancestry of the five largest Latino subgroups in the United States: Puerto Ricans, Cubans, Mexicans, Dominicans, and Salvadorans.

Throughout the 1920s, a series of immigration laws placed caps on the number of immigrants that could settle in the United States. Individuals from the Western Hemisphere, however, were omitted from these formal restrictions.[2] The 1965 Immigration Act repealed these earlier national-origin quotas and introduced a new approach to immigration policy. For the first time, immigrants from the Western Hemisphere were subject to the federal limits. In determining immigrant admissions, the 1965 law prioritized the principles of family reunification and meeting the employment needs of the U.S. However, due to a patchwork quilt of immigration, citizenship, and asylum provisions that extend beyond the 1965 law, as well as legal arrangements preceding this act, some Latino national-origin subgroups have fared differently than others in the citizenship regime.

Puerto Ricans became Americans "by conquest," when the island was awarded to the U.S. under the 1898 Treaty of Paris in the aftermath of the Spanish-American War. All Puerto Ricans were granted U.S. citizenship by statute under the 1917 Jones Act, and the island of Puerto Rico became a U.S. Commonwealth in 1952. Particularly among early migrants, Puerto Ricans coming to the U.S mainland tended to be from the lower economic strata (Portes and Grosfoguel 1994). Consequently, Puerto Ricans on the mainland have consistently demonstrated higher levels of poverty in comparison to other Latino groups (Ramirez and de la Cruz 2003).

While some Cubans settled in the U.S. before the Cuban Revolution, large waves of migrants arrived as a result of Fidel Castro's rise to power in 1959. Cubans in the U.S. have historically viewed themselves as an exile community rather than as long-term settlers in the United States (de los Angeles Torres 1999; Rieff 1995). Those arriving prior to the 1980s were primarily white and middle or upper class, though recent immigrants are more diverse (Rieff 1995).

Because of Cuba's enduring communist government, the U.S. has treated Cuban immigrants differently than other arrivals from Latin America and the Caribbean. Starting with the 1966 Cuban Adjustment Act (CAA) and subsequently under the current "Wet Foot / Dry Foot" policy,[3] Cubans have maintained a distinct advantage with respect to U.S. immigration policy. Early arrivals also received significant resettlement assistance from the U.S. government, and many exiles collaborated with the U.S. administration during the Cold War (Portes and Grosfoguel 1994; Wilson and Portes 1980). This preferential treatment has resulted in a different relationship with the U.S. government than that of other Latino groups. While many early Cuban and Puerto Rican arrivals experienced discrimination in the U.S., given their privileged legal status, I hypothesize that members of both of these subgroups will have more open attitudes about what it means to be American than other Latinos will.

Compared to that of other Latino groups, the migration of Mexicans to the United States is notable both for its extended history as well as the large number and duration of migrants crossing the border. Many Mexicans "became" American due to territorial acquisitions in the mid-nineteenth century, with nearly 75,000 becoming U.S. citizens as a result of the 1848 Treaty of Guadalupe Hidalgo (García Bedolla 2009). Since that time, large numbers of Mexicans have come to the U.S. as economic migrants, with the first major wave of arrivals in the 1910s–1920s. Prior to the civil rights movement, many Mexicans experienced significant discrimination, violence, and in some cases, even forced deportation under the Mexican "Repatriation" program of the 1930s and "Operation Wetback" in the 1950s (Balderrama and Rodriguez 2006). Between the 1940s and 1960s, hundreds of thousands of Mexicans came to the U.S. under the *Bracero* program, through which Mexican workers were employed as contract workers in the agriculture and railroad sectors (García Bedolla 2009). The extensive history of Mexican Americans in the U.S. suggests significant diversity within this community, highlighting the importance of immigrant generation and broader measures of incorporation.

Under the 1965 Immigration Act, Mexicans became subject to formal visa caps for the first time. As a result of the family-preference provision of the act, coupled with the vast number of Mexicans living in the U.S. who have family abroad, in recent years, Mexicans have constituted the largest legal immigrant group in the U.S. The 1986 Immigration Reform and Control Act (IRCA) also provided a path to citizenship for nearly 3 million undocumented immigrants, mostly Mexican (García Bedolla 2009). Additionally, as of 2009, an estimated 6,650,000 Mexicans lived in the United States without proper documents, constituting nearly 62% of the overall estimated unauthorized population (Hoeffer, Rytina, and Baker 2010).

Most early Dominican migrants were political exiles, aided in their settlement by the U.S. government (Itzigsohn 2009). The vast majority of Dominicans currently in the U.S., however, are economic migrants arriving since 1970, with most entering through the work-certification process. Only a small number of political asylees have come to the U.S. since that time (Portes and Grosfoguel 1994; Migration Policy Institute 2004).

Immigrants from El Salvador have a more complicated history. During the 1980s, the U.S. was actively involved in the Salvadoran civil war, aligning itself with that country's repressive government. Estimates indicate that more than 75,000 Salvadorans were killed during the nation's brutal civil war, with hundreds of thousands of individuals internally displaced (Karl 1992). Additionally, by 1987, an estimated 10% of the country's population had fled to the U.S. to escape the violence. A subsequent International Truth Commission determined that the Salvadoran government was responsible for 85% of the deaths that took place in that conflict, while just 15% were attributed to insurgent activity (Wood 2008).

Elisabeth Wood (2008) highlights the polarization of political identities that occurs over the course of civil wars. She argues that such shifts may persist over time and space, as refugees flee the violence of war and bring their experiences with them to their new homes. Focusing on El Salvador, she finds that the extreme violence caused many who were previously pacifists to join the antigovernment insurgency. Given the close association of the U.S. with the Salvadoran regime's atrocities, an extension of Wood's theory suggests that Salvadoran immigrants may hold a more negative view of the U.S. than their Latino counterparts do. This perception could translate into a distinct view of what it means to be American.

Likewise, throughout the civil war, as the U.S. government supported the Salvadoran state abroad, at home, it denied asylum claims from Salvadoran refugees.[4] Since 1990, hundreds of thousands of Salvadorans have received legal protection under provisions including Temporary Protected Status (TPS),[5] Deferred Enforced Departure (DED), and the Nicaraguan Adjustment and Central American Relief Act (NACARA) (Gammage 2007; Wasem and Ester 2008). According to 2010 estimates, after Mexicans, Salvadorans constitute the second-largest undocumented population in the U.S., totaling approximately 530,000 (Hoeffer, Rytina, and Baker 2010). Given the experience of the Salvadoran civil war and the early struggles faced by asylum seekers in the U.S., I anticipate that this group will have the most restrictive view of what it means to be American.

Methods

To explore differences in Latino perspectives about what it means to be American, I examine responses to a series of questions that gauge where individuals think the boundaries of American group membership lie.[6] Specifically, the analysis focuses on responses to the following questions: "When you think of what it means to be fully American in the eyes of most Americans, do you think it is very important, somewhat important, or not important to: be born in the U.S.; speak English; be white; and be Christian?" These questions provide the opportunity to study the extent to which different segments of the Latino population understand or define American in ascriptive terms.

One limitation of the present study is the ambiguous phrasing of the survey question, in that respondents may be referring both to their own definition of "American" as well as to perceptions of discrimination or attitudes of others. As McClain and her colleagues (2009) suggest, however, a combination of these factors is likely to be important in shaping perceptions of group identity. Additionally, these four characteristics represent classic ascriptive views regarding who is included in the category of "American" (see Theiss-Morse 2009), and the responses provide a unique opportunity to better understand varying Latino perspectives. Moreover, with the exception of being born in the United States, these are the categories most emphasized by Huntington in his discussion of the Latino "challenge." Consequently, a better understanding of Latino views on these particular characteristics will help to assess the validity of Huntington's argument. If, as Huntington suggests, Latinos threaten the classical ascriptive features of the United States, in particular with regard to language and religion, we would expect Latinos to place relatively little importance on these characteristics.

Similar questions regarding birthplace, religion, and language appeared on the 2004 version of the General Social Survey (GSS). This data provides the opportunity to establish a baseline of comparison with a large population of whites and a smaller sample of African Americans and English-speaking Latinos.[7] Notably, the GSS question is more straightforward, with respondents asked, "Some people say the following things are important for being truly American. Others say they are not important. How important do you think each of the following is . . . ?" Respondents were then given a number of characteristics, including to be a Christian, to have been born in America, and to be able to speak English. Race was not included among the list of ascriptive characteristics on the GSS.[8]

Table 6.1 presents a comparison of responses from the 2004 GSS and the 2006 LNS. As the table reflects, using raw data from both surveys, Latino respondents in the GSS and the LNS place even more importance on speaking English than whites do. These numbers defy Huntington's fears that Latinos in the U.S. do not wish to learn English.[9] With respect to being a Christian, Latinos are less likely to think this attribute is very important than are other respondents. However, across both surveys, a similar minority of white and Latino respondents think Christianity is *not* important to being defined as American. Perhaps most striking in this category is the very high percentage of African Americans emphasizing the importance of Christianity, compared to whites and Latinos.

Finally, with respect to birthplace, looking only at the GSS data, African American respondents are most likely to place importance on being born in the U.S., followed by Latinos and then whites. Comparing Latino respondents across the surveys, those in the LNS place far less emphasis on birthplace. This difference may, in part, stem from the larger proportion of LNS respondents born outside the U.S (64.6%) than Latino respondents in the GSS (33.8%).[10] With the exception of the birthplace question in the LNS, however, Latino and white respondents have similar perspectives on what it means to be American. Overall, echoing the findings of Deborah Schildkraut (2011), more similarities than differences exist when looking at the ways that members of distinct racial and ethnic groups conceptualize "American."

Table 6.1: The Importance of Ascriptive Characteristics for Being American, GSS (2004) and LNS (2006)

Ascriptive characteristic	GSS, whites	GSS, blacks	GSS, Latinos	LNS
Speak English	N = 971	N = 164	N = 112	N = 8634
Very important	82.2%	90.2%	90.2%	84.9%
Somewhat/fairly important	14.5%	7.9%	8.0%	11.1%
Not important	3.3%	1.8%	1.8%	4.0%
Christian	N = 948	N = 159	N = 104	N = 8634
Very Important	47.3%	75.5%	35.6%	41.3%
Somewhat/fairly important	17.2%	6.9%	26.0%	22.0%
Not important	35.6%	17.6%	38.5%	36.7%
Born in U.S.	N = 961	N = 157	N = 107	N = 8,634
Very Important	55.9%	70.1%	60.8%	44.4%
Somewhat/fairly important	22.0%	12.7%	24.3%	25.6%
Not important	22.1%	17.2%	14.9%	30.0%
White				N = 9,834
Very Important				18.5%
Somewhat/fairly important				18.8%
Not important				62.7%

Note: This table presents a comparison among different populations of the importance of ascriptive characteristics for being defined as American, using raw data from the 2004 General Social Survey and the 2006 Latino National Survey. In the GSS, respondents were asked, "Some people say the following things are important for being truly American. Others say they are not important. How important do you think each of the following is?" Respondents were given four potential options (very important, fairly important, not very important, not important at all). In the LNS, respondents were asked, "When you think of what it means to be fully American in the eyes of most Americans, do you think it is very important, somewhat important, or not important to: Have been born in the United States? To speak English well? To be White? To be Christian?," with three possible responses (very important, somewhat important, and not very important). In this table, the GSS categories "not very important" and "not important at all" are combined to facilitate comparability between the datasets.

Defining "American"

*[handwritten note: * variation appears in the importance of birthplace & Christianity]*

A bivariate analysis of raw survey data from the LNS reveals interesting differences in the ways that members of Latino subgroups define the boundaries of Americanness. In looking at each of the four ascriptive categories, the most variation occurs with respect to the importance of birthplace and Christianity to being American. For each of these characteristics, over 40% of respondents indicate that these characteristics are very important, around one-quarter say they are somewhat important, and one-third say they are not important. In contrast, clear majorities indicate that speaking English is very important (85%) and being white is not important (62%). Consequently, there is far less variation to explain with respect to these latter categories.

Birthplace

Puerto Ricans, who have birthright citizenship, are the least likely (38.9%) to say that being born in the U.S. is very important for being American. This figure suggests that for Puerto Ricans, being American means something far beyond birthplace. Nearly 44% of Mexicans and Cubans say birthplace is very important, followed by 47.5% of Dominicans. Salvadorans by far placed the most emphasis on being born in the U.S., with 56.5% of respondents indicating that it is very important.

In addition to the more challenging immigration experience faced by many Salvadorans, the vast majority of Salvadorans in the survey (92.4%) were born outside the U.S. Interestingly, however, survey-wide, there appears to be an inverse relationship between a respondent's place of birth and the importance placed on

[handwritten margin note, top: non-native immigrants place more importance on birthplace]

nativity. For the nonnative population, defined here as those born outside the U.S. and Puerto Rico, 42.4% indicate that being American-born is very important. This figure compares to 49.6% of first-generation respondents (those born in the U.S. but with both parents born elsewhere) and 50.3% of second-generation respondents (those with at least one parent born in the U.S.) These numbers suggest that birthplace alone is unlikely to account for the distinct views of Salvadoran respondents.

For region, I divide respondents from the fifteen LNS states and the Washington, D.C., metro area into four categories, following the U.S. Census. Accordingly, the South is defined as Arkansas, Georgia, North Carolina, Texas, and Florida; the West includes Arizona, California, Colorado, New Mexico, Nevada, and Washington; the Midwest includes Illinois, notable for a history of "immigrant-friendly" policies, and Iowa; and the Mid-Atlantic includes New York, New Jersey, and the Washington, D.C., metropolitan area. Respondents from the Midwest placed the least emphasis on birthplace, with only 38% saying this characteristic is very important. Almost no difference was evident in the remaining regions, with an estimated 45% of respondents from the West, South, and Mid-Atlantic placing the most importance on birthplace.

Christianity

[handwritten margin note: religion is most important for immigrants born outside the US]

Since the founding of the U.S., America has paradoxically been grounded in ideas of both religious freedom and the importance of Protestantism. As Theiss-Morse (2009) explains, from John Jay to Joseph McCarthy to John McCain, political leaders throughout American history have repeatedly asserted that the U.S. is a Christian nation. Likewise, Huntington argues, "Religion has been and still is a central, perhaps the central, element of American identity" (2004b, 20). Even as the ideals of religious freedom underscore American philosophy, Protestantism has repeatedly been cited as an important ethnocultural characteristic.

Perhaps demonstrating this tension, significant variation exists in response to questions about the importance of being Christian. Again, Salvadorans are the most likely (57.5%) to say this ascriptive characteristic is very important for being perceived as American, compared to 45.2% of Cubans, 47.8% of Puerto Ricans, and 50.7% of Dominicans. Mexicans are far less likely (37.6%) than other subgroups to indicate that Christianity is very important.

Looking at immigrant generation, religion is most important for nonnative respondents, with 44% choosing the highest category. This figure may in part be a reflection of the important role played by the church to mobilize and incorporate new immigrants (Wong 2006). By comparison, 32.1% of first-generation respondents and 35.7% of second-generation respondents indicate that being a Christian is very important for being perceived as American. Regionally, Christianity is seen as most important in the Mid-Atlantic (46.2%) and the "Bible Belt" region of the South (45.3%). An estimated 36%–37% of respondents from the West and the Midwest responded in the highest category.

Language

Despite the ideas of Huntington and others who suggest that Latinos seek to make Spanish the second official language of the United States, there is little to no variation in the raw survey data with respect to the importance of speaking English. Rather, across all national-origin categories, nearly 85% of respondents indicate that speaking English is very important to being American. Once more, Puerto Ricans hold the least restrictive views of what it means to be American, with 82.5% indicating that English is very important. As with birthplace, Puerto Ricans are followed by Mexicans (83.7%), then Cubans (85.7%) and Dominicans (88.7%). Once again, respondents from El Salvador retain the most restrictive view regarding group boundaries, with 92.6% indicating that language abilities are very important. Overall, higher numbers of respondents from this subgroup appear to see American as an exclusive category, based on one's place of birth, religion, and language abilities.

Interestingly, both first- and second-generation immigrants are far less likely to say that English abilities are very important (77.5% and 78.1%, respectively) than are nonnatives (87.9%). Little difference is evident by region: across all regions, 83%–87% of respondents view English proficiency as fundamentally important to being fully American.

> English is most important to non-native immigrants

Race

Because the traditional racial categories of newcomers often do not align with their experiences in U.S. society, the interaction between race and ethnicity for migrants to the United States can be complex (Itzigsohn 2009; Itzigsohn, Giorguli, and Vazquez 2005; Rodríguez 2000). Historically, the largest numbers of black Latino immigrants have come from the Dominican Republic and Puerto Rico (Lavariega Monforti and Sanchez 2010; Logan 2003). In contrast, Cuban exiles included only a very small number of nonwhite immigrants prior to 1980 (Rieff 1995).

In line with the idea of a multiracial, multiethnic United States, majorities across all populations agree that skin color is not central to being seen as American. However, Cubans are the most likely (26.4%) to indicate that being white is very important to being American. By comparison, 23.3% of Salvadorans, 20.9% of Dominicans, 19.5% of Puerto Ricans, and 17.1% of Mexicans indicate that skin color is very important. In contrast to other ascriptive categories in which answers may stem from a respondent's own insecurities or experiences of discrimination, here subgroup members appear to favor their own attributes.

When looking by generation, those living in the U.S. the longest seem most open to the idea of a racially inclusive society. Specifically, just 14.7% of second-generation respondents indicate that being white is very important, compared to 17.4% of those in the first generation and 19.6% of nonnative immigrants. Comparing by region, relatively little variation is evident. Respondents from the Mid-Atlantic are most likely (19.9%) to place high importance on race, compared to 18.9% in the South, 17.8% in the West, and 17.2% in the Midwest.

those living in the US seem to be most racially inclusive

Overall, based on these descriptive statistics, a few interesting puzzles emerge. Puerto Ricans and Cubans, who both have different forms of preferential status in comparison to other Latino subgroups, and Mexicans, who are second most likely among LNS respondents to be born in the U.S., are paradoxically the *least* likely to emphasize the importance of being born in the United States. In three out of four ascriptive categories, as predicted, respondents from El Salvador have the most restrictive perceptions of what it means to be American. These trends indicate tentative support for the political learning hypothesis.

The bivariate analysis also demonstrates preliminary support for the integration hypothesis. As anticipated, when we look by immigrant generation, individuals born outside the U.S. have the most restrictive views of what it means to be American in terms of race, English abilities, and religion. In contrast, second-generation respondents tend to have the most open perception of group boundaries. However, with respect to birthplace, the pattern switches. Here, second-generation respondents place the most emphasis on being born in the U.S., while nonnative respondents are the least restrictive. Finally, the raw data show limited support for the regional hypothesis, with little variation among respondents regarding the importance of birthplace and language skills. On race and Christianity, respondents in the Mid-Atlantic tend to place the most emphasis on ascriptive categories, followed by those from the South. Respondents in the West and Midwest demonstrate the most open perspectives of what it means to be American.

Multivariate Analysis

In order to take into account a range of independent variables that may have a relationship with the dependent variables of interest, this section uses multivariate analysis to test the political socialization, integration, and regional hypotheses. In the subsequent models, dummy variables are used for subnational groups. Because Mexicans are by far the largest subgroup in both the survey and the overall Latino population, they are used as the reference category. To control for context, regional dummy variables are used, with the West excluded as the reference category. Given the large and longstanding Mexican immigrant population in the United States, political science research on Latinos frequently focuses on Mexicans residing in California. Using these reference categories allows us to test whether the broader Latino population has similar understandings of what it means to be American.

As the integration hypothesis suggests, I anticipate that respondents who are more incorporated into U.S. society are more likely to see "American" as a permeable category. In addition to the dummy variables described earlier for immigrant generation, additional variables are included to measure an individual's level of acculturation. Socioeconomic variables include a continuous measure of years of education as well as a continuous measure of income, which is separated into three categories: below $25,000, $25,000–$45,000, and above $45,000.[11] Additional dummy variables are included for a respondent's language preference (based on the language of the interview), as well as for new arrivals, referring to those who have been in the U.S. for less than five years.

Finally, drawing on literature from African American politics, I employ the concept of "linked fate," a phenomenon whereby individuals perceive their interests to be connected to other members of the same in-group (Dawson 1994). I anticipate that respondents who have a high sense of linked fate with other Latinos will have a more restricted definition of "American." To measure how much respondents believe their fate is linked to other Latinos, a variable is included from the LNS, with responses ranging from 1 (nothing) to 4 (a lot).

In addition to the hypotheses outlined earlier, I expect that a number of other variables will contribute to the perceived permeability of the boundaries of Americanness. A tradition of literature on immigrant incorporation emphasizes the different experiences of Latino men and women in the U.S. (Jaramillo 2010; Jones-Correa 1998a, 1998b). Additionally, existing research indicates that Latinas are less likely than Latino men to self-identify as American (Golash-Boza 2006; Silber Mohamed 2013). Consequently, I include a dummy variable for gender, with the expectation that women will have a more closed perception of what it means to be American.

Given the questions on Christianity and race, I also anticipate that one's own characteristics are likely to affect responses. Thus, control variables are used for skin color (measured 1–5, with 1 being very dark) and religiosity, measured by attendance at religious services (from 1–5, with 1 being more than once a week and 5 being never). Both of these measures are self-reported. Additionally, a continuous variable is used for age, measured by decade (1 = respondents nineteen and under; 2 = respondents twenty to twenty-nine, etc.), with the expectation that younger respondents will have the most open perspective on what it means to be American.

Because the dependent variables are ordinal, meaning that the possible outcomes can be ordered but the distance between each category is unknown, ordinal logistic regression is used in the analysis.[12] Predicted probabilities are based on the model in table 6.2 and are calculated with continuous independent variables moving from their minimum to maximum values, holding all other continuous independent variables constant at their means. For dummy variables, a prototypical respondent is used with the following characteristics: male, Mexican, from the Southwest, non-native but arrived in the U.S. more than five years ago, with survey responses in English. (For tables of all predicted probabilities and confidence intervals for significant variables, see appendix 6B.)

The analysis in table 6.2 finds mixed support for the *political learning hypothesis*, which predicted that distinct political learning and socialization experiences of different national-origin groups would impact subgroup members' perceptions of identity categories. Based on previous experiences, history, and immigration/citizenship status, this hypothesis anticipated that Cubans and Puerto Ricans would have the most open perception of what it means to be American. In contrast, Salvadoran immigrants, who have arguably had the most negative experiences with the U.S. government, were expected to demonstrate the most closed perspective. The Salvadoran case represents the strongest support for this hypothesis; Salvadorans have the most restrictive views of what it means to be American in three out of four categories. With high degrees of statistical significance, Salvadorans are 8% more likely to think it is very important to be born in the United States, 9% more likely to emphasize speaking English, and 14% more likely to emphasize being Christian than is the prototypical respondent.

Despite expectations that Cubans would have a more open perception of what it means to be American, however, no statistically significant difference is evident across most categories. The only exception is skin color, which moves *against* the predicted direction; Cuban exiles, who are historically more likely to have lighter phenotypes, also place the most importance on being white; compared to

Table 6.2: Ordered Logistic Regression: Ascriptive Characteristics of Being American (LNS 2006)

	Born in U.S.	Christianity	English	White
Female	0.00	0.04	−0.05	−0.06
	(0.05)	(0.05)	(0.07)	(0.05)
Skin color	−0.03	−0.02	0.00	−0.02
	(0.02)	(0.02)	(0.03)	(0.02)
Age	0.52***	2.04***	1.30***	0.46***
	(0.13)	(0.14)	(0.20)	(0.14)
Subnational groups				
Cuban	0.07	0.19	0.14	0.48***
	(0.13)	(0.14)	(0.20)	(0.14)
Dominican	0.02	0.37**	0.35	−0.16
	(0.14)	(0.14)	(0.22)	(0.15)
Puerto Rican	−0.20*	0.47***	0.08	0.25*
	(0.10)	(0.10)	(0.14)	(0.11)
Salvadoran	0.35**	0.56***	0.67**	0.11
	(0.11)	(0.12)	(0.20)	(0.12)
Region				
Mid-Atlantic	0.05	0.17	0.07	−0.04
	(0.09)	(0.09)	(0.14)	(0.10)
Midwest	−0.21**	−0.18*	−0.05	0.08
	(0.08)	(0.08)	(0.14)	(0.08)
South	0.03	0.33***	−0.02	−0.02
	(0.06)	(0.06)	(0.08)	(0.06)
Incorporation				
Income	−0.35***	−0.26***	−0.11	−0.15*
	(0.07)	(0.07)	(0.09)	(0.07)
Years of education	−0.66***	−1.32***	−0.20	−0.26
	(0.16)	(0.16)	(0.24)	(0.17)
New arrival	0.04	0.00	0.32**	−0.15
	(0.07)	(0.07)	(0.12)	(0.08)
First generation	0.81***	0.09	−0.11	−0.07
	(0.08)	(0.08)	(0.10)	(0.08)
Second generation	0.72***	0.13	−0.06	−0.22**
	(0.08)	(0.08)	(0.10)	(0.08)
Prefer Spanish	0.24***	0.19**	0.71***	−0.10
	(0.07)	(0.07)	(0.09)	(0.08)
Linked fate	0.33***	0.50***	0.01	0.30***
	(0.07)	(0.07)	(0.03)	(0.07)
Attend church	−0.09	−1.3***	−0.02	−0.09
	(0.08)	(0.08)	(0.03)	(0.08)
N	6401	6401	6401	6401
Pseudo R^2	0.02	0.07	0.04	0.01

Two-tailed tests; significance levels: * $p < 0.05$, ** $p < 0.01$, *** $p < 0.001$

Note: The unit of observation is an individual respondent. Standard errors in parentheses. Estimation is done using ordered logistic regression, using the revised national-level weights provided in the dataset. Analysis is limited to Cubans, Dominicans, Mexicans, Puerto Ricans, and Salvadorans. The dependent variables are responses to the following question: "When you think of what it means to be fully American in the eyes of most Americans, do you think it is very important, somewhat important, or not important to: Have been born in the United States? To speak English well? To be White? To be Christian?" where 1 = not important, 2 = somewhat important, and 3 = very important. Female is a dummy variable for gender. Skin color is self-reported on a scale of 1 (very dark) to 5 (very light). Age is coded continuously by decade (e.g., 2 = ages twenty to twenty-nine). Mexicans are the omitted subnational group. For region, Mid-Atlantic is defined as NY, NJ, and the D.C. metro area; Midwest includes IL and IA; South is defined as AR, GA, NC, TX, and FL; and West is AZ, CA, CO, NM, NV, and WA, with West as the omitted category in the analysis. Income is defined continuously, with respondents divided into three categories: under $25,000, $25,000–$44,999, and $45,000 and above, and income imputed in cases where respondents did not provide a response (see Lavariega Monforti and Michelson, chap. 4 in this volume). Years of education is coded continuously with 0 = none, 8 = eighth grade or below, 10 = some high school / GED, 12 = high school graduate, 14 = some college, 16 = four-year college degree, and 19 = graduate or professional degree. *New arrival* is a dummy variable for respondents living in the U.S. less than five years. For immigrant generation, the omitted category is those born outside the U.S. Immigrant generation is defined as first generation = respondent born in U.S. but parents born elsewhere, second generation = respondent and at least one parent born in U.S. *Prefer Spanish* is a dummy variable for language of interview, where 1 = Spanish. *Linked fate* is a continuous variable asking respondents how much their "doing well" depends on other Latinos/Hispanics doing well, where 1 = nothing, 2 = a little, 3 = some, and 4 = a lot. Religiosity is a self-reported measure of attending religious services, measured continuously from 1 (more than once a week) to 5 (never). Before running the multivariate analysis, all continuous variables were rescaled from 0 to 1 to facilitate comparability in evaluating predicted probabilities.

Mexicans, Cubans are 6% more likely to indicate that skin color is very important to being American.

Interestingly, Puerto Ricans, who are born U.S. citizens, are 4% less likely to think that birthplace is very important to being American, suggesting that being American means more than just birthright for this population. Surprisingly, though, compared to Mexicans, Puerto Ricans are 8% more likely to emphasize Christianity, which counters expectations that this group would have a more inclusive perspective of the American category.

In testing the *integration hypothesis*, stronger relationships are evident between an individual's level of incorporation and one's opinions about what it means to be American. Again, however, the results indicate mixed support depending on the characteristic. Questions about the importance placed on being born in the U.S. and Christianity suggest a clear correlation with a respondent's level of income and education. For instance, compared to respondents in the lowest income category, those in the highest category are 8% less likely to emphasize being born in the U.S., 4% less likely to emphasize Christianity, and 2% less likely to emphasize skin color. Similarly, when compared to the least educated respondents, those with a graduate or professional degree are 15% less likely to say birthplace is very important and 21% less likely to say Christianity is very important.

Surprisingly, however, holding everything else constant, length of time in the U.S. has a relatively weak effect across the models. The variable for being in the U.S. less than five years reaches statistical significance only in the case of speaking English, with newcomers 5% more likely to emphasize this ability. Similarly, immigrant generation is statistically significant in only a few cases. The importance of birthplace is the only question for which first- and second-generation respondents are significantly different, statistically and substantively, from their immigrant counterparts. In both cases, however, the relationship moves opposite the predicted direction: first- and second-generation respondents are *more* likely to emphasize birthplace as very important for being American (19% and 17%, respectively), reflecting a less permeable view of Americanness than that of nonnatives. Yet second-generation respondents are also slightly less likely (3%) to emphasize the importance of skin color, suggesting that length of time in the U.S. may correlate with more open attitudes about the importance of race.

As expected, the measures for preferring Spanish and feeling that one's fate is strongly linked with other Latinos are both associated with more restrictive views of what it means to be American across three out of four ascriptive categories. For instance, respondents who report having the highest feelings of linked fate are 7% more likely to emphasize the importance of birthplace and Christianity and 5% more likely to indicate that light skin color is very important to being American. Similarly, Spanish-speaking respondents are 17% more likely to emphasize birthplace, 3% more likely to emphasize religion, and 12% more likely to say that English skills are very important than are their English-speaking counterparts. These results lend support for the other side of the incorporation hypothesis: those respondents who are less integrated into life in the United States are more likely to feel that "American" is a closed category from which they are excluded.

As for the *regional hypothesis*, few differences are evident across these categories, with the largest variation demonstrated regarding opinions on the role of Christianity. The increased importance of religion for respondents from the traditional Bible Belt states is relatively unsurprising, with Latinos in the South being 4% more likely to indicate that Christianity is very important. Respondents from the Midwest, including Iowa and immigrant-friendly Illinois, are 4% less likely to say that being born in the U.S. and Christianity are very important. Despite extant literature regarding the distinct nature of race relations in the South (see chapter 9 by Sanchez and Barreto), no regional differences are evident with respect to the importance of skin color. However, moving to a smaller level of analysis, such as county or census tract, may help to further parse out the role of local context in developing identity boundaries.

The additional control variables also present a few surprises. Using the raw LNS data, women are less likely to "very strongly" self-identify as American (36%) than are their male counterparts (44%). Despite this gap, however, there is no apparent difference in the way that being American is defined, ascriptively, across the genders. In other words, while Latinas and Latino men have a similar understanding of what it means to be American, they adopt this identity to varying degrees. This finding suggests that something beyond ascriptive perceptions of group boundaries is driving the difference in self-identification between Latinas and Latino men and points to the need for future research to better understand this gender gap in identification. Unfortunately, the lack of further survey questions on this topic represents one limitation of this dataset.

Similarly, the variable for skin color has no significant effect across the categories. However, this result may be attributed, at least in part, to lack of diversity among respondents. Indeed, just 10% of respondents place themselves in the two darkest categories in response to the question regarding one's own phenotype.

As expected, younger respondents have a far more open interpretation of what it means to be American, with the age variable statistically significant across all four categories. As age increases, respondents are more likely to emphasize the importance of each of the various ascriptive categories. Specifically, the oldest respondents are 10% more likely to indicate that birthplace is very important, 45% more likely to emphasize Christianity, 19% more likely to emphasize English skills, and 8% more likely to say skin color is very important than are their younger counterparts.

Finally, the measure of religiosity is statistically significant in the predictable direction with respect to Christianity only: respondents who are more likely to attend religious services are also 18% more likely see religion as a very important part of being American. Given the important role played by the church to incorporate new immigrants (Wong 2006), the absence of a relationship between religiosity and the other categories is unexpected.

Conclusion

This chapter focuses on variation in understandings of what it means to be American, exploring differences in perception across the heterogeneous Latino population. I hypothesize that one's national origin / ancestry, level of incorporation, and region of residence in the U.S. will affect a respondent's perspectives on the

Key Findings

- Latinos and non-Latino whites have very similar perceptions of what it means to be American.

- Reflecting the diversity of the Latino population, respondents demonstrate significant variation in opinion regarding the boundaries of Americanness, particularly with respect to birthplace and religion.

- Large majorities of Latinos believe that speaking English is very important and race is unimportant to being defined as American.

- Some support exists for the political learning hypothesis, which posited that variance in U.S. history and immigration policy toward members of different Latino subgroups would influence group members' sense of belonging in the U.S.

- Salvadorans have the most restrictive view of what it means to be American in three out of four ascriptive categories.

- Cubans are more likely to emphasize skin color than is the baseline respondent.

- Mexicans and Dominicans have the most similar view of Americanness.

- Overall support exists for the integration hypothesis, which predicted that broader indicators of immigrant incorporation are associated with a more open understanding of what it means to be American, and vice versa.

- Respondents with higher levels of income and education generally perceive ascriptive categories as less essential in their definition of "American."

- Spanish-speakers and respondents reporting high levels of linked fate with other Latinos see these categories as more important, yielding a more restrictive view of what it means to be American.

- Immigrant generation is the exception. Respondents born in the U.S. are more likely to see birthplace as essential to being American, compared to nonnatives.

- Limited support exists for the regional hypothesis, which predicted that region of residence in the U.S. would impact one's definition of what it means to be American.

- Respondents from the Midwest see "American" as a more open category, while respondents from the South are more likely to emphasize the importance of religion.

- Younger respondents are more open in defining Americanness.

- Age is the only variable statistically significant across all four ascriptive categories, and the values are substantively significant as well.

- Gender and skin color are insignificant in shaping one's definition of "American." Men and women and respondents of different phenotypes similarly perceive what it means to be American.

extent to which being American is a permeable category that he or she may be able to join.

In multivariate analysis, I find mixed support for the hypotheses presented earlier. With respect to the political learning hypothesis, while some variation exists in the ways that individuals from different national-origin subgroups conceptualize American, these differences are not always in the anticipated direction. When looking at distinct Latino subgroups, in terms of skin color, Cubans, who tend to have the lightest phenotype, place more importance on this ascriptive characteristic than do members of other subgroups. While Puerto Ricans have more open views on the importance of birthplace, compared to Mexicans, they place significantly more emphasis on religion and race.

Salvadorans maintain the most restrictive view of what it means to be American across three out of four categories, with members of this subgroup placing greater emphasis on birthplace, religion, and English proficiency than do other ancestral-origin groups. I posit that this result may be the byproduct of the memory of that nation's bloody U.S.-backed civil war, the contentious experience of many Salvadorans upon arrival in the U.S., and the large undocumented population. However, future qualitative research would help to elucidate the specific reasons behind this relationship.

Interestingly, among the different subgroups in the LNS, Salvadorans are the least likely to self-identify as American. In contrast, Elizabeth Theiss-Morse (2009) finds that among the general population, those who most strongly identify as American have the most restrictive views about what being American means. I suggest that for minority communities, the construction of identity boundaries with respect to their host society may work in the opposite direction, with those who are least likely to feel American holding the most restrictive view. Many of the findings with respect to immigrant incorporation support this idea. Indeed, immigrants who are less incorporated into American society, socioeconomically and linguistically, hold more closed views about the boundaries of American identity. Likewise, respondents who see their fate as closely linked with other Latinos are more likely to perceive Americanness as tied to ascriptive definitions, from which they may be excluded.

The findings presented in this chapter represent an initial attempt to better understand the ways in which different subsets of the Latino population conceptualize the boundaries of American society, as well as some of the factors that may impact one's broader sense of belonging and citizenship. As the Latino population in the United States grows, the potential for this community to act as a political and cultural force will likewise increase, as is evident by the widely noted role of the Latino electorate in the 2012 election. How group members understand what it means to be American, and whether they believe they can join that category, will undoubtedly influence both the decision to participate politically and the nature of Latino participation in the years ahead. The mixed results outlined here illustrate the need for future research to better understand how political learning, socialization, incorporation, and context can influence perceptions regarding the boundaries of Americanness by different immigrant groups.

[handwritten margin note: immigrants who are less incorporated into American Society hold more closed views about American identity]

① the majority of Latinos
 believe English is important
 to being American   THE BOUNDARIES OF AMERICANNESS >> 151

Study Questions

1. How do the results in this chapter support or debunk claims of a Latino "challenge"?

2. How might immigrants' experience from their home country (or country of origin, for later generations) impact their perceptions of what it means to be American? In what other ways could political learning affect a minority's experience?

3. What are the strengths and weaknesses of using a prototypical respondent to interpret results? What other statistical tools could be used?

4. Discuss some of the counterintuitive findings outlined in this chapter (i.e., gender, skin color, region, etc.).

5. Based on the findings of this chapter, what are the varying ways that a respondent's individual characteristics appear to shape his or her definition of "American"? Specifically, what characteristics might be associated with a more permeable (or restrictive) categorization? → facing more adversity as a subgroup
(Salvadorans)

Appendix 6A: Question Wording and Variable Coding for *Americanness*

Dependent Variable

AMERICANNESS   "When you think of what it means to be fully American in the eyes of most Americans, do you think it is very important, somewhat important, or not important to: Have been born in the United States? To speak English well? To be white? To be Christian?" 1 = not important; 2 = somewhat important; 3 = very important

Independent Variables

FEMALE   1 = yes; 0 = no

SKIN COLOR   "(Latinos/Hispanics) can be described based on skin tone or complexion shades. Using a scale from 1 to 5 where 1 represents very dark and 5 represents being very light, where would you place yourself on that scale?"

AGE   "What year were you born?" Responses are coded continuously by decade: 1 = less than 20 years old; 2 = 20–29; 3 = 30–39; 4 = 40–49; 5 = 50–59; 6 = 60–60; 7 = 70–79; 8 = 80–89; 9 = 90–97

SUBNATIONAL GROUPS   "Families of Latino/Hispanic origin or background in the United States come from many different countries. From which country do you trace your Latino heritage?" *If more than one response given, read,* "Which country does most of your family come from?" Dummy variables are assigned for each subnational group such that 1 = yes and 0 = no. Analysis is limited to five main demographic groups: Mexicans, Cubans, Dominicans, Puerto Ricans, and Salvadorans.

REGION	South = Arkansas, Georgia, North Carolina, Texas, and Florida; West = Arizona, California, Colorado, New Mexico, Nevada, and Washington; Midwest = Illinois and Iowa; Mid-Atlantic = New York, New Jersey, and the Washington, D.C., area.
INCOME	"Which of the following best describes the total income earned by all members of your household during 2004?" 1 = under $25,000; 2 = $25,000–$44,999; 3 = $45,000 and above
YEARS OF EDUCATION	"What is your highest level of formal education completed?" Coded continuously such that 0 = none; 8 = eighth grade or below; 10 = some high school / GED; 12 = high school graduate; 14 = some college; 16 = four-year college degree; 19 = graduate or professional degree
NEW ARRIVAL	"When did you first arrive to live in the U.S. [mainland]?" 1 = 2000 and above; 0 = prior to 2000
NON-NATIVE	1 = respondents born elsewhere; 0 = respondents born in mainland U.S. / Puerto Rico
FIRST GENERATION	1 = respondents born in the U.S. with both parents born outside the U.S.; 0 = all others
SECOND GENERATION	1 = respondents born in the U.S. with at least one parent born in the U.S.; 0 = all others
PREFER SPANISH	Language of interview. 1 = Spanish; 0 = English
LINKED FATE	"How much does your 'doing well' depend on other Latinos/Hispanics also doing well? A lot, some, a little, or not at all?" 1 = nothing; 2 = a little; 3 = some; 4 = a lot
RELIGIOSITY	"How often do you attend religious services? Do you attend . . . ?" 1 = more than once a week; 2 = once a week; 3 = once a month; 4 = only major religious holidays; 5 = never

Appendix 6B: Predicted Probabilities of Significant Variables and Ascriptive Definitions of *Americanness*

To be fully American in the eyes of most Americans, do you think it is very important, somewhat important, or not important to be/have been . . .	Not important	Somewhat important	Very important
. . . born in U.S.			
Age	−0.10	0.00	0.10
	[−0.2, −0.06]	[−0.02, 0.00]	[0.06, 0.18]
Puerto Rican	0.05	0.00	−0.04
	[0.00, 0.09]	[−0.02, 0.00]	[−0.08, 0.00]
Salvadoran	−0.08	0.00	0.08
	[−0.123 −0.03]	[−0.01, 0.01]	[0.03, 0.13]
Midwest	0.05	−0.01	−0.04
	[0.01, 0.09]	[−0.02, 0.00]	[−0.08, −0.01]
Income	0.08	−0.01	−0.08
	[0.05, 0.11]	[−0.02, 0.00]	[−0.10, −0.05]
Years of education	0.15	0.01	−0.15
	[0.08, 0.22]	[−0.02, 0.00]	[−0.21, −0.08]
First generation	−0.17	−0.02	0.19
	[−0.20, −0.14]	[−0.04, −0.01]	[0.16, 0.23]

To be fully American in the eyes of most Americans, do you think it is very important, somewhat important, or not important to be/have been . . .	Not important	Somewhat important	Very important
. . . born in U.S. (*continued*)			
Second generation	−0.15	−0.02	0.17
	[−0.18, −0.12]	[−0.03, −0.01]	[0.14, 0.21]
Prefer Spanish	−0.06	0.00	0.06
	[−0.09. −0.03]	[0.00, −0.01]	[0.03, 0.08]
Linked fate	−0.08	0.01	0.07
	[−0.11, −0.05]	[0.00, 0.02]	[0.04, 0.10]
. . . Christian			
Age	−0.44	−0.01	0.45
	[−0.48, −0.39]	[−0.04, 0.02]	[0.39, 0.51]
Dominican	−0.09	0.03	0.06
	[−0.16, −0.02]	[0.01, 0.05]	[0.01, 0.11]
Puerto Rican	−0.12	0.04	0.08
	[−0.17, −0.07]	[0.02, 0.05]	[0.04, 0.12]
Salvadoran	−0.14	0.04	0.10
	[−0.20, −0.08]	[0.03, 0.05]	[0.05, 0.14]
Midwest	0.05	−0.01	−0.04
	[0.00. 0.09]	[−0.02, 0.00]	[−0.07. 0.00]
South	−0.08	0.03	0.05
	[−0.11, −0.05]	[0.02, 0.04]	[0.03. 0.07]
Income	0.06	−0.02	−0.04
	[0.03, 0.09]	[−0.04, −0.01]	[−0.06, −0.02]
Education	0.31	−0.10	−0.21
	[0.24, 0.39]	[−0.12, −0.08]	[−0.28, −0.16]
Prefer Spanish	−0.05	0.02	0.03
	[−0.08, −0.01]	[0.1, 0.03]	[0.01, 0.05]
Linked fate	−0.12	0.05	0.07
	[−0.15, −0.09]	[0.03, 0.06]	[0.05, 0.09]
Church attendance	0.30	−0.12	−0.18
	[0.26, 0.33]	[−0.13, −0.10]	[−0.21, −0.15]
. . . English-speaking			
Age	−0.05	−0.14	0.19
	[−0.07, −0.04]	[−0.17, −0.10]	[0.14, 0.24]
Salvadoran	−0.02	−0.07	0.09
	[−0.04, −0.01]	[−0.10, −0.03]	[0.04, 0.14]
New arrival	−0.01	−0.03	0.05
	[−0.02. 0.00]	[−0.06, −0.01]	[0.02, 0.08]
Prefer Spanish	−0.03	−0.09	0.12
	[−0.04, −0.02]	[−0.12, −0.07]	[0.09, 0.16]
. . . white			
Age	−0.11	0.04	0.08
	[−0.18, −0.04]	[0.02, 0.05]	[0.03, 0.13]
Cuban	−0.12	0.03	0.09
	[−0.18, −0.05]	[0.02, 0.05]	[0.03, 0.14]
Puerto Rican	−0.06	0.02	0.04
	[−0.11, −0.01]	[0.00, 0.03]	[0.00, 0.08]
Income	0.04	−0.01	−0.02
	[0.00, 0.07]	[−0.02, 0.00]	[−0.05, 0.00]
Second generation	0.05	−0.02	−0.03
	[0.01, 0.09]	[−0.03, −0.01]	[−0.06, −0.01]
Linked fate	−0.07	0.03	0.05
	[−0.11, −0.04]	[0.01, 0.04]	[0.02, 0.07]

Note: Each independent variable of interest varies from its minimum to maximum value, holding all dummy variables constant and the other continuous variables at their mean. The baseline respondent is male, Mexican, living in the West, born outside the U.S., arriving more than five years ago, and responding to the survey in English. Brackets indicate the 95% confidence interval.

Notes

1. The full report, "U.S. Census Bureau Projections Show a Slower Growing, Older, More Diverse Nation a Half Century from Now," was released December 12, 2012, and can be accessed online at https://www.census.gov/newsroom/releases/archives/population/cb12 -243.html.

2. See Ngai 2005 for a discussion of informal restrictions that nevertheless limited Western Hemisphere immigration during this period.

3. Under the CAA, those who arrived in the U.S. illegally became eligible for legal resident status after 366 days. In 1996, this policy was replaced with the "Wet Foot / Dry Foot" policy, under which Cubans found at sea are returned to Cuba unless they have sufficient evidence for an asylum claim. However, all those who make it to U.S. soil are able to qualify for legal resident status.

4. To protest these refusals, in the mid-1980s, the "sanctuary" movement emerged in the United States, in which a number of religious organizations and activists declared their communities safe spaces for these political refugees. In 1985, activists sued the U.S. government for discrimination against asylum applicants from El Salvador and Guatemala in what became known as the ABC case (for American Baptist Church, the lead plaintiff in the lawsuit); the following year, the government convicted eight religious activists of conspiracy and alien-smuggling for their protection of refugees from El Salvador and Guatemala (for details, see Coutin 2000).

5. TPS essentially provides a renewable safe haven for those who cannot return home due to extraordinary circumstances such as natural disaster or civil war. To be covered under TPS, nationals must meet a number of conditions, including continual residence in the U.S. prior to the country's designation.

6. Following initial data collection, each respondent was assigned three weights: national, state, and urban/rural. These weights were subsequently revised in March 2010. Bivariate analyses in this chapter use raw data, while the multivariate analysis employs the revised, nationally weighted figures, which attempt to make the survey more representative of the Latino population in all fifty states.

7. Unfortunately, the question was not repeated on the 2006 version of the GSS, which marked the first time the survey specifically targeted the Spanish-speaking population.

8. Race and ethnicity were treated as separate categories in the GSS. Consequently, respondents could identify as both white, black, or other and Latino. Reported race of Latino respondents in the survey is as follows: 61% white, 4% black, 35% other. While LNS respondents did not report race, they were asked questions about both ethnicity and skin color.

9. Indeed, existing research demonstrates that Mexicans are learning English at the same rate or faster than other immigrant groups (see Citrin et al. 2007).

10. The GSS question on birthplace is dichotomous, asking respondents whether or not they were born in this country, while the LNS includes Puerto Rico as a separate, third category. Because those born in Puerto Rico also have birthright citizenship, the statistic cited in the text includes those born in Puerto Rico as born in the U.S.

11. Because of the large number of respondents who did not answer the income question, following Michelson and Lavariega Monforti (chap. 4 in this volume), I use an imputation of income for respondents with missing data. For a full discussion of this imputation, see the previous chapter.

12. While ordinary least squares regression is more straightforward and easier to interpret, having a dependent variable with ordinal outcomes can violate the assumptions underlying linear regression and may result in inaccurate conclusions. As an alternative, ordered

logistic regression is used to estimate these nonlinear models. Because the results of ordered logistic regression are more difficult to interpret, predicted probabilities are also included for certain "prototype" respondents. The use of predicted probabilities allows us to measure the effects of a change in one independent variable, holding all other independent variables constant at some predefined level. See Long and Freese 2006 for a discussion of these techniques. In addition, in the subsequent analysis, all variables are recoded from 0 to 1 to facilitate comparison of the effects of different independent variables.

References

Balderrama, Francisco E., and Raymond Rodriguez. 2006. *Decade of Betrayal: Mexican Repatriation in the 1930s.* Albuquerque: University of New Mexico Press.

Brewer, Marilynn B. 2003. *Intergroup Relations.* Milton Keynes, UK: Open University Press.

Citrin, Jack, Amy Lerman, Michael Murakami, and Kathryn Pearson. 2007. "Testing Huntington: Is Hispanic Immigration a Threat to American Identity?" *Perspectives on Politics* 5 (1): 31–48.

Citrin, Jack, Beth Reingold, and Donald P. Green. 1990. "American Identity and the Politics of Ethnic Change." *Journal of Politics* 52 (4): 1124–1154.

Citrin, Jack, Cara Wong, and Brian Duff. 2001. "The Meaning of American National Identity: Patterns of Ethnic Conflict and Consensus." In *Social Identity, Intergroup Conflict, and Conflict Reduction*, ed. Richard D. Ashmore, Lee Jussim, and David Wilder, 71–100. New York: Oxford University Press.

Corbridge, Stuart, Glyn Williams, Manoj Srivastava, and Réne Véron. 2005. *Seeing the State: Governance and Governmentality in India.* Cambridge: Cambridge University Press.

Coutin, Susan Bibler. 2000. *Legalizing Moves: Salvadoran Immigrants' Struggle for U.S. Residency.* Ann Arbor: University of Michigan Press.

Dawson, Michael C. 1994. *Behind the Mule: Race and Class in African-American Politics.* Princeton: Princeton University Press.

de los Angeles Torres, María. 1999. *In the Land of Mirrors: Cuban Exile Politics in the United States.* Ann Arbor: University of Michigan Press.

Ennis, Sharon R., Merarys Rios-Vargas, and Nora G. Albert. 2011. "The Hispanic Population: 2010." U.S. Census Bureau, May. http://www.census.gov/prod/cen2010/briefs/c2010br-04.pdf.

Gammage, Sarah. 2007. "El Salvador: Despite End to Civil War, Emigration Continues." Migration Information Source, July. http://www.migrationinformation.org/Profiles/display.cfm?ID=636.

García, John. 1981. "Political Integration of Mexican Immigrants: Explorations into the Naturalization Process." *International Migration Review* 15 (4): 608–625.

García Bedolla, Lisa. 2005. *Fluid Borders: Latino Power, Identity, and Politics in Los Angeles.* Berkeley: University of California Press.

García Bedolla, Lisa. 2009. *Latino Politics.* Cambridge, UK: Polity.

Golash-Boza, Tanya. 2006. "Dropping the Hyphen? Becoming Latino(a)-American through Racialized Assimilation." *Social Forces* 85 (1): 27–55.

Hartz, Louis. 1950. *The Liberal Tradition in America.* New York: Harcourt Brace Jovanovich.

Higham, John. 1988. *Strangers in the Land: Patterns of American Nativism, 1860–1925.* New Brunswick: Rutgers University Press.

Hochschild, Jennifer L. 1995. *Facing Up to the American Dream: Race, Class, and the Soul of the Nation.* Princeton: Princeton University Press.

Hoeffer, Michael, Nancy Rytina, and Bryan C. Baker. 2010. "Estimates of the Unauthorized Immigrant Population Residing in the United States: January 2009." Population Estimates, Department of Homeland Security, Office of Immigration Statistics, January. http://www.dhs.gov/xlibrary/assets/statistics/publications/ois_ill_pe_2009.pdf.

Huckfeldt, Robert. 1996. *Politics in Context: Assimilation and Conflict in Urban Neighborhoods.* New York: Agathon.

Huddy, Leonie. 2001. "From Social to Political Identity: A Critical Examination of Social Identity Theory." *Political Psychology* 22 (1): 127–156.

Huddy, Leonie, and Nadia Khatib. 2007. "American Patriotism, National Identity, and Political Involvement." *American Journal of Political Science* 51 (1): 63–77.

Huntington, Samuel P. 1981. *American Politics: The Promise of Disharmony.* Cambridge: Belknap Press of Harvard University Press.

Huntington, Samuel P. 2004a. "The Hispanic Challenge." *Foreign Policy,* March–April, 30–45.

Huntington, Samuel P. 2004b. *Who Are We? The Challenges to America's National Identity.* New York: Simon and Schuster.

Itzigsohn, José. 2009. *Encountering American Faultlines: Race, Class, and the Dominican Experience in Providence.* New York: Russell Sage Foundation.

Itzigsohn, José, Silvia Giorguli, and Obed Vazquez. 2005. "Immigrant Incorporation and Racial Identity: Racial Self-Identification among Dominican Immigrants." *Ethnic and Racial Studies* 28 (1): 50–78.

Jaramillo, Patricia A. 2010. "Building a Theory, Measuring a Concept: Exploring Intersectionality and Latina Activism at the Individual Level." *Journal of Women, Politics and Policy* 31 (3): 193–216.

Jones-Correa, Michael. 1998a. *Between Two Nations, The Political Predicament of Latinos in New York City.* Ithaca: Cornell University Press.

Jones-Correa, Michael. 1998b. "Different Paths: Gender, Immigration and Political Participation." *International Migration Review* 32 (2): 326–349.

Karl, Terry L. 1992. "El Salvador's Negotiated Revolution." *Foreign Affairs* 71 (2): 147–164.

Lakoff, George. 1987. *Women, Fire, and Dangerous Things: What Categories Reveal about the Mind.* Chicago: University of Chicago Press.

Lavariega Monforti, Jessica, and Gabriel R. Sanchez. 2010. "The Politics of Perception: An Investigation of the Presence and Sources of Perceptions of Internal Discrimination among Latinos." *Social Science Quarterly* 91 (1): 245–265.

Lieske, Joel. 1993. "Regional Subcultures of the United States." *Journal of Politics* 55 (4): 888–913.

Logan, John. 2003. "How Race Counts for Hispanic Americans." Lewis Mumford Center for Comparative Urban and Regional Research, July 14. http://mumford.albany.edu/census/BlackLatinoReport/BlackLatino01.htm.

Long, J. Scott, and Jeremy Freese, eds. 2006. *Regression Models for Categorical Dependent Variables Using Stata.* College Station, TX: Stata.

McClain, Paula D., Jessica D. Johnson Carew, Eugene Walton, Jr., and Candis S. Watts. 2009. "Group Membership, Group Identity, and Group Consciousness: Measures of Racial Identity in American Politics?" *Annual Review of Political Science* 12: 471–485.

Migration Policy Institute. 2004. "The Dominican Population in the United States: Growth and Distribution." Report commissioned by Aeropuertos Dominicanos Siglo XXI. September. http://www.migrationpolicy.org/pubs/MPI_Report_Dominican_Pop_US.pdf.

Myrdal, Gunnar. 1944. *An American Dilemma: The Negro Problem and Modern Democracy.* New York: Harper and Brothers.

Newton, Lina Y., and Brian E. Adams. 2009. "State Immigration Policies: Innovation, Cooperation or Conflict?" *Publius: The Journal of Federalism* 39 (3): 408–431.

Ngai, Mae. 2005. *Impossible Subjects: Illegal Aliens and the Making of Modern America.* Princeton: Princeton University Press.

Portes, Alejandro, and Ramón Grosfoguel. 1994. "Caribbean Diasporas: Migration and Ethnic Communities." *Annals of the American Academy of Political and Social Science* 533:48–69.

Ramakrishnan, S. Karthick. 2005. *Democracy in Immigrant America*. Stanford: Stanford University Press.

Ramirez, Roberto R., and G. Patricia de la Cruz. 2003. "The Hispanic Population in the United States: March 2002." U.S. Census Bureau, U.S. Department of Commerce, Economics and Statistics Administration, June. http://www.census.gov/prod/2003pubs/p20-545.pdf.

Rieff, David. 1995. "From Exiles to Immigrants." *Foreign Affairs* 74 (4): 76–89.

Rodríguez, Clara E. 2000. *Changing Race: Latinos, the Census, and the History of Ethnicity in the United States*. New York: NYU Press.

Sapiro, Virginia. 2004. "Not Your Parents' Political Socialization: Introduction for a New Generation." *Annual Review of Political Science* 7:1–23.

Schildkraut, Deborah J. 2005. *Press One for English: Language Policy, Public Opinion, and American Identity*. Princeton: Princeton University Press.

Schildkraut, Deborah J. 2011. *Americanism in the Twenty-First Century: Public Opinion in the Age of Immigration*. New York: Cambridge University Press.

Segura, Gary M., and Helena Alves Rodrigues. 2006. "Comparative Ethnic Politics in the United States: Beyond Black and White." *Annual Review of Political Science* 9:375–395.

Silber Mohamed, Heather. 2013. "Can Protests Make Latinos 'American'? Identity, Immigration Politics, and the 2006 Marches." *American Politics Research* 41 (2): 298–326.

Smith, Rogers. 1988. "The 'American Creed' and American Identity: The Limits of Liberal Citizenship in the United States." *Western Political Quarterly* 41 (2): 225–251.

Soss, Joe. 1999. "Lessons of Welfare: Policy Design, Political Learning, and Political Action." *American Political Science Review* 93:363–380.

Tajfel, Henri. 1970. "Experiments in Intergroup Discrimination." *Scientific American* 223:96–102.

Tam Cho, Wendy K., James G. Gimpel, and Joshua J. Dyck. 2006. "Residential Concentration, Political Socialization, and Voter Turnout." *Journal of Politics* 68 (1): 156–167.

Theiss-Morse, Elizabeth. 2009. *Who Counts as an American? The Boundaries of National Identity*. New York: Cambridge University Press.

Turner, John C., Michael Hogg, Penelope J. Oakes, Stephen D. Reicher, and Margaret S. Wetherell. 1987. *Rediscovering the Social Group: A Self-Categorization Theory*. Oxford, UK: Blackwell.

Wasem, Ruth Ellen, and Karma Ester. 2008. *Temporary Protected Status: Current Immigration Policy and Issues*. Washington, DC: Congressional Research Service.

Weaver, Vesla M., and Amy E. Lerman. 2010. "Political Consequences of the Carceral State." *American Political Science Review* 104 (4): 817–833.

Wilson, Kenneth L., and Alejandro Portes. 1980. "Immigrant Enclaves: An Analysis of the Labor Market Experience of Cubans in Miami." *American Journal of Sociology* 86 (2): 295–312.

Wong, Janelle S. 2006. *Democracy's Promise: Immigrants and American Civic Institutions*. Ann Arbor: University of Michigan Press.

Wood, Elisabeth J. 2008. "The Social Processes of Civil War: The Wartime Transformation of Social Networks." *Annual Review of Political Science* 11:539–561.

Zimbardo, Philip G., Christina Maslach, and Craig Haney. 2000. "Reflections on the Stanford Prison Experiments: Genesis, Transformations, Consequences." In *Obedience to Authority: Current Perspectives on the Milgram Paradigm*, ed. Thomas Blass, 193–237. Mahwah, NJ: Lawrence Erlbaum.

PART IV

Negrura, Linked Fate, and Interminority Relations

7

Black and Latino Coalition Formation in New England

Perceptions of Cross-Racial Commonality

MARION ORR, DOMINGO MOREL, AND KATRINA GAMBLE

One enduring puzzle in political analysis is whether diverse populations of "minority" Americans will see themselves, or can see themselves, as political allies—socialized through similar experiences of social exclusion and sharing common interests and policy goals. During the 2008 elections, this question took on real-world significance in the Democratic presidential primaries. Several of candidate Hillary Clinton's high-profile Hispanic supporters, including the pollster Sergio Bendixen, suggested that Latino voters simply would not vote for Black candidate Barack Obama. Bendixen told the *New Yorker* magazine, "The Hispanic voter—and I want to say this very carefully—has not shown a lot of willingness or affinity to support black candidates" (Lizza 2008). In retrospect, of course, this was a foolish claim, and in both the primaries and general election of 2008, and in the general election of 2012, Latino voters gave Obama strong support. Yet it may be true that Latino political relations with African Americans vary by region, issue, and ethnonational population. In this chapter, Marion Orr, Domingo Morel, and Katrina Gamble make use of the Latino National Survey's New England extension to measure the racial attitudes of Latino respondents in Massachusetts, Connecticut, and Rhode Island. In their analysis, Orr, Morel, and Gamble consider prospects for Black-Latino alliance building in the region and whether those prospects may depend on Latinos' perceptions of social commonality with African Americans, linked fate with other Latinos, and experiences of social integration within American society.

Political Minorities and Political Coalitions

While Latinos have experienced significant population growth in recent decades, they remain a numerical and political minority, which means if they are to leverage their growing power, they must build viable coalitions with other racial and ethnic groups. One area that requires further study is cross-racial coalition building between Blacks and Latinos under this new political and demographic dynamic. Given the changes in racial demographics and the diversity of the Latino community in New England, we believe it is important to better understand Black-Latino relations in this region (Filindra and Orr 2013; Orr and West 2007). Most research on African American and Latino coalition formation focuses on conflict rather than cooperation (Bobo and Hutchings 1996; McClain and Karnig 1990; McClain 1993; Meier et al. 2004). For example, some observers argue that changing demographics and divergent policy preferences made it difficult to build Black-Latino coalitions in the late 1980s and 1990s (Falcón 1988; Mollenkopf 2003). Instead of viewing each other as allies, Blacks and Latinos may see the other group as competition for limited resources. For example, Nicolas Vaca's (2004) analysis of local politics in Los Angeles, Miami, New York, and Houston found that Blacks and Latinos

---

Research Questions

- What contexts may encourage African American and Latino coalition building?
- What factors lead Latinos in New England to believe that they share political or economic commonalities with African Americans?
- Are there differences between perceptions of economic commonality and political commonality that may affect the potential for Latino–African American coalition building?

---

were in direct competition over jobs, housing, and educational opportunities. This zero-sum conflict, combined with negative stereotypes associated with Blacks, led some observers to argue that it would be more rational for Latinos to join in coalitions with whites than with Blacks (Kaufmann 2007). In short, conflict is the central theme in much of the literature on cross-racial coalition building.

In this chapter, we shift the focus from competition between Blacks and Latinos to political and economic *commonality*. Instead of analyzing potential hurdles to coalition building, we seek to understand what contexts encourage coalition building. If Blacks and Latinos recognize that they are both politically and economically marginalized, they may decide to work together rather than fight over limited resources. In particular, we are interested in determining what factors make Latinos more likely to believe they have something politically or economically in common with African Americans.

Rufus Browning, Dale Marshall, and David Tabb (1984), in their now-classic analysis of city politics, found that Latinos and African Americans were more likely to become politically incorporated if they formed coalitions. In previous decades, Blacks would likely have been the dominant partner in Black-Latino coalitions because of their size, organization, and existing political ties. Many of the nation's first Black mayors were elected by forging coalitions with Latinos and liberal whites (Sonenshein 1993; Sonenshein and Pinkus 2002; Tedin and Murray 1994; Pinderhughes 2003; Kleppner 1985; Rivlin 1993). In many of these cases, the Black community was the largest of the two minority groups. Latinos were considered junior partners in these coalitions, in part, because they were numerically a smaller part of the coalition. Black leaders built coalitions with Latinos because they were a small but crucial part of the city's electorate. However, with Latinos' increased political influence and organization, the structural context for Latino-Black coalitions are shifting. Today, nationally and in many states and localities, Latinos have replaced African Americans as the largest minority group. Nicolas Vaca (2004) contends that the "Latino tsunami," or tremendous growth in the Latino population, threatens African Americans as the dominant minority group in the United States.

Or as Karen Kaufmann writes, Latinos "have gone from being perennial bridesmaids of urban politics to becoming powerful independent forces in many cities" (2007, 4). If Black-Latino coalitions are to form, Latinos must want to work with Blacks—Latinos may or may not see the need to join with Blacks to gain political leverage (Kaufmann 2007). Under the current population dynamics, African Americans are likely to be the junior partners in a coalition led by Latinos. Given this shift in cross-racial coalition dynamics, it is crucial to understand what factors are likely to lead Latinos to build coalitions with African Americans.

We contend that an important foundation for cross-racial coalition is perception of shared interests. While this is not the only factor, we argue that Blacks and Latinos must have some sense of shared commonality from which elites and organizations can build sustainable political and economic coalitions. Objectively, on many measures from education to unemployment, Blacks and Latinos have shared interests, but individuals on the ground within communities must acknowledge those points of commonality to build sustainable and effective coalitions. In this chapter, we analyze Latinos' perceptions of political and economic commonality with African Americans. We view this as a crucial and formative step toward bettering our understanding of how to build and maintain Latino-Black coalitions.

We examine public opinion among Latinos to determine what explains belief in political and economic commonality between Blacks and Latinos because we believe mass opinion is central to building durable political coalitions. Raphael Sonenshein (1993) argues that ideology, interests, and leadership are key components to interracial coalition building. He maintains that groups that share similar ideological beliefs on the liberal-to-conservative spectrum are more likely build coalitions. He also contends that shared interests are a necessary condition for coalition development; if two groups are marginalized from political power, then they are likely to work together to gain political influence. Finally, Sonenshein argues that elites play a significant role in coalition formation—community leaders can hinder or help coalition building by the way they frame community interests and concerns.

While we agree that ideology and elite behavior are important to coalition building, we argue that durable political coalitions must be supported at the mass level —if most Latinos do not believe they have shared interests with Blacks, it will be quite difficult to form sustainable cross-racial political coalitions. In this chapter, we analyze what factors predict Latino perceptions of political and economic commonality with Blacks. Political behavior scholarship demonstrates that individuals do not always act in support of what seem to be their objective political interests. For example, Michael Dawson, in his seminal work *Behind the Mule* (1994), finds that middle-class African Americans often act against their objective economic interests. While middle-class and upper-class Blacks would, often, benefit from more conservative economic policies supported by the Republican Party, they overwhelmingly vote for the Democratic Party. Dawson argues that Blacks often see their fate linked to the larger Black community and therefore use the group's interest as a proxy for individual interests; a simple rational-choice model would not be able to explain this political behavior. Similarly, the support of working-class whites for the Republican Party, despite the likely benefit from more progressive Democratic policies, seems counterintuitive. What these examples demonstrate is that individuals' political behavior can be influenced by many different factors. While Blacks and Latinos may share objective economic and political interests, this does not mean individual members of the communities will perceive a shared interest. Scholars have found that economic competition, disparities in material well-being, distrust, and negative stereotypes between Blacks and Latinos may prevent coalition building (Bobo and Hutchings 1996; Gay 2006; McClain et al. 2006; Bobo et al. 1994).

This chapter contributes to cross-racial-coalition literature in two ways. First, our analysis focuses on factors that contribute to perceptions of commonality versus conflict. Only a few scholars have analyzed perceived commonality between Blacks and Latinos (Sanchez 2008; Kaufmann 2003; Mindiola, Niemann, and Rodriguez 2002). Furthermore, we analyze political and economic commonality as two separate processes. While Latinos may not perceive economic commonality with Blacks because of job competition, they may believe in political commonality because both groups are politically marginalized. We contend that variables that predict Latinos' perceived political commonality with Blacks may not be the same items that drive perceived economic commonality. We believe that an examination of political commonality and economic commonality as independent processes will provide significant information toward understanding cross-racial coalition development. Our results suggest that Latino linked fate and Latino-Black linked fate are positively correlated with perceptions of political and economic commonality. This indicates that group connection may influence individuals' views about political and economic power. We show that social networks tend to play a more significant role in Latinos' perception in economic commonality than they do in perceptions of political commonality. We also show that social integration is positively linked to both economic and political commonality. One of the big differences in the way Latinos in New England view economic and political commonality with Blacks is the role of competition. We show, for example, that political competition is not necessarily a barrier to Black-Latino political commonality and coalition formation.

Theoretical Background: Minority Coalition Hypotheses

African Americans and Latinos are expected to form coalitions because they share similar economic circumstances. Following Sonenshein (1993), it is considered to be in the economic interests of both groups to form a coalition. Both are poor relative to white Americans. The expectation of Black-Latino coalitions is often encouraged by Latino and African American leaders who make public pronouncements to their respective communities to coalesce around minority political candidates. In addition, Latinos and African Americans are expected to form coalitions because they share similar views about experiencing discrimination in employment, housing, education opportunities, and police-community relations. Our research, however, focuses on mass attitudes. From a theoretical perspective, we maintain that perceptions of commonality are critical for the formation and maintenance of political coalitions. In the next sections, we lay out our theoretical arguments and hypotheses about what factors are likely to influence Latino perceptions of political and economic commonality.

Social Integration

There are a number of theories of social integration that help explain the mass belief systems of Latinos toward African Americans. One theory centers on the process of assimilation and acculturation (Park 1950; Park and Burgess 1969; Gordon 1964;

Glazer and Moynihan 1963). Some scholars argue that the amount of time immigrants spend in the U.S. has a significant impact on their worldview and how they see themselves within the broader U.S. society. There are two competing theories on the effect of Latino acculturation. Some argue that the longer Latino immigrants stay in the U.S., the less they identify as "minority" (Gordon 1964; Sears et al. 1999; Hood, Morris, and Shirkey 1997). Scholars contend that as Latinos become more educated and their economic status improves and as their perceptions of discrimination and social isolation lessen, the more their political behaviors and attitudes will resemble the majority group, whites.

However, a number of other scholars have challenged the assimilation theory. Researchers argue that the longer Latinos are in the U.S. and more acculturation results in a greater connection with their minority status (Glazer and Moynihan 1963; Alba and Nee 2003; Portes and Zhou 1993; Jones-Correa and Leal 1996). Ethnic conflict theory argues that as minorities, in this case Latinos, become more aware of discrimination, social inequalities, and white privilege, the more connected they become to minority struggles and marginalization. *We hypothesize that as Latinos become more acculturated, they are more likely to find political and economic commonality with Black Americans; therefore, we suspect that second-generation Latinos will be more likely to perceive political and economic commonality with Blacks than will first-generation Latino immigrants. We also believe that Latinos who prefer English as their primary language are more likely to perceive both political and economic commonality with Blacks.*

Intra-Latino Linked Fate and Black Linked Fate

Dawson (1994) found that African Americans have strong notions of "linked fate" between themselves and other African Americans. Dawson argues that African Americans employ a "Black utility heuristic" which informs the way they act politically. "Within the realm of mainstream American partisan politics," he explains, "African American political behavior remains powerfully influenced by African Americans' perceptions of group interests" (204–205). When African Americans believe that their own self-interest is associated with the interest of Blacks as a group, they are exhibiting linked fate. Research has shown that African Americans' perception that Blacks have historically been discriminated against is a strong determinant in their conception of Black group consciousness and linked fate (Shingles 1981). Some scholars have examined linked fate among Latinos in the U.S., as well. However, much of this research suggests that high levels of group consciousness or linked fate do not exist among Latinos (de la Garza et al. 1992; Hero 1992; DeSipio 1996; Jones-Correa and Leal 1996; Kaufmann 2003). Latinos have extremely diverse cultural, historical, and national backgrounds that create barriers for panethnic identity. While Mexican Americans constitute the largest group of Latinos, there are also large numbers of Puerto Ricans, Cubans, Dominicans, Salvadorans, Colombians, and Guatemalans living in the U.S. Latino immigrants arrive in the U.S. with different cultural backgrounds, including variation in language. Latinos also have varied racial characteristics—lighter-skinned, presumably more "Euro" Latinos; those of mixed heritage (African and European descent, or Indigenous and European descent); and those with darker skin and/or self-conscious African or

Indigenous heritage—and tend to see and experience life in the United States in measurably different ways (Affigne 2007). Nevertheless, previous research has suggested that "Latinos must develop group consciousness internally before engaging in any meaningful political relationship with another group" (Sanchez 2008, 431). Scholars have found that Latinos with high levels of group consciousness are more likely to perceive commonality with Blacks (Sanchez 2008; Kaufmann 2003).

One unexplored component of linked fate is the extent to which Latinos believe that their social, political, and economic interests are connected to what happens to African Americans. We argue that because Latinos and Blacks share similar social and economic status, there should be increased levels of linked fate between the two groups. In median income, housing, and education, Latinos have a status that is similar to, if not worse than, that of African Americans. Moreover, research has shown that minority perception of racial and ethnic discrimination is a central component of racial/ethnic-group consciousness. National surveys have shown that high percentages of Latino respondents believe that African Americans face discrimination (de la Garza et al. 1992). In fact, when asked, 64 percent of Cubans, 83 percent of Mexican Americans, and 85 percent of Puerto Ricans believe that the group most likely to face a lot of discrimination is African Americans (de la Garza et al. 1992, 93). We develop two hypotheses from the group consciousness and linked fate literature. First, *we expect that Latinos who express a sense of linked fate with other Latinos will be more likely to perceive a political and economic commonality with Blacks. We also hypothesize that Latinos who have a strong sense of linked fate with Blacks will also be more likely to perceive political and economic commonality with Blacks.*

Group Competition

Many scholars have examined whether Blacks and Latinos see each other as competition for employment and political power (McClain 1993; McClain and Karnig 1990; McClain and Tauber 1998; Meier et al. 2004; Bobo and Hutchings 1996; Mindiola, Niemann, and Rodriguez 2002). Research that examines objective measures of competition find that Latinos and African Americans do not engage in harmful socioeconomic competition with each other (McClain and Karnig 1990). Paula McClain and Albert Karnig found that as Blacks improved in education, income, and employment, Latinos also prospered. However, some research on school boards and education systems has found that competition does exist between Latinos and African Americans for positions as teachers, principals, and other school administrators. This competition arises because of scarce resources. "There is after all only one principal in each school. If the principal is African American, she cannot be a Latina" (Meier et al. 2004, 407).

Black-Latino competition may be muted if there is a white majority (McClain and Karnig 1990). If Blacks and Latinos perceive the white majority as limiting access to public-sector resources, then they may view each other as allies rather than competition. Scholars have also examined how Latinos and African Americans perceive each other regardless of whether competition actually exists or not. Both African Americans and Latinos view each other as competition (Bobo and

Hutchings 1996). Furthermore, studies have found that foreign-born Latinos are more likely than second-generation Latinos to view Blacks negatively or as competitors (Bobo and Hutchings 1996; Mindiola, Niemann, and Rodriguez 2002). Some contend that group competition makes it quite difficult to build Black-Latino coalitions (Kaufmann 2007). Given the significance of group competition theory in the cross-racial-coalition literature, we also control for group competition in both our political and economic commonality models. *We hypothesize that Latinos who view Blacks as competition for political, economic, or government resources are less likely to perceive political or economic commonality with Blacks.*

Social Networks

Social networks—one's family, friends, and work colleagues—provide information and influences on public life that can shape vote choice and issue preference (Huckfeldt and Sprague 1987). Social networks provide for social interaction as individuals share information and their stories, concerns, and interpretations and ideas about public life (Zuckerman 2005). Sociological research posits that these interactions influence our understanding of politics and public opinion (Kotler-Berkowitz 2005). "Friends variably affect each other's political preferences by reinforcing or challenging current views on parties, politicians, and policy issues" (Kotler-Berkowitz 2005, 153). In addition to family members, friends are a component of social networks that can have a tremendous influence on the daily decisions that people must make and the preferences they adopt (Kotler-Berkowitz 2005, 153; Huckfeldt and Sprague 1995; Zuckerman 2005). Moreover, research has shown that greater diversity in one's friendship networks increases the likelihood that one will have knowledge about political issues relevant to the racial group to which one's friends belong (Kotler-Berkowitz 2005). Additionally, scholarship on linked fate and group consciousness has argued that one's social networks have a significant influence on one's feelings of group connectedness (Dawson 1994, 10–13). Given the significance of social networks and their diversity on political perceptions and group identity, we believe it is important to understand how they influence Latino perceptions of political and economic commonality with Blacks. *We hypothesize that Latinos with friendship networks that consist of Blacks and Latinos are more likely to perceive political or economic commonality with Blacks than are those who have friendship networks that are mostly Latino or Latino and white.*

Data and Methods

We used the Latino National Survey–New England project conducted in 2007 and 2008 for our analysis. The survey was conducted as an extension of the Latino National Survey. Respondents were selected from a random sample of Latino households in the three New England states with the largest populations: Connecticut, Massachusetts, and Rhode Island. Survey data was collected through 1,200 telephone interviews with self-identified Latinos in each of the three states (400 in each state). The sample was completed by Geospace International, a marketing research and sampling firm, drawn from its household database of approximately 11 million households in the United States that are identified as Latino or Hispanic. Interviews were composed of 165 distinct items ranging from basic demographic inquiries to questions concerning opinions toward local and national policies, religiosity, and levels of acculturation.

As mentioned, the size of the Latino population in New England has grown considerably, especially in Massachusetts, Connecticut, and Rhode Island (Torres 2006; Hardy-Fanta and Gerson 2002). In fact, 95 percent of New England's Latinos live in these three states (Marcelli and Granberry 2006). The number of Latinos living in New England rose by 60 percent between 1990 and 2000, from 545,000 to over 871,000. By 2010, that number grew to over 1.3 million Latinos in New England. And in Rhode Island alone, the Latino population grew by 44 percent between 2000 and 2010. In fact, the growth of the Latino population in Rhode Island prevented the state from losing a congressional seat (Parker 2011). When you compare this growth to that of the population of non-Latinos in the region, it is even more remarkable: non-Hispanics grew only 3.2 percent between 2000 and 2006. The Latino population in New England is younger than the general population, so as this group ages, we are likely to see the Latino community shape the region in dramatic ways in the future. Large percentages of the Latino population in Connecticut, Massachusetts, and Rhode Island are of Puerto Rican and Dominican descent, with sizable percentages with heritages from Colombia and Guatemala. Puerto Ricans and Dominicans are Latino subgroups that previous research has shown to have a closer affinity to African Americans (Affigne 2007). Despite Latinos' growing presence in New England, most research on Latino–African American relations and coalition building focuses on the West, the South, or New York (McClain and Stewart 2006). With few exceptions, analysis of cross-racial coalitions in New England is completely absent from the literature.

Modeling Political and Economic Commonality

There are a number of factors that could shape Latinos' perceptions of commonality with Blacks. In this analysis, we focus our analysis of Latinos' perception of political and economic commonality with Blacks on four major factors: (1) group consciousness, (2) group competition for resources, (3) Latino social integration, and (4) social networks. We also control for partisanship and demographic characteristics, including gender, education, and income. In this section, we explain in more detail how we operationalize Latinos' perception of political and economic commonality with Blacks. We then briefly discuss the independent variables included in the analysis. For more detailed information about the coding and survey questions used to operationalize the independent variables in our models, please see appendix 7A.

We analyze four models, two concerned with the factors that predict Latino perceptions of political commonality with Blacks and two that focus on Latino perceptions of economic commonality with Blacks. The political commonality item was measured using the question, "Now I'd like you to think about the political situation of Hispanics/Latinos in society. Thinking about things like government services and employment, political power and representation, how much do Hispanics/Latinos have in common with other racial groups in the United States today? Would you say

Hispanics/Latinos have a lot in common, some in common, little in common, or nothing at all in common with Blacks?" Economic commonality is measured using the following question: "Thinking about issues like job opportunities, educational attainment or income, how much do Hispanics/Latinos have in common with other racial groups in the United States today? Would you say Hispanics/Latinos have a lot in common, some in common, little in common, or nothing at all in common with Blacks?" Given that the dependent variables in our models are nominal, we use multinomial logit to estimate the models.

Independent Variables

We analyze the social integration theory using generational status and English proficiency. We included two linked fate measures in the models. One measures linked fate among Latinos, and the other captures individual Latinos' sense of linked fate with Blacks. We found a collinearity problem between the two linked fate variables but thought it substantively important to include them both; therefore, for each dependent variable, we run a model with both linked fate variables and a model without the Black-Latino linked fate variable. To test theories about social networks, we used questions that asked the racial/ethnic composition of the respondent's friendship network. Our models include economic and political measures of group competition, including questions about private-sector jobs and elected officials. Both models also control for various demographic characteristics such as gender, education, and income.

Results

Our findings in some ways support what previous research has found, and they also reveal some new areas for future investigation. While competition between Blacks and Latinos continues to pose an obstacle for cross-racial coalitions, our research suggests that there is some common ground for building Latino-Black coalitions. In fact, initial analyses suggest that perceptions of shared concerns between Blacks and Latinos may be more prevalent than perceptions of competition. More than 66 percent of Latino respondents in the survey indicated moderate or high levels of linked fate with Blacks (see table 7.1 for details). In other words, many believed that Latinos "doing well" also depended on African Americans "doing well." The survey of Latinos in New England seems to indicate that Latinos see more commonality than conflict with African Americans. More than 50 percent of Latino respondents saw no competition with Blacks in getting jobs, and we see similar patterns regarding education (see table 7.2 for details).

Table 7.1: Measures of Linked Fate

	Latino linked fate	Latino-Black linked fate
Not at all	15.27%	15.92%
A little	14.02%	17.67%
Some	23.72%	25.83%
A lot	46.99%	40.58%

Table 7.2: Percentage of Latinos Who Perceive Political and Economic Competition with Blacks

	Getting jobs	Access to education	Getting jobs with city or state	Representatives in public office
Strong competition	28.42%	31.08%	35.33%	36.58%
Weak competition	20.25%	21.92%	23.33%	28.08%
No competition	51.33%	47.00%	41.33%	35.30%

Table 7.3: Latino-Black Linked Fate and Political and Economic Commonality

	High or moderate Latino-Black linked fate	No Latino-Black linked fate
"Nothing or little" in common politically with African Americans	33.06%	52.80%
"Some or a lot" in common politically with African Americans	66.94%	47.20%
"Nothing or little" in common economically with African Americans	31.95%	50.00%
"Some or A Lot" in common economically with African Americans	68.05%	50.00%

Our initial analysis suggests that Latinos who believe Blacks' and Latinos' well-being is connected are also likely to perceive both political and economic commonality with Blacks. Sixty-eight percent of respondents who indicated a moderate or high sense of linked fate with Blacks perceived economic commonality with Blacks, and 67 percent believed Blacks and Latinos had similar political concerns (see table 7.3 for details).

We found that many of the same factors that influence belief in political commonality also influence belief in economic commonality, but the degree of that influence varies across the two models. In other words, individual Latinos seem to view economic and political shared interests differently. While similarities exist, coalition building on economic issues should not be viewed in the same way as coalition building on political issues.

Economic and Political Commonality

We found that group consciousness measures and social integration measures are significant and function in the way expected for both the political and economic commonality models. Our findings for the group competition variables are not as one might expect. We found that perception of group competition is positively correlated with belief in both economic and political commonality. However, the group competition variables are statistically significant only in the political commonality model. Our analysis indicates that Latinos' perception of political competition with African Americans actually increases the probability of belief in political commonality. We found that having mostly Black and Black and Latino friends had a positive and significant impact on belief in economic commonality but no statistical influence on perception of political commonality.

Group Consciousness and Friendship Networks

We present the findings about group consciousness and the friendship network variables together. While they are separate, they do complement each other. In

Dawson's (1994) discussion of linked fate, an important factor in maintaining linked fate is one's social networks. In both the economic and political commonality models, the linked fate measures were positive and statistically significant. In other words, Latinos who have a stronger sense of linked fate are more likely to believe that Blacks and Latinos have economic and political commonality.

Latinos who believe that what happens to other Latinos has a lot to do with what happens to them—that is, a strong sense of linked fate—have a 25.7 percent probability of believing that Blacks and Latinos have a lot in common politically,

Table 7.4: Explaining Perceptions of Economic Commonality with Blacks

	Model 1			Model 2		
	Little in common	Some in common	A lot in common	Little in common	Some in common	A lot in common
Group Consciousness						
Latino linked fate	−0.012	0.085	0.155	0.055	0.200**	0.293***
	(0.107)	(0.103)	(0.114)	(0.105)	(0.100)	(0.109)
Latino-Black linked fate	0.258**	0.457***	0.582***			
	(0.108)	(0.107)	(0.121)			
Group Competition						
Weak job competition	0.551*	0.844***	0.238	0.501	0.742**	0.097
	(0.320)	(0.301)	(0.328)	(0.321)	(0.300)	(0.326)
Strong job competition	0.437	0.370	0.429	0.400	0.333	0.400
	(0.288)	(0.282)	(0.284)	(0.287)	(0.275)	(0.275)
Weak political competition	0.283	0.292	0.124	0.278	0.296	0.149
	(0.295)	(0.283)	(0.294)	(0.300)	(0.282)	(0.291)
Strong political competition	0.095	0.064	0.092	0.131	0.127	0.180
	(0.287)	(0.277)	(0.286)	(0.283)	(0.270)	(0.275)
Social Integration						
2+ generation	0.750***	0.589**	0.871**	0.740***	0.578**	0.862***
	(0.249)	(0.243)	(0.247)	(0.251)	(0.242)	(0.245)
Prefer English	0.483	1.180***	1.230***	0.385	1.021***	1.030***
	(0.327)	(0.310)	(0.321)	(0.323)	(0.302)	(0.308)
Social Networks						
Mostly Latino friends	−0.277	0.144	−0.254	−0.261	0.162	−0.231
	(0.281)	(0.276)	(0.287)	(0.279)	(0.272)	(0.281)
Other friends	0.060	0.483*	0.128	0.055	0.473*	0.119
	(0.281)	(0.275)	(0.281)	(0.281)	(0.272)	(0.274)
Mostly Black / Black and Latino friends	1.601	2.220**	1.760*	1.610	2.230**	1.770*
	(1.051)	(1.030)	(1.040)	(1.050)	(1.030)	(1.031)
Demographics/SES						
Education	0.158	0.189	−0.059	0.123	0.125	−0.139
	(0.320)	(0.299)	(0.319)	(0.316)	(0.295)	(0.311)
Male	0.209	0.306	0.213	0.203	0.304	0.214
	(0.232)	(0.225)	(0.239)	(0.232)	(0.224)	(0.229)
Income	−0.042	0.079	0.085	−0.050	0.066	0.071
	(0.077)	(0.074)	(0.076)	(0.075)	(0.072)	(0.074)
Constant	−0.796	−2.230	−2.740	−0.211	−1.220	−1.341
	(0.544)	(1.340)	(0.600)	(0.491)	(0.486)	(1.349)
Observations		984			984	
Pseudo R²		0.0554			0.0430	

*** $p < 0.01$, ** $p < 0.05$, * $p < 0.1$

Note: Base is "nothing in common"; robust standard errors in parentheses; estimated with multinomial logit

Source: Latino National Survey–New England (2006)

Table 7.5: Explaining Perceptions of Political Commonality with Blacks

	Model 1			Model 2		
	Little in common	Some in common	A lot in common	Little in common	Some in common	A lot in common
Group Consciousness						
Latino linked fate	−0.092	−0.039	0.065	−0.016	0.102	0.212*
	(0.111)	(0.112)	(0.128)	(0.106)	(0.106)	(0.121)
Latino-Black linked fate	0.262**	0.529***	0.556***			
	(0.106)	(0.105)	(0.124)			
Group Competition						
Weak job competition	0.339	0.144	−0.173	0.300	0.050	−0.280
	(0.299)	(0.294)	(0.329)	(0.295)	(0.287)	(0.320)
Strong job competition	0.662**	−0.051	0.262	0.624**	−0.072	0.244
	(0.282)	(0.280)	(0.297)	(0.283)	(0.278)	(0.294)
Weak political competition	0.500*	0.821***	0.116	0.508*	0.843***	0.150
	(0.278)	(0.273)	(0.298)	(0.279)	(0.271)	(0.296)
Strong political competition	0.295	0.708**	0.622**	0.341	0.778***	0.703**
	(0.281)	(0.276)	(0.296)	(0.278)	(0.271)	(0.289)
Social Integration						
2+ generation	0.560**	0.755***	1.050***	0.564**	0.755***	1.050***
	(0.238)	(0.232)	(0.249)	(0.237)	(0.228)	(0.244)
Prefer English	0.530	1.046***	0.986***	0.421	0.848***	0.776**
	(0.295)	(0.288)	(0.310)	(0.296)	(0.386)	(0.304)
Social Networks						
Mostly Latino friends	0.164	0.145	−0.088	0.187	0.171	−0.057
	(0.281)	(0.273)	(0.297)	(0.279)	(0.270)	(0.292)
Other friends	0.386	0.159	0.254	0.369	0.139	0.235
	(0.278)	(0.271)	(0.285)	(0.277)	(0.266)	(0.278)
Mostly Black / Black and Latino friends	0.238	−0.334	0.281	0.237	−0.324	0.295
	(0.558)	(0.545)	(0.550)	(0.552)	(0.550)	(0.561)
Demographics/SES						
Education	−0.091	−0.022	−0.275	−0.114	−0.082	−0.352
	(0.314)	(0.302)	(0.326)	(0.308)	(0.295)	(0.318)
Male	0.152	0.237	0.562**	0.145	0.231	0.560**
	(0.228)	(0.220)	(0.236)	(0.227)	(0.218)	(0.231)
Income	0.035	0.078	0.168**	0.024	0.063	0.155**
	(0.071)	(0.070)	(0.074)	(0.068)	(0.068)	(0.071)
Constant	−0.986	−1.990	−3.100	−0.429	−0.780	−1.830
	(0.532)	(0.546)	(0.633)	(0.485)	(0.492)	(0.542)
Observations		1,002			1,002	
Pseudo R^2		0.060			0.050	

*** $p < 0.01$, ** $p < 0.05$, * $p < 0.1$

Note: Base is "nothing in common"; robust standard errors in parentheses; estimated with multinomial logit

Source: Latino National Survey–New England (2006)

compared to those with no sense of linked fate, who have a 17.7 percent probability of believing that Blacks and Latinos have a lot in common politically. It is a difference of 8.0 percent. When we examine the same measure in the economic commonality model, we find that Latinos with very high linked fate with other Latinos have a 36.18 percent probability of believing that Blacks and Latinos have a lot in common economically, compared to 25.66 percent probability for those with no sense of linked fate with other Latinos—a difference of 10.52 percent. We find a similar pattern for those Latinos who have a high sense of linked fate with Blacks. Latinos who have the highest level of Latino-Black linked fate have a 27.06 percent probability of believing that Blacks and Latinos have a lot in common politically, compared to 17.82 percent probability for those Latinos with no sense of Latino-Black linked fate—a difference of 9.22 percent. These findings indicate that Latino-Black linked fate has a large influence on perceptions of political commonality. When holding all other variables constant, having Black-Latino linked fate is a more powerful predictor of perceived economic and political commonality with Blacks than is having Latino linked fate.

The findings for the economic model are similar. Latinos with the highest level of Latino-Black linked fate have a 39.60 percent probability of perceiving Blacks and Latinos as having a lot in common economically, compared to 23.91 percent probability for Latinos with no sense of Latino-Black linked fate—a difference of 15.69 percent.

While there are not significant differences in how the linked fate measures function on the economic and political commonality models, our findings do suggest that increased Latino group consciousness is more likely to have an influence on building political commonality than on building economic commonality, but both would be benefited from increased levels of group consciousness among Latinos. More importantly, Latino-Black group connectedness is likely to have a large impact on both political and economic commonality.

An area that has gotten little attention in previous studies is individuals' social networks. Research has long shown that our social interactions with family members, friends, co-workers, and neighbors can exert an important influence on political behavior and policy preferences (Lazarsfeld, Berelson, and Gaudet [1944] 1968; Campbell et al. 1960, 76). Our results show that those Latinos whose friendship networks are mostly Latino, a mix of Latino and Black, or mostly Black are more likely to believe that Blacks and Latinos have a lot in common economically than are those Latinos whose friendship networks are mostly white or a mix of Latino and white. However, we found friendship networks had no impact on perception of political commonality. In fact, those Latinos who responded that their friendship networks are composed of mostly Blacks or a mix of Blacks and Latinos had a 37.12 percent probability of believing that they had a lot in common politically with Blacks. On the other hand, those respondents who described their friendship network as mostly Latino had a 24.26 percent probability of believing that they had a lot politically in common with Blacks. Latinos whose friendship network is composed of mostly whites and whites and Latinos had only a 28.51 percent probability

Table 7.6: Group Consciousness Predicted Probabilities

	High Latino linked fate	No Latino linked fate	High Latino-Black linked fate	No Latino-Black linked fate
"A lot" of political commonality with African Americans	25.70%	17.72%	27.06%	17.82%
"A lot" of economic commonality with African Americans	36.18%	25.66%	39.60%	23.91%

Table 7.7: Friendship Networks Predicted Probabilities

	Mostly Latino friends	Mostly Black / mix of Black and Latino friends	Mostly white / mix of white and Latino friends
"A lot" of political commonality with African Americans	24.26%	37.12%	28.51%
"A lot" of economic commonality with African Americans	34.41%	36.71%	40.16%

of perceiving political commonality with Blacks. The difference in perceived political commonality between Latinos with mostly Black or Black and Latino friendship networks and Latinos with mostly white or white and Latino friendship networks is 8.61. In other words, Latinos who have few Blacks in their friendship network are less likely to perceive that they have anything in common with Blacks politically (see table 7.7 for details).

Interestingly, we also found that there is a bivariate relationship between diverse friendship networks and age. That is, younger Latinos are more likely to have friendship networks with Blacks. Although we do not present the findings, the chi-square and ANOVA tests we conducted suggest that the differences across age groups are statistically significant; however, the correlation coefficients were small. While we note a pattern, we do caution that the relationship is not very strong. With that said, we believe it is important to recognize this pattern and examine it in future research. Demographics show that in 2010, 35 percent of the Latinos in the U.S. were under eighteen, compared to 24 percent for the overall U.S. population (U.S. Census 2011). Young Latinos' openness to Blacks may indicate a stronger foundation for building Latino-Black coalitions in the future. If as these young people age they maintain their friendships or remain open to friendships with Blacks, it may mean important shifts in how the Black and Latino communities view each other.

Social Integration

In both the economic and political commonality models, we find that most of the social integration measures are statistically significant and indicate that as Latinos become more socially integrated, they are more likely to perceive economic and political shared interests with Blacks. In both models, generational differences exist in perceptions of political and economic commonality. Second-generation and greater Latinos are more likely than first-generation Latinos to believe that Latinos and Blacks have a lot in common economically and politically. Second-generation or greater Latinos have a 34.41 percent probability of believing that Blacks and Latinos have a lot in common economically, compared to a 27.40 percent probability for first-generation Latinos. Similarly, second-generation and greater Latinos have a 24.26 percent probability of perceiving that Latinos have a lot in common politically with Blacks, compared to only a 16.72 percent probability for first-generation Latinos.

In our analysis of economic and political commonality, we found that language preference is also a predictor of an increased sense of shared interests economically and politically with Blacks. We assume that Latinos who used English as their preferred language for the interview are more socially integrated into U.S. society.

It is assumed that as Latinos become more integrated, they become more aware of their minority status and will recognize the shared experiences they have with Blacks as another marginalized group in U.S. society. In fact, we found that Latinos whose preferred language is English are more likely to perceive economic and political commonality with Blacks. Those whose preferred language is English have a 24.26 percent probability of perceiving that Blacks and Latinos have a lot in common politically with Latinos, compared to only a 19.61 percent probability for those whose preferred language is Spanish. We found a similar pattern in the perception of economic commonality between Latinos and Blacks—those whose preferred language is English have a 34.41 percent probability of believing that Blacks and Latinos have a lot in common economically, versus a 24.56 percent probability for those whose preferred language is Spanish.

Group Competition

Scholars have maintained that competition among Latinos and Blacks over jobs and public resources reduces the potential for broad-based Black-Latino coalitions. Our findings cast doubts on these findings. In fact, our results show that Latinos' belief that there is strong competition for jobs between Blacks and Latinos does not negatively influence their perception of political or economic commonality. There is a positive relationship between Latinos' belief that there is competition with Blacks for jobs and political resources and their perceptions of economic and political commonality. While the competition variables are not statistically significant in the economic commonality model, they are for the political commonality model. Latinos who believe that Latinos are in strong competition with Blacks for jobs have a 36.10 percent chance of believing that Blacks and Latinos have a lot in common economically, compared to only 34.41 percent for those who see no competition for jobs. Similarly, Latinos who perceive strong competition with Blacks for political resources are more likely to perceive political commonality between Blacks and Latinos.

Table 7.8: Social Integration Predicted Probabilities

	1st generation	2nd+ generation	Prefer English	Prefer Spanish
"A lot" of political commonality with African Americans	16.72%	24.26%	24.26%	19.61%
"A lot" of economic commonality with African Americans	27.40%	34.41%	34.41%	24.56%

Table 7.9: Group Competition Predicted Probabilities

	No job competition	Strong job competition	No political competition	Strong political competition
"A lot" of political commonality with African Americans	24.26%	25.53%	24.26%	25.67%
"A lot" of economic commonality with African Americans	34.41%	36.10%	34.41%	34.99%

It may be that perceptions of political competition are a byproduct of institutional structures that result from Latinos and Blacks sharing residential and political space. Latinos' fervent desire to elect one of their own to public offices is an expected norm and pattern in American politics. However, because of the prevalence of single-member electoral districts, Latinos have to compete with African Americans (who happen to share the same residential and political space) to make it happen. While perceptions of competition between Blacks and Latinos are found to exist, our research suggests that rather than hindering perceptions of commonality, competition actually magnifies Latinos' perceptions of economic and political commonality with Blacks. Commonality and competition seem to work together. The challenge in using this finding for coalition building is to appeal to feelings of commonality and shared interests, despite competition. It is also important to note that most Latinos surveyed perceived little or no competition with Blacks for economic and political resources.

Overall, our results suggest that there are some clear paths to building Black-Latino coalitions in New England. Our research suggests that despite the emphasis on conflict and competition between Blacks and Latinos, there appears to be a solid foundation of shared concerns and connections. Our analysis shows that significant numbers of Latinos in New England see themselves as linked to African Americans. And far fewer see Blacks as competition for jobs and other resources. We are not arguing that competition does not exist but that it may not be as large a barrier to Black-Latino coalitions as previously suggested. We note that in the 2012 U.S. Senate election, Democratic challenger Elizabeth Warren strongly courted African American and Latino voters, and with a little help from President Obama (who was on the ballot for reelection), they came through for her, helping her defeat Republican incumbent Scott Brown. Voter turnout in Massachusetts's heavily minority cities and towns increased significantly in 2012 over the 2010 special election that sent Brown to Washington to fill the Senate seat once held by Democrat Edward Kennedy. Black and Latino voters overwhelmingly voted for Warren.

Our research also raises the question of whether coalition building among Latinos and Blacks in the U.S. might occur differently in different regions of the country. The term "Latino," although a means to underscore the commonality of a Latin American heritage and Spanish language, hides vast diversity. The rapid rise of the Latino population in North Carolina and other southern states has been attributed to immigration from Mexico (McClain et al. 2006). Many of the western and southwestern states also have heavy concentrations of Latinos with Mexican heritage. As mentioned, New England's Latino population is much more diverse than the Latino communities in other parts of the country that have gotten the attention of the bulk of the literature. According to the 2010 Census, only 8.7 percent of New England's Latinos are of Mexican descent. While nearly half of Latinos in New England are of Puerto Rican descent, the other half come from almost all countries in Latin America. In Rhode Island, for example, nearly 30 percent of the Latino population is Dominican, and nearly 15 percent is Guatemalan. There are historical and cultural differences among the different groups. There are also significant differences in their reasons for, and experiences in, migrating to the U.S. Our research

---

Key Findings

- Our findings suggest that Latinos see more commonality than conflict with African Americans.

- We find that Latinos who believe that Blacks' and Latinos' well-being is connected are likely to perceive both political and economic commonality with African Americans.

- Our findings support previous research that shows that Latinos who have a high sense of linked fate with other Latinos are more likely to perceive political commonality with African Americans. We also find that Latinos who have a high sense of linked fate with other Latinos are also more likely to perceive economic commonality with African Americans.

- Our findings suggest that despite political competition, Latinos often perceive political commonality with African Americans.

- We find that social integration is positively linked to perceptions of both economic and political commonality. Latinos who are second generation or greater are more likely than first-generation Latinos to perceive political and economic commonality with African Americans. Likewise, Latinos who preferred to have the survey conducted in English are more likely than Latinos who preferred Spanish to perceive political and economic commonality with African Americans.

- We find that having a diverse social network tends to play a more significant role in Latinos' perception of economic commonality than in their perceptions of political commonality.

---

on New England's Latinos suggests that scholars should pay closer attention to these differences.

Finally, we find that scholars cannot think about coalition building as a universal concept—how one works to build a successful coalition will depend, in part, on what issues are on the table. We note that diverse friendship networks can play a central role in building coalitions around economic issues. However, diverse friendship networks influence Latinos' perceptions of political commonality with African Americans at a different level. When it comes to perception of political commonality between Blacks and Latinos, we find that demographic characteristics are strong predictors. Men, second-generation and greater Latinos, and those with higher income are likely to perceive political commonality with Blacks. These demographic factors have no statistically significant influence on Latinos' perception of economic commonality with Blacks.

Understanding the relationship between Blacks and Latinos is becoming increasingly important, given the changing demographics of American cities and states. This chapter is a step toward understanding how Latinos view Black Americans and what leads individual Latinos to see common ground between themselves and Black Americans, which may serve as building blocks for Latino-Black coalitions in the future.

Study Questions

1. Why is it important to focus on African American–Latino coalition building in New England?

2. What are some of the factors that increase the likelihood that Latinos will perceive of themselves as having political and economic commonality with African Americans?

3. Do perceptions of competition for elected office present a barrier for Latino and African American coalition building?

Appendix 7A: Variable Construction and Frequency Distributions

Dependent Variables: Economic Commonality and Political Commonality

ECONOMIC COMMONALITY

"Thinking about issues like job opportunities, educational attainment or income, how much do Hispanics/Latinos have in common with other racial groups in the United States today? Would you say Hispanics/Latinos have a lot in common, some in common, little in common, or nothing at all in common with Blacks?"

Value	Label	Frequency	%
1	Not at all	149	14.10
2	A little	249	23.56
3	Some	349	33.02
4	A lot	310	29.33

Obs.	Mean	Std. Dev.	Min.	Max.
1,057	2.78	1.02	1	4

POLITICAL COMMONALITY

"Thinking about things like government services and employment, political power and representation, how much do Hispanics/Latinos have in common with other racial groups in the United States today? Would you say Hispanics/Latinos have lot in common, some in common, little in common, or nothing at all in common with Blacks?"

Value	Label	Frequency	%
1	Not at all	151	14.18
2	A little	268	25.16
3	Some	370	34.74
4	A lot	276	25.92

Obs.	Mean	Std. Dev.	Min.	Max.
1,065	2.72	1.00	1	4

Independent Variables: Measures of *Linked Fate*
Group Consciousness

LATINO LINKED FATE

"How much does your 'doing well' depend on other Latinos/Hispanics also doing well? A lot, some, a little, or not at all?" 1 = not at all; 2 = a little; 3 = some; 4 = a lot

Value	Label	Frequency	%
1	Not at all	170	15.27
2	A little	156	14.02
3	Some	264	23.72
4	A lot	523	46.99

Obs.	Mean	Std. Dev.	Min.	Max.
1,113	3.02	1.11	1	4

LATINO-BLACK LINKED FATE

"How much does Latinos/Hispanics 'doing well' depend on African-Americans also doing well? A lot, some, a little, or not at all?" 1 = not at all; 2 = a little; 3 = some; 4 = a lot

Value	Label	Frequency	%
1	Not at all	191	15.92
2	A little	212	17.67
3	Some	310	25.83
4	A lot	487	40.58

Obs.	Mean	Std. Dev.	Min.	Max.
1,200	2.91	1.10	1	4

Social Integration

GENERATIONAL STATUS

Constructed using "born in the U.S." variable. "Were you born in the mainland United States, Puerto Rico or some other country?" 0 = some other country (first generation); 1 = mainland U.S. and Puerto Rico (second generation or greater)

Value	Label	Frequency	%
0	1st generation	633	52.75
1	2nd generation or greater	567	47.25

Obs.	Mean	Std. Dev.	Min.	Max.
1,200	.473	.499	0	1

LANGUAGE PREFERENCE

"Would you prefer I speak in English or Spanish?" 0 = Spanish; 1 = English

Value	Label	Frequency	%
0	Spanish	800	66.67
1	English	400	33.33

Obs.	Mean	Std. Dev.	Min.	Max.
1,200	1.67	.472	0	1

Group Competition

JOBS

"How much does Latinos/Hispanics getting jobs compete with African Americans getting jobs?" 1 = no competition; 2 = weak competition; 3 = strong competition

Value	Label	Frequency	%
1	no competition	616	51.33
2	weak competition	243	20.25
3	strong competition	341	28.42

Obs.	Mean	Std. Dev.	Min.	Max.
1,200	1.77	.863	1	3

PUBLIC REPRESENTATION

"How much does Latinos/Hispanics having representatives in elected office compete with African Americans having representatives in office?" 1 = no competition; 2 = weak competition; 3 = strong competition

Value	Label	Frequency	%
1	no competition	424	35.33
2	weak competition	337	28.08
3	strong competition	439	36.58

Obs.	Mean	Std. Dev.	Min.	Max.
1,200	2.01	.848	1	3

Social Networks and Information Sources

FRIENDSHIP NETWORKS

0 = mix/other; 1 = mostly Latino/Portuguese speaking; 2 = mostly white / mix white and Latino; 3 = mostly Black / mix Black and Latino

Value	Label	Frequency	%
0	Mix/other	408	34.90
1	Mostly Latino	343	29.34
2	Mostly white / mix white and Latino	357	30.54
3	Mostly Black / mix Black and Latino	61	5.22

Obs.	Mean	Std. Dev.	Min.	Max.
1,169	1.06	.927	0	3

SES/Demographics

GENDER

"Are you male or female?" 0 = female; 1 = male

Value	Label	Frequency	%
0	Female	723	60.25
1	Male	477	39.75

Obs.	Mean	Std. Dev.	Min.	Max.
1,200	.398	.490	0	1

EDUCATION

"What is your highest level of formal education completed?" 0 = less than four-year degree; 1 = four-year degree or higher

Value	Label	Frequency	%
0	Less than four-year degree	995	82.92
1	four-year degree or higher	205	17.08

Obs.	Mean	Std. Dev.	Min.	Max.
1,200	.171	.377	0	1

INCOME

"Which of the following best describes the total income earned by all members of your household during 2004?"

Value	Label	Frequency	%
1	below $15,000	224	18.67
2	$15,000–24,999	220	18.33
3	$25,000–34,999	265	22.08
4	$35,000–44,999	193	16.08
5	$45,000–54,999	138	11.50
6	$55,000–64,999	56	4.67
7	above $65,000	104	8.67

Obs.	Mean	Std. Dev.	Min.	Max.
1,200	3.32	1.80	1	7

References

Affigne, Tony. 2007. "Negrura en Política: The Politics of Blackness in Latino Communities." Paper presented at the annual meeting of the American Political Science Association. Chicago, IL, August 30–September 2.

Alba, Richard, and Victor Nee. 2003. *Remaking the American Mainstream: Assimilation and Contemporary Immigration*. Cambridge: Harvard University Press.

Bobo, Lawrence D., and Vincent Hutchings. 1996. "Perceptions of Racial Group Competition: Extending Blumer's Theory of Group Position to a Multiracial Social Context." *American Sociological Review* 61:951–972.

Bobo, Lawrence D., James H. Johnson, Jr., Melvin L. Oliver, and Camille L. Zubrinsky. 1994. "Public Opinion before and after the Spring of Discontent." In *The Los Angeles Riots: Lessons for the Urban Future*, ed. Mark Baldassare, 103–133. Boulder, CO: Westview.

Browning, Rufus P., Dale Rogers Marshall, and David H. Tabb. 1984. *Protest Is Not Enough: The Struggle of Blacks and Hispanics for Equality in Urban Politics*. Berkeley: University of California Press.

Campbell, Angus, Philip E. Converse, Warren E. Miller, and Donald E. Stokes. 1960. *The American Voter*. New York: Wiley.

Dawson, Michael C. 1994. *Behind the Mule: Race and Class in African-American Politics*. Princeton: Princeton University Press.

de la Garza, Rodolfo O., Louis DeSipio, F. Chris Garcia, John García, and Angelo Falcón. 1992. *Latino Voices: Mexican, Puerto Rican, and Cuban Perspectives on American Politics*. Boulder, CO: Westview.

DeSipio, Louis. 1996. *Counting on the Latino Vote: Latinos as a New Electorate*. Charlottesville: University of Virginia Press.

Falcón, Angelo. 1988. "Black and Latino Politics in New York City." In *Latinos in the Political System*, ed. F. Chris Garcia, 171–194. South Bend, IN: Notre Dame.

Filindra, Alexandra, and Marion Orr. 2013. "Anxieties of an Ethnic Transition: The Election of the First Latino Mayor in Providence, Rhode Island." *Urban Affairs Review* 49:3–31.

Gay, Claudine. 2006. "Seeing Difference: The Effect of Economic Disparity on Black Attitudes toward Latinos." *American Journal of Political Science* 50 (4): 982–997.

Glazer, Nathan, and Daniel Patrick Moynihan. 1963. *Beyond the Melting Pot: The Negroes, Puerto Ricans, Jews, Italians, and Irish of New York City*. Cambridge: MIT Press.

Gordon, Milton M. 1964. *Assimilation in American Life: The Role of Race, Religion, and National Origins*. New York: Oxford University Press.

Hardy-Fanta, Carol, and Jeffrey Gerson, eds. 2002. *Latino Politics in Massachusetts: Struggles, Strategies, and Prospects*. New York: Routledge.

Hero, Rodney E. 1992. *Latinos and the U.S. Political System: Two-Tiered Pluralism*. Philadelphia: Temple University Press.

Hood, M. V., III, Irwin L. Morris, and Kurt A. Shirkey. 1997. "'¡Quedate o Vente!': Uncovering the Determinants of Hispanic Public Opinion toward Immigration." *Political Research Quarterly* 50 (3): 627–647.

Huckfeldt, Robert, and John Sprague. 1987. "Networks in Context: The Social Flow of Political Information." *American Political Science Review* 81 (4): 1197–1216.

Huckfeldt, Robert, and John Sprague. 1995. *Citizens, Politics, and Social Communication: Information and Influence in an Election Campaign*. New York: Cambridge University Press.

Jones-Correa, Michael, and David Leal. 1996. "Becoming 'Hispanic': Secondary Pan-ethnic Identification among Latin American-Origin Populations in the United States." *Hispanic Journal of Behavioral Sciences* 18:214–255.

Kaufmann, Karen M. 2003. "Cracks in the Rainbow: Group Commonality as a Basis for Latino and African-American Political Coalitions." *Political Research Quarterly* 56:199–210.

Kaufmann, Karen M. 2007. "Immigration and the Future of Black Power in U.S. Cities." *DuBois Review* 4:1–18.

Kleppner, Paul. 1985. *Chicago Divided: The Making of a Black Mayor*. DeKalb: Northern Illinois University Press.

Kotler-Berkowitz, Laurence. 2005. "Friends and Politics: Linking Diverse Friendship Networks to Political Participation." In *The Social Logic of Politics*, ed. Alan S. Zuckerman, 152–170. Philadelphia: Temple University Press.

Lazarsfeld, Paul F., Bernard Berelson, and Hazel Gaudet. (1944) 1968. *The People's Choice: How the Voter Makes Up His Mind in a Presidential Campaign*. New York: Columbia University Press.

Lizza, Ryan. 2008. "Minority Reports: After New Hampshire, a Hint of Racial Politics." *New Yorker*, January 21.

Marcelli, Enrico A., and Phillip J. Granberry. 2006. "Latino New England: An Emerging Demographic and Economic Portrait." In *Latinos in New England*, ed. Andrés Torres, 25–52. Philadelphia: Temple University Press.

McClain, Paula D. 1993. "The Changing Dynamics of Urban Politics: Black and Hispanic Municipal Employment—Is There Competition?" *Journal of Politics* 55:399–414.

McClain, Paula D., Niambi M. Carter, Victoria M. DeFrancesco Soto, Monique L. Lyle, Jeffrey D. Grynaviski, Shayla C. Nunnally, Thomas J. Scotto, J. Alan Kendrick, Gerald F. Lackey, and Kendra Davenport Cotton. 2006. "Racial Distancing in a Southern City: Latino Immigrants' Views of Black Americans." *Journal of Politics* 68 (3): 571–584.

McClain, Paula D., and Albert Karnig. 1990. "Black and Hispanic Socioeconomic and Political Competition." *American Political Science Review* 84:535–545.

McClain, Paula D., and Joseph Stewart, Jr. 2006. *"Can We All Get Along?" Racial and Ethnic Minorities in American Politics*. Boulder, CO: Westview.

McClain, Paula D., and Steven C. Tauber. 1998. "Black and Latino Socioeconomic and Political Competition: Has a Decade Made a Difference?" *American Politics Quarterly* 26:237–252.

Meier, Kenneth J., Paula D. McClain, J. L. Polinard, and Robert D. Wrinkle. 2004. "Divided or Together? Conflict and Cooperation between African Americans and Latinos." *Political Research Quarterly* 57:399–409.

Mindiola, Tatcho, Jr., Yolanda F. Niemann, and Nestor Rodriguez. 2002. *Black-Brown Relations and Stereotypes*. Austin: University of Texas Press.

Mollenkopf, John. 2003. "New York: Still the Great Anomaly." In *Racial Politics in American Cities*, ed. Rufus P. Browning, Dale Rogers Marshall, and David H. Tabb, 115–139. New York: Longman.

Orr, Marion, and Darrell M. West. 2007. "Power and Race in Cross-Group Coalitions." *National Political Science Review* 11:52–72.

Park, Robert E. 1950. *Race and Culture*. Glencoe, IL: Free Press.

Park, Robert E., and Ernest W. Burgess. 1969. *Introduction to the Science of Sociology*. Stud. ed. abridged by Morris Janowitz. Chicago: University of Chicago Press.

Parker, Paul Edward. 2011. "Census: Hispanic Growth Saves RI Seat in Congress." *Providence Journal*, March 23.

Pinderhughes, Dianne M. 2003. "Urban Racial and Ethnic Politics." In *Cities, Politics, and Policy: A Comparative Analysis*, ed. John P. Pelissero, 97–125. Washington, DC: CQ.

Portes, Alejandro, and Min Zhou. 1993. "The New Second Generation: Segmented Assimilation and Its Variants." *Annals of the American Academy of Political and Social Science* 530:74–96.

Rivlin, Gary. 1993. *Fire on the Prairie: Harold Washington and the Politics of Race*. New York: Holt.

Sanchez, Gabriel R. 2008. "Latino Group Consciousness and Perceptions of Commonality with African Americans." *Social Science Quarterly* 89 (2): 428–444.

Sears, David O., Jack Citrin, Sharmaine V. Cheleden, and Colette van Laar. 1999. "Cultural Diversity and Multicultural Politics: Is Ethnic Balkanization Psychologically Inevitable?" In *Cultural Divides: Understanding and Overcoming Group Conflict*, ed. Deborah A. Prentice and Dale T. Miller, 35–79. New York: Russell Sage Foundation.

Shingles, Richard D. 1981. "Black Consciousness and Political Participation: The Missing Link." *American Political Science Review* 75 (1): 76–91.

Sonenshein, Raphael J. 1993. *Politics in Black and White*. Princeton: Princeton University Press.

Sonenshein, Raphael J., and Susan H. Pinkus. 2002. "The Dynamics of Latino Political Incorporation: The 2001 Los Angeles Mayoral Election as Seen in *Los Angeles Times* Exit Polls." *PS: Political Science and Politics* 35 (March): 67–74.

Tedin, Kent L., and Richard W. Murray. 1994. "Support for Biracial Political Coalitions among Blacks and Hispanics." *Social Science Quarterly* 75:772–789.

Torres, Andrés, ed. 2006. *Latinos in New England*. Philadelphia: Temple University Press.

U.S. Census. 2011. *American Community Survey*. Washington, DC: U.S. Census Bureau.

Vaca, Nicolas C. 2004. *The Presumed Alliance: The Unspoken Conflict between Latinos and Blacks and What It Means for America*. New York: HarperCollins.

Zuckerman, Alan S., ed. 2005. *The Social Logic of Politics: Personal Networks as Contexts for Political Behavior*. Philadelphia: Temple University Press.

8

Racial Identities and Latino Public Opinion

Racial Self-Image and Policy Preferences among Latinos

ATIYA KAI STOKES-BROWN

In January 2003, the Census Bureau reported a demographic bombshell: for the first time, Hispanics were more numerous than Blacks in the U.S. The news spread quickly, generating headlines proclaiming that Hispanics would "surpass," "overtake," or "pass" Blacks in the American polity. An Associated Press report, for example, began with a declaration that "Hispanics have surged past blacks and now constitute the largest minority group in the United States, a status that Latino leaders are sure to use to push for political and economic advances." Another journalist wrote that Latinos would need to "exercise their potential clout or risk falling further behind in employment, education and other indicators of success."[1] However, because it takes time to calculate and report new data, the reversal of the nation's number-two and number-three population ranking (whites remained the largest ethnoracial grouping) had actually occurred more than a year earlier, probably sometime in early 2001. More significantly, the bureau's definitions of "Hispanic" and "Black" treated the two groups as completely distinct —despite the fact that at least 1.1 million Americans at the time were *Afro-Latinos*. In the Census report, however, people who self-identified as both Hispanic *and* Black were counted as Hispanic but *not* Black; nor, in the other direction, were Blacks who reported more than one race included in the Black population estimates. In this chapter, Stokes-Brown explores how complex racial realities, and the varied ways Latinos—especially Black Latinos—self-identify racially, may be shaping policy preferences.

Racially Distinct Policy Attitudes among Latinos

A number of scholars have explored Latino attitudes about public policies (e.g., de la Garza et al. 1993; Hood. Morris, and Shirkey 1997; Sanchez 2006; Branton 2007), yet few of them have explored the relationship between Latinos' policy attitudes and their *racial* identities. I hypothesize that because race is central in determining the life chances and social positions of groups in the United States, social and economic differences among Latino racial groups may create distinct policy attitudes among these groups. Thus, it is expected that feelings of closeness and commonality (due to similar social and economic positions) may lead to distinct policy preferences among Latino racial groups. However, it is important to recognize that the Latino population consists of immigrants (nonnaturalized and naturalized) and native-born citizens. Because extant research has shown that there are significant differences in Latino public opinion among immigrants and their native-born counterparts (e.g., Branton 2007; García Bedolla 2005; Hood, Morris, and Shirkey 1997), I also examine how the effect of generational status varies across Latino racial groups.

After reviewing extant literature on Latino policy attitudes and the role of racial

---

Research Questions

- How do Latinos racially self-identify in the U.S.? What are the most common racial categories chosen by Latinos?

- What is the social reality of race for Latinos? How might the social realities created by racial identities influence policy attitudes?

- How does generational status condition the influence of racial identity on Latino policy attitudes?

---

identity in Latino politics, this chapter will discuss the methods used to examine Latino public opinion, present the findings, and discuss the implications of the results. This study fills an important gap in the political science literature, providing a rare opportunity to understand Latino public opinion using the lens of race (but see Nicholson, Pantoja, and Segura 2005). Highlighting the politics of identity in the Latino community, this research also raises important questions about the meaning of racial identification as measured by surveys and the implications of survey formats for studying the Latino population. This is particularly important given ongoing debates about the "best" way to ask questions about race and ethnicity for those who trace their origins to countries where racial boundaries are loosely drawn, racial mixing is common, and race has ethnocultural connotations.

Latinos, Public Opinion, and Racial Identity

Much of the research on Latino public opinion centers largely on Latino attitudes toward immigration and abortion. Several studies have examined the impact of acculturation[2] on Latino attitudes toward immigration and found that immigrants and individuals with stronger cultural ties to their country of origin are more supportive of policies that benefit immigrants (de la Garza et al. 1993; Miller, Polinard, and Wrinkle 1984). Latinos more acculturated into U.S. society are more likely to support restrictive immigration policies (Hood, Morris, and Shirkey 1997; Binder, Polinard, and Wrinkle 1997) and are less likely to support policies that provide benefits to immigrants and refugees (de la Garza et al 1993; Branton 2007). There are also significant differences in opinion on immigration among Latino national-origin groups—Cubans tend to be most concerned about illegal immigration, whereas Mexicans are more likely to believe that the government is already doing too much to stop illegal immigration (Michelson 2001). Cubans and Central Americans also tend to support increasing levels of legal immigration into the U.S. (Hood, Morris, and Shirkey 1997; Martinez-Ebers et al. 2000; Sanchez 2006), and Latinos of Caribbean origin are less likely to believe that immigration should remain unchanged rather than be decreased (Sanchez 2006).

Extant research also shows that Latinos are more likely than Anglos to oppose abortion (Leal 2004a). In a study of religion and abortion attitudes, Sean Bolks and colleagues (2000) found that committed (i.e., regularly attending) Catholic Latinos and Latinos who receive a great deal of guidance from their faith tend to express greater opposition to abortion rights, while less devout Catholics exhibit greater acceptance of legalized abortion. Christopher Ellison et al. (2005) also found that committed Protestant Latinos are more likely to be prolife and are more likely to support a total abortion ban. There is also substantial subgroup variation in Latino opinion about abortion. Cubans are more likely to be prochoice than are Mexicans and Puerto Ricans (Bolks et al. 2000; Leal 2004a; Ellison, Echevarría, and Smith 2005; Sanchez 2006). Central/South Americans are also more likely to believe that abortions should be legal in all or most cases (Sanchez 2006).

Recently, scholars have conducted analyses that expand our knowledge of Latino policy attitudes across a wide range of issues. Regina Branton (2007) found that acculturation is an important explanatory factor in understanding Latino attitudes toward nonimmigration policy issues. In a study of Latino public opinion toward Latino salient issues (immigration and bilingual education) and issues not directly tied to Latinos (abortion and the death penalty), Gabriel Sanchez (2006) found that perceived discrimination, a dimension of group consciousness, plays the greatest role in determining Latino attitudes on Latino salient issues.

This study adds to this body of literature by investigating Latino policy attitudes across several issue areas. However, whereas extant research suggests that a multitude of factors including acculturation, citizenship, national origin, and other demographic factors drive Latino political attitudes, this study considers the political consequences of racial identity. While we generally discuss Latino group identity in ethnic terms, variations in racial self-identification are prevalent. According to the 2000 U.S. Census, 49.9 percent of Latinos self-identified as White, 2.7 percent self-identified as Black, and 47.4 percent self-identified as some other race (see Logan 2003). How do Latinos come to choose these racial categories? It is certainly the case that foreign-born Latinos enter the country with their own notions of race formed by different historical processes in their countries of origin (Marrow 2003). Latinos often describe their race as equivalent to their nationality, culture, familial socialization, birthplace, skin color, ethnicity, or a combination of these (Montalvo and Codina 2001, 322; Rodríguez 2000, 152). Coming from backgrounds where racial boundaries are loosely drawn and racial mixing is common, many Latinos often see themselves deriving from more than one race (Rodriguez 2000). Once in the United States, they are immersed in a culture where the dominant racial paradigm exists around Black and White (Itzigsohn, Giorguli, and Vazquez 2005). Thus, it is assumed that migrating to the United States alters the racial identities of some Latinos, who are presumed to be, and treated by others as, Black or White based on their phenotype. Nonimmigrant Latinos also tend to reorder their racial identity as they navigate between the system of racial classification of their immigrant parents and relatives and that of mainstream U.S. society (see Bonilla-Silva 2003; Marrow 2003). This is clearly the case for many second- and third-plus-generation Latinos who "gr[o]w up in two cultures, belonging simultaneously to both and to neither of them and experiencing discrimination as Latinos" (Itzigsohn and Dore-Cabral 2000, 228; also see Oboler 1992). Because native-born Latinos are experiencing race differently than other Latinos, they may adopt the standard racial categories provided on surveys. It may even be the case that for some, "Latino" and "Hispanic" may become a racialized category.

The diversity of racial identities in the Latino community and the social realities these identities create suggests that racial self-identification within the Latino community will influence individual policy attitudes. White Latinos have the lowest rates of poverty and highest incomes, followed sequentially by "some other race" Latinos and Black Latinos. Despite having more education, Black Latinos also appear to have fewer opportunities than other Latino racial groups (e.g., Logan 2003). That race could be a growing fissure in Latino life increases the possibility that race could be a key component of Latino identity and, therefore, *politically significant*. The social implications attached to a racial identity influence an individual's worldview, which then frames that individual's political perceptions. Thus, because an individual perceives that his or her life chances are shaped by race, the individual is more likely to rely on his or her racial identity to make political judgments (see Dawson 1994 for greater discussion).

Recent studies of Latino racial identity have found that race is an important explanatory factor in understanding political behavior. For example, we know from research that race is significantly related to Latino vote choice (Stokes-Brown 2006; Basler 2008). Racial identity is also a significant predictor of political efficacy, trust, and participation among Latinos (Stokes-Brown 2009). To date, only one paper explores the relationship between racial identity and Latino policy attitudes. Using the 1999 Harvard Kennedy School / Kaiser Family Foundation / Washington Post Latino Survey, Stephen Nicholson et al. (2005) find that Black Latinos tend to be more supportive of government-sponsored health care and less supportive of the death penalty as compared to White Latinos. Thus, they find this clear difference in Latino opinion by race on implicitly racial policies and issues concerning social welfare that generally tend to polarize non-Hispanic Blacks and Whites.

This study revisits and expands this prior research in distinct ways. First, this study makes use of a source specifically designed to provide more detailed information about Latino racial identification and Latino policy attitudes than any other publicly available source. Using the LNS, I move beyond the Black-White divide and include both standard and innovative racial identification choices. This is particularly important given that the political amalgamation of race and ethnicity has changed the way in which many Latinos view themselves. A growing number of Latinos identify themselves outside of standard racial categories, often writing in "Hispanic," "Latino," or "some other race" on Census forms and surveys (Logan 2003; also see Rodriguez 1992; Tafoya 2004). The data also include questions about a wide range of policy issues. This is noteworthy given that the Nicholson et al. study only includes two implicitly racial policies (government-sponsored health insurance and capital punishment). We know from previous research that differences between non-Hispanic Whites and Blacks are less apparent for non-race-related issues because perspectives on racial inequality play less of a role in determining one's position on these issues. It remains unclear whether differences in opinion between Latino racial groups will also follow this trend or whether variability in attitudes among Latinos as a function of race exists across a wide range of policy items, including issues that are directly tied to ethnicity (i.e., immigration). Lastly, the substantial growth of the Latino population since 1999 intensifies the need for timely, reliable data.

Measurement: Policy Attitudes

The LNS includes three sets of issues. The first set of questions deal with one Latino salient issue: immigration. The *immigrants* item asked respondents whether they believe immigrants strengthen the country or are a burden. The *illegal immigration* item asked respondents to identify their preferred policy on illegal immigration: sealing/closing off the border; a guest-worker program designed for temporary entrance; a guest-worker program leading to legalization; or immediate legalization. The second grouping contains questions about implicitly racial/social welfare policies: government spending and health care. The *government spending* item asked respondents whether they strongly oppose, oppose, support, or strongly support governmental income support for those who need it. The *health care* item asked whether respondents strongly oppose, oppose, support, or strongly support governmental intervention to reform health care. The remaining set of policy issues are not directly tied to the Latino community but are high-profile political issues. Two education policy issues asked respondents to state their level of support for the use of standardized tests to determine whether a child is promoted to the next grade or graduates from high school (*standardized tests*) and for vouchers that pay a portion of the cost to send children to private schools (*vouchers*).[3] A third question asked whether same-sex couples should receive no legal recognition, be permitted to enter into civil unions, or be permitted to legally marry (*same-sex marriage*) and whether abortion should be illegal in all circumstances, legal only to save the life of the mother and in cases of incest, legal in most circumstances, or legal in all circumstances.

Because the dependent variables—*immigrants, illegal immigration, government spending, health care, standardized tests, vouchers, same-sex marriage*, and *abortion* —range in scale, various estimation techniques are used. *Immigrant* is a dichotomous variable, meaning that the response has only two categories. In addition, the responses are not ranked, so the appropriate method to model the relationship between Latino racial identity and this dependent variable is logistic regression (see Aldrich and Nelson 1984). For the remaining variables, the data are categorical (the data can be divided into groups) and ordered (the data are ranked). Thus, the appropriate method to model the relationship between Latino racial identity and these dependent variables is ordered probit regression (see Greene 2003).

Measurement: Latino Racial Identity

How to define (and measure) race and ethnicity remains a highly contentious issue. The tradition in social science has been to conceptually separate ethnicity from race. Race is defined as "a group of human beings socially defined on the basis of physical characteristics," whereas ethnicity is defined as "a collectivity within a larger society having real or putative common ancestry, memories of a shared historical past, and a cultural focus on one or more symbolic elements defined as the epitome of their peoplehood" (Cornell and Hartmann 1998, 24, 19; also see Schermerhorn 1978). The standards adopted by the U.S. Office of Management and Budget (OMB) for the federal collection of racial and ethnic data reinforce this tradition, treating race and Hispanic origin as separate measures and questions.[4] Under this two-question scheme, Latinos can be identified by race (White, Black, etc.) and as a distinct group (Hispanic vs. non-Hispanic).

Some scholars argue that this strategy for enumerating the Latino population is problematic because it distorts Latinos' understanding of race as a cultural, social, and/or political concept that differs from the largely mainstream U.S. conception of race (Rodriguez 2000). Latinos trace their origins to Latin American and Caribbean countries populated by phenotypically diverse descendants of Spanish, African, and indigenous peoples and are often accustomed to a ternary model of race relations that formally acknowledges intermediary populations of multiracial individuals (Daniels 1999). Arguing that "Latinos straddle the divide, being both a race, in some common understandings, and an ethnic group" (Cornell and Hartmann 1998, 33) and that race and ethnicity are presumed by most people to be linked and equivalent, some have called for the creation of a combined race/ethnicity question in which Latino is included in the list of races.[5]

The analysis presented here relies on closed-ended questions that measure race and Hispanic heritage separately. Relying on survey questions that are modeled after the Census permits direct comparisons across multiple sources of data. For example, 2000 Census data show that most Latinos self-identified as White or "some other race" (Logan 2003; also see Tafoya 2004). The most common racial identity chosen by LNS respondents was "some other race" (66 percent). Twenty-three percent of the respondents self-identified as White, while 1 percent of respondents self-identified as Black.[6] Yet it should be noted that the LNS data are somewhat unique in that additional effort was made to clarify some responses. While the categories Black and White are self-explanatory given the existing racial hierarchy, it is not clear what it means to be "some other race." Because this racial category is vague and inclusive, respondents were asked by interviewers to explain their response. Of those who initially self-identified as "some other race," approximately 75 percent reported "Hispanic" or "Latino" as their race (SOR_Latino). This finding suggests that there is a growing conflation of race and ethnicity in the way that Latinos define their identities. This is further supported by the reality that almost 4 percent of the "some other race" respondents who report their race to be Hispanic/Latino *also* believe that Latinos are a distinctive race category in the U.S. (Latino_R).[7] More so than for another other Latino racial group, there is seemingly little contradiction for these Latinos between their ethnic and racial group identities.

Although this analysis is focused primarily on the relationship between racial identity and Latino public opinion, the model also includes several control variables shown to be predictive of Latino policy attitudes including national origin (*Mexican, Puerto Rican, Cuban, Dominican*), self-reported phenotype (ranges from very dark to very light), gender, age, income, and education.[8] For example, we know from extant research that there is considerable variation in opinion about immigration policy among national-origin groups. It is possible that Latino public opinion may also vary by phenotype. Skin color is the feature that people in the U.S. are most likely to use to determine another's race and thus categorize the person as a member of a particular racial group (e.g., Brown, Dane, and Durham 1998). Given that skin color is an important component of how race shapes life chances, the social implications attached to skin color may also influence one's worldview and political perceptions. It is also reasonable to suggest that gender and age will influence political attitudes. The likelihood of holding a prolife stance about abortion increases as Latinos become older and if they are women (e.g., Bolks et al. 2000; Sanchez 2006). Latino political attitudes are also influenced by one's level of educational attainment and income. Bolks et al. (2000) found socioeconomic status to be a significant predictor of attitudes about abortion, as respondents with higher education and income levels are more likely to adopt a prolife stance. Highly educated Latinos are much more likely to express support for restricting immigration (Hood, Morris, and Shirkey 1997). It is also the case that Latinos with higher levels of income are more likely to believe that immigration policies should remain the same as opposed to being decreased (Sanchez 2006).

I also include controls for generational status, discrimination and perceptions of commonality, and other measures of acculturation. Immigrants often possess a different set of orientations and reactions to the same situation and context from their U.S.-born counterparts. This is indeed the case with immigration policy, as native-born Latinos tend to favor more restrictive policies than do foreign-born Latinos (Binder, Polinard, and Wrinkle 1997). As might be expected, the perception that racial discrimination exists in society and that these inequalities are based on ethnicity and phenotype may facilitate racial group attachment, which could lead to varying opinions. In a study of Latino public opinion, Sanchez (2006) found that Latinos who believe that discrimination against Latinos in society is a problem are more likely to favor increasing immigration and are more likely to support bilingual education than are those who believe that discrimination is not a problem. Similarly, we might also expect Latinos who feel a sense of commonality with a specific racial group to develop attitudes closer to the group they feel attached to (*Political/socioeconomic commonality with Whites/Blacks*). *Discrimination* is a five-point scale that ranges from 0 to 4. Perceptions that discrimination is a result of being Latino or because of skin color are binary variables. I also control for perceptions of linked fate with African Americans and Latinos.

Several works also note the significant relationship between acculturation and Latino policy attitudes (e.g., Miller, Polinard, and Wrinkle 1984; Polinard, Wrinkle, and de la Garza 1984; Branton 2007). When compared to less acculturated Latinos, English-language-dominant Latinos furthest removed from the immigrant experience tend to be less supportive of increased government spending, are less likely to believe that the government is doing the best job of providing services to the needy, are less likely to support affirmative action, and are less likely to think that parents' top priority is to help a failing school (Branton 2007, 298). Thus, one might expect to find that language competence is highly predictive of Latino public opinion. In addition to generational status, acculturation includes two measures of respondent language preferences measuring whether the interview was conducted in English (*English interview*) and the respondent's desire to preserve Spanish-language skills (*Keep Spanish language*).[9]

Predicting Latino Public Opinion

The first set of multivariate results are presented in table 8.1. The key independent variables are measures of racial identity (White Latino is the category of reference). Here we see that racial identity influences Latino policy attitudes, yet this influence is not consistent across all measures of public opinion. While there is no difference in opinion among Latino racial groups about a preferred policy on illegal immigration, the results show that Latinos who racially self-identify as "some other race" are significantly more likely to believe that immigrants strengthen the country. This provides some evidence to suggest that differences in opinion exist beyond issues on which White-Black attitudes have long been bifurcated and that there are clear racial differences in opinion on Latino salient issues. "Some other race" Latinos are also more likely to believe that government should provide income support and believe that the health care system needs government intervention. This is consistent with previous research that has found clear racial differences in Latino opinion on implicitly racial policies (Nicholson, Pantoja, and Segura 2005).

The results also demonstrate that variability in attitudes among Latinos as a function of race exists across a range of policy issues.[10] Respondents' attitudes about vouchers, same-sex marriage, and abortion are all significantly related to racial identity. "Some other race" Latinos are more likely to support vouchers. This finding is particularly interesting because while it is often assumed that African American and Latino educational interests are closely related or even identical because they share similar objective circumstances, Latinos tend to be more supportive than African Americans of voucher programs and standards-based education reforms including high-stakes testing (Leal 2004b; Moe 2001; Lay and Stokes-Brown 2009). The fact that most Latinos self-identify as "some other race," coupled with the finding that "some other race" Latinos are more supportive of this reform than are other Latino racial groups, may help us better understand why we see differences in African American and Latino opinion on this issue. There are also significant racial differences in Latino opinion about same-sex marriage and abortion. Predicted probabilities (not shown) reveal that Black Latinos express the highest levels of support for legalizing same-sex marriage. Also, while the opinions of "some other race" and White Latinos are more similar to each other than to the opinions of Black Latinos, "some other race" Latinos are significantly more likely to believe that same-sex marriage should receive no legal recognition. "Some other race" Latinos are also more likely to have prolife attitudes.

Other general patterns are clear from this table. Whereas extant research shows that generational status impacts Latino opinions toward Latino salient issues like immigration (e.g., Branton 2007; García Bedolla 2005; Hood, Morris, and Shirkey 1997), the results show that generational status is also predictive of Latino attitudes about implicitly racial issues. Later-generation Latinos are less likely to have a positive view of immigrants and support liberal immigration policies but are more

Table 8.1: The Impact of Racial Identity on Latino Policy Attitudes

	Immigrants	Illegal immigration	Government spending	Health care	Standardized tests	Support for vouchers	Same-sex marriage	Abortion
Black	−.24	−.12	−.07	−.04	.01	.56	.70*	−.19
	(.75)	(.27)	(.19)	(.23)	(.35)	(.45)	(.38)	(.54)
Some other race	.43***	.07	.08*	.12**	−.03	.12*	−.22**	−.15*
	(.15)	(.05)	(.04)	(.05)	(.06)	(.06)	(.09)	(.07)
Mexican	.30*	.10*	−.05	−.03	−.10	−.10	−.05	.04
	(.19)	(.05)	(.06)	(.06)	(.07)	(.07)	(.10)	(.09)
Puerto Rican	−.24	−.04	.34***	.24**	−.06	.02	.23	.21
	(.26)	(.09)	(.09)	(.10)	(.13)	(.13)	(.17)	(.15)
Cuban	.19	.00	.04	.25**	−.19	−.22*	.02	.16
	(.30)	(.10)	(.09)	(.10)	(.14)	(.14)	(.15)	(.14)
Dominican	−.10	−.09	.12	.13	−.08	.13	−.03	−.05
	(.37)	(.11)	(.11)	(.10)	(.15)	(.15)	(.20)	(.14)
Skin color	−.10	−.05**	−.00	−.04*	−.01	.05*	.06	−.04*
	(.06)	(.02)	(.02)	(.02)	(.03)	(.03)	(.04)	(.03)
Female	.07	.17***	.02	.08*	−.13**	−.04	.14*	.02
	(.12)	(.04)	(.04)	(.04)	(.05)	(.06)	(.07)	(.06)
Age	−.01**	−.01**	−.00	.01**	.01***	.00	−.02***	−.01**
	(.00)	(.00)	(.01)	(.00)	(.00)	(.01)	(.00)	(.00)
Generation	−.30***	−.14***	.04*	−.03	−.03	−.04	.09*	.06
	(.07)	(.02)	(.02)	(.02)	(.04)	(.03)	(.04)	(.04)
Income	.00	−.01**	−.01***	.00	.00	−.01*	.00	.01***
	(.01)	(.00)	(.00)	(.01)	(.01)	(.00)	(.01)	(.00)
Education	.00	−.04***	−.02*	.00	−.03*	−.01	.04	.07***
	(.05)	(.01)	(.01)	(.01)	(.01)	(.02)	(.02)	(.02)
Social commonality with Blacks	−.01	.05**	.04*	.01	−.04	−.01	.10*	.06*
	(.07)	(.02)	(.02)	(.02)	(.03)	(.03)	(.04)	(.03)
Social commonality with Whites	−.08	−.02	−.05**	−.03	.09**	.04	−.10*	−.03
	(.09)	(.03)	(.02)	(.02)	(.03)	(.03)	(.05)	(.05)
Political commonality with Blacks	.09	−.01	.01	.05*	−.02	−.03	.06	.04
	(.08)	(.25)	(.03)	(.02)	(.03)	(.02)	(.04)	(.05)
Political commonality with Whites	−.03	−.02	.00	−.08**	−.04	.08**	.00	−.02
	(.08)	(.03)	(.02)	(.03)	(.03)	(.03)	(.05)	(.04)
Discrimination (scale)	−.06	.02	.01	.10***	−.04	−.01	.08*	.03
	(.07)	(.03)	(.03)	(.03)	(.03)	(.03)	(.04)	(.04)

	(1)	(2)	(3)	(4)	(5)	(6)	(7)
Discrimination because respondent is Latino	.39*	.05	.03	.02	-.05	-.14	-.01
	(.20)	(.07)	(.07)	(.09)	(.10)	(.11)	(.09)
Discrimination because of color	.37	-.07	-.04	-.04	.00	-.11	.03
	(.27)	(.09)	(.10)	(.14)	(.13)	(.16)	(.12)
Linked fate with Blacks	.05	.06**	.06**	-.02	-.01	-.01	-.07**
	(.06)	(.02)	(.02)	(.03)	(.03)	(.04)	(.03)
Linked fate with Latinos	.11*	.06**	.06**	.03	.04	.04	-.03
	(.07)	(.02)	(.03)	(.03)	(.03)	(.05)	(.04)
English interview	-1.32***	-.21***	-.23***	.32***	-.72***	.17*	.31***
	(.21)	(.05)	(.06)	(.07)	(.07)	(.10)	(.08)
Keep Spanish language	.34***	.07*	-.01	.02	-.00	.01	-.17**
	(.10)	(.05)	(.04)	(.05)	(.05)	(.07)	(.06)
Constant/Cut1	1.85	-1.42	-1.56	-.87	-1.00	.01	-1.52
	(.57)	(.23)	(.22)	(.28)	(.30)	(.40)	(.32)
Cut 2	—	-.89	-1.12	-.32	-.27	.38	.15
		(.22)	(.22)	(.26)	(.29)	(.40)	(.32)
Cut 3	—	.30	.04	.53	.48	—	.57
		(.22)	(.22)	(.27)	(.29)		(.31)
Wald χ²	298.16	244.53	148.13	70.95	297.48	128.74	236.56
Observations	4225	4291	4310	2057	2066	1472	2025

* significant at p < .05, ** significant at p < .01 *** significant at p < .001

Note: Estimates are logit and ordered probit coefficients. Standard errors are in parentheses.

likely to support government spending and same-sex marriage. National origin and phenotype are also significantly related to Latino policy attitudes. Mexicans are more likely to have positive views about immigration, believing that immigrants strengthen the country and favoring immigration reforms. Puerto Ricans are significantly more supportive of government spending for income support and health care. Cubans are also more likely to support government spending for health care but are less likely to support the use of vouchers. The results also show that skin color influences public opinion, as Latinos with lighter skin tones are less supportive of immigration efforts, government intervention to improve health care, and abortion but are significantly more likely to support the use of vouchers to send children to private schools. Furthermore, there are significant gender differences in Latino opinion. Latinas tend to hold more liberal attitudes than Latino males—women are significantly more likely to favor legalization for illegal immigrants and government spending for health care. Being a woman is also associated with greater support for same-sex marriage, but Latinas tend to be less supportive of standardized tests. Age is also a significant predictor of Latino opinion, as older Latinos are much more likely to oppose policies that favor immigrants, same-sex marriage, and abortion but are more likely than younger Latinos to support government intervention for health care and standardized tests.

There is also evidence to suggest that predictions of Latino policy attitudes should take into account socioeconomic factors. Respondents with higher levels of income and education are less likely to support liberal immigration policies and are more likely to oppose government spending. Yet these respondents tend to have more liberal, prochoice attitudes about abortion. Interestingly, the results also show that education attainment negatively predicts support for standardized tests, and income negatively predicts support for vouchers. Highly educated Latinos are much more likely to oppose the use of standardized tests to determine promotion or graduation, and affluent Latinos are more likely to oppose the use of vouchers to send children to private schools.

It is also the case that intergroup perceptions, experiences with discrimination, and feelings of linked fate are important contributing factors to Latino policy attitudes. Latinos who perceive socioeconomic commonality with Blacks have more liberal attitudes about illegal immigration, government spending, same-sex marriage, and abortion. Perceived socioeconomic commonality with Whites negatively predicts support for same-sex marriage but is a positive predictor of support for standardized tests. Political commonality is also predictive of Latino attitudes—Latinos who express political commonality with Blacks are more likely to support government intervention to improve health care, whereas Latinos who express political commonality with Whites are less supportive of that policy. Political commonality with Whites is also a significant and positive predictor of support for vouchers.

The linked fate variables are also significant for some policy issues. A sense of linked fate with African Americans negatively predicts Latinos' support for abortion. While Latinos who believe that the success of their national-origin group is tied to other national-origin groups are more likely to believe that immigrants strengthen the nation, Latinos who feel a sense of linked fate with African Americans are more likely to support more liberal immigration policies. It is also worth noting that a sense of linked fate with both other Latinos and African Americans positively predicts support for both implicitly racial policies—governmental income support and government intervention to reform health care. Perceived discrimination is also significant, as Latinos who have experienced some level of discrimination are more likely to support government intervention to improve health care and have more liberal attitudes toward same-sex marriage. Latinos who believe that being Latino was the reason for a discriminatory experience are more likely to believe that immigrants strengthen the country.

Finally, consistent with extant research (e.g., Branton 2007), measures of acculturation have a significant impact on Latino attitudes. Preferring to be interviewed in English (commonly noted as a measure of language proficiency) is highly predictive across almost every policy item. These respondents are more likely to hold negative views of immigrants and are less likely to favor liberal immigration policies. They are also less likely to favor government spending and government intervention for health care reform. Most of these attitudes are opposite of those who are attached to Spanish-language use. These respondents are much more likely to think that immigrants strengthen the country and are supportive of government spending. English-dominant speakers also have distinct opinions about education, as they are more likely to favor standardized tests but oppose vouchers. Language preference also divides Latino opinion on abortion and same-sex marriage. Respondents who prefer to be interviewed in English are more likely to adopt prochoice attitudes and be supportive of same-sex marriage, while respondents who are concerned about maintaining the ability to speak Spanish are more likely to be prolife.

Differences in Opinion among "Some Other Race" Latinos?

Recall that while a majority of Latinos choose to identify as "some other race," a majority of respondents clarified their response and racially self-identified as "Hispanic" or "Latino." Furthermore, almost half of these respondents also believe that Latinos are a distinctive race category. The multivariate analyses in table 8.2 show the coefficient for the variables of interest (racial identity) from regression analyses predicting levels of support for each public policy. Each regression model includes the independent variables listed in table 8.1. Conceptually, each racial category represents a point on the continuum of racialized Latino identity. Whereas "some other race" is a general, nondescript category, the other categories represent an increasing awareness and acceptance of "Hispanic/Latino" as a distinct race in the U.S. racial hierarchy.

The results show that the patterns of racial difference in Latino public opinion are somewhat similar among these three "some other race" groups. Much like "some other race" Latinos, respondents who when prompted self-identified as "Hispanic/Latino" (SOR_Latino) and those who also believe that Latinos are a distinct racial group (Latino_R) are significantly more likely to support the use of vouchers and oppose same-sex marriage. However, there are some important differences. "Some other race" Latinos and SOR_Latinos are more likely to have positive views of immigrants, are more likely to favor government intervention to improve health care, and more are likely to hold prolife attitudes. Interestingly, for the aforementioned issue

Table 8.2: "Some Other Race" Latinos' Policy Attitudes

	Some other race	SOR_Latino[a]	Latino_R[b]
Immigrants strengthen country	.43**	.41***	.12
	(.15)	(.13)	(.13)
Illegal immigration	.07	.05	−.02
	(.05)	(.04)	(.04)
Government spending	.08*	.05	.03
	(.05)	(.04)	(.04)
Health care	.12**	.09**	.06
	(.05)	(.04)	(.04)
Standardized tests	−.03	.04	.14**
	(.06)	(.05)	(.06)
Support for vouchers	.12*	.11*	.10*
	(.06)	(.06)	(.06)
Same-sex marriage	−.22**	−.17**	−.18**
	(.09)	(.07)	(.08)
Abortion	−.14*	−.10*	−.06
	(.07)	(.06)	(.07)

* significant at p < .05, ** significant at p < .01, *** significant at p < .001

Note: Model was estimated with the variable representing Black identity (White identity is the reference category) and the following control variables: Mexican, Puerto Rican, Cuban, Dominican, Skin color, Female, Age, Generation, Income, Education, Socioeconomic commonality with Blacks, Socioeconomic commonality with Whites, Political commonality with Blacks, Political commonality with Whites, Discrimination, Discrimination because respondent is Latino, Discrimination because of skin color, Linked fate with Blacks, Linked fate with Latinos, English interview, Keep Spanish language. Estimates are logit and ordered probit coefficients. Standard errors are in parentheses.

[a] Represents respondents who self-identified as "Latino/Hispanic" after initially self-identifying as "some other race."

[b] Represents respondents who self-identified as "Latino/Hispanic" after initially self-identifying as "some other race" and believe that Latinos/Hispanics make up a distinctive racial group in America.

areas, the opinions of Latinos in the third group (in which a racialized conceptualization of Latino identity is most evident) are not statistically different from those of White Latinos. It is also worth noting that some groups have uniquely different perspectives. While "some other race" Latinos are significantly more likely to support governmental income support for those who need it, the opinions of respondents in the other "some other race" categories are not statistically different from those of white Latinos. This pattern also holds for attitudes about standardized tests—only those with a racialized conceptualization of "some other race" identity are significantly more likely to support the use of these tests for promotion and graduation.

The Interactive Effect of Racial Identity and Generational Status

Thus far, the results suggest that racial identity has political meaning for Latinos. However, in light of immigration's seminal role in shaping the Latino population, generational status is a key characteristic. Because immigrants may possess a different set of orientations and reactions to the same situation and context from their U.S.-born counterparts, it may be useful to also examine how generational status conditions the influence of racial identity on Latino policy attitudes.[11] The multivariate analyses in table 8.3 show the coefficients for the variables of interest (race variables, generation, and interaction variables). Although not shown, each regression model includes the independent variables listed in table 8.1. Here we see statistically discernable differences in the effect of generational status across Latino racial groups. The effect of generational status among Black Latinos is larger than that for White Latinos (the reference group). In other words, as generation level increases (moving from first to fourth), so too does the belief among Black Latinos that immigrants strengthen the nation. A similar statistically significant effect for Black Latinos is present in the vouchers model.

Why do we see the effect of generation vary between White and Black Latinos? It is somewhat difficult to answer this question because very little political science literature explores the role of Black Latinos in Latino politics (but see Nicholson, Pantoja, and Segura 2005; Stokes-Brown 2006, 2009). While the literature is limited (for greater discussion, see Affigne 2007), we do know that the nation's Black Latino population is partly the result of intermarriage. Black Latinos are less likely to be immigrants than are Latinos from other racial groups (Logan 2003) and are often the children of non-Hispanic Black and Latino parents (Logan 2003; Nicholson, Pantoja, and Segura 2005). The Black Latino population is also a result of immigration. Thus, it is possible that for Black Latinos (more so than for other Latino racial groups), generational status creates a distinct cleavage between those who are immigrants (and express norms from their home country) and those who are native-born (and have perhaps a uniquely different experience and perspective as the children of native-born African Americans and second- and third-plus-generation Latinos). This cleavage may be more pronounced because the Black Latino sample contains a higher proportion of immigrants (63 percent) than those in Census data (28 percent) (Logan 2003). Thus, the highly unrepresentative

Table 8.3. The Impact of Racial Identity and Generational Status on Latino Policy Attitudes

	Immigrants	Illegal imm.	Gov. spending	Health care	Stand. tests	Support for vouchers	Same-sex marriage	Abortion
Black	−2.84***	−.28	−.17	−.41	−.29	−.84	.25	−1.52
	(.98)	(.49)	(.34)	(.36)	(.71)	(.56)	(.84)	(1.03)
Some other race	.39	.01	.03	.14	.10	.06	−.11	−.11
	(.14)	(.09)	(.08)	(.09)	(.12)	(.11)	(.16)	(.12)
Generation	−.33***	−.17***	.03	−.02	.03	−.06	.14*	.07
	(.11)	(.04)	(.04)	(.04)	(.05)	(.05)	(.07)	(.06)
Black*Generation	1.33**	.08	.06	.20	.10	.69*	.27	.82
	(.45)	(.16)	(.16)	(.21)	(.30)	(.32)	(.37)	(.57)
Some other race*Generation	.02	.03	.02	−.01	−.08	.03	−.05	−.01
	(.12)	(.05)	(.04)	(.05)	(.05)	(.05)	(.07)	(.07)
Constant/Cut1	1.84	−2.19	−1.46	−1.54	.73	−1.04	.10	−1.52
	(.59)	(.24)	(.23)	(.23)	(.29)	(.30)	(.41)	(.32)
Cut 2	—	−1.38	−.94	−1.10	−.18	−.30	.46	.15
		(.24)	(.24)	(.22)	(.29)	(.31)	(.42)	(.33)
Cut 3	—	−.14	.26	−.01	.67	.45	—	.58
		(.24)	(.23)	(.23)	(.28)	(.30)		(.33)
Wald χ²	322.54	600.53	244.79	150.65	73.70	305.89	133.77	237.68
Observations	4532	4225	4291	4310	2057	2066	1472	2025

* significant at p < .05, ** significant at p < .01, *** significant at p < .001

Note: Model was estimated with the following control variables: Mexican, Puerto Rican, Cuban, Dominican, Skin color, Female, Age, Generation, Income, Education, Socioeconomic commonality with Blacks, Socioeconomic commonality with Whites, Political commonality with Blacks, Political commonality with Whites, Discrimination, Discrimination because respondent is Latino, Discrimination because of skin color, Linked fate with Blacks, Linked fate with Latinos, English interview, Keep Spanish language. Estimates are logit and ordered probit coefficients. Standard errors are in parentheses.

percentage of first-generation Black Latinos in the sample may further heighten the effect of racial identity.

To the extent that the effect of generational status varies among Latino racial groups, this finding has important implications, providing additional evidence that Black Latino identity matters. When the interaction between racial identity and generation is excluded, the only significant relationship between Black racial identity and policy attitudes is found for the issue of same-sex marriage. However, as the results in table 8.3 show, when generational diversity within Latino racial groups is considered, Black Latinos have a unique perspective on some Latino salient and high-profile political issues.

Conclusion

Drawing on recent works that show distinct differences among Latino racial groups, this chapter contributes to this body of research, examining the influence of racial identity on Latino policy attitudes. The results show that the personal and social construction of one's identity has implications for Latino public opinion, as race is a significant determinant of Latino attitudes about Latino salient, racially implicit, and high-profile political issues. "Some other race" Latinos are significantly more likely to believe that immigrants strengthen the country and are more likely to support governmental income support for the poor, government intervention for the health care system, and vouchers and are less likely to support same-sex marriage and abortion. Black Latinos are significantly more likely to support same-sex marriage. The results also show that there are significant differences in the effect of generational status across Latino racial groups. More so than for any other group, generational shifts among Black Latinos are related to more positive views of immigrants and support for vouchers. These findings are an important contribution to the growing Latino politics literature which embraces the salience of multiple identities in shaping political attitudes.

This research has several implications. First, it informs scholarly debates about how "best" to measure and classify the Latino population. Some scholars argue that it is best to solicit Latino identification in a separate question to maximize Latino identification and population count (e.g., Campbell and Rogalin 2006).[12] However, a severe disadvantage of this strategy is that most Latinos racially self-identify as "some other race," a term that is not ordinarily used by individuals to describe themselves. So as Sonya Tafoya notes in her study of Latinos, "who are the some-other-race Hispanics? And, what are they trying to tell us with their choice of this label?" (2004, 1). The survey design adopted in the LNS provides a rare opportunity to examine this racial group in-depth. Undoubtedly the use of closed-ended questions asks respondents to self-identify from a list of externally imposed racial categories—categories that are ultimately used for political purposes including the allocation of resources and documenting inequality. However, allowing respondents to express in their own words what "some other race" identification means provides detailed responses that can then be used to better understand who these Latinos are and how their understanding of that racial label influences their perspectives and beliefs. Question formats influence identification patterns (e.g.. Campbell and

Key Findings

- Latinos who self-identify as "some other race" are significantly more likely than others, to believe that (1) immigrants strengthen the country; (2) government should provide income support; and (3) the health care system needs government intervention. They are also more likely to support vouchers, oppose same-sex marriage, and have prolife attitudes.

- Black Latinos are more likely to express support for the legalization of same-sex marriage.

- There are significant differences in opinion, however, even among Latinos who self-identify as "some other race," depending on whether they have a racialized conceptualization of Latino identity; those who think of themselves in racial terms do not have statistically different views from White and Black Latinos on immigrants, health care, and abortion. These Latinos are also more likely to support the use of standardized tests for promotion and graduation.

- Generational status mediates the views of Black Latinos. Among later cohorts of Black Latinos, moving from the first to the fourth generation, the belief that immigrants strengthen the nation and support for school vouchers both become more prevalent.

Rogalin 2006), and the LNS survey design clearly shows that it is possible using externally imposed racial categories to further disaggregate the Latino population —a goal that most scholars would agree is desired and necessary.

This research also has significant implications for the future study of U.S. race relations. As a result of the changing population, scholarly debates have ensued over how racial self-identification within the Latino community might affect future racial identification patterns. One perspective predicts that the existing racial hierarchy of White/non-White will prevail, as Latinos will incorporate as racialized minorities who exist as part of a large community made up of "people of color" (e.g., Skrentny 2002). A second perspective suggests that the U.S. will maintain a binary system, yet our understanding of who is White will shift as this category expands to incorporate Latinos and Asian Americans (e.g., Warren and Twine 1997; Yancey 2003; Gans 1999; Lee and Bean 2007). A third perspective suggests that the existing racial hierarchy will evolve into a three-tier racial model of race relations in which Latinos will be an intermediate category between Whites and Blacks (Forman, Goar, and Lewis 2002; Duany 2005; Bonilla-Silva et al. 2003; Bonilla-Silva 2004). The fact that a significant number of "some other race" respondents racially self-identify as Latino or Hispanic is supportive of others' claim that Latinos can develop unique conceptions of their racial identities as they learn to adapt to the rigid racial categories they encounter in the United States. Thus, the data from the LNS provide some support for predictions that Latinos may eventually occupy a unique position in the U.S. racial structure.

Finally, the results and implications of this research should not be lost on those who seek to bridge Latinos together through common interests (García 2003). Efforts to advance and sustain Latino political power will not be effective unless political and community actors better understand how Latinos view themselves and how their identities inform political judgments. Just as there are contradictory interests among Latinos of different national origins, the growing racial divide among Latinos suggests that it may become necessary to address contradictory interests among Latinos who self-identify with various racial categories.

Study Questions

1. What is the most common racial identity chosen by LNS respondents? How does the author attempt to better understand that racial identity?

2. The chapter uses a social identity framework and suggests that racial self-identification within the Latino community influences individual policy attitudes. How useful is this theory in helping us understand the relationship between Latino racial identity and political attitudes and behaviors?

3. The chapter suggests that the current strategy adopted by the government to measure and classify the Latino population can be improved on, to further disaggregate this population. What improvements are suggested? Do you find them to be useful? Why or why not?

4. Given the multivariate results presented in table 8.1, how does racial identity influence Latino policy attitudes? How are respondents' attitudes about these issues related to racial identity?

5. The chapter suggests that Latinos may eventually occupy a unique position in racial structure, negotiating the racial middle. How does the reality of this racial middle differ from the existing racial hierarchy? Do you agree with this conclusion? Why or why not?

Appendix 8A: Variable Construction for Independent Variables

BLACK	Indicates Black self-identification (0,1)
SOME OTHER RACE	Indicates "some other race" identification (0,1)
SOR_LATINO	Initial "some other race" identification; when prompted "Hispanic/Latino" identification (0,1)
SOR_LATINO (R)	Initial "some other race" identification; when prompted "Hispanic/Latino" identification (0,1) *and* belief that Latinos are a distinctive racial category in the U.S. (0,1)
MEXICAN	Mexican ancestry (0,1)
CUBAN	Cuban ancestry (0,1)
PUERTO RICAN	Puerto Rican ancestry (0,1)
DOMINICAN	Dominican ancestry (0,1)
SKIN COLOR	Respondent skin color (self-report) (0 = very light, 1 = light, 2 = medium, 3 = dark, 4 = very dark)
FEMALE	Indicates respondent gender (1,0)
AGE	Indicates respondent age (18–98)

GENER	Indicates generational status. First-generation Latinos are those born outside the United States or on the island of Puerto Rico, naturalized U.S. citizens, legal immigrants, and undocumented immigrants. Second-generation Latinos are those born in the U.S. to at least one foreign-born parent. Third- or higher-generation Latinos are those born in the U.S. to U.S.-born parents.
INCOME	Indicates household income (ranges from 0 = below $15,000 to 6 = above $65,000)
EDUCATION	Indicates respondent education level (ranges from 0 = no formal education to 7 = graduate or professional degree)
SOCIOECONOMIC COMMONALITY WITH BLACKS/WHITES	Indicates perceived commonality with other racial groups concerning issues including job opportunities, educational attainment, and income (ranges from 0 = nothing to 3 = a lot)
POLITICAL COMMONALITY WITH BLACKS/WHITES	Indicates perceived commonality with other racial groups concerning political issues including government services and employment, political power, and representation (ranges from 0 = nothing to 3 = a lot)
DISCRIMINATION	Indicates perceived level of discrimination. Respondents were asked, "In the following questions we are interested in your beliefs about the way other people have treated you in the U.S. Have you ever been 1) unfairly fired or denied a job or promotion? 2) unfairly treated by the police? 3) unfairly prevented from moving into a neighborhood (vecindario or barrio) because the landlord or a realtor refused to sell or rent you a house or apartment? 4) treated unfairly or badly at restaurants or stores?" (affirmative responses were coded 1 and added together to create a discrimination scale that ranges from 0 = no experience with discrimination to 4 = experience discrimination in all four areas)
DISCRIMINATION B/C R IS LATINO	Indicates perceived explanation for discrimination experience. Respondents were asked, "There are lots of possible reasons why people might be treated unfairly. What do you think was the main reason for your experience(s)? Would you say . . . ?" (0,1)
DISCRIMINATION B/C R'S SKIN COLOR	Indicates perceived explanation for discrimination experience (0,1)
LINKED FATE WITH BLACKS	Indicates belief that Latinos' ability to "do well" is dependent on African Americans doing well (ranges from 0 = nothing to 3 = a lot)
LINKED FATE WITH LATINOS	Indicates belief that respondent's national-origin group's ability to "do well" is dependent on other Latinos doing well (ranges from 0 = nothing to 3 = a lot)
ENGLISH INTERVIEW	Indicates the language of interview (1,0)
KEEP SPANISH LANGUAGE	Indicates desire to preserve Spanish-language skills (ranges from 0 = not at all important to 3 = very important)

Notes

1. Genaro C. Armas, "Census: Hispanics Pass Blacks as Largest U.S. Minority Group," Associated Press, FoxNews.com, January 21, 2003, http://www.foxnews.com/story/ 0,2933,76183,00.html; John Iwasaki, "The 2000 Census: Hispanics Surpass Blacks," *Seattle Post-Intelligencer*, January 21, 2003, http://www.seattlepi.com/news/article/The-2000 -Census-Hispanics-surpass-blacks-1105754.php.

2. While no one definition of "acculturation" exists, the existing research tends to measure acculturation by factors such as generational status, English-language competence, length of residency in the U.S., feelings toward one's native country, and commitment to native-country traditions.

3. It can be argued that the issue of school vouchers may be perceived as an implicitly racial issue by those who believe that vouchers may further exacerbate racial segregation in schools.

4. The first asks individuals to identify any Hispanic or Latino ethnic origin, while the second question asks individuals to identify with one or more racial categories.

5. Supporters also suggest that Latinos would maintain the opportunity like other respondents to choose more than one racial category. So Latino respondents could theoretically choose only the "Latino" racial category or choose the "Latino" racial category and another racial category (White, Black, etc.).

6. White, Black, and "some other race" Latinos make up 90 percent of the sample.

7. Respondents were asked to respond yes or no to the following question: "In the U.S., we use a number of categories to describe ourselves racially. Do you feel that Latinos/Hispanics make up a distinctive racial group in America?" It should be noted that this question follows the initial race question in the survey.

8. While persons of Mexican origin form the largest Latino population group in the U.S., sizable segments of the population also trace their ancestry to a wide range of countries and territories including Puerto Rico, Cuba, and the Dominican Republic (Pew Hispanic Center 2009).

9. See appendix 8A for the variable construction of independent variables.

10. It should be noted that the education policy questions (standardized tests, vouchers) and social issue questions (same-sex marriage, abortion) were asked of only half the respondents. It is not clear from the survey materials why this was done. In an effort to make sure that the results are not an artifact of which respondents were chosen to respond to these questions, each model was run a second time, using only those respondents who were asked about their overall evaluation of immigrants (*immigrants*). The use of this sample did not cause the regression results to change; thus, we can be confident that the survey's randomization process was successful.

11. Here the use of interaction terns is analogous to running separate regression models within each racial subgroup of interest (Friedrich 1982).

12. Using a combined race/ethnicity question lowers Latino population counts (Campbell and Rogalin 2006).

References

Affigne, Tony. 2007. "Negrura en Política: The Politics of Blackness in Latino Communities." Paper presented at the annual meeting of the American Political Science Association, Chicago, IL, August 30–September 2.

Aldrich, John H., and Forrest D. Nelson. 1984. *Linear Probability, Logit, and Probit Models.* Beverly Hills, CA: Sage.

Basler, Carleen. 2008. "White Dreams and Red Voters: Mexican Americans and the Lure of Inclusion in the Republican Party." *Ethnic and Racial Studies* 31 (1): 123–166.

Binder, Norman E., J. L. Polinard, and Robert D. Wrinkle. 1997. "Mexican American and Anglo Attitudes toward Immigration Reform: A View from the Border." *Social Science Quarterly* 78:324–337.

Bolks, Sean M., Diana Evans, J. L. Polinard, and Robert D. Wrinkle. 2000. "Core Beliefs and Abortion Attitudes: A Look at Latinos." *Social Science Quarterly* 81 (1): 253–260.

Bonilla-Silva, Eduardo. 2003. "From Bi-racial to Tri-racial: Towards a New System of Racial Stratification in the U.S.A." Paper presented at the Color Lines Conference, Harvard Law School, Cambridge, MA, 2003.

Bonilla-Silva, Eduardo. 2004. "From Bi-racial to Tri-racial: Towards a New System of Racial Stratification in the U.S.A." *Ethnic and Racial Studies* 27 (6): 931–950.

Bonilla-Silva, Eduardo, Tyrone Forman, Amanda Lewis, and David Embrick. 2003. "It Wasn't Me: How Will Race and Racism Work in 21st Century America." *Research in Political Sociology* 12:111–134.

Branton, Regina. 2007. "Latino Attitudes toward Various Areas of Public Policy: The Importance of Acculturation." *Political Research Quarterly* 60:293–303.

Brown, Terry D., Jr., Francis C. Dane, and Marcus D. Durham. 1998. "Perception of Race and Ethnicity." *Journal of Social Behavior and Personality* 13:295–306.

Campbell, Mary E., and Christabel L. Rogalin. 2006. "Categorical Imperatives: The Interaction of Latino and Racial Identification." *Social Science Quarterly* 87:1030–1052.

Cornell, Stephen, and Douglas Hartmann. 1998. *Ethnicity and Race: Making Identities in a Changing World*. Thousand Oaks, CA: Pine Forge.

Daniels, G. Reginald. 1999. "Either Black or White: Race Relations in Contemporary Brazil." In *Latin America: An Interdisciplinary Approach*, ed. Gladys M. Varona-Lacey and Julio López-Arias. New York: Peter Lang.

Dawson, Michael C. 1994. *Behind the Mule: Race and Class in African-American Politics*. Princeton: Princeton University Press.

de la Garza, Rodolfo O., Angelo Falcón, F. Chris Garcia, and John García. 1993. "Attitudes toward U.S. Immigration Policy." *Migration World Magazine* 21:13–16.

Duany, Jorge. 2005. "Neither White nor Black: The Representation of Racial Identity among Puerto Ricans on the Island and in the U.S. Mainland." In *Neither Enemies nor Friends: Latinos, Blacks, Afro-Latinos*, ed. Anani Dzidzienyo and Suzanne Oboler. New York: Palgrave Macmillan.

Ellison, Christopher G., Samuel Echevarría, and Brad Smith. 2005. "Religion and Abortion Attitudes among U.S. Hispanics: Findings from the 1990 Latino National Political Survey. *Social Science Quarterly* 86 (1): 192–208.

Forman, Tyrone, Carla Goar, and Amanda E. Lewis. 2002. "Neither Black nor White? An Empirical Test of the Latin Americanization Thesis." *Race & Society* 5:65–84.

Friedrich, Robert J. 1982. "In Defense of Multiplicative Terms in Multiple Regression Equations." *American Journal of Political Science* 26 (4): 797–833.

Gans, Herbert J. 1999. "The Possibility of a New Racial Hierarchy in the Twenty-First Century United States." In *The Cultural Territories of Race*, ed. Michele Lamont. Chicago: University of Chicago Press and Russell Sage Foundation.

García, John A. 2003. *Latino Politics in America: Community, Culture, and Interests*. Lanham, MD: Rowman and Littlefield.

García Bedolla, Lisa. 2005. *Fluid Borders: Latino Power, Identity, and Politics in Los Angeles*. Berkeley: University of California Press.

Greene, William H. 2003. *Economic Analysis*. 5th ed. Upper Saddle River, NJ: Prentice-Hall.

Hood, M. V., III, Irwin L. Morris, and Kurt A. Shirkey. 1997. "'¡Quedate o Vente!': Uncovering the

Determinants of Hispanic Public Opinion toward Immigration." *Political Research Quarterly* 50 (3): 627–647.

Itzigsohn, José, and Carlos Dore-Cabral. 2000. "Competing Identities? Race, Ethnicity and Pan-ethnicity among Dominicans in the United States." *Sociological Forum* 15 (2): 225–247.

Itzigsohn, José, Silvia Giorguli, and Obed Vazquez. 2005. "Immigrant Incorporation and Racial Identity: Racial Self-Identification among Dominican Immigrants." *Ethnic and Racial Studies* 28 (1): 50–78.

Lay, J. Celeste, and Atiya Kai Stokes-Brown. 2009. "Put to the Test: Racial and Socioeconomic Differences in Support for High-Stakes Testing." *American Politics Research* 37:429–448.

Leal, David L. 2004a. "Latino Public Opinion?" Paper presented at the Latino Politics: The State of the Discipline, conference sponsored by Texas A&M University and the University of Texas at Austin, College Station, TX, April 30–May 1.

Leal, David L. 2004b. "Latinos and School Vouchers: Testing the 'Minority Support' Hypothesis." *Social Science Quarterly* 85:1227–1237.

Lee, Jennifer, and Frank D. Bean. 2007. "Reinventing the Color Line: Immigration and America's New Racial/Ethnic Divide." *Social Forces* 86:561–586.

Logan, John. 2003. "How Race Counts for Hispanic Americans." Lewis Mumford Center for Comparative Urban and Regional Research. July 14. Available online at http://mumford.albany.edu/census/BlackLatinoReport/BlackLatino01.htm.

Marrow, Helen B. 2003. "To Be or Not to Be (Hispanic or Latino): Brazilian Racial and Ethnic Identity in the United States." *Ethnicities* 3:427–464.

Martinez-Ebers, Valerie, Luis Fraga, Linda Lopez, and Arturo Vega. 2000. "Latino Interests in Education, Health, and Criminal Justice Policy." *PS: Political Science & Politics* 33:547–554.

Michelson, Melissa R. 2001. "The Effect of National Mood on Mexican American Political Opinion." *Hispanic Journal of Behavioral Sciences* 23:57–70.

Moe, Terry. 2001. *Schools, Vouchers, and the American Public.* Washington, DC: Brookings Institution Press.

Montalvo, Frank F., and G. Edward Codina. 2001. "Skin Color and Latinos in the United States." *Ethnicities* 1:321–341.

Nicholson, Stephen P., Adrian D. Pantoja, and Gary M. Segura. 2005. "Race Matters: Latino Racial Identities and Political Beliefs." Paper presented at the annual meeting of the American Political Science Association, Washington, DC, September 1–4.

Oboler, Suzanne. 1992. "The Politics of Labeling: Latino/a Cultural Identities of Self and Others." *Latin American Perspectives* 19:18–36.

Pew Hispanic Center. 2009. *Statistical Portrait of Hispanics in the United States, 2007.* http://pewhispanic.org/factsheets/factsheet.php?FactsheetID=46.

Polinard, Jerry, Robert D. Wrinkle, and Rodolfo de la Garza. 1984. "Attitudes of Mexican Americans toward Irregular Mexican Immigration." *International Migration Review* 18:782–799.

Rodríguez, Clara E. 1992. "Race, Culture, and Latino 'Othernesss' in the 1980 Census." *Social Science Quarterly* 73:931–937.

Rodríguez, Clara E. 2000. *Changing Race: Latinos, the Census, and the History of Ethnicity in the United States.* New York: NYU Press.

Sanchez, Gabriel R. 2006. "The Role of Group Consciousness in Latino Public Opinion." *Political Research Quarterly* 59:435–446.

Schermerhorn, Richard A. 1978. *Comparative Racial and Ethnic Relations: A Framework for Theory and Research.* Chicago: University of Chicago Press.

Skrentny, John D. 2002. *The Minority Rights Revolution.* Cambridge: Harvard University Press.

Stokes-Brown, Atiya Kai. 2006. "Racial Identity and Latino Vote Choice." *American Politics Research* 34 (5): 627–652.

Stokes-Brown, Atiya Kai. 2009. "The Hidden Politics of Identity: Racial Self Identification and Latino Political Engagement." *Politics and Policy* 37:1281–1305.

Tafoya, Sonya M. 2004. *Shades of Belonging*. Washington, DC: Pew Hispanic Center.

Warren, Jonathan, and France Winddance Twine. 1997. "White Americans, the New Minority? Non-Blacks and the Ever-Expanding Boundaries of Whiteness." *Journal of Black Studies* 28 (2): 200–218.

Yancey, George. 2003. *Who Is White? Latinos, Asians, and the New Black/Nonblack Divide*. Boulder: CO: Lynne Rienner.

9

A "Southern Exception" in Black-Latino Attitudes?

Perceptions of Competition with African Americans and Other Latinos

MATT A. BARRETO AND GABRIEL R. SANCHEZ

One of the more surprising revelations in the 2010 Census was a dramatic increase in the number of Latinos living in the South. Between 2000 and 2010, the Hispanic population of the southern states grew by 57.3 percent, to 18.2 million persons. Georgia is now home to the nation's tenth-largest Latino population, and North Carolina is not far behind. At the same time, the Black population of the South grew less quickly, by 18.3 percent, but at 23.1 million persons, it is greater than the combined Black populations in the rest of the country and remains greater than that of southern Hispanics. Given the African American population's historic presence in the South, and its significant political empowerment there as well, what do these major demographic changes mean for the future of Black-Latino relations in the South? In this chapter, Barreto and Sanchez explore whether Hispanics in southern states perceive lesser, or greater, competition with African Americans and ask whether social proximity and Black concentration play roles in shaping those Latino perceptions.

The Latino Emergence in Southern States

Recent dramatic growth in Latino populations across the United States has captured the interest of academics and political observers, with special attention to the movement of Latinos, and particularly Latino immigrants, into regions of the country previously not associated with this population. In 1990, for example, Hispanics accounted for less than 2% of the population in twenty-two states (Garcia and Sanchez 2008). By 2000, however, there were only eleven states in which Hispanics constituted only 2% or less of the population, and Hispanics are now found in numbers above 1,000 in every one of the fifty states. This demographic shift has been most pronounced in the southern United States, as Latinos have almost doubled in numbers within this region from 1990 to 2000—from 6.8 million to almost 12 million (Guzmán 2001). In this same period, for example, the Latino population grew by an average of 308% in Arkansas, North Carolina, Georgia, Tennessee, South Carolina, and Alabama (Kochhar, Suro, and Tafoya 2005). This dramatic surge in population has led the Pew Hispanic Center to report that "the Hispanic population is growing faster in much of the South than anywhere else in the United States" (Kochhar, Suro, and Tafoya 2005).

The demographic trends associated with the Latino population in the South may have a marked impact on this region, an environment which has been defined historically by race relations. Although scholars and political observers have noted the importance of this demographic change, little work to date has examined the social and political consequences of the incorporation of a new ethnic group, neither

---

Research Questions

- Do Latinos living in the South, as compared to Latinos living outside the South, perceive greater competition with African Americans?

- Does having Black friends or Black co-workers improve Latino attitudes toward Blacks, with respect to perceptions of social, economic, and political competition?

- How does the existence of a large Black population at the county level impact Latino attitudes toward Blacks?

Black nor White, in a region where for nearly four centuries, social interactions have been based on a White-Black paradigm.

With this context in mind, we focus attention on relationships between Latinos and African Americans, using data from the Latino National Survey (LNS) to evaluate Latinos' perceptions of competition with African Americans. Our analysis is multifaceted, and in this chapter we test several distinct research hypotheses. We are particularly interested in identifying any possible differences in perceptions and attitudes toward Blacks, comparing Latinos who live in the South to those who live in other regions. We utilize the national LNS sample to determine if Latinos in the South are more or less likely to see African Americans as competitors or as a community with common interests with Latinos. One of the primary advantages of using the LNS is that we can conduct analyses within specific regions or individual states, using the survey's robust state-level sample sizes. This chapter capitalizes on this opportunity by isolating the LNS respondents from the southern states of Arkansas (n = 401), North Carolina (n = 401), Georgia (n = 400), and Florida (n = 800), in an additional investigation of determinants of perceptions of competition with Blacks within the region. The large Black population of these southern states—in the 2000 Census, the African American population share was 16.0% in Arkansas, 22.1% in North Carolina, 29.2% in Georgia, and 15.5% in Florida[1]—and the fact that virtually all social, cultural, and economic structures in the region have historically been defined by race provide an important and unique context to study Black-Latino relations.

Moreover, we contend that when assessing Latinos' attitudes toward African Americans, it may be important to take into account the attitudes of Latinos toward *other* groups—including Latino coethnics. In an earlier analysis utilizing the LNS (Barreto and Sanchez 2007) we suggested that a key feature of LNS data is the opportunity they provide to isolate Latino perceptions of competition with African Americans, while comparing them to perceptions of overall competition. In the current analysis, we build on that earlier working paper and illustrate the depth of the LNS, by utilizing our comparative perception measure in an analysis of the South. This research design will allow a comparison of results generated with the conventional approach to measurement of racial attitudes to results based on perceptions of competition between Latinos and African Americans relative to similar perceptions of competition with other Latinos.

Results from the full LNS sample suggest that Latinos actually view coethnics as a greater source of competition than they do Blacks when our standardized measure is used to interpret Latinos' perceptions of competition with African Americans. Similarly, perceptions of competition do not vary by region when the standard measure is utilized, but interestingly, when the relative competition measure is employed, we find that Latinos who live in southern states do have higher perceptions of competition with Blacks than do Latinos more generally. We believe that these trends provide a valuable addition to the extant literature focused on intergroup relations, by emphasizing that place and context matters to these dynamics. Finally, we find evidence that supports the notion that social interactions help influence Latinos' attitudes toward Blacks. However, our results build on the extant literature by emphasizing that it is critical to take into account the nature of the interactions that take place between groups, not just the extent to which these interactions are occurring. This is reflected in our finding that having African American friends leads to more positive attitudes toward Blacks in general, particularly in the South.

Race Relations in the New South

The regional dynamics of the South provide a unique opportunity to examine perceptions of competition among Latinos and African Americans. Political scientists have noted the unique political culture of the South, particularly the distinctive voting behavior of southern residents (Frymer, Kim, and Bimes 1997; Burden and Kimball 2002; Wattenberg 2002). Scholars have discussed the recent transformation of the "New South" due to overall population growth (a 17% increase in population from 1990 to 2000) and increases in education, income, and age over time as well (Hillygus and Shields 2008; Cobb 1993). Arguably, the greatest demographic change in this region, however, has been the explosion of the Latino population. This demographic shift has led Roberto Suro and Audrey Singer (2002) of the Pew Hispanic Center to refer to many cities in the South as "New Latino Destinations." Specifically, many locations throughout the South saw some of the largest increases in Latino population from 1980 to 2000, including 538% in Sarasota, 995% in Atlanta, 859% in Orlando, and 630% in Nashville. The state of North Carolina is a great example of this population growth, as Raleigh-Durham saw a striking 1,180% increase in Latino population from 1980 to 2000, Charlotte an increase of 932%, and a 962% increase in Greensboro. Suro and Singer contend that "these metropolitan areas epitomize the new economy of the 1990s with rapid development in the finance, business services, and high tech sectors" (2002, 5), which are responsible for a large share of this population growth.

This is an important point, as the influx of Latinos entering into the South is due to the region's fairly recent economic success. In comparison to other regions of the United States, employment in the South increased in six southern states by an average of 2.4%—larger than the national employment average (Kochhar, Suro, and Tafoya 2005). Given the size of the employment rate, employers across a variety of industries have sought unskilled and inexpensive labor (Torres 2000). While the majority of Latinos took jobs performing services, expansions in manufacturing and construction provided additional opportunities for Latinos to migrate from other areas in the U.S. as well as to immigrate directly to the South from Latin America (Kochhar, Suro, and Tafoya 2005). In South Carolina, for example, "Latinos held 20 percent of the state's meat industry jobs" (Torres 2000, 6). Furthermore, "in North Carolina and Georgia, increased labor demands in industry and construction led to a 75 percent increase in the Latino population" (Torres 2000, 6). The poultry-processing industry has been particularly successful in the South, with approximately half of all poultry processing in the country occurring in Georgia, Alabama, Arkansas, and North Carolina (Odem and Lacey 2009). Creating over 400,000 new jobs for Latinos in the areas of manufacturing, construction, and services, the South has provided job opportunities not present elsewhere in the United States (Kochhar, Suro, and Tafoya 2005).

Although the majority of Hispanic workers throughout the South have been concentrated in blue-collar occupations, it is important to note that Latinos are making rather significant inroads into white-collar occupations in this region as well. For example, between 1995 and 2005, just over 15,000 Hispanic workers filled jobs in office and administrative support occupations. Another 17,000 Hispanic workers filled jobs in professional, management, business, and financial occupations in North Carolina during the same period (Johnson and Kasarda 2009).

We consider whether the demographic changes fueled by this labor demand have impacted race relations within this region. While there have been some studies focused on the impact of Latino migration to the South on the region's economy (Murphy, Blanchard, and Hill 2001; Mohl 2003; Ciscel, Smith, and Mendoza 2003; Torres 2000; Kandel and Parrado 2004; Johnson and Kasarda 2009; Mohl 2009), there has been limited research exploring how the marked increases of Latinos have influenced intergroup relations in the South. We draw, however, from a growing literature focused on race relations in the South to develop our theory of Latino attitudes toward Blacks in this region.

In comparison to other regions of the United States, the South is populated by a large number of Blacks who have a long historical residence in this area and a relatively smaller but rapidly growing Latino population. Given the rate at which Latinos are entering into the region, social interaction between the two groups is likely to be higher than in areas with more traditional Latino neighborhoods. Thus, in sharp contrast to traditional Latino migration to southwestern cities with small African American populations and comparatively larger Hispanic populations, African Americans across the South outnumber Latinos (Schmidley 2003). More importantly, the South is a region where race has historically defined the social, economic, and political life of its residents (McClain et al. 2006; Stuesse 2009).

Latino newcomers to the South, however, are often unaware of these historical realities, which may have a direct impact on their perceptions of African Americans. This trend is reflected well from the following quote: "Many [Hispanic migrants] also lack knowledge of the social and political histories of the South and often find it difficult to empathize with the life experiences of their coworkers and neighbors who are often African American" (Stuesse 2009, 92). This lack of understanding may lead Hispanic workers in the South to have negative attitudes about their Black co-workers and neighbors. For example, Angela Stuesse's (2009) focus-group work in Mississippi indicates that most Hispanics accept the dominant ideology that Blacks are responsible for their disadvantaged economic condition.

The structural conditions of the South impact both African Americans and Latino newcomers individually as well as the intergroup relations between these groups. For example, the economic gap between Blacks and Whites, particularly in the rural South, has led to greater levels of both perceived and real competition between Latinos and Blacks in this region (McClain et al. 2009; Dunn, Aragonez, and Shivers 2005; Rich and Miranda 2005; Marrow 2009). Previous research has shown that these competitive environments can lead to greater levels of intergroup discrimination (Kasinitz et al. 2008; Marrow 2009). So while Latino immigrants report being discriminated against by Whites in the South, qualitative work in the region suggests that due to a perceived economic threat from immigrants, the hostility from poor Blacks is even greater (Marrow 2009).

Ongoing research by Paula McClain and her colleagues has illustrated this dynamic well within Raleigh-Durham, North Carolina. Raleigh-Durham is a city with a large Black population that lives below the poverty line (22% in 2000), along with a growing Latino population that is generally composed of unskilled workers with low levels of educational attainment (McClain et al. 2009). The economic gap between both groups and Whites led McClain et al. (2009) to suggest that Latino immigrants and the Black underclass of this city are likely to be in competition for the same low-paying jobs as well as social services. They found support for this contention, as survey data collected by the authors indicate that Blacks in Raleigh-Durham feel that Latino immigration threatens both their economic and political positions (McClain et al. 2009). In a related study, McClain et al. (2006) found that Latinos' stereotypes of Blacks in Raleigh-Durham are more negative than White stereotypes of Blacks. Specifically, nearly 57% of Latinos in this study felt that few or almost no Blacks could be trusted, and nearly 59% believed that few or almost no Blacks are hardworking (McClain et al. 2006, 578). Particularly when contrasted with Latinos' significantly less negative perceptions of Whites in the study, it appears as though Latinos (at least those in Raleigh-Durham) do not have strong feelings of commonality with Blacks. Furthermore, qualitative interviews from the state indicate that these attitudes are not confined to the metropolitan city of Raleigh-Durham. Helen Marrow's (2009) article finds that Latinos living in the more rural southeastern segment of the state share some of these stereotypical views of Blacks. Interviews with Latino immigrants from this study illustrate stereotypical views of African Americans in the state as "loud, violent, lazy, uneducated, dependent, and lacking in family values" (Marrow 2009, 1045). We are able to determine if these trends hold across a larger sample of Latino respondents in North Carolina, as well as whether Latinos in North Carolina are unique from those living in other southern states, through the large sample sizes of the LNS.

We believe that the unique cultural dynamics associated with the South as well as the recent Latino influx may heighten real and perceived competition among Latinos and African Americans. Given the size of the LNS nationwide sample, the LNS provides an opportunity to examine whether Latinos' perceptions of competition are distinct in the South as well as the ability to isolate respondents from several southern states to conduct multivariate analyses with this split sample. Our preceding discussion of this important region of the country motivates the following hypothesis:

> *Southern Hypothesis*: We anticipate that Latinos living in the South will have higher perceptions of competition with African Americans than those living outside of the South due to the unique demographic and cultural dynamics of this region.

The Impact of Social Interactions on Racial Attitudes

While our primary focus in this project is to examine the impact of region on Latino's attitudes toward African Americans, we are also interested in addressing another major question in the race-relations literature: what is the impact of social interaction on intergroup relations? Previous research focused on the relationship between the social contexts and the racial attitudes of Whites has produced mixed results. A number of studies exploring the *racial threat hypothesis* have found that larger populations of minority groups correspond with greater White racial animosity and/or prejudicial attitudes (Frisbie and Niedert 1977; Glaser 1994; Taylor 1998; Wright 1977). However, other studies report that racial contact lessens racial antagonism (Sigelman and Welch 1993; Welch et al. 2001; Powers and Ellison 1995). There is much less published research focused on the role of social interaction on minority attitudes toward each other. However, J. Eric Oliver and Janelle Wong (2003) find that negative stereotypes and perceptions of competition among both Blacks and Latinos decrease as their neighborhoods become more diverse. The authors speculate that this trend is a result of social interaction leading to greater tolerance among racial and ethnic groups. Scholars have added to this framework by finding that negative attitudes toward Latinos increase with higher concentrations of Latinos in the neighborhoods in which Black respondents live (Bobo and Hutchings 1996; Bobo and Johnson 2000; Cain, Citrin, and Wong 2000; Oliver and Wong 2003; Branton and Jones 2005) and when Blacks are disadvantaged economically relative to Latinos (Gay 2005; Oliver and Wong 2003).

We believe that the lack of clarity in this area of research is at least partially due to the inability of the typical research design to account for two important factors. First, most of the work in this area assumes a linear relationship between population increases and attitudes. Using a measure for the percentage or overall population of the target group within a geographical unit (city, county, neighborhood, etc.), such work hypothesizes that as this population increases, so will hostile or positive attitudes toward that target group. We question this assumption, as it seems likely that the impact of social context must vary according to the *relative* magnitude of change—not in some linear, arithmetic way. To illustrate, imagine that a county's Black population doubles from 10% to 20%. How could a similar change —measured as absolute or percentage increases—yield the same racial threat effect, if the starting point were, for example, much higher, as in a county whose 50% Black population increased to 60%? To the contrary, we believe that Latino perceptions of competition with African Americans will diminish significantly in majority and supermajority Black counties. Our argument is based on the notion that in areas where Blacks are the clear majority, Latinos will not see themselves as a viable challenger to the dominant African American population—thus decreasing perceptions of competition. Such contexts may also diminish hostility in the other direction, toward Latinos among Blacks, as any perceived threat from a rise in Latino population will be offset by the African American community's perception of its own strength in numbers. We are able to test this inference by applying a quadratic term to our Black population measure.

Second, the extant literature has not been able to account for the nature of perceived interactions among the populations under study. Specifically, this approach does not allow for the distinction of whether the presumed interactions between members of different racial and ethnic groups are positive or negative in nature. We contend that this is a critical yet often overlooked point. For example, having friendships with people of different racial and ethnic backgrounds may temper more general perceptions of competition with that group. There is evidence that accounting for this distinction is important, as having Black friends does in fact influence Whites' attitudes toward minority populations (Wilner Walkley, and Cook 1955; Cook 1963; Jackman and Crane 1986). This is reinforced by findings that suggest friendship with Whites has motivated more positive racial attitudes among African Americans (Ellison and Powers 1994; Sigelman and Welch 1993). This distinction has yet to be made, however, within the Latino population.

Contrary to interactions through friendship, high levels of social interaction in other contexts, including within the workplace, may heighten perceptions of competition due to this type of social interaction being more naturally competitive. Stuesse's (2009) focus-group work in Mississippi indicates that most Hispanics do not see much in common with their African American co-workers, often perceiving Blacks to be privileged and themselves and other Latinos to be exploited in the workforce. The most troubling outcome of Stuesse's work in the South is that these racial stereotypes are often advanced by management in an effort to divide the workforce along racial lines to prevent the formation of alliances. We therefore test the following hypotheses through the LNS, as this effort may provide important clarifications to our extant knowledge regarding the impact of social context and social interactions on Latinos' attitudes toward Blacks.

> *Social Interaction Hypothesis*: We anticipate finding a differential impact for our Black friends and Black co-workers measures, with Black friends producing positive attitudes and Black co-workers leading to greater perceptions of competition.
>
> *Nonlinear Hypothesis*: We anticipate that the impact of Black population on Latino attitudes toward Blacks will be nonlinear, possibly producing a curvilinear pattern in which the impact of Black population becomes less pronounced at levels beyond 50%.

The Impact of Relative Perceptions of Competition on Latinos' Attitudes toward Blacks

Finally, in addition to the ability to explore the impact of region and social interactions on Black-Latino relations, the LNS provides the opportunity to account for

Latinos' perceptions of competition with Blacks relative to perceptions of competition with other groups—including other Latinos. Previous work has found Latinos to have high perceptions of conflict and competition with African Americans. However, this research has not been able to control for general perceptions of conflict and/or competition. We contend that while it is plausible that Latinos maintain high levels of competition with Blacks, this trend may be tempered by perceptions of competition in general—including internal competition. Research interested in the contextual determinants of racial animosity among Whites has found that individuals faced with economic adversity tend to exhibit not only a generic distrust of out-groups but also feelings of relative deprivation, anxiety, and alienation (Oliver and Mendelberg 2000). Similarly, African Americans in urban ghettos tend to have a "deep suspicion of the motives of others, a marked lack of trust in the benevolent intentions of people and institutions" (Massey and Denton 1993, 172). Claudine Gay (2004) has also found that African Americans living in low-income neighborhoods tend to believe that racism limits their individual life chances, as well as the overall socioeconomic attainment of Blacks as a group. We contend that it is likely that Latinos, primarily those who are foreign-born, may have similar worldviews marked with perceptions of competition.

During the 1980s, many of the nation's major cities went through rapid demographic transformations, while government cutbacks left new immigrants and older residents in poor sections of these cities directly engaged in competition for scarce resources (Jones-Correa 2001). The upward concentration of wealth in the U.S. in the past two decades has been coupled with declines in real wages and lack of investments in urban neighborhoods, putting the Black and Latino working class in a disadvantaged position (Jennings 2003). Not surprisingly, foreign-born Latinos have been found to perceive greater competition with African Americans than do their native-born counterparts (Bobo and Hutchings 1996; Rodrigues and Segura 2004; Jones-Correa 2001; McClain et al. 2006).[2] However, we contend that this trend does not necessarily reflect hostility toward Blacks among Latinos but possibly a more general worldview that includes high perceptions of competition. Thus, Latinos may be just as likely (if not more likely) to perceive competition with other Latinos as they do with Blacks. By accounting for this important trend, we are able to isolate competitive attitudes toward African Americans from competitive perceptions more generally.

Due to these trends identified in the extant literature, we believe that it is vital to assess Latinos' perceptions of competition with Blacks relative to those same attitudes toward coethnics. Testing of the following hypothesis will therefore add significantly to our working knowledge of not only coalition politics among Latinos and African Americans but the nature of internal competition among Latinos as well.

> *Relative Perception of Competition Hypothesis*: We anticipate finding that seemingly high levels of perceived competition with Blacks among Latinos will become significantly tempered when perceptions of competition with coethnics is taken into account.

Data and Methods

As previously noted, the data for this study are from the 2006 Latino National Survey (LNS). The LNS was a national, bilingual, stratified-random-sample telephone survey of 8,634 Latino residents of the United States, with more than 165 question items to assess the qualitative nature of political and social life for Latinos in America. In this chapter, we utilize the national data but focus on responses from Latinos living in southern states,[3] including 1,440 interviews with respondents in Georgia, Arkansas, North Carolina, Virginia, and Washington, D.C. The universe for the survey was all adult Latinos (eighteen years of age and older), with surveys conducted in the preferred language of the respondent (English, Spanish, or both languages). The survey is particularly useful for our purposes because it contains a large sample of foreign-born Latinos, a group previously hypothesized to perceive, or to actually be in, greater competition with African Americans. Overall, 6,184 foreign-born Latinos are in the sample, including 1,219 in the South.

With the ability to account for perceptions of commonality and competition across various contexts, as well as the ability to analyze Latinos' perceptions of competition with African Americans relative to other Latinos, the LNS is the only dataset available to address the research questions driving this analysis. To take advantage of the unique approach and rich sample sizes of the LNS, we implement a wide range of statistical analyses to provide a comprehensive investigation of Latino perception of social and political competition with Blacks. The first stage of the analysis consists of a series of descriptive statistics to determine the degree to which Latinos perceive commonality or perceive African Americans to be competitors for economic and political resources relative to Latinos' perceived competition with other Latinos. Results are provided for South/non-South comparisons, as well as for specific southern states of interest.

We then present results from multivariate regression models to test a host of explanatory variables on overall perceptions of Black-Latino competition nationally and also in the South. In particular, we are interested in whether Latinos who regularly interact with African Americans as co-workers or friends or live in heavily Black areas are more or less likely to perceive competition with Blacks. The regression models provide the opportunity to determine whether the trends we identify with descriptive statistics hold true when other factors are accounted for. For example, we are able to directly test whether Latinos in the South have higher perceptions of competition with African Americans than do Latinos from other areas in the country when we control for other important factors, such as social class (income) and social interactions.

Although there has been a significant increase in the Latino population throughout the entire southern United States, the impacts of these demographic changes are likely to be mediated by preexisting political and social structures in specific southern states, as well as the characteristics of the Latino population that has migrated to specific location within the South. In short, there is a need to explore any potential differences across this region that may influence perceptions of competition and commonality among Latinos and Blacks. North Carolina, for example, is a very intriguing location to study Black-Latino relations, as this state has been defined as the premier "new destination," posting the greatest Latino population growth during the 1990s (Marrow 2009). There is also evidence that this state may be more institutionally receptive to Latino immigrants than other areas in the South are. For example, Marrow (2005) finds that North Carolina may have greater resources available to better incorporate Latino migrants to the state, specifically in the realms of the education and judicial systems. One of the primary advantages of the use of LNS for this project is the large sample of southern residents, which allows for the inclusion of dummy variables for multiple southern states. This will provide the opportunity to determine if Latino attitudes vary across the region.

Variable Construction

We think two important advances appear in our study. First, we conduct in-depth analyses of the South as compared to the non-South, a comparative feature absent from previous studies, perhaps for reasons of data limitations. Second, our dependent variables are *relative* measures of perceived competition. Most studies cited earlier rely on a single, unidirectional measure or index of Black-Latino competition, quantifying how Latinos perceive Blacks or how Blacks perceive Latinos. However, a Latino respondent's perception of Blacks alone is difficult to interpret without some knowledge of that same respondent's perceptions of a reference group. In this study, we construct a relative measure of Black-Latino competition on the basis of how much competition Latinos perceive with African Americans, compared to how much competition they see with other Latinos. For example, for the dependent variable "social trust," when on a 0–10 scale a respondent assigned "trust in Blacks" a value of 3, that response on its face would appear to be low and could be interpreted as an "anti-Black" attitude. However, if we asked that respondent how much she trusts other Latinos, and she reported the same value of 3, the full context suggests that the attitudes are not anti-Black but reflect low levels of trust in general, for both her own in-group and an out-group. Almost every previous study of Black-Latino conflict has relied on a single measure of positive or negative viewpoints toward just one group, either toward Blacks or toward Latinos. In this project, we utilize two series of questions within the LNS to create relative, comparative measures for Black-Latino competition, a potentially significant improvement for understanding race relations in the real world.

First, respondents were asked,

> Some have suggested that Latinos are in competition with African-Americans. After each of the next items, would you tell me if you believe there is strong competition, weak competition, or no competition at all with African-Americans? How about . . .
> . . . in getting jobs?
> . . . having access to education and quality schools?
> . . . getting jobs with the city or state government?
> . . . having Latino representatives in elected office?

From these four questions, we created an overall index of competition with African Americans, with a Cronbach alpha interitem covariance of .354 and a scale reliability of .793. However, this is only half of the story. We are interested in knowing whether the perceived competition is a unique Latino-versus-Black phenomenon or if competition is also perceived with other Latinos. Thus, we used the exact same series of questions asked later in the survey with respect to competition among Latinos: "Some have suggested that [respondent's country-of-ancestry group][4] are in competition with other Latinos. After each of the next items, would you tell me if you believe there is strong competition, weak competition, or no competition at all with other Latinos?" The same four items were used: jobs, education, government jobs, and elected representation. By combining the Black competition index with the Latino competition index, we are able to arrive at an overall relative measure of Black-Latino competition.

The combined index ranges from −8 to +8, where a value of −8 represents "high competition" with Latinos and "low competition" with Blacks. In contrast, a value of +8 represents "high competition" with Blacks and "low competition" with Latinos. Respondents who had the same value for both groups, regardless of what that value was, are scored as a zero because they see no difference in the amount of competition between Blacks and Latinos.

Independent Variables

We rely on a variety of well-known, as well as some new, independent variables in predicting Black-Latino competition. Several variables related to social interaction, contact, and association with African Americans are included, to determine whether exposure to the Black community has a positive or negative impact on how Latinos view competition with Blacks. The first of these variables are two items related to social interactions; Black friends and Black co-workers are included as dummies and measure whether the respondent's friends or co-workers are mostly Black or mixed Black and Latino or if these social circles do not include any African Americans. In contrast to these two social interaction variables, a variable related to self-reported negative experiences with African Americans, whether the respondent has been the victim of a crime or has experienced discrimination by an African American, is included and called "Black discrimination." Last, we include a preimmigration variable of exposure to Black populations in Latin America, controlling for whether the Latino respondent traces his or her ancestry to a country in Latin America with a noticeable "Black" population such as the Dominican Republic, Puerto Rico, Venezuela, or any other country in Latin America with at least a 10% Black population.[5]

Finally, we control for region-related variables that are particularly relevant to this study. First, we include a simple dummy variable for whether the respondent resides in one of four southern states: Georgia, North Carolina, Arkansas, D.C./Virginia. Separately, we also include dummy variables for each of these states to test whether all southern states are similar or if one or two may be driving an effect. Next, we include two measures of the percent population which is Black within the county that the Latino respondent resides. We include percent-Black and also percent-Black-squared to assess any nonlinear effects. These variables allow us to test whether population dynamics contribute to feelings of competition and if Latinos view greater competition as the Black population increases. For example, Latinos in counties with a very small Black population may not see much competition with Blacks because they do not come into frequent contact, whereas Latinos residing in majority-Black areas may see Blacks as their competitors, both in the South and in Los Angeles. In full, we employ five variables specifically related to race.

Finally, standard demographic variables include age, education, income, gender, marital status, and home-ownership status. Here, we are particularly interested in class-based variables, such as income, and also variables which evaluate the respondent's personal financial situation. We also include many standard ethnic variables to test cultural-based hypotheses, which include religion (Catholic or born-again), immigrant generation, Spanish usage, Latino linked fate, importance of maintaining Latino culture, and identification as American. With respect to political variables, we include interest in politics and party identification. (Complete coding instructions for all independent variables can be found in appendix 9A.)

The Results

The first level of results is a comparison of mean averages for the Black-Latino competition dependent variable. Using the perceived relative competition measure, we compare means of several different geographic subgroups of Latinos. Looking to table 9.1, a negative mean value demonstrates that the group perceives more competition with other Latinos than with Blacks (i.e., low competition with Blacks), while mean values greater than zero demonstrate that the group perceives more competition with African Americans. The second column of table 9.1 reveals more interesting patterns by region and state. Overall, for all states in the sample, Black-Latino competition is low, with an average of −0.183. For states in the South, the overall average is positive, 0.047, suggesting perceived competition with African Americans is higher in this region than in the non-South, which has a mean of −0.295. Further, the state results indicate that the perceived competition is particularly strong in North Carolina (0.155) and Arkansas (0.129). Averages in Georgia and the D.C. metro are still "higher" than for the non-South, though they both register negative

Table 9.1: The Relationship between Region and Perceptions of Competition with Blacks Relative to Coethnics among Latinos

State-region	Relative competition (−8–8)
All states	−0.183
Southern	0.047
Georgia	−0.023
Carolina	0.155
Arkansas	0.129
D.C. metro	−0.094
Non-South	−0.229
California	−0.295
Florida	−0.080
Texas	−0.501
New York	−0.070
Illinois	−0.342

Note: The statistics reported here reflect mean competition levels on our *Relative competition* scale for each location. Negative coefficients indicate greater perceived competition with other Latinos, while positive coefficients indicate greater perceived competition with African Americans.

values. Outside of the old South, states such as California, Texas, and Illinois appear to have among the lowest levels of perceived Black-Latino competition. To illustrate the impact of region on perceptions of competition graphically, we replicate the frequencies of the relative perception of competition measure for the states in the South. Consistent with the trends in table 9.1, Latinos in the South are more likely to view African Americans (38%) as competitors relative to other Latinos (36%), a difference from the trends of the full sample. Although the gap here is rather limited, when compared to the frequencies of the full sample and the comparison of means in table 9.1, it is clear that Latinos' attitudes toward African Americans are distinct in the South. There is therefore support for our *Southern Hypothesis*, as the unique social, demographic, and cultural context in this region of the country appears to create the context for greater levels of perceived competition among Latinos.

Building on the descriptive statistics, we next move to a multivariate regression analysis in which we test our hypotheses through a more rigorous set of models. Here, we look for statistically significant results related to contributors to intergroup attitudes that may be driven by region and the Black social context variables by isolating data from southern states. We conclude the analysis with a direct test of the *Nonlinear Hypothesis* with our Black county population variables. Overall, the regression results point to a consistent finding that the social context reflected through region matters greatly.

While we have determined through descriptive statistics that there is a distinct regional effect among Latinos in the South, we are also interested in whether this trend holds after accounting for other factors that may influence Latinos' attitudes toward Blacks. We therefore start our regression analysis by examining perceptions of relative competition (table 9.2) using the full sample, with control variables for the southern region. Table 9.2 contains results for two OLS regressions using the two-item index of perceived competition between Latinos and Blacks. Looking first to our key independent variables, we find that when it comes to understanding perceptions of competition, having Black friends plays an important role. Latinos with Black friends are less likely to perceive Black-Latino competition compared to those without Black friends, all other things being equal. In contrast, working with Blacks leads to higher perceptions of competition. Consistent with our *Social Interaction Hypothesis*, while friendship is a great resource in alleviating any social pressures that may contribute to competitiveness between Latinos and Blacks, it seems that workplace coexistence only further reinforces perceptions of competition.

Further, the variable Black ancestry, which accounts for the presence of large Black populations in Latin American countries, also contributes to perceived competitiveness, perhaps building on learned notions of competition between Mestizo and Afro-Latinos in Latin America. Finally, we note that Latinos in southern states are statistically more likely to perceive competition with Blacks when compared to Latinos in other regions. This is in line with the descriptive statistics and further supports the *Southern Hypothesis*. In order to take full advantage of the robust sample sizes of the LNS, we take a closer look at this regional influence by isolating individual states to see if elevated perceptions of competition are present across the entire southern region. Looking to column two, we see that this is largely driven by heightened perceived competition in the states of Georgia and North Carolina in

Table 9.2: Predictors of Competition with Blacks Relative to Coethnics among Latinos (Full Sample)

	Coef.	SE		Coef.	SE	
Black friends	−0.295	0.169	†	−0.294	0.169	†
Black co-workers	0.558	0.180	***	0.554	0.180	***
Black discrimination	−0.144	0.148		−0.150	0.148	
Black ancestry	0.374	0.094	***	0.373	0.094	***
Southern state	0.388	0.157	***			
Georgia				0.470	0.260	†
Carolina				0.504	0.276	†
Arkansas				0.510	0.572	
D.C. metro				0.214	0.232	
Latino linked fate	−0.048	0.037		−0.048	0.037	
Identify as Latino	−0.085	0.048	†	−0.085	0.048	†
Identify as American	−0.088	0.038	*	−0.088	0.038	*
Maintain Latino culture	0.097	0.070		0.097	0.070	
Age	0.002	0.003		0.002	0.003	
Education	−0.024	0.010	*	0.024	0.010	*
Income	5.4E−06	2.3E−06	*	5.4E−06	2.3E−06	*
Personal finances better	0.078	0.048		0.077	0.048	
Female	0.041	0.070		0.041	0.070	
Married	−0.139	0.073	†	−0.141	0.073	*
Home owner	−0.026	0.080		−0.029	0.080	
Years at address	0.003	0.004		0.003	0.004	
Catholic	0.137	0.078	†	0.138	0.078	†
Born again	−0.064	0.070		−0.064	0.070	
Generation	−0.014	0.042		−0.014	0.042	
Spanish ability	−0.149	0.037	***	−0.149	0.037	***
Political interest	0.090	0.046	*	0.091	0.046	*
Party 7-pt.	−0.014	0.020		−0.015	0.020	
Constant	0.397	0.412		0.389	0.412	
N	6,920			6,920		
Adj R²	.0120			.0118		

† p > .100, * p > .050, ** p < .010, *** p <.001

Note: The dependent variable in these models is the *Relative competition* variable. Negative coefficients indicate greater perceived competition with other Latinos, while positive coefficients indicate greater perceived competition with African Americans.

particular. Tested independently, Arkansas and the D.C. metro are not statistically different from nonsouthern states such as California or Illinois. Our analysis has therefore indicated that not only is it critical to account for region when analyzing intergroup attitudes, but when possible, scholars should also control for state and/or local context as well.

While we have determined that there is a distinct effect among Latinos in the South, we are also interested in knowing whether the key covariates related to Black-Latino interactions work the same or differently in the South. Thus, in table 9.3, we turn to a split sample analysis of data from only the southern states to assess these relationships. Consistent with findings from the full model, and in line with the *Social Interaction Hypothesis*, we find that Latinos who have Black friends are statistically less likely to view competition with Blacks. We are also interested in whether the effects for Black-Latino friendship are more pronounced in southern states. We therefore directly compare the substantive impact of having Black friends in the South versus the impact of this type of social interaction outside of this region. Outside the South, the presence of Black friends does reduce perceptions of competition by −.30. In contrast, for Latinos living in the South, having

*Table 9.3: Predictors of Competition with Blacks
Relative to Coethnics among Latinos in the South*

	Relative competition		
	Coef.	SE	
Black friends	−0.693	0.373	†
Black co-workers	0.152	0.361	
Black discrimination	0.084	0.286	
Black ancestry	0.285	0.247	
Latino linked fate	0.063	0.085	
Identify as Latino	−0.092	0.112	
Identify as American	−0.162	0.087	†
Maintain Latino culture	0.079	0.172	
Age	−0.004	0.008	
Education	0.031	0.023	
Income	−1.9E−06	5.9E−06	
Personal finances better	0.143	0.115	
Female	−0.015	0.165	
Married	−0.149	0.172	
Homeowner	0.311	0.197	
Years at address	0.045	0.020	*
Catholic	0.021	0.185	
Born again	0.182	0.167	
Generation	0.128	0.125	
Spanish ability	−0.038	0.095	
Political interest	−0.047	0.111	
Party 7-pt.	−0.061	0.052	
Constant	−0.004	1.006	
N	1,130		
Adj. R²	.090		

† $p > .100$, * $p > .050$, ** $p < .010$, *** $p < .001$

Note: The dependent variable in these models is the *Relative competition* variable. Negative coefficients indicate greater perceived competition with other Latinos, while positive coefficients indicate greater perceived competition with African Americans.

Black friends reduces perceived competition by −.80. More interestingly, the effect in the South is substantively meaningful. Those who have no Black friends actually perceive a positive (above zero) degree of competition with Blacks (.10); however, this drops to a negative value (−.70) for those with Black friends—reversing the direction of perceived competition altogether.

In addition to the measures directly related to our hypotheses, the ethnic-specific variables offer some interesting patterns. Latinos with a heightened sense of linked fate with other Latinos also tend to perceive that they have more in common with African Americans, perhaps out of a shared minority experience. It does not seem to be the case that Latino-based ethnic-identity variables are driving a wedge between Blacks and Latinos; in fact, the opposite appears to be the case. In addition to linked fate, Latinos who think it is important to maintain a clear Latino culture also view higher levels of commonality with Blacks, as do Latinos who subscribe to the label "Latino or Hispanic" and also those who identify more as "American." It could be that these variables, taken together, point to Latinos' acceptance of their status as an American minority group, distinct from the dominant White population, and therefore they see themselves more closely aligned with African Americans. In regard to relative perceptions of competition, Latinos who self-identify as American are less likely to view African Americans as a source of competition; however, living at the same address for a longer duration yields higher levels of perceived competition with Blacks relative to other Latinos.

Lastly, we examine how the demographic context of where Latinos live affects their perceptions of competition with Blacks. Previous work has relied on population counts at the neighborhood, city, county, or state level to assess whether, and how, the degree of racial diversity impacts minority viewpoints toward each other. Here, we include data about the Black population at the county level to determine how Latinos within the South view competition with Blacks on the basis of whether they live in proximity to African Americans. However, building on the contradictory findings of previous studies, we do not necessarily believe this relationship is a linear one. Therefore, we include both a direct continuous variable and a squared (quadratic) version of the population variable. Regression results are presented in table 9.4 and show that Latinos are impacted by the surrounding Black population —however, not in a linear fashion. The effect for the linear term is positive, suggesting that as the Black population in a county increases, Latinos begin to perceive more competition. However, the effect for the squared term is negative, suggesting that at some point, this pattern changes and Latinos begin to perceive less competition in high-density Black counties, something akin to an *n*-curve. In the full

Table 9.4: Predictors of Competition with Blacks Relative to Coethnics among Latinos— Black County Population Models

	Full LNS dataset			Southern states only		
	Coef.	SE		Coef.	SE	
Black friends	−0.194	0.166		−0.652	0.362	†
Southern state	0.293	0.160	†			
% county Black	0.017	0.006	***	0.035	0.017	*
% county Black squared	−1.8E−04	1.0E−04	†	−5.5E−04	2.8E−04	*
Latino linked fate	−0.054	0.037		0.065	0.085	
Identify as Latino	−0.087	0.048	†	−0.090	0.112	
Identify as American	−0.080	0.038	*	−0.148	0.086	†
Maintain Latino culture	0.103	0.070		0.098	0.172	
Age	0.004	0.003		−0.001	0.007	
Education	−0.018	0.010	†	0.036	0.022	
Income	5.9E−06	2.3E−06	**	−1.4E−06	5.9E−06	
Personal finances better	0.072	0.049		0.142	0.115	
Female	0.059	0.070		−0.011	0.164	
Married	−0.156	0.073	*	−0.161	0.172	
Homeowner	−0.027	0.080		0.325	0.196	†
Years at address	0.002	0.004		0.044	0.019	*
Catholic	0.135	0.078	†	0.023	0.185	
Born again	−0.058	0.070		0.177	0.166	
Generation	−0.017	0.042		0.137	0.124	
Spanish ability	−0.152	0.037	***	−0.046	0.094	
Political interest	0.085	0.046	†	−0.043	0.110	
Party 7-pt.	−0.010	0.020		−0.059	0.052	
Constant	0.159	0.412		−0.555	1.030	
N	6,675			6,909		
Adj R²	.115			.099		

† p > .100, * p > .050, ** p < .010, *** p < .001

Note: The dependent variable in these models is the *Relative competition* variable. Negative coefficients indicate greater perceived competition with other Latinos, while positive coefficients indicate greater perceived competition with African Americans.

Key Findings

- We find that rates of perceived competition with Blacks are lower overall when compared to perceptions of competition with other Latinos.

- We find, however, that perceived competition with Blacks is mediated by region, with Latinos living in the South having higher rates of perceived competition with African Americans. This trend holds even when other factors are accounted for in our regression models.

- We also find that social interactions help to explain perceptions of relative competition with African Americans, as having Black friends leads to lower levels of perceived competition, while having Black co-workers increases perceived competition. Further, the positive impact of having Black friends is more pronounced in the South.

- Finally, we find that there is a positive relationship between living around African Americans and perceptions of competition with Blacks. However, there is not a linear relationship here, as perceptions of competition with Blacks actually begin to decrease in counties with greater than 50% African American density.

---

sample, Latinos who live in counties with almost no Blacks view very low levels of Black-Latino competition, yet this steadily rises in medium-density Black counties, only to begin dropping again as the Black population increases. Results for the southern states are once again more robust than those in the full sample. Competition starts at a higher level in the South, increases slowly as the Black population increases, but then sharply drops off to a much lower level. That is, Latinos who live in very high-density Black counties in the South perceive very little competition with Blacks.

Conclusion

In conclusion, we have identified several new dimensions to the study of Black-Latino relations in this chapter. First, it is clear that place matters, as it appears as though Latinos' perceptions of competition with Blacks are higher in the South when compared to other region of the U.S. The significant rise of the Latino population in this region provides a very interesting context in which to study intergroup attitudes. We hope that scholars build on our work to explore other dimensions of relations between groups in this region of the country. Our analysis in this chapter suggests that Latinos' perceptions of competition are particularly high in the southern states of Georgia and North Carolina, and our chapter's literature review provides some speculation to explain this more specific regional trend. However, this is one area where scholars can expand on our work by conducting further research in this important region.

Second, our study finds that social interactions play a major role in how Latinos view African Americans. However, our study provides some new insights regarding this relationship. For example, we find that while Black population concentration impacts Latinos' views toward African Americans, there is not a linear impact on perceptions of competition. Further, the nature of social interactions also matters here; working alongside African Americans does not influence attitudes toward Blacks for Latinos in the South, while having Black friends leads to lower levels of competition and higher rates of perceived commonality.

Finally, it is important to note that this chapter has only examined the viewpoints of Latinos toward perceived competition with Blacks. As Latinos now represent the largest minority group in America, surpassing African Americans in thirty states, it may be that Blacks actually view more competition with Latinos than Latinos do with Blacks. While reliable data for this investigation are an obstacle, future studies should examine both groups simultaneously to fully understand the dynamics of Black-Latino relations.

Study Questions

1. Why is it important to study Black-Latino relations?

2. What are the principal variables used by scholars to investigate Latino attitudes toward Blacks?

3. How do demographic factors (e.g., age, education, religion, gender, etc.) affect Latino attitudes toward Blacks?

4. How do southern Latinos' perceptions of Blacks compare and contrast with those of Latinos living in other regions of the country?

Appendix 9A: Variable Coding for Analysis of *Relative Competition*

Independent Variables

AGE	Continuous; 18–98
EDUCATION	Categorical; 0 = none; 4.5 = less eighth; 10.5 = some HS; 12 = HS grad.; 14.5 = some college; 16 = college grad.; 18 = graduate school
INCOME	Categorical with missing income replaced using Barreto and Espino (2008) income imputation
FINANCES BETTER	Personal financial situation; 1 = worse; 2 = same; 3 = better
UNEMPLOYED	Dummy; 1 = currently unemployed
FEMALE	Dummy; 1 = female
MARRIED	Dummy; 1 = married
HOME OWNER	Dummy; 1 = home owner
YEARS ADDRESS	Continuous; number of years lived at current address; 0–90
CATHOLIC	Dummy; 1 = Catholic
BORN AGAIN	Dummy; 1 = born again (includes any religious denomination)
GENERATION	Categorical; 0 = foreign noncitizen; 1 = foreign citizen; 2 = second; 3 = third; 4 = fourth

SPANISH (SCALE)	Categorical; 1 = English only; 2 = English, a little Spanish; 3 = English, decent Spanish; 4 = fully bilingual; 5 = Spanish, decent English; 6 = Spanish, a little English; 7 = Spanish only
SPANISH SERVICES	Index, see question L23 of LNS; 0 = no Spanish services available in community; 1 = one of three services in Spanish; 2 = two of three services in Spanish; 3 = three of three services in Spanish
POL INTEREST	Categorical; interested in politics; 1 = low; 4 = high
POL KNOWLEDGE	Index, see J10, J11, J12; 0 = zero of three correct; 1 = one of three correct; 2 = two of three correct; 3 = three of three correct
PARTY (7 POINT)	Categorical; 1 = strong Dem.; 2 = weak Dem.; 3 = lean Dem.; 4 = indep.; 5 = lean GOP; 6 = weak GOP; 7 = strong GOP
BLACK SKIN	Dummy; 1 = self-identify as having very dark or dark skin (see E16)
BLACK FRIENDS	Dummy; 1 = friends are mostly Black or mix of Black and Latino (see G6)
BLACK WORKERS	Dummy; 1 = co-workers are mostly Black or mix of Black and Latino (see G7)
BLACK CRIME	Dummy; 1 = victim of crime committed by Black (see L18/L19)
BLACK DISCRIMINATION	Dummy; 1 = experienced discrimination by Black (see N2/N4)
BLACK ANCESTRY	Dummy; 1 = ancestry is to one of eight Latin American countries with large Black populations
BLACK COMMONALITY	Index, see G1A/G2A; 1 = nothing at all in common; 8 = a lot in common
LINKED FATE–LATINO	Categorical; 1 = none; 2 = little; 3 = some; 4 = lot
AMERICAN ID	Categorical; 1 = not at all; 2 = not strong; 3 = somewhat strong; 4 = very strong
MAINTAIN CULTURE	Categorical; 1 = not at all; 2 = somewhat important; 3 = very important
RANK BLACKS	Relative rank of Blacks on commonality vis-à-vis Whites, Asians, and other Latinos; 4 = rank Blacks highest; 3 = rank Blacks second; 2 = rank Blacks third; 1 = rank Blacks lowest
TIME LIVED IN US	Scale measuring percentage of life lived in U.S.; 1%–25%, 26%–50%, 51%–75%; 76%–100%

Notes

1. U.S. Census Bureau, "Table 6. Race Alone or in Combination, for States, Puerto Rico, and Places of 100,000 or More Population: 2000," in *Population by Race and Hispanic or Latino Origin for the United States, Regions, Divisions, States, Puerto Rico, and Places of 100,000 or More Population (PHC-T-6)*. http://www.census.gov/population/www/cen2000/briefs/phc-t6.

2. The McClain et al. (2006) study also confirms the role of nativity in Latinos' attitudes toward African Americans, as approximately 93% of the sample utilized in this study is foreign-born. However, this study suggests that this trend may be a result of Latino immigrants arriving in the U.S. with negative stereotypes regarding Blacks that were formulated

in their country of origin. In fact, a sizable literature focused on discrimination and racial stereotypes in Latin America is cited to address this issue (de la Cadena 2001; Dulitzky 2005; Guimaraes 2001; Hanchard 1994; Mörner 1967; Sweet 1997; Wade 1993, 1997; Winant 1992).

3. Respondents from Maryland are not included in our interpretation of southern states.

4. For example, the question might have read, "Some have suggested that Puerto Ricans are in competition with other Latinos. After each of the next items, would you tell me if you believe there is strong competition, weak competition, or no competition at all with other Latinos?"

5. Eight countries were identified as having the highest percentage Black or Afro-Latino population based on data from the *Latin American Almanac* and the CIA *World Factbook*. While the exact "Black" population is not known due to differences in how race is measured in Latin America, the estimates for these eight countries range from a low of 10% of the total population to a high of 60%. These countries include Colombia, Costa Rica, Cuba, Dominican Republic, Nicaragua, Panama, Puerto Rico, and Venezuela.

References

Barreto, Matt A., and Rodolfo Espino. 2008. "Estimating Income When Income Is Missing: A New Approach for Latino Public Opinion Data." Paper presented at annual meeting of the American Political Science Association, Boston, MA, August 30.

Barreto, Matt A., and Gabriel Sanchez. 2007. "Social and Political Competition between Latinos and Blacks: Exposing Myths, Uncovering New Realities." Paper presented at the Latino National Survey Conference, Cornell University, Ithaca, NY, November.

Bobo, Lawrence D., and Vincent Hutchings. 1996. "Perceptions of Racial Group Competition: Extending Blumer's Theory of Group Position to a Multiracial Social Context." *American Sociological Review* 61 (6): 951–972.

Bobo, Lawrence D., and Devon Johnson. 2000. "Racial Attitudes in the Prismatic Metropolis: Identity, Stereotypes, and Perceived Group Competition in Los Angeles." In *Prismatic Metropolis: Inequality in Los Angeles*, ed. Lawrence D. Bobo, Melvin L. Oliver, James H. Johnson, Jr., and Abel Valenzuela, Jr. New York: Russell Sage Foundation.

Branton, Regina, and Bradford Jones. 2005. "Reexamining Racial Attitudes: The Conditional Relationship between Diversity and Socio-Economic Environment." *American Journal of Political Science* 49:359–372.

Burden, Barry C., and David C. Kimball. 2002. *Why Americans Split Their Tickets: Campaigns, Competition, and Divided Government*. Ann Arbor: University of Michigan Press.

Cain, Bruce, Jack Citrin, and Cara Wong. 2000. *Ethnic Context, Race Relations, and California Politics*. San Francisco: Public Policy Institute of California.

Ciscel, David H., Barbara Ellen Smith, and Marcela Mendoza. 2003. "Ghosts in the Global Machine: New Immigrants and the Redefinition of Work." *Journal of Economic Issues* 37 (June): 333–341.

Cobb, James. 1993. *The Selling of the South*. 2nd ed. Urbana: University of Illinois Press.

Cook, Stuart W. 1963. "Desegregation: A Psychological Analysis." In *Readings in the Social Psychology of Education*, ed. W. W. Charters, Jr., and N. L. Gage, 40–50. Boston: Allyn and Bacon.

de la Cadena, Marisol. 2001. "Reconstructing Race: Racism, Culture and Mestizaje in Latin America." *NACLA Report on the Americas* 34 (6): 16–23.

Dulitzky, Ariel E. 2005. "A Region in Denial: Racial Discrimination and Racism in Latin America." In *Neither Enemies nor Friends: Latinos, Blacks, Afro-Latinos*, ed. Anani Dzidzienyo and Suzanne Oboler, 39–60. New York: Palgrave Macmillan.

Dunn, Timothy J., Ana Maria Aragonez, and George Shivers. 2005. "Recent Mexican

Immigration in the Rural Delmarva Peninsula: Human Rights versus Citizenship Rights in a Local Context." In *New Destinations: Mexican Immigration to the United States*, ed. Victor Zúñiga and Rubén Hernández-León, 155–183. New York: Russell Sage Foundation.

Ellison, Christopher G., and Daniel A. Powers. 1994. "The Contact Hypothesis and Racial Attitudes among Black Americans." *Social Science Quarterly* 75 (2): 385–399.

Frisbie, W. Parker, and Lisa J. Niedert. 1977. "Inequality and the Relative Size of Minority Populations: A Comparative Analysis." *American Journal of Sociology* 82 (5): 1007–1030.

Frymer, Paul, Thomas Kim, and Terri Bimes. 1997. "Party Elites, Ideological Voters, and Divided Party Government." *Legislative Studies Quarterly* 22 (May): 195–216.

Garcia, F. Chris, and Gabriel R. Sanchez. 2008. *Hispanics and the U.S. Political System: Moving into the Mainstream*. Upper Saddle River, NJ: Prentice Hall.

Gay, Claudine. 2004. "Putting Race in Context: Identifying the Environmental Determinants of Black Racial Attitudes." *American Political Science Review* 98 (4): 547–562.

Gay, Claudine. 2005. "Your Blues Ain't Like Mine: The Effect of Economic Disparity on Black Attitudes toward Latinos." Paper presented at the annual meeting of the American Political Science Association, Washington, DC, September.

Glaser, James. 1994. "Back to the Black Belt: Racial Environment and White Racial Hostility in the South." *Journal of Politics* 56 (1): 21–41.

Guimaraes, Antonio Sergio. 2001. "Race, Class, and Color: Behind Brazil's 'Racial Democracy.'" *NACLA Report on the Americas* 34 (6): 38–41.

Guzmán, Betsy. 2001. "The Hispanic Population: Census 2000 Brief." Washington, DC: U.S. Census Bureau, Department of Commerce. http://www.census.gov/prod/2001pubs/c2kbr01-3.pdf.

Hanchard, Michael G. 1994. *Orpheus and Power: The "Movimento Negro" of Rio de Janeiro and São Paulo, Brazil, 1945–1988*. Princeton: Princeton University Press.

Hillygus, D. Sunshine, and Todd Shields. 2008. "Southern Discomfort? Regional Differences in Voter Decision Making in the 2000 Presidential Election." *Presidential Studies Quarterly* 38 (3): 506–520.

Jackman, Mary R., and Marie Crane. 1986. "'Some of My Best Friends Are Black . . .': Interracial Friendship and Whites' Racial Attitudes." *Public Opinion Quarterly* 50:459–486.

Jennings, James. 2003. *Welfare Reform and the Revitalization of Inner City Neighborhoods*. East Lansing: Michigan State University Press.

Johnson, James H., Jr., and John D. Kasarda. 2009. "Hispanic Newcomers to North Carolina: Demographic Characteristics and Economic Impact." In *Latino Immigrants and the Transformation of the U.S. South*, ed. Mary E. Odem and Elaine Lacy, 70–90. Athens: University of Georgia Press.

Jones-Correa, Michael. 2001. "Institutional and Contextual Factors in Immigrant Naturalization and Voting." *Citizenship Studies* 5 (1): 41–56.

Kandel, William, and Emilio A. Parrado. 2004. "Hispanics in the American South and the Transformation of the Poultry Industry." In *Hispanic Spaces, Latino Places: Community and Cultural Diversity in Contemporary America*, ed. Daniel D. Arreola. Austin: University of Texas Press.

Kasinitz, Philip, John Mollenkopf, Mary Waters, and Jennifer Holdaway. 2008. *Inheriting the City: The Children of Immigrants Come of Age*. New York and Cambridge, MA: Russell Sage Foundation and Harvard University Press.

Kochhar, Rakesh, Roberto Suro, and Sonya Tafoya. 2005. "The New Latino South: The Context and Consequences of Rapid Population Growth." Pew Hispanic Center Report.

Marrow, Helen. 2005. "New Destinations and Immigration Incorporation." *Perspectives on Politics* 3 (4): 781–799.

Marrow, Helen. 2009. "New Immigration Destinations and the American Colour Line." *Racial and Ethnic Studies* 32 (6): 1037–1057.

Massey, Douglas S., and Nancy A. Denton. 1993. *American Apartheid.* Cambridge: Harvard University Press.

McClain, Paula D., Niambi M. Carter, Victoria M. DeFrancesco Soto, Monique L. Lyle, Jeffrey D. Grynaviski, Shayla C. Nunnally, Thomas J. Scotto, J. Alan Kendrick, Gerald F. Lackey, and Kendra Davenport Cotton. 2006. "Racial Distancing in a Southern City: Latino Immigrants' Views of Black Americans." *Journal of Politics* 68 (3): 571–584.

McClain, Paula D., Gerald F. Lackey, Efrén O. Peréz, Niambi M. Carter, Jessica Johnson Carew, Eugene Walton, Jr., Candis S. Watts, Monique L. Lyle, and Shayla C. Nunnally. 2009. "Intergroup Relations in Three Southern Cities: Black and White Americans and Latino Immigrants' Attitudes." Working paper.

Mohl, Raymond A. 2003. "Globalization, Latinization, and the Nuevo New South." *Journal of American Ethnic History* 22 (Summer): 31–66.

Mohl, Raymond A. 2009. "Globalization and Latin American Immigration in Alabama." In *Latino Immigrants and the Transformation of the U.S. South*, ed. Mary E. Odem and Elaine Lacy, 51–69. Athens: University of Georgia Press.

Mörner, Magnus, ed. 1967. *Race Mixture in the History of Latin America.* Boston: Little, Brown.

Murphy, Arthur D., Colleen Blanchard, and Jennifer A. Hill. 2001. *Latino Workers in the Contemporary South.* Athens: University of Georgia Press.

Odem, Mary E., and Elaine Lacey, eds. 2009. *Latino Immigrants and the Transformation of the U.S. South.* Athens: University of Georgia Press.

Oliver, J. Eric, and Tali Mendelberg. 2000. "Reconsidering the Environmental Determinants of White Racial Attitudes." *American Journal of Political Science* 44 (3): 574–589.

Oliver, J. Eric, and Janelle Wong. 2003. "Inter-group Prejudice in Multiethnic Settings." *American Journal of Political Science* 47 (4): 567–582.

Powers Daniel A., and Christopher G. Ellison. 1995. "Interracial Contact and Black Racial Attitudes: The Contact Hypothesis and Selectivity Bias." *Social Forces* 74:205–226.

Rich, Brian L., and Marta Miranda. 2005. "The Sociopolitical Dynamics of Mexican Immigration in Lexington, Kentucky, 1977 to 2002: An Ambivalent Community Responds." In *New Destinations: Mexican Immigration to the United States*, ed. Victor Zúñiga and Rubén Hernández-León, 187–219. New York: Russell Sage Foundation.

Rodrigues, Helena Alves, and Gary M. Segura. 2004. "A Place at the Lunch Counter: Latinos, African-Americans, and the Dynamics of American Race Politics." Paper presented at the "Latino Politics: The State of the Discipline" conference, Texas A&M University, College Station, TX, April 30–May 1.

Schmidley, A. Dianne. 2003. "The Foreign-Born Population in the United States." *Current Population Reports*, March 2002. P20-539. Washington, DC: U.S. Census Bureau.

Sigelman, Lee, and Susan Welch. 1993. "The Contact Hypothesis Revisited: Black-White Interaction and Positive Racial Attitudes." *Social Forces* 71 (3): 781–795.

Stuesse, Angela. 2009. "Race, Migration, and Labor Control: Neoliberal Challenges to Organizing Mississippi's Poultry Workers." In *Latino Immigrants and the Transformation of the U.S. South*, ed. Mary E. Odem and Elaine Lacy, 91–111. Athens: University of Georgia Press.

Suro, Roberto, and Audrey Singer. 2002. "Latino Growth in Metropolitan America: Changing Patterns, New Locations." Center on Urban & Metropolitan Policy. July.

Sweet, James H. 1997. "The Iberian Roots of American Racist Thought." *William and Mary Quarterly* 54 (1): 143–166.

Taylor, Marylee C. 1998. "How White Attitudes Vary with the Racial Composition of Local Populations: Numbers Count." *American Sociological Review* 63 (4): 512–535.

Torres, Cruz C. 2000. "Emerging Latino Communities: A New Challenge for the Rural South." Southern Rural Development Center, Policy Brief No. 12, August, 1–8.

Wade, Peter. 1993. *Blackness and Race Mixture: The Dynamics of Racial Identity in Colombia*. Baltimore: Johns Hopkins University Press.

Wade, Peter. 1997. *Race and Ethnicity in Latin America*. London: Pluto.

Wattenberg, Martin P. 2002. *Where Have All the Voters Gone?* Cambridge: Harvard University Press.

Welch, Susan, Lee Sigelman, Timothy Bledsoe, and Michael Combs. 2001. *Race and Place: Race Relations in an American City*. New York: Cambridge University Press.

Wilner, Daniel M., Rosabelle Price Walkley, and Stuart W. Cook. 1955. *Human Relations in Interracial Housing*. Minneapolis: University of Minnesota Press.

Winant, Howard. 1992. "Rethinking Race in Brazil." *Journal of Latin American Studies* 24 (1): 173–192.

Wright, Gerald. 1977. "Contextual Models of Electoral Behavior: The Southern Wallace Vote." *American Political Science Review* 71 (2): 497–508.

PART V

Conclusion

10

Latino Politics and Power in the Twenty-First Century

Insights from Political Analysis

MANNY AVALOS AND TONY AFFIGNE

When clear winter skies rise over New England—more than 2,000 miles from the Rio Grande River—the sun's pale rays illumine richly colored images of La Virgen de Guadalupe in thousands of Mexican American homes, in cities like Bridgeport, Hartford, Providence, Worcester, and Boston. In fact, by the time of the 2010 Census, several thousand Mexican American people could be found as far into the northeast as Bangor, Maine—the easternmost city in the United States.[1] Maine is not unique; in the first years of the twenty-first century, the nation's Latino[2] population has grown to more than 53 million persons, living and working in every region and every state, transforming local polities of all kinds, from rural towns of the central plains and deep South to the very largest East and West Coast cities.[3]

The Latino Emergence

The rise of a large and powerful Latino political community at the end of the twentieth century—the *Latino emergence*—followed closely on two crucial reversals of longstanding federal policy. First came the Immigration and Naturalization Act of 1965, which eliminated racial, ethnic, and regional quotas, offering legal entry to previously excluded Latin American applicants. A few years later in 1970 and 1975, extensions of the Voting Rights Act of 1965 (VRA) for the first time established federally protected voting rights for Latinos, comparable to those enacted in 1965 to ensure free participation by African American voters. In particular, these VRA extensions made exclusion and suppression of Latino votes illegal—throwing out more than a century of "No Mexicans Allowed" voting laws.[4] Shortly after these policy shifts, a rapid growth in Latino population and political participation occurred, ultimately bringing Latino representatives to power within Congress, state and municipal legislatures, the judiciary and executive branches, and at every level of American federalism. In some places, Latino population size, suffrage, cohesion, or resources were insufficient to elect Latino politicians, but even there, Latinos hold significant influence as coalition partners and swing electorates.

For example, in New York City, the Latino population of Harlem is now larger than that historic neighborhood's Black community, reshaping New York's political dynamic. In many places, African American populations have been growing more slowly than Latinos'. Black populations actually fell in New York, Detroit, Cleveland,

and St. Louis.[5] In this light, the 2012 contest between venerable (but increasingly vulnerable) Rep. Charles Rangel, a leader of the Congressional Black Caucus, and New York State Senator Adriano Espaillat, a rising star in Latino politics, promised to show how the new urban dynamic sometimes plays out.[6] After counts and recounts, Rangel narrowly prevailed. The two campaigns' political bases were, not surprisingly, different. Espaillat's coalition included some African Americans, but Rangel's political family has always included Latinos, many of whom were prominent in his campaign. In addition, like many other Black New Yorkers, Rangel's late father was Puerto Rican. Not surprisingly, then, in his political career Rangel has reached out to Afro-Latinos, including many in the Puerto Rican and Dominican communities. This was not just an accident of practical politics. Not many years ago, Rangel helped orchestrate a pan-American conference on Afro-*latinidad*, held at Hunter College in Manhattan, bringing together Afro-descent community leaders from across Latin America with their counterparts in New York. The Latino electorate's regard for Rangel is genuine, and his victory came as no surprise. Still, at some point Rep. Rangel's career will end, and his successor will likely be *hijo de la comunidad*, with even deeper roots than Rangel's among Latino voters.

Many urban areas are undergoing this transformation. As a result of rapid Latino population growth and concentration in the national metropole, where African American and Latino populations share common spaces, patterns of Black-Latino competition and cooperation will become more important in urban, state, and national politics. Scholars of Latino politics often work at the nexus of these politics, exploring what form the Black-Latino relationship will take at different times and in different contexts. Some argue that distance and competition may be inevitable, while others find evidence of and reasons for significant Black-Latino cooperation.[7] We should not be surprised to find political and economic competition while Latino populations were dispersing across the country between 1965 and 2012. By 2010, Latinos had become the largest minority population not only for the nation as a whole (a threshold they crossed in 2001) but also in more than half of the nation's metropolitan areas (191 of 366 urban centers), conurbations where a record 83.7% of the total population, and 92.5% of Latinos, now live.[8]

In fact, every one of the fifty states and the District of Columbia saw growth in the Latino population from 2000 to 2010.[9] Far into the heartland, along the Missouri River Valley, for example, softly spoken Spanish, punctuated with children's laughter, can be heard at Cub Scout pack meetings. In Columbia, Pack 121 was formed in 2012, as the city's first Hispanic pack, where young Latino boys (and girls), recruited into the Boy Scouts of America's "Hispanic Initiative," start each pack meeting the same way Cub Scouts have done for decades—reciting the Pledge of Allegiance.[10]

Even in the South, where cities and towns may still be resolving centuries-old Black-White racial tensions, new challenges confront political systems as they struggle to incorporate America's fastest-growing Hispanic communities. Between 1990 and 2000, Latino populations in southern states nearly doubled—from 6.8 million to 12 million, then to more than 18 million in 2010. This pace of Latino population growth was far quicker than in the Northeast, Midwest, or West. Latinos were not the only newcomers to the South. In fact, non-Hispanic Whites increased

numbers by only 4.2% from 2000 to 2010, while the combined minority population (Black, Asian, Native, and Latino) grew by 33.6%—likewise the fastest overall
minority population growth rate in the nation. By 2010, the Latino population had
more than doubled in Alabama, Arkansas, Kentucky, Mississippi, North Carolina,
Tennessee, South Carolina, and Maryland, and the state of Georgia now has the
tenth-largest Latino population (853,689) in the United States.[11]

Around Houma, Louisiana, for example—in a state whose overall Latino population grew by 79%—a doubling of the local Hispanic population led to most of the
area's growth, and the many Latino-owned businesses serving new Hispanic residents have become that rural economy's most dynamic sector.[12] Similar patterns are
seen throughout the South. Finally, in the western states, home to America's oldest
and largest Hispanic communities (California was, after all, northern Mexico until
1848), both old and new Latino communities—hailing from Mexico and Central
and South America—are embroiled in bitter political debates over immigration
policy, education, and criminal justice, even as their growing numbers fuel insistent
demands for increased political power and representation.[13]

In Los Angeles—the nation's second-largest city—Hispanics constitute the single
largest share of the population. The city's nearly 4 million people in 2010 were 48.5%
Latino, 28.6% White, 11.3% Asian, and 9.2% Black. Agitation to make Los Angeles city government more representative of its diverse population has intensified,
and Latinos are—as they have been since 1970—the main force in this debate.[14] By
2020, Hispanics are projected to be a plurality of the population in the country's
largest state, California (40.7 %), and grow to 48% there by 2060.[15] A pattern of
Latino population growth and demands for empowerment—and a corresponding
backlash, as in Arizona—recurs throughout the West and Southwest.[16]

In every corner of the nation, then, we see evidence of a Latino emergence
unprecedented for its speed and breadth, driven by new immigration as well as
youthful, growing families, posing challenges to both scholars and participants in
U.S. politics, for whom understanding the character and potential of Latino politics remains a work in progress. The 2010 Census made clear the extent and pace
of change which is occurring, finding that between 2000 and 2010, the Hispanic
population grew by 43%, while the non-Hispanic population grew by only 5% and,
significantly, the non-Hispanic White population by just 1%.[17]

It is important to remember that while recent growth may be unprecedented, the
presence of Latinos in U.S. society—even in smaller numbers—has been a reality
for the body politic for a very long time. Much of Latinos' experience with American politics, however, has been bitter. Since the days of the Texas Revolution (1836)
and Mexican War (1846–1848), Mexicans living in the United States have frequently
been subject to abuse and treated as foreigners—long after they had demonstrated,
both individually and as a group, their loyalty to the United States, their contributions to national development, culture, and politics, and their commitment to
the core values of the national community.[18] Caught in the strange zone between
nationality and conquest, many Puerto Ricans since 1898 have likewise found themselves simultaneously included (as U.S. "citizens" and subjects) and excluded (cast
in U.S. political culture as untrustworthy aliens, dark-skinned, Spanish-speaking
jibaros, or political subversives). "Chicanos and Puerto Ricans in the U.S., the

present pillars of the so-called 'Hispanic' minority," wrote Juan Flores, "stand at the same juncture, straddling North and South America and embodying the unequal, oppressive relation between them."[19] The world of the Latino in the United States, however, has changed. A return to the old system of exclusion seems impossible, despite recent controversies over voter-identification laws, as many such efforts (largely, but not exclusively, by Republicans) have been abandoned or nullified and seemed only minimally effective, if at all, in reducing Latino participation.

Even in early Republican presidential primaries of 2012, despite GOP support for immigration and education policies which were broadly unpopular with Latinos, aspirants for the party's nomination found it imperative to tailor some messages to skeptical Latino electorates, in constituencies as different as Florida and Nevada.[20] Even in such nontraditional states for Hispanic influence as Montana, Nebraska, and Missouri, Latino vote choices in 2012's U.S. Senate elections were crucial in tightly balanced contests, not just for individual races but for partisan control of the Senate itself, which remained in the hands of the Democratic Party—with strong support from Latino voters.[21] In the run-up to the 2012 elections, many a late-night strategy session struggled with the challenge of winning Latino votes, a task made more difficult by Latinos' exclusion from much of the twentieth century's political analysis.

The Impact of the Latino Vote in the 2012 Presidential Election

Only after the election, however, was the true scope of Latino influence evident, and only afterward could we calculate the *precise* risk in not taking Latino impact more seriously, both in practical politics and in political analysis. A record number of Latinos voted (12.2 million) in the 2012 presidential election and are considered to be "the leading edge of an increasing ethnic voting bloc" that is likely to double in size within a generation, according to a Pew Hispanic Center analysis. The increase in the Latino electorate has been rapid. In 1988, Latinos were only 3.7% of the electorate, but by 2012, their share had grown to almost 10%. This rapid increase is partly accounted for by the fact that Latinos are by far the nation's youngest ethnic-group percentage of the population. The percentage of Latinos who will be of eligible voting age will continue to rise quickly over the coming decades. The Pew Hispanic Center estimates that by 2030 Latinos will account for 40% of the growth in the electorate (up from 23.7 million in 2012 to 40 million).[22]

For many pundits, the election of 2012 was a "watershed" moment for the Latino electorate.[23] A record 75% of the Latino vote went for President Obama, and Latinos were decisive in the final outcome. The net Latino popular-vote contribution to Obama was a +5.4% margin, while the national popular-vote margin for Obama was +2.3%. For the first time in U.S. history, Latinos can plausibly claim to have had a decisive impact on the final outcome.[24]

A further analysis of the 2012 election exit polling done by Latino Decisions indicates extraordinarily high levels of Latino support for President Obama in the western swing states. In Nevada, eight out of every ten Latino votes went for the president (a net contribution of 9.3% of the Obama vote). In Colorado, 87% of the Latino vote went for Obama (9.5% of the Obama vote). With overall winning margins for Obama of 3.2% in Colorado and 6.7% in Nevada, the Latino vote clearly influenced his victory in these crucial swing states.[25]

Even in swing states where the Latino vote was a small percentage of the electorate, such as Virginia (5%) and Ohio (3%), their vote for President Obama helped tilt the outcome of the election. As we have seen, the Latino population has been migrating in record numbers toward what one might consider nontraditional destinations in the Midwest and the Southeast. Within the next two decades, we expect the expansion of the Latino electorate in these regions will bring them above 10%, furthering Latinos' impact in a wide range of election scenarios, especially where tightly balanced partisan and ideological shares have created opportunities for small swing electorates—a phenomenon we will see in congressional as well as statewide and presidential elections.[26]

In the end, President Obama did not need Florida to win the election this time, but still, the Latino vote in that state reveals a significant shift among Latinos. Today Latinos are nearly 18% of the electorate in Florida. Historically, Florida's Latino electorate has been predominantly Cuban American and politically aligned with conservative Republicans. This trend, however, is changing. Over the past decade, we have seen a significant growth in the Puerto Rican population particularly along the I-4 corridor from Tampa to Orlando. Unlike the conservative Republican Cuban American electorate in Miami-Dade County, the Puerto Rican electorate in Florida identifies largely as Democrat. While close to two-thirds of Cuban Americans in Florida voted for Mitt Romney, 72% of Puerto Ricans voted for President Obama, helping him to win the overall Latino vote by 58%–40% in Florida.[27]

Yet despite the growth in the Latino population nationally and the growth in the size of the Latino electorate, the potential electoral impact could be much larger. In 2012, it is estimated that 2.5 million Latinos who were registered did not vote and another 8.6 million were eligible to vote but were not registered. Together these 11.1 million potential voters almost equal the actual number (12.2 million) of Latinos who voted. The more politically engaged the Latino electorate becomes, the greater will be their impact in various states such as Texas and California (where 2 million are not registered in each state). In two other highly contested states, Arizona (400,000 unregistered voters) and Florida (638,000 unregistered voters), the increase in registration and turnout could have significant implications for the outcomes of state and federal races. If one considers the millions of permanent resident aliens who are currently eligible for citizenship and if comprehensive immigration reform becomes a reality in 2013, this could potentially add 11 million new Latino voters in the near future.[28]

Finally, it is crucial to note that the true impact of the Latino vote in the 2012 election goes well beyond its contribution to the reelection of President Obama. With recent and prospective changes in the racial and ethnic demographics of the United States, the Republican Party finds itself with significant support coming only from older white males. As one of our colleagues, Professor Gary Segura, has said, if the Republican Party is not able to reach out to Latinos, Asians, African Americans, and young female voters, it will go the way of the dinosaur.[29] So it is not so surprising that for the first time since 2007 the Republican Party seemed in mid-2013 to be on board to engage in the possibility for comprehensive immigration reform, in no small part because of its dismal performance with Latino voters in November 2012. It is also no small wonder why Congressman Marco Rubio (R-Florida) was chosen to give the Republican response to the 2013 State of the Union Address. *Time* magazine's February 13, 2013, front cover proclaims Cuban American Marco Rubio as "the Republican Savior."[30]

Insights from Political Analysis: A Review of Findings

These lessons from presidential and congressional politics demonstrate why more robust analysis of Latino political behavior, policy preferences, and social contexts is necessary. The Latino presence in America is deeply rooted in the nation's past and is increasingly salient for the nation's future as well. If we are to meet coming national challenges with a fully engaged and effective citizenry, American political institutions, the media, commercial enterprises, schools, and more will need to adjust to the Latino emergence. Old expectations about Latino turnout, partisanship, and electoral power may no longer be valid, but new models and expectations have yet to be widely accepted. Will Latinos work together as a quasi-racial group, or will existing potential fault lines, especially national origin, intraethnic racial identity, and social class, prove more able to fracture the Latino community than linked fate and practicality are able to bring Latinos together as a unified political community? Questions like these allow us to *explain* and *predict* Latino behavior, by exploring attitudes toward the home country, "the American dream," alliances and competition with other "minority" groups, the meaning of "Latino" and the meaning of "American," regionally distinct social environments, linked fate with other Latinos and with African Americans, and the nation's policy debates, and they are exactly the questions other contributors to this volume have asked—and answered.

Lavariega Monforti (chapter 2) and Gershon and Pantoja (chapter 3) illuminate the contributions that panethnicity and immigrant transnational ties might make in increasing mobilization of the Latino electorate. If we learn that sentiments of panethnic commonality are real, for significant numbers of Latinos, and that transnational engagements sometimes *facilitate* engagement in the U.S., then we can turn to the question of just how political candidates seeking Latino support might best tap those sentiments and provide corresponding benefits as they can, should they reach public office. We know from the ImpreMedia/Latino Decisions presidential-election-eve poll that many campaigns are not reaching out very effectively, on panethnic, transnational, or other grounds: during the 2012 campaigns, only 31% of Latino voters were contacted by a campaign, political party, or community organization to either register to vote or cast a ballot. Even in key swing states, only three out of every ten Latino voters were contacted—meaning that seven in ten were ignored![31]

Such differential mobilization clearly impacts Latino voter turnout. As we approach the congressional midterm elections in 2014, and the 2016 presidential race, it will behoove political parties and candidates to pay greater attention to the growing pool of soon-to-be-eligible Latino voters and invest heavily in voter registration and mobilization efforts. These efforts could have a significant impact on Latino turnout now and long into the future.[32]

A look at our contributors' other findings makes several interesting things clear. Beyond the implication that panethnic appeals may be increasingly effective, as Latino citizens experience a variety of reinforcing influences, Lavariega Monforti's reanalysis of Louis DeSipio's approach to panethnicity suggests that "Hispanic" and "Latino" identity may actually arise from different sources. Given the Latino community's composition, made up as it is of diverse national-origin subgroups, is there evidence of persistent ethnic-group solidarity? Like DeSipio before her, but using the newer LNS data, Lavariega Monforti concludes that the answer is a qualified yes. Her findings are important because they demonstrate that perceptions of group identity can have real-world consequences. Panethnic identity for Latinos may have direct impacts on the development and durability of multiethnic coalitions, allowing them to shape public policies for which no individual group would have sufficient influence.

Taking Lavariega Monforti's findings about correlates and apparent strength of panethnicity one step farther, and considering the most recent elections, in which Obama won the support of a solid 75% bloc of Latino votes—*in spite of* the extreme diversity we know exists among Latinos—what should we conclude about the role panethnic identity played in 2012 or might continue to play in future elections? Moreover, as discussed by Orr, Morel, and Gamble in chapter 7, what might intra-Latino solidarity tell us about the future of *broader* ethnic coalitions, involving Latinos, Blacks, and Asian Americans, who similarly voted overwhelmingly for the Democratic candidate? Is this a one-time occurrence, or are there social and economic commonalities which will encourage greater interracial, interethnic cooperation, leading to joint political empowerment, ongoing mobilization, continued participation, and greater "minority" influence, both in elections and in policy disputes?

Gershon and Pantoja, for their part, raise the question of whether transnational ties among Latino immigrants might be an impediment to political incorporation, pursuit of citizenship, and civic engagement. The answer, they report, is no. This is good news for anyone experiencing national and cultural anxiety in the face of ongoing binational engagement and activism among Latinos for whom the home country—with its elections, remittances, sports teams, TV personalities, and the like—is just an email away. Immigrants who maintain strong connections with their country of origin, Gershon and Pantoja found, *also* engage socially, culturally, and politically in the U.S. In particular, Gershon and Pantoja provide evidence that transnational ties encourage immigrant incorporation, especially in nonelectoral and civic activities. So one way to increase naturalization rates and political incorporation, paradoxically, is to encourage and facilitate immigrants' maintaining their connections to their home country. For those who see cultural attachments and political engagement efforts as zero-sum, they will be disturbed or disoriented by these findings, but if you trust the data and the analysis, the conclusion is clear.

Another important contribution of Gershon and Pantoja's chapter is that it reminds us that "incorporation" and "transnationalism," as applied to immigrants, are contested ideas. How one measures and operationalizes these concepts also matters, and so another key contribution is the way Gershon and Pantoja specify multiple measures of these concepts. Their analysis offers a more optimistic outlook for the role transnational ties play domestically in facilitating immigrants' civic engagements in the U.S. An immigrant simply does not have to cast aside his or her transnational ties to become politically incorporated in the U.S. The immediate relevance of these findings is clear, as Congress deliberates the possibility, and the limits, of comprehensive immigration reform. The fear on the part of observers such as Samuel Huntington, that immigrants would fail to fully integrate into the political culture of the United States, is not supported by the analysis in chapter 3. Rather, we should find ways to celebrate the opportunity to create a more effective pathway to full citizenship and political incorporation.

Just as importantly, Lavariega Monforti and Michelson (chapter 4) have reported that Latinos who strongly identify as "American" or have strong feelings of linked fate are more trusting of government and of other Latinos, whereas those who have experienced discrimination become less trusting of government. These are not surprising findings. However, their work also tells us that acculturation into the mainstream is *not* a factor driving cynicism among Latinos; rather, it is the lack of a sense of belonging and community, the absence or breakdown of social capital and interpersonal trust, which are increasing cynicism among Latinos. This finding is important, in light of earlier, somewhat simplistic assumptions that those who become more acculturated will become more like the modal, cynical "American," less trusting of government, more prone to political alienation. Trust, Lavariega Monforti and Michelson remind us, is a complex concept. For Latinos, trust reflects both political identity and the sense of belonging to a broader community. Again, this is not a discouraging finding at all. If anything, knowing that community, acceptance, and social resources can help *reduce* political alienation among Latinos is as reassuring in its way as were Gershon and Pantoja's findings about the positive influence of transnational ties. Sometimes what we think we know simply is not true.

In chapter 5, Branton, Franco, and Wrinkle teach some important lessons about how Latinos come to hold, and change, their policy views. In particular, as with chapter 4's findings on political trust, chapter 5 tells us that acculturation is positively associated with greater tolerance and willingness to entertain a range of social welfare and moralistic policies not generally associated with Latinos—school vouchers, egalitarian school funding, guaranteed income, abortion rights, and same-sex marriage. In other words, while their findings may not reassure social and economic conservatives, who have been looking high and low to find millions of theologically doctrinaire, family-values, small-government Latino voters, they *will* give some comfort at the other end of the spectrum, relieving concerns that as Latinos become more acculturated—as must inevitably occur—they will not simply drift to the right. Given the extreme hostility toward immigrants in general, and Latinos in particular, which has lately emanated from conservatives, Republicans, and the Tea Party, a rightward drift has always been unlikely; but Branton, Franco, and Wrinkle offer empirical evidence which seems to explain *why* this will not happen. In brief, they report that Latinos are much more liberal on moralistic policy issues than has been suggested in previous work and that as acculturation increases, Latinos are even more likely to hold liberal views. The authors also find that that among the most acculturated Latinos, gaining more *political knowledge strengthens liberal attitudes* on such questions as same-sex marriage and abortion rights. Their work thus refutes much of the extant conventional wisdom regarding Latino attitudes on Latino-centric as well as social welfare policies. Once again, findings such as these may help explain why Latinos are really not the social conservatives that many people would like to believe. Heretofore, many political observers and politicians have posited that Latino values (importance of family and religion, for example) would be aligned with more conservative ideologies and positions on policy issues. Future research might explore how attitudes on social policy issues vary, by gender, generation, region, and Latino subgroup.

Silber Mohamed's chapter 6 asks the basic question, what do Latinos think it means to be American? More specifically, Silber Mohamed delves into the question of how we define what it means to be American in terms of ascriptive characteristics such as language, birthplace, race, and religion and under what conditions Latinos view the term "American" as an open and accessible or a rigid and closed category. Individual Latinos' experiences, she finds, shape what it means to be American, and country of origin, level of integration in the U.S., and region of residence impact the extent to which Latinos view "American" as an ascriptive category.

This is an important question because the perception of "American" as an open identity which anyone may claim, as opposed to the idea that being American is something one either is or is not based on ascriptive characteristics, can either discourage or encourage full engagement by immigrants seeking to incorporate and integrate into U.S. society. Very little literature explores how members of racialized ethnic immigrant groups understand what it means to be American. Silber Mohamed's findings show a great deal of variation, by country of origin, in opinions regarding what it means to be American. Large majorities of Latinos believe that to be fully entitled to the mantle of "Americanness," speaking English is very important, while race is less so and need not prevent one from identifying, and being identified, as an American. Interestingly, she found that Salvadorans have the most restrictive view of what it means to be American and that Cubans are most likely to emphasize skin color.

Orr, Morel, and Gamble (chapter 7) utilized one of the unique aspects of the Latino National Survey. With large subsamples at the state level, the dataset makes possible finely grained analyses like theirs, which considers Latinos in the New England states, a region whose Latino communities tend to be more racially diverse than those of other regions of the United States, with large numbers of Salvadorans, Guatemalans, Puerto Ricans, Colombians, and Dominicans but fewer Mexican and Cuban Americans. Using the three New England state samples thus allows the authors to examine one of the least understood and researched topics in the field, concerning cross-ethnic coalition building, linking African Americans and Latinos. The authors indeed find that Latinos in New England have more in common than in conflict with African Americans. Despite the fact that electoral structures and shared urban space means political competition is inevitable, Latinos still perceive significant political commonality with African Americans. Moreover, Latinos who believe that their well-being is connected with African Americans (linked fate) are much more likely to perceive political and economic commonality. This research

contributes to the literature on cross-racial coalition building by focusing on commonality rather than conflict. In essence, the authors find that political competition between Latinos and Blacks is not necessarily an insurmountable obstacle to
political commonality (as previously thought) and that conditions exist, at least in
these regions, for coalition formation based on political commonality. In addition,
they find that Latinos who have a strong sense of linked fate with other *Latinos* are
more likely to perceive political and economic commonality with *African Americans* as well.

Somewhat differently, in chapter 8, Stokes-Brown finds that Latinos appear to
be conflating "race" and "ethnicity" when they define their own identities. She
also finds that there are significant differences of opinion regarding public policies
among Latinos who self-identify as "White," "Black," or "some other race." In this
chapter, the depth of the Latino National Survey is plain. Not only does the dataset
include a variable for racial self-identification; it also allows analysis of self-reported
skin color, which is different from "race" and may yield different findings. In Stokes-
Brown's work, she identifies racial-identity differences on questions of immigration,
social welfare, and non-Latino specific but high-profile issues, such as abortion and
support for school vouchers. Beyond the chapter's substantive findings, it contributes to the debate on how best to measure and operationalize the concept of identity
using survey data.

Finally, in chapter 9, Barreto and Sanchez explore Latino perceptions of competition with African Americans, relative to their perception of competition with
other Latinos, and like Orr, Morel, and Gamble, they take advantage of the survey's
unique design, which is deep enough to allow comparisons, on the question of perceptions of African Americans, between Latinos who live in the South and those
who live in other regions. Do Latinos in the South see greater competition with
African Americans? Beyond this chapter's creative and unique research design, it
raises the very important question, what is the impact of social interactions and
social proximity on intergroup relations? However, there is a twist: very few studies look at social interaction effects on *minority-group attitudes toward one other*
(usually the comparison is with the white population). One major contribution here
is that the authors develop more flexible, comparative measures for Black-Latino
competition, rather than a single measure as is used in most studies of this kind.

Barreto and Sanchez's findings are fascinating. Latinos' perceived competition
with African Americans is found to be higher in the South than in other regions,
particularly in North Carolina and Georgia. Social context within regions, they
discover, matters greatly, as do state and local context. In their multivariate model,
the authors find support for a positive view of the effects of social contact. When
Latinos have Black friends, they are less likely to perceive Black-Latino competition, as compared to Latinos without Black friends. This social contact factor has
a more significant effect in the South than elsewhere. Friendship, then, just as we
have always been taught, can be an important resource in alleviating the negative
effects of social contexts which might otherwise contribute to competition. A final
important finding is that Latinos with a heightened sense of linked fate with other
Latinos also seem to feel more in common with African Americans—perhaps a
shared minority experience?

Suggested Directions: The Future of Latino Political Studies

These chapters have offered new findings and should give the reader much to think about. Beyond their specific conclusions, they have also demonstrated the power and the versatility of the LNS dataset. No other extant database includes the depth and breadth of respondent populations, contexts, and substantive variables that is offered by the LNS. We encourage you to consider how you might use these data in your own work. There is much to be done! While scholarship on Latino politics has grown exponentially in the past decade, after a slow start in the 1970s, there is a need for additional research in many areas. New survey data have become available from sources such as the Latino National Survey, the Pew Hispanic Center, and the General Social Survey, but to date there are few comparative studies which analyze data across surveys from the same time period. This is especially important because many of the items on the LNS questionnaire were adopted directly from other instruments, specifically to make such comparisons possible. Moreover, we encourage you to consider ways you might use other data, generated from panel and cohort designs across time (such as the National Longitudinal Survey of Youth), and to incorporate available data from pre- and postelection surveys such as the ImpreMedia/Latino Decisions polls and the 2008 Hispanic Pew surveys which were deployed just before, and just after, the seminal presidential election that year.

Chapters in this volume also suggest that there is room for additional theory and model building, in the areas of inter- and intraracial attitude formation and change, spatial and contextual analysis testing for competition and cooperation at the community level. In particular, the LNS offers abundant opportunities for comparative analysis at the state and local levels; several metropolitan areas were sampled sufficiently to allow regional and substate comparisons as well. Case studies have limitations, if we aim to truly understand community empowerment and coalition building, but by using substate data, robust comparisons of urban communities are feasible. In addition, there is work to be done analyzing policy in states, including immigration, health care, gun violence, and more. Finally, as boundaries between disciplines becomes less relevant, there is a great need for more interdisciplinary Latino political research, cutting across disciplines such as political science, economics, history, and psychology, and you hold in your hand a wealth of ideas and resources to begin your work on any of these important projects.

Notes

1. Maine's Latino population growth of nearly 81% between 2000 and 2010 seems extraordinary but was only enough to rank nineteenth fastest in the nation. The ten fastest-growing Latino populations were in South Carolina (148%), Alabama (145%), Tennessee (134%), Kentucky (122%), Arkansas (114%), North Carolina (111%), Maryland (106%), Mississippi (106%), South Dakota (103%), and Delaware (96%). Ennis, Ríos-Vargas, and Albert 2011; Passel, Cohn, and Lopez 2011.
2. "Hispanic" and "Latino" are used rather interchangeably throughout this book. We are aware of significant distinctions of meaning and nuance, but since these are rarely significant in this discussion, so we have used both terms, except where the point in question clearly calls for one or the other. For discussion of the historical roots of the contemporary

Latino emergence and the diversities which underlie the politics of naming, see Affigne, Jackson, and Avalos 1999.

3. Data from the 2010 U.S. Census show that the total U.S. population grew by 23.7 million (9.7%) during the prior decade, the number of Hispanics/Latinos grew by 15.2 million (43.0%), the non-Hispanic white population grew only slightly, and the combined minority population increased by 28.8%. Indeed, as the Census Bureau reported in March 2011, "The vast majority of the growth in the total [U.S.] population came from increases in those who reported their race(s) as something other than White alone and those who reported their ethnicity as Hispanic or Latino" (Humes, Jones, and Ramirez 2011, 3).

4. For discussion of the 1965 immigration reforms, see Douglas S. Massey, "The New Immigration and Ethnicity in the United States," *Population and Development Review* 21 (3) (September 1995): 631–652. On the VRA's impacts, see John A. García, "The Voting Rights Act and Hispanic Political Representation in the Southwest," *Publius* 16 (4) (Autumn 1986): 49–66.

5. Hope Yen, "Hispanics Now Exceed African-Americans In Most Urban Areas," Associated Press, *Boston.com*, April 15, 2011, http://www.boston.com/news/nation/articles/2011/04/15/hispanics_now_exceed_african_americans_in_most_urban_areas/

6. Thomas Kaplan, "Rangel Fends Off Challengers to Win a Congressional Primary," *New York Times*, June 27, 2012, A19; David A. Love, "Does Rise of Latino Population Spell Doom for the Congressional Black Caucus?," *TheGrio.com*, http://www.thegrio.com/politics/does-rise-of-latino-population-spell-doom-for-the-congressional-black-caucuss.php.

7. Paula D. McClain, Niambi M. Carter, Victoria M. DeFrancesco Soto, Monique L. Lyle, Jeffrey D. Grynaviski, Shayla C. Nunnally, Thomas J. Scotto, J. Alan Kendrick, Gerald F. Lackey, Kendra Davenport Cotton, "Racial Distancing in a Southern City: Latino Immigrants' Views of Black Americans," *Journal of Politics* 68 (3) (2006): 571–584.

8. U.S. Census Bureau, *Patterns of Metropolitan and Micropolitan Population Change: 2000 to 2010*, Census Special Reports, C2010SR-01 (Washington, DC: U.S. Government Printing Office, 2012), 34.

9. Sharon R. Ennis, Merarys Ríos-Vargas, and Nora G. Albert, "Table 2. Hispanic or Latino Population for the United States, Regions, and States, and for Puerto Rico: 2000 and 2010," in *The Hispanic Population: 2010* (Washington, DC: U.S. Census Bureau, May 2011), 34.

10. McKenzie Kramer, "Hispanic Cub Scout Pack Comes to Columbia," *Columbia Missourian*, January 16, 2012, http://www.columbiamissourian.com/stories/2012/01/16/hispanic-cub-scout-pack-comes-columbia.

11. Jeffrey S. Passel, D'Vera Cohn, and Mark Hugo Lopez, "Hispanics Account for More than Half of Nation's Growth in Past Decade" (Washington, DC: Pew Hispanic Center, 2011).

12. Cara Bayles, "Latino-Owned Businesses Cater to Communities," *HoumaToday.com*, January 8, 2012, http://www.houmatoday.com/article/20120108/ARTICLES/120109699/1026/news01?p=1&tc=pg&tc=ar.

13. Abby Sewell, "Lawsuit Alleging Compton Elections Unfair to Latinos Going to Trial," *L.A. Now* (blog), *Los Angeles Times*, January 6, 2012, http://latimesblogs.latimes.com/lanow/2012/01/latino-voting-lawsuit-compton-ruling.html.

14. Stephen Ceaser, "Residents Balk at L.A. Council District 4's Proposed New Shape," *Los Angeles Times*, January 29, 2012, http://articles.latimes.com/2012/jan/29/local/la-me-redistricting-labonge-20120129.

15. Juliet Williams and Elliot Spagnat, "Hispanics in California Will Soon Be a Majority," *Huffington Post*, January 31, 2013, http://www.huffingtonpost.com/2013/01/31/hispanics-in-california-will-soon-be-majority_n_2593033.html.

16. "The Backlash Begins: A New State Law Has Galvanised Latinos Nationwide, and Others Too," *Economist*, May 6, 2010, http://www.economist.com/node/16060133.

17. Karen R. Humes, Nicholas A. Jones, and Roberto R. Ramirez, "Overview of Race and Hispanic Origin: 2010" (Washington, DC: U.S. Census Bureau, March 2011).

18. For the history of anti-Mexican prejudice, see Rodolfo Acuña's *Occupied America: A History of Chicanos*, 7th ed. (New York: Longman, 2010). See Rodolfo O. de la Garza, Angelo Falcón, and F. Chris Garcia, "Will the Real Americans Please Stand Up? Anglo and Mexican-American Support of Core American Political Values," *American Journal of Political Science* 40 (2) (May 1996): 335–351.

19. Juan Flores, *Divided Borders: Essays on Puerto Rican Identity* (Houston: Arte Público, 1993), 182.

20. Matt O'Brien, "As Republicans Shift West, Attracting Latinos a Challenge," *San Jose Mercury News*, February 1, 2012, http://www.mercurynews.com/presidentelect/ci_19870807.

21. Sean J. Miller, "Hispanic Vote Crucial in Critical 2012 States Could Hold Key to GOP Senate Majority," *Ballot Box* (blog), *The Hill*, March 24, 2011, http://www.thehill.com/blogs/ballot-box/senate-races/151611-hispanic-vote-may-hold-key-to-gop-senate-majority.

22. Paul Taylor, Ana Gonzalez-Barrera, Jeffrey S. Passel, and Mark Hugo Lopez, "An Awakened Giant: The Hispanic Electorate is Likely to Double by 2030" (Washington, DC: Pew Hispanic Center, November 14, 2012).

23. Gabriel Sanchez, "The Untapped Potential of the Latino Electorate," *Latino Decisions Blog*, January 15, 2013, http://www.latinodecisions.com/blog/2013/01/15/the-untapped-potential-of-the-latino-electorate/.

24. If Latinos had split their vote evenly, President Obama would have lost the election, and if Mitt Romney had captured even 35% of the Latino vote, he would have won the election. See election-eve analysis: Matt A. Barreto and Gary M. Segura, "2012 Latino Election Eve Poll," ImpreMedia/Latino Decisions webinar slides, *Latino Decisions*, November 7, 2012, http://www.latinodecisions.com/files/3513/5232/9137/LEE_PRESENTATION_2012.pdf.

25. See Barreto and Segura, "2012 Latino Election Eve Poll."

26. See Victoria De Francesco Soto, "Obama's Re-election Sets Record Support for Latino Voters," *Latino Decisions Blog*, November 13, 2012, http://www.latinodecisions.com/blog/2012/11/13/obamas-re-election-sets-record-for-support-latino-voters/.

27. See ImpreMedia/Latino Decisions 2012 election-eve poll data, November 7, 2012, http://www.latinovote2012.com/app/#puerto_rican-fl-all.

28. Sanchez, "Untapped Potential."

29. Gary M. Segura, "Latino Public Opinion & Realigning the American Electorate," *Dædalus: The American Academy of Arts & Sciences* 141 (4) (Fall 2012): 98–113. Also see Gwen Ifill's *PBS NewsHour* interview with Gary Segura at http://www.pbs.org/newshour/rundown/2012/05/pollster-democrats-should-bait-gop-on-latino-issues.html.

30. See *Time*, February 18, 2013, cover: http://www.time.com/time/covers/0,16641,20130218,00.html.

31. See ImpreMedia/Latino Decisions 2012 Latino election-eve poll data: http://www.latinovote2012.com/app/#all-national-all.

32. See Sanchez, "Untapped Potential."

References

Affigne, Tony, M. Njeri Jackson, and Manuel Avalos. 1999. "Latino Politics in the United States: Building a Race-Conscious, Gendered, and Historical Analysis." Paper presented at the annual meeting of the American Political Science Association, Atlanta, GA. September 2–5.

Bayles, Cara. 2012. "Latino-Owned Businesses Cater to Communities." *HoumaToday.com*, January 8. http://www.houmatoday.com/article/20120108/ARTICLES/120109699/1026/news01?p=1&tc=pg&tc=ar.

Ceaser, Stephen. 2012. "Residents Balk at L.A. Council District 4's Proposed New Shape." *Los Angeles Times*, January 29. http://articles.latimes.com/2012/jan/29/local/la-me-redistricting-labonge-20120129.

Ennis, Sharon R., Merarys Ríos-Vargas, and Nora G. Albert. 2011. *The Hispanic Population: 2010*. Washington, DC: U.S. Census Bureau, May.

Flores, Juan. 1993. *Divided Borders: Essays on Puerto Rican Identity*. Houston: Arte Público.

Humes, Karen R., Nicholas A. Jones, and Roberto R. Ramirez. 2011. *Overview of Race and Hispanic Origin: 2010*. Washington, DC: U.S. Census Bureau, March.

Kaplan, Thomas. 2012. "Rangel Fends Off Challengers to Win a Congressional Primary." *New York Times*, June 27, A19.

Kramer, McKenzie. 2012. "Hispanic Cub Scout Pack Comes to Columbia." *Columbia Missourian*, January 16. http://www.columbiamissourian.com/stories/2012/01/16/hispanic-cub-scout-pack-comes-columbia.

Love, David A. 2012. "Does Rise of Latino Population Spell Doom for the Congressional Black Caucus?" *TheGrio.com*, http://www.thegrio.com/politics/does-rise-of-latino-population-spell-doom-for-the-congressional-black-caucuss.php.

McClain, Paula D., Niambi M. Carter, Victoria M. DeFrancesco Soto, Monique L. Lyle, Jeffrey D. Grynaviski, Shayla C. Nunnally, Thomas J. Scotto, J. Alan Kendrick, Gerald F. Lackey, and Kendra Davenport Cotton. 2006. "Racial Distancing in a Southern City: Latino Immigrants' Views of Black Americans." *Journal of Politics* 68 (3): 571–584.

Miller, Sean J. 2011. "Hispanic Vote Crucial in Critical 2012 States Could Hold Key to GOP Senate Majority." *Ballot Box* (blog), *The Hill*, March 24. http://www.thehill.com/blogs/ballot-box/senate-races/151611-hispanice-vote-may-hold-key-go-gop-senate-majority.

O'Brien, Matt. 2012. "As Republicans Shift West, Attracting Latinos a Challenge." *San Jose Mercury News*, February 1. http://www.mercurynews.com/presidentelect/ci_19870807.

Passel, Jeffrey S., D'Vera Cohn, and Mark Hugo Lopez. 2011. "Hispanics Account for More than Half of Nation's Growth in Past Decade." Washington, DC: Pew Hispanic Center.

Sanchez, Gabriel. 2013. "The Untapped Potential of the Latino Electorate." *Latino Decisions Blog*, January 15. http://www.latinodecisions.com/blog/2013/01/15/the-untapped-potential-of-the-lationo-electorate/.

Segura, Gary. M. 2012. "Latino Public Opinion & Realigning the American Electorate." *Dædalus: The Journal of American Academy of Arts & Sciences* 141 (4) (Fall): 98–113.

Sewell, Abby. 2012. "Lawsuit Alleging Compton Elections Unfair to Latinos Going to Trial." *L.A. Now* (blog), *Los Angeles Times*, January 6. http://latimesblogs.latimes.com/lanow/2012/01/latino-voting-lawsuit-compton-ruling.html.

Taylor, Paul, Ana Gonzalez-Barrera, Jeffrey S. Passel, and Mark Hugo Lopez. 2012. "An Awakened Giant: The Hispanic Electorate Is Likely to Double by 2030." Washington, DC: Pew Hispanic Center, November 14.

U.S. Census Bureau. 2012. *Patterns of Metropolitan and Metropolitan Change: 2000 to 2010*. Census Special Reports, C2010SR-01. Washington, DC: U.S. Government Printing Office.

Williams, Juliet, and Elliot Spagnat. 2013. "Hispanics in California Will Soon Be a Majority." *Huffington Post*, January 31. http://www.huffingtonpost.com/2013/01/31/hispanics-in-california-will-soon-be-majority_n_2593033.html.

Yen, Hope. 2011. "Hispanics Now Exceed African-Americans in Most Urban Areas." Associated Press. *Boston.com*, April 15. http://www.boston.com/news/nation/articles/2011/04/15/hispanics_now_exceed_african_americans_in_most_urban_areas/.

Appendix A

Latino National Survey Questionnaire (LNS/LNS-NE, 2005–2008)

Screeners

1. Would you prefer that I speak in English or Spanish?
2. Do you consider yourself Hispanic or Latino or a person of Spanish origin?
3. (S4) The most frequently used terms to describe persons of Latin American descent living in the United States are "Hispanic" and "Latino." Of the two, which do you prefer, or do you not care about this terminology [Hispanic or Latino]?

Section A—Political Knowledge

4. How frequently would you say you watch television news? Would it be daily, most days, only once or twice a week, or almost never?
5. How often would you say you read a daily newspaper? Would it be daily, most days, only once or twice a week, or almost never?
6. For information about public affairs and politics, would you say you rely more heavily on Spanish-language television, radio, and newspapers, or on English-language TV, radio, and newspapers?
7. Do you have regular internet access at home, somewhere else, or not at all?
8. How interested are you in politics and public affairs? Would you say you are very interested, somewhat interested, or not at all interested?

Section B—Demographics

9. What year were you born?
10. Are you male or female (ask only if necessary)?
11. How many people, including yourself, currently live in your household? We don't need their names, just the number.
12. How many of these people are 18 years of age or older?
13. (B4) Families of [Hispanic or Latino] origin or background in the United States come from many different countries. From which country do you trace your Latino heritage [Respondent's country of origin]?
14. Were you born in the mainland United States, Puerto Rico, or some other country?
15. Where were you born?
16. If Mexican born, can you tell me, what state you were born?
17. What would you say is the main reason you came to live in the United States?
18. When did you first arrive to live in the U.S. (mainland)?
19. Are you a naturalized American citizen?
20. Where were your parents born? Were they both born in the U.S., was one born in the U.S., or were both born in another country?
21. How many of your grandparents, if any, were born outside the U.S.A.?

Section C—Assimilation, Acculturation, and Language

Asked only of Spanish-language respondents.

22. How good is your spoken English? Would you say you could carry on a conversation in English (both understanding and speaking) very well, pretty well, just a little, or not at all?

Asked only of English-language respondents.

23. How good is your spoken Spanish? Would you say you could carry on a conversation in Spanish (both understanding and speaking) very well, pretty well, just a little, or not at all?

24. How important do you think it is for you or your family to maintain the ability to speak Spanish?

25. How important do you think it is that everyone in the United States learn English?

Section D—Civic Engagement

26. Do you participate in the activities of one social, cultural, civic or political group, more than one such group, or do you not participate in the activities of any such groups?

27. How would you describe these groups? Are they: Mostly Latino; Mixed Latino/White; Mostly Black; Mixed Latino/Black; Mostly Asian; Mixed Latino/Asian; Other; Don't know?

28. When an issue or problem needs to be addressed, would you work through existing groups or organizations to bring people together, would you get together informally, or would you do nothing to deal with this matter?

29. Have you ever tried to get government officials to pay attention to something that concerned you, either by calling, writing a letter, or going to a meeting?

30. Have you done this more than once?

31. Was the official you contacted a Latino or Hispanic?

Section E—Marital Status and Family

32. What is your current marital status?

33. What is your [spouse or partner's] race and national origin?

34. How many children do you have, if any?

If R was foreign-born . . .

35. Do you have children under 18 that you assist financially living in another country?

If R's spouse/partner was non-Latino and couple have children . . .

36. Do you consider your children Latina/o?

Section F—Education

37. What is your highest level of formal education completed?

If R was foreign-born or born on island of Puerto Rico . . .

38. Where did you complete your highest level of education? U.S. or elsewhere?

If R was U.S.-born . . .

39. Which of the following best describes your parents' educational attainment. Did they . . . ?

40. What grade would you give your community's public schools—A, B, C, D, or Fail?

41. Did you have children enrolled in elementary or secondary / high school last year?

"Now I want to ask you about a particular child. Think about your child who had the most recent birthday and was enrolled in school last year. For the following questions, please focus on this child."

42. Is this child enrolled in public or private school?

43. Is this child a boy or girl?

44. During the school year that just ended, what grade was your child in?

45. How far would you like to see this child go in school?

"Here is a list of things that some parents have done and others have not regarding their children's school. Which of these things have you done? Have you . . ."

46. Met with your child's teacher?
47. Attended a PTA meeting?
48. Acted as a school volunteer for your child's school?
49. When you have had contact with school officials, would you say your experience has been very good, somewhat good, not too good, or not good at all?

    If Spanish speaking . . .
50. Was there a specialized program for teaching English to Spanish-speaking children in your child's school?
51. Was your child ever in that program?
52. How far do you think your child will actually go in school?

Section G—Race and Skin Color

53. What is your race? Are you White, Black, American Indian, Asian, Native Hawaiian / Pacific Islander, some other race, or more than one?
54. In the U.S., we use a number of categories to describe ourselves racially. Do you feel that [Hispanics or Latinos] make up a distinctive racial group in America?
55. [Hispanics or Latinos] can be described based on skin tone or complexion shades. Using a scale from 1 to 5 where 1 represents very dark and 5 represents being very light, where would you place yourself on that scale?

Section H—Religiosity

56. With what religious tradition do you most closely identify? [Catholic; Assemblies of God; Southern Baptist; Pentecostal; other Protestant; Mormon; Jewish; Jehovah's Witness; Don't identify with any religious denomination; Other]
57. Do you consider yourself a born-again, spirit-filled Christian, or involved in the charismatic movement?
58. How often do you attend religious services? Do you attend [read list].

Section I—Naturalization and Citizenship

59. Have you or any close member of your family ever served in the U.S. military?

    If foreign-born . . .
60. Now we would like to ask you about U.S. citizenship. Are you a U.S. citizen, currently applying for citizenship, planning to apply to citizenship, not planning on becoming a citizen?

    If foreign-born and a naturalized citizen . . .
61. What would you say is the main reason you chose to become a U.S. citizen? (open ended, interviewer code into categories)
62. In what year did you become a U.S. citizen?
63. What would you say is the main reason for becoming a citizen of the United States? (open ended, interviewer code into categories)

    If foreign-born and not a naturalized citizen . . .
64. What would you say is the main reason you have not naturalized? (open ended, interviewer code into categories)

Section J—Interethnic and Group Relations

"Thinking about issues like job opportunities, educational attainment or income, how much do [Hispanics or Latinos] have in common with other racial groups in the United States

today? Would you say [Hispanics or Latinos] have a lot in common, some in common, little in common, or nothing at all in common with . . ."

65. African Americans?
66. Whites?
67. Asian Americans?

"Now I'd like you to think about the political situation of [Hispanics or Latinos] in society. Thinking about things like government services and employment, political power and representation, how much do [Hispanics or Latinos] have in common with other racial groups in the United States today? Would you say [Hispanics or Latinos] have a lot in common, some in common, little in common, or nothing at all in common with . . ."

68. African Americans?
69. Whites?
70. Asian Americans?
71. How much does [Hispanics or Latinos] "doing well" depend on African Americans also doing well? A lot, some, a little, or not at all?

"Some have suggested that [Hispanics or Latinos] are in competition with African Americans. After each of the next items, would you tell me if you believe there is strong competition, weak competition, or no competition at all with African Americans? How about . . ."

72. In getting jobs?
73. Having access to education and quality schools?
74. Getting jobs with the city or state government?
75. Having [Hispanic or Latino] representatives in elected office?

"How important is it for [Hispanics or Latinos] to . . ."

76. Change so that they blend into the larger American society?
77. Maintain their distinct cultures?
78. How would you describe your friends? Are they [list racial and ethnic identities]?
79. How would you describe your co-workers? Are they [list racial and ethnic identities]?

Section K—Gender

"People frequently have different opinions about the status of women in society including the nature of relationships between men and women. Please tell me if you strongly agree, somewhat agree, somewhat disagree, disagree strongly, or have no opinion about the following statements."

80. Men and women should get equal pay when they are in the same jobs.
81. Mothers should be more responsible for caring for children than fathers.
82. Women should have easy access to birth control / contraception.
83. Men are better qualified to be political leaders than women.

Section L—Electoral Participation

If a U.S. citizen . . .

84. Are you currently registered to vote in the U.S.?
85. About how old were you when you first registered in the U.S.?
86. In talking to people about elections, we often find that a lot of people were not able to vote because they weren't registered, they were sick, or they just didn't have time. How about you—did you vote in the presidential election last November?
87. In the 2004 elections, were you ever contacted to vote for or contribute money to a candidate or political campaign?

88. a. For voters: Who did you vote for in this past election? b. For nonvoters and noncitizen respondents: Whom did you favor or prefer for president in this past election?

89. If a party or candidate was trying to contact you about an election, which of the following would you pay the most attention to [campaign contact, media]?

Asked only of nonvoting but registered U.S. citizens—open-ended response . . .

90. People were not able to vote because of a variety of reasons. How about you? What was the main reason for not voting in this past November election?

If registered . . .

91. Are you registered as a Republican, a Democrat, an independent, or some other party? [Rotated order]

Asked of citizens, if not yet registered . . .

92. Do you know how and where to register to vote?

Section M—Party Identification

93. Generally speaking, do you usually consider yourself a Democrat, a Republican, an Independent, some other party, or what?

If Democrat or Republican . . .

94. Would you consider yourself a strong [Democrat or Republican], or a not very strong [Democrat or Republican]?

If independent . . .

95. Do you think of yourself as closer to the Republican or Democratic Party?

If other . . .

96. Do you think of yourself as closer to the Republican or Democratic Party?

97. Which of the following best describes how your feelings about the parties have changed in recent years?

98. Generally speaking, in politics do you consider yourself as conservative, liberal, middle-of-the-road, or don't you think of yourself in these terms?

If conservative . . .

99. Do you consider yourself a strong, or not very strong, conservative?

If liberal . . .

100. Do you consider yourself a strong, or not very strong, liberal?

If neither liberal nor conservative . . .

101. Do you consider yourself more like a liberal, or more like a conservative, or truly middle-of-the-road?

102. Which political party, Democrat or Republican [alternate order], has a majority in the United States House of Representatives?

103. In the United States, presidential elections are decided state-by-state. Can you tell me, in the election of 2004, which candidate, Bush or Kerry, won the most votes in [respondent's current state of residence]?

104. Which one of the political parties is more conservative than the other at the national level, the Democrats or the Republicans?

Section N—Leadership and Representation

"People can prefer a candidate for a variety of different reasons. How important is it for you that a candidate . . ."

105. is [Hispanic or Latino]?
106. speaks Spanish?
107. shares your positions on issues?

"People have different ideas about the government in the United States. Please tell me how strongly you agree or disagree with each of these statements."

108. "Government is pretty much run by just a few big interests looking out for themselves, and not for the benefit of all the people."
109. "People like me don't have any say in what the government does."
110. "Sometimes politics and government seem so complicated that a person like me can't really understand what's going on."
111. "People are better off avoiding contact with government."
112. How much of the time do you trust the government to do what is right—just about always, most of the time, some of the time, or never?

"Would you strongly agree, somewhat agree, somewhat disagree, or strongly disagree with the following statements, or do you have no opinion?"

113. "No matter what a person's political beliefs are, they are entitled to the same legal rights and protections as anyone else."
114. "Most people who don't get ahead should not blame the system; they have only themselves to blame."
115. "It is not really that big of a problem if some people have more of a chance in life than others."
116. Now I would like to ask you about your feelings towards President Bush. Thinking about the kind of person he is, would you say you view him very favorably, somewhat favorably, somewhat unfavorably, very unfavorably, or do you have no feeling toward him one way or another?
117. I am going to read you a list of characteristics about President Bush. From the following list, which is the most important reasons why you view him favorably?
118. How strongly do you approve or disapprove of how President Bush is doing as president? Would you say you strongly approve, somewhat approve, somewhat disapprove, strongly disapprove, or don't you have strong feelings on that?
119. Now thinking about the economy in the country as a whole, would you say that over the past year the nation's economy has gotten better, stayed about the same, or gotten worse?
120. What about your personal financial situation? Over the past year, has it gotten better, stayed about the same, or gotten worse?

Section O—Employment and Residential Status

121. What is your employment status? Are you [employed full-time; working more than one job; employed part-time; engaged in occasional labor or day labor; currently unemployed; a full-time student; retired or permanently disabled; not working outside the home]?

Asked of U.S.-born . . .

122. What kind of work do you usually do? For example, are you primarily a carpenter, teacher, sales clerk, bricklayer, meat processor, farm worker, etc.?

Asked of foreign-born . . .

123. What kind of work do you usually do in the U.S.? For example, are you primarily a carpenter, teacher, sales clerk, bricklayer, meat processor, farm worker, etc.?
124. Are you or anyone in your household a member of a union?
125. Where you currently live, have you ever been paid less than you were promised, or not paid at all, for work you completed?

126. Do you own, or rent, your residence in the United States?
127. How many years have you lived at your current address?

Asked of foreign-born . . .
128. Have you lived in another state in the U.S. previously?
129. If yes, which state was that?

Section P—Intra-Latino Relations and Panethnicity

"Earlier, you indicated that your family was originally from [R's country of origin]."
130. Thinking about issues like job opportunities, educational attainment or income, how much do you have in common with other [Hispanics or Latinos]? Would you say you have a lot in common, some in common, little in common, or nothing at all in common?
131. Now thinking about things like government services and employment, political power, and representation, how much do you have in common with other [Hispanics or Latinos]? Would you say you have a lot in common, some in common, little in common, or nothing at all in common?
132. How much does your "doing well" depend on other [Hispanics or Latinos] also doing well? A lot, some, a little, or not at all?
133. Thinking about issues like job opportunities, education or income, how much do [R's ethnic subgroup] have in common with other Latinos or Hispanics? Would you say [R's ethnic subgroup] share a lot in common, some things in common, little in common, or nothing in common with other Latinos?
134. Now thinking about things like government services and employment, political power and representation, how much do [R's ethnic subgroup] have in common with other Hispanics or Latinos? Would you say [R's ethnic subgroup] share a lot in common, some things in common, little in common, or nothing in common with other Latinos?
135. How much does [R's ethnic subgroup] "doing well" depend on how other Hispanics or Latinos also doing well? A lot, some, a little, or not at all?

"Some have suggested that [R's ethnic subgroup] are in competition with other Latinos. After each of the next items, would you tell me if you believe there is strong competition, weak competition, or no competition at all with other Latinos . . ."
136. In getting jobs?
137. Having access to education and quality schools?
138. Getting jobs with the city or state government?
139. Having [R's ethnic subgroup] representatives in elected office?

"I am going to read a list of labels describing people, and I want you to tell me how strongly you identify with each."
140. In general, how strongly or not do you think of yourself as "American"?
141. In general, how strongly or not do you think of yourself as [national-origin descriptor]?
142. Finally, in general, how strongly or not do you think of yourself as Hispanic or Latino?
143. Of the three previous terms, Latino or Hispanic, [national-origin descriptor], or American, which best describes you?

"When you think of what it means to be fully American in the eyes of most Americans, do you think it is very important, somewhat important, or not important to . . ."
144. Have been born in the United States?
145. To speak English well
146. To be White?
147. To be Christian?

Section Q—Partisanship, Ideology, and Public Policy

148. What do you think is THE one most important problem facing the country today? [Response categories not provided; open-ended response.]

149. Which political party do you think has a better approach to address this problem? Is it [rotated: the Republicans or the Democrats], or is neither party better than the other?

150. What do you think is THE one most important problem facing the Latino community today? [Response categories not provided; open-ended response.]

151. Which political party do you think has a better approach to address the problem you have identified? Is it [rotated: the Republicans or the Democrats], or is neither party better than the other?

152. Do you think the police in your community treat [Hispanics or Latinos] fairly?

153. Have you ever been the victim of a crime in this country?

154. Was the person who committed the crime Hispanic, White, Black, or don't you know?

"I'm going to ask you about some policy issues. Please tell me how strongly you support or oppose the following policies. Your response can be strongly support, support, oppose, or strongly oppose. If you are not sure how you feel or don't know, feel free to say so. How about . . ."

155. "Keep U.S. military troops in Iraq as long as it takes to stabilize their government."

156. "Government should provide income support to those who need it."

157. "The current health-care system needs government intervention to improve access and reduce costs."

158. "Undocumented immigrants attending college should be charged a higher tuition rate at state colleges and universities, even if they grew up and graduated from high school in the state."

159. "Use of matrícula consular—as an ID issued by foreign countries—is an acceptable form of identification for immigrants in the U.S."

160. "Use standardized tests to determine whether a child is promoted to the next grade or graduates from high school."

161. "Fund public education so that all school districts have about the same amount of money to spend per student."

162. "Provide school vouchers to pay for a portion of the cost to send children to private schools, even if that would take some money away from public schools."

163. "Replace multiyear bilingual instruction in schools with instruction only in English after one year."

164. "Government should provide income support to those who try to provide for themselves but who cannot adequately do so."

165. What is your view about same-sex couples? Should they be permitted to legally marry; enter into civil unions; receive no legal recognition; no opinion?

166. Generally speaking, do you think abortion should be [legal in all circumstances; legal in most circumstances; legal only when necessary to save the life of the woman or in cases of rape or incest; illegal in all circumstances; unsure]?

"Are the following government services available in Spanish in your community? Answer yes or no for each type of service."

167. Social services including public health clinics or hospitals?

168. Police or law enforcement, courts / legal representation?

169. Information from public schools?

170. Looking around at conditions in your neighborhood, how impacted is your neighborhood today by pollution, toxic waste, landfills?

171. Do you believe that pollution, toxic waste, etc. are less likely, more likely, or equally likely to be located in minority neighborhoods?

172. Which comes closer to your own views? Immigrants today strengthen our country because of their hard work and talents, OR Immigrants today are a burden on our country because they take our jobs, housing, and health care?

173. What is your preferred policy on undocumented or illegal immigration? Should there be [immediate legalization of current undocumented immigrants; a guest-worker program leading to legalization eventually; a guest-worker program that permits immigrants to be in the country, but only temporarily; an effort to seal or close off the border to stop illegal immigration; none of these]?

Section R—Transnationalism

174. How often do you have contact with friends and family in [R's country of origin]?

If foreign-born . . .

175. Since coming to the U.S., how often have you returned to [R's country of origin]?

176. Have you ever returned to live (rather than just visit) there for a portion of time?

177. How long do you think you will remain in the U.S.?

178. Are you the owner of land, a house or a business in [R's country of origin]?

179. How often do you visit [R's country of origin]?

180. Do you have plans to go back to [R's country of origin] to live permanently?

181. How often do you send money?

If R sends money . . .

182. What is the average amount you send each time?

183. Do you participate in the activities of a club, association or federation connected to the town or province your family came from in [R's country of origin]?

184. How much attention would you say you pay to politics in [R's country of origin]? Would you say you pay a lot of attention, some attention, a little attention, or none at all?

If R not born in U.S. . . .

185. Before coming to the U.S., did you ever vote in [R's country of origin] elections?

186. Have you ever voted in [R's country of origin] elections since you've been in the U.S.?

187. Did you cast your vote from the U.S. or from [R's country of origin]?

188. Since coming to the U.S., have you contributed money to a candidate or party in your country of origin?

189. Before you came to the United States, how active were you in a political party, a political organization, or in any other type of organizations such as labor unions, student organizations, or paramilitary organizations?

190. Some people believe that it is appropriate that people from [R's country of origin] living in the United States be able to cast their ballot in [R's country of origin] national elections, from the United States. Would you strongly agree, somewhat agree, somewhat disagree, or strongly disagree, or haven't you thought much about that?

Section S—Discrimination

"For the following questions, please indicate how much you agree with each statement."

191. "Poor people can get ahead in the United States if they work hard."

192. "Latinos can get ahead in the United States if they work hard."

"In the following questions, we are interested in your beliefs about the way other people have treated you in the U.S. Have you ever . . ."

193. "Been unfairly fired or denied a job or promotion?"
194. "Been unfairly treated by the police?"
195. "Been unfairly prevented from moving into a neighborhood (*vecindario o barrio*) because the landlord or a realtor refused to sell or rent you a house or apartment?"
196. "Been treated unfairly or badly at restaurants or stores?"
197. There are lots of possible reasons why people might be treated unfairly. What do you think was the main reason for your experience(s)? Would you say the main reason was [being Latino; being an immigrant; your national origin; your language or accent; your skin color; your gender; your age; other; don't know]?
198. In the most recent incident you experienced, what was the race or ethnicity of the person(s) treating you unfairly?

Section T—Income

199. Which of the following best describes the total income earned by all members of your household during 2004?
200. How many people work to contribute to this combined income?
201. How many people are currently supported by this combined income?
202. Do you receive now or have you ever received any kind of government assistance?

Appendix B

Latino National Survey Questionnaire (*en Español*)

S3. ¿Usted preferiría que yo hable en inglés o en español?

1   Inglés
2   Español

Alternative Phrasing for Introduction

Hola, mi nombre es _____. Estoy llamando desde Interviewing Service of America en nombre de un equipo de investigadores universitarios. Estamos conduciendo una encuesta pública acerca de la opinión de personas como usted acerca de asuntos importantes. Su participación es voluntaria, puede negarse a responder a cualquier pregunta, y la confidencialidad de sus respuestas será mantenida.

S1. ¿Usted se consdidera ser hispano(a) o latino(a) o una persona de origen español?

1   Si
2   No
3   NS/Rehusa

S2. Ahora podemos comenzar la encuesta

S4. Los términos más frequentemente usados para describir a las personas de descendencia latino-americana que viven en los EE.UU. son "Hispano" y "Latino." ¿De los dos, cuál prefiere usted, o no le interesa esta terminología?

1   Hispano
2   Latino
3   Los dos son aceptables
4   No le interesa
5   NS/NA

For Residents of New Mexico

S5. Muchos Hispanos en Nuevo México se refieren a sí mismos [se identifican como o usan el término, o se denominan] como Nuevomexicanos, Hispanos, o Nuevomexicanos en lugar de Mexicanos, Latinos o Hispanos. Desde su punto de vista, ¿son estos términos . . . ?

1   Igual que Latino o Hispano
2   Igual, pero significando Hispanos de Nuevo México
3   Algo diferente

A1. ¿Qué tan seguido mira usted noticias por televisión? Diría que diariamente, la mayoría de los días, solo una o dos veces por semana, o casi nunca?

1   Diariamente
2   La mayoría de los días
3   Una o dos veces por semana
4   Casi nunca

A2. ¿Qué tan seguido diría usted que lee periódicos diarios? ¿Diría que diariamente, la mayoría de los días, solo una o dos veces por semana, o casi nunca?

1   Diariamente
2   La mayoría de los días
3   Una o dos veces por semana
4   Casi nunca

A4. Para información acerca de asuntos públicos y políticos, ¿usted diría que depende más en televisión, radio y periódicos en español, o en televisión, radio y periódicos en inglés?

1   Inglés mas
2   Español mas
3   Ambos por igual (Bilingual)
4   Otro, NS/NA

A5. ¿Tiene usted acceso regular al Internet en su hogar, en otro lugar, o no tiene acceso?

1   Hogar
2   Otro lugar
3   Ambos
4   No tiene acceso

A6. ¿Qué tan interesado(a) está usted en la política y los asuntos públicos? ¿Diría que está muy interesado(a), algo interesado(a), o nada interesado(a)?

4   Muy interesado(a)
3   Algo interesado(a)
2   Nada interesado(a)
1   No está seguro(a)/ No sabe
5   Rehusa

B1. ¿En qué año nació usted? (RECORD 4-DIGIT YEAR, REFUSED = 9999)
_____ Año de nacimiento

B2. (INTERVIEWER: ENTER GENDER OF RESPONDENT)

1   Hombre
2   Mujer

B3a. ¿Cuántas personas, incluyéndose usted, viven actualmente en su hogar? No necesitamos sus nombres, solo el número. (RECORD EXACT NUMBER OF PEOPLE, DO NOT ACCEPT A RANGE) (REFUSED = 99)
Número de personas en el hogar _____

B3b. ¿Cuántas de estas personas tienen 18 años de edad o más? (RECORD EXACT NUMBER OF PEOPLE, DO NOT ACCEPT A RANGE) (REFUSED = 99)
Número de personas en el hogar que tienen 18 años de edad o más _____

B4. Familias de origen o ascendencia hispana/latina/española en los EE.UU. vienen de diferentes países. ¿De qué país viene su herencia latina? (Si la respuesta es "Estados Unidos," pregunta: Delinea su heréncia latina, ya hace varias generaciones pasadas, a algún país que no es los Estados Unidos?)

1   Argentina
2   Bolivia
3   Chile
4   Colombia
5   Costa Rica
6   Cuba
7   República Dominicana
8   Ecuador

9	El Salvador	17	Puerto Rico
10	Guatemala	18	España
11	Honduras	19	Uruguay
12	México	20	Venezuela
13	Nicaragua	23	(NO LEA) EE.UU.
14	Panamá	21	No sabe
15	Paraguay	22	Rehusa
16	Perú		

B5. ¿Nació usted en los EE.UU. continental, en Puerto Rico o en algún otro país?

1 EE.UU. continental (SKIP TO B11)
2 Puerto Rico (SKIP TO B8)
3 Otro país (CONTINUE)

B6. (IF SOME OTHER COUNTRY:) ¿Dónde nació usted?

1	Argentina	11	Honduras
2	Bolivia	12	México
3	Chile	13	Nicaragua
4	Colombia	14	Panamá
5	Costa Rica	15	Paraguay
6	Cuba	16	Perú
7	República Dominicana	17	Puerto Rico
8	Ecuador	18	España
9	El Salvador	19	Uruguay
10	Guatemala	20	Venezuela

(IF RESPONDENT BORN IN MEXICO, CONTINUE)
(IF RESPONDENT NOT BORN IN MEXICO, SKIP TO B8)

B7. Puede decirme, ¿en qué estado nació usted?

1	Aguacaliente	18	Nayarit
2	Baja California Norte	19	Nuevo Leon
3	Baja California Sur	20	Oaxaca
4	Campeche	21	Puebla
5	Coahuila	22	Querétaro
6	Colima	23	Quintana Roo
7	Chiapas	24	San Luis Potosí
8	Chihuahua	25	Sinaloa
9	Districto Federal	26	Sonora
10	Durango	27	Tabasco
11	Guanajuato	28	Tamaulipas
12	Guerrero	29	Tlaxcala
13	Hidalgo	30	Veracruz
14	Jalisco	31	Yucatán
15	Estado de México	32	Zacatecas
16	Michoacán	33	No sabe
17	Morelos	34	Rehusa

B8. ¿Cuál diría que es el motivo principal por el que usted vino a vivir en los EE.UU.?

1 Educación
2 Reunificación de la familia

3   Escapar malestar político
4   Mis padres me trajeron cuando era niño
5   Mejorar la situación económica
6   Otro (ESPECIFICADO) _____

B9. ¿En qué año llego por primera vez a los EE.UU.? [add "continental" if born in PR]? (RECORD 4-DIGIT YEAR, REFUSED = 9999)

_____ Año de llegada

B10. ¿Es usted un(a) ciudadano(a) americano(a) naturalizado(a)?

1   Si
2   No

B11a. ¿Dónde nacieron sus padres? ¿Nacieron los dos en los EE.UU., solo uno de ellos nació en los EE.UU., o ambos nacieron en otro país?

1   Uno de los padres
2   Ambos padres
3   Ninguno de los dos
4   No sabe
5   Rehusa

B11b. ¿Cuántos de sus abuelos, si alguno, nacieron fuera de los Estado Unidos?

0   Ninguno
1   Uno
2   Dos
3   Tres
4   Todos
5   No sabe
6   Rehusa

ASK ONLY OF ENGLISH INTERVIEWEES:

C2. ¿Qué tan bien habla en inglés? ¿Diría que usted puede mantener una conversación en inglés (ambos entendiendo y hablando) muy bien, bastante bien, solo un poco, o nada?

4   Muy bien
3   Bastante bien
2   Solo un poco
1   Nada
5   Otro
6   NS
7   NA

C4. ¿Qué tan importante piensa usted que es para usted y su familia mantener la habilidad de hablar en español?

4   Muy importante
3   Algo importante
2   No muy importante
1   Nada importante

C5. Qué tan importante usted piensa que es que todos en los EE.UU. aprendan inglés?

4   Muy importante
3   Algo importante

2 No muy importante
1 Nada importante

D1. ¿Usted participa en las actividades de un grupo social, cultural, cívico o político, más de uno de tales grupos, o no participa en ningún grupo como tales?

1 Si, uno
2 Sí, más de un grupo
3 Ningún
4 NS
5 Rehusa

D2. Deténgame cuando yo llegue a su respuesta. ¿Cómo describiría a estos grupos? Diría que son . . . (READ LIST)

1 Mayormente latinos
2 Mezcla de latinos y blancos
3 Mayormente negros
4 Mezcla de latinos y negros
9 Mayormente blancos

[IN CA, TX, NY, IL ADD THESE CATEGORIES]

5 Mayormente asiáticos
6 Mezcla de latinos y asiáticos
7 (NO LEA) Otro
8 NS/NA
0 Mezcla de todos mencionados

D3. Cuando es necesario hallar una solución para un asunto o problema en su comunidad, ¿usted trabajaría con grupos u organizaciones existentes para reunir a la gente, se reunirían informalmente, o usted no haría nada para resolver este asunto?

1 Usaría organizaciones existentes
2 Se reunirían informalmente
3 Ambos
4 No haría nada
5 No sabe
6 Rehusa

D4. ¿Ha usted tratado alguna vez de hacer que los oficiales del gobierno presten atención a algo que le preocupa a usted, ya sea llamando, escribiendo una carta, o yendo a una reunión?

1 Si
2 No
3 NS/NA

D5. ¿Ha hecho esto más de una vez?

2 Si, más de una vez
3 No
4 No sabe (SKIP NEXT QUESTION)
5 Rehusa (SKIP NEXT QUESTION)

D6. ¿Era latino o hispano el oficial con quien usted se puso en contacto?

1 Si, latino o hispano
2 No, otra raza/etnicidad

3   No sabe

4   Rehusa

D7. ¿Cuál es su estado civil/matrimonial actual?

1   Soltero(a)

3   No casado(a) pero viviendo juntos en

4   Casado(a) pero no viviendo juntos

5   Casado(a)

6   Divorciado(a)

7   Viudo(a)

D8. ¿Cuál es la raza o etnicidad de su (Respuesta para la pregunta D7)?

1   LATINO

2   Negro(a)

3   Blanco(a)

4   Indio(a) Americano(a), nativo(a) de Alaska o Indígena

5   Asiático(a) o Isleño(a) del Pacífico

6   Otra (Por favor especifique:)

7   LSNS

8   Rehusa

D9. ¿Cuántos niños tiene usted, si tiene hijos? (RECORD EXACT NUMBER OF CHILDREN, DO NOT ACCEPT A RANGE) (REFUSED = 99)

_____Cantidad de niños.

D10. ¿Tiene usted niños menores de 18 a quienes usted asiste financieramente y que viven en otro país?

1   Si

2   No

D11. ¿Usted considera que sus niños son latinos?

1   Si

2   No

3   Rehusa

4   NS/No tiene importancia

D12. ¿Cuál es el nivel más alto de educación formal que usted ha completado?

0   Ninguno

1   Octavo grado o menos

2   Algo de escuela secundaria

3   GED

4   Graduado de escuela secundaria

5   Algo de colegio universitario

6   Diploma de universidad de 4 años

7   Diploma de Graduado o Professional

D13. ¿Dónde completó su nivel más alto de educación? ¿En los EE.UU. o en otro lugar?

1   EE.UU.

2   Puerto Rico

3   Otro lugar

D14. ¿Cuál de lo siguiente describe mejor el nivel de educación de sus padres? ¿Diría que . . . ?
(LEA LISTA)

   1   Ninguno de ellos finalizó escuela secundaria
   2   Al menos uno de ellos finalizó escuela secundaria
   3   Al menos uno de ellos asistió a la universidad
   4   Al menos uno de ellos obtuvo un diploma de universidad
   5   Al menos uno de ellos recibió un diploma
   6   No sabe

E1. ¿Qué calificación le daría usted a las escuelas públicas de su comunidad? ¿A, B, C, D, o Falla?

   1   A
   2   B
   3   C
   4   D
   5   Falla

E2. ¿Usted tuvo niños matriculados en la escuela primaria o secundaria el año pasado?

   1   Si
   2   No (SKIP TO E13)

Ahora quisiera hacerle preguntas acerca de un niño en particular. Piense en el niño que fue el último en cumplir años y que estaba matriculado en la escuela el año pasado. Para las próximas preguntas, por favor enfoquemos nos en este niño.

E3. ¿Estaba este niño matriculado en una escuela pública o privada?

   1   Pública
   2   Privada

E4. ¿Es este un niño o una niña?

   1   Niño
   3   Niña

E5. Durante el año escolar que recién finalizó, ¿en qué año escolar estaba su niño(a)? (RECORD THE NUMBER OF THE GRADE OR "K" FOR KINDERGARTEN)

_____ año escolar

E6. ¿Hasta qué nivel usted quisiera ver que este(a) niño(a) vaya a la escuela?

   1   Graduarse de escuela secundaria u obtener diploma GED
   2   Recibir algún entrenamiento
   3   Graduarse de colegio universitario
   4   Recibir un diploma avanzado de graduado

E7. Aqui hay una lista de cosas que algunos padres han hecho y que otros no han hecho, relacionadas con la escuela de sus niños. ¿Cuál de estas cosas ha hecho usted? ¿Diría que usted ha . . . (READ ITEM)? (MARK "SI, NO, NO LO SABE, REHUSA")

E7.A ¿Tenido una reunión con el maestro de su niño(a)?

   1   Si
   2   No
   3   Sabe
   4   Rehusa

E7.B ¿Asistido a una reunión de PTA (Asociación de Padres y Maestros)?

1 Si
2 No
3 Sabe
4 Rehusa

E7.C ¿Actuado como voluntario(a) para la escuela de su niño(a)?

1 Si
2 No
3 Sabe
4 Rehusa

E8. Cuando usted ha estado en contacto con oficiales de la escuela, ¿diría que su experiencia fue muy buena, algo buena, no muy buena, o nada buena?

5 Muy buena
4 Algo buena
3 No muy buena
2 Nada buena
1 No ha tenido contacto con oficiales de la escuela

E9. ¿Había un programa especializado para enseñar inglés a niños de habla hispana en la escuela de su niño(a)?

1 Si
2 No

E10. ¿Estuvo su niño(a) en ese programa alguna vez?

1 Si
2 No
3 Rehusa

E11. ¿Hasta qué nivel piensa que su niño(a) irá a la escuela?

1 Algo de escuela secundaria
2 Obtener diploma GED
3 Graduarse de la escuela secundaria
4 Recibir algún entrenamiento
5 Graduarse de colegio universitario
6 Recibir diploma avanzado de graduado o profesional

E13. ¿Cuál es su raza? ¿Es usted blanco(a), negro(a), indio(a) americano(a), asiático(a), nativo(a) de Hawaii/isleño(a) del Pacífico, o alguna otra raza o más de una?

1 Blanco(a)
2 Negro(a), Afro-Americano(a)
3 Indio(a) americano(a) o nativo(a) de Alaska
4 Nativo de la India (Asia)
5 Nativo(a) de Hawaii o isleño(a) del Pacífico
6 Alguna otra raza (especifique)
9 (DO NOT READ) Rehusa

E14. En los EE.UU., usamos un número de categorías para describirnos racialmente. ¿Usted siente que los latinos/hispanos son un grupo racial distinto en America?

1 Si

2 No
3 (NO LEA) Quizás
4 NS/No responde

E16. Los latinos pueden ser descritos en base al tono de la piel o cutis. Usando una escala del 1 al 5, donde 1 representa muy oscuro y 5 es muy claro, ¿donde se ubicaría usted en esa escala? (Respuesta del 1 al 5; REFUSED = 9)

E17. Deténgame cuando o llegue a la respuesta correcta. ¿Con qué tradición religiosa se identifica más usted?

1 Católica
2 Asambleas de dios
3 Bautista de sur
4 Pentecostal
5 Otra Protestante (Cristiana o Protestante)
6 Mormona
7 Judía
8 No se identifica con ninguna denominación religiosa
0 Testigos De Jehova
9 Otra

E18. ¿Usted se considera Cristiano(a) Nacido(a)-de Nuevo [" born-again"], Cristiano(a) Lleno del Espíritu ["spirit-filled Christian"], o involucrado(a) en el Movimiento Carismático?

1 Si
2 No
3 No sabe
4 Rehusa

E19. ¿Qué tan seguido asiste usted a servicios religiosos? ¿Diría que asiste . . . ? (READ LIST)

1 Más de una vez por semana
2 Una vez por semana
3 Una vez por mes
4 Solo en fiestas religiosas mayores
5 Nunca
6 NS
7 Rehusa

E20. ¿Ha servido usted o algún miembro de su familia en las fuerzas armadas de los EE.UU.?

1 Si
2 No

IF US BORN, SKIP TO G1.

IF THE ANSWER IN B10 IS NATURALIZED, SKIP TO F2.

IF NON-CITIZEN, ASK . . .

IF RESPONDENT IS PUERTO RICAN ALSO SKIP TO G1.

F1. Ahora quisiéramos hacerle preguntas acerca de la ciudadanía de EE.UU. ¿Es usted ciudadano(a) de EE.UU., está actualmente tramitando su ciudadanía, está planeando hacer trámites para obtener su ciudadanía, o no está planeando en convertirse en ciudadano(a)?

2 Actualmente tramitando su ciudadanía (SKIP TO F4)
3 Planeando hacer trámites para su ciudadanía (SKIP TO F4)

4 No está planeando en convertirse en ciudadano(a) (SKIP TO F4)

5 NS/Rehusa

F2. ¿Cuál diría que es el motivo principal por el cual usted escogió convertirse en ciudadano(a)?

[OPEN ENDED, INTERVIEWER CODE INTO CATEGORIES]

1 Para que le sea posible votar

2 "Derechos legales, políticos o civiles" o "Para que la gente no me trate injustamente"

3 Oportunidad económica

4 Para recibir beneficios del gobierno

5 Para reunirse con su esposa(o), familiares, y/o niños

6 Para ser más americano(a)

7 Otro (ESPECIFICA POR FAVOR)

F3. ¿En qué año se convirtió en ciudadano de EE.UU.? (RECORD 4-DIGIT YEAR, CAN'T RECALL = 9999)

_____ año que se conviertió

F4. ¿Cuál diría que es el motivo principal para convertirse en ciudadano de EE.UU.?

1 Para que le sea posible votar

2 Derechos

3 Oportunidad económica

4 Para recibir beneficios del gobierno

5 Para reunirse con su esposa(o), familiares, y/o niños

6 Para ser más americano(a)

7 Otro (ESPECIFICA POR FAVOR)

F5. ¿Cuál diría que es el motivo principal por el que usted no se ha naturalizado?

1 Cuesta demasiado

2 No sabe como hacerlo

3 Lleva demasiado tiempo

4 Esta aquí sin los

5 Planea regresar a su país

6 Afección/lealtad a su propio país

7 No tiene la habilidad necesaria con el idioma

8 Otro (ESPECIFICA POR FAVOR)

9 NS/Reh

G1. Pensando en asuntos como oportunidades para empleo, progreso educacional o ingreso monetario, ¿cuánto tienen los latinos en común con otros grupos raciales en los EE.UU., ahora? ¿Usted diría que los latinos tienen mucho en común, algo en común, poco en común, o nada en común . . .

G1.A con Afro-Americanos?

4 Mucho

3 Algo

2 Poco

1 Nada

5 NS/NA

con blancos?

4 Mucho

3 Algo

2 Poco

1 Nada

5 NS/NA

(ASK ONLY IN CA, TX, NY, IL):

con Asiático-Americanos?

4 Mucho

3 Algo

2 Poco

1 Nada

5 NS/NA

G2. Ahora quisiera que piense en la situación política de los latinos en la sociedad. Pensando en cosas como los servicios del gobierno y empleo con el gobierno, poder político y la representación politica, ¿cuánto tienen los latinos en común con otros grupos raciales en los EE.UU., ahora? ¿Usted diría que los latinos tienen mucho en común, algo en común, poco en común, o nada en común . . .

G2.A con Afro-Americanos?

4 Mucho

3 Algo

2 Poco

1 Nada

5 NS/NA

G2.B con blancos?

4 Mucho

3 Algo

2 Poco

1 Nada

5 NS/NA

(ASK ONLY IN CA, TX, NY, IL):

G2.C con Asiático-Americanos?

4 Mucho

3 Algo

2 Poco

1 Nada

5 NS/NA

G3. ¿En qué medida depende que los latinos avanzaran, de que tambien los Afro-Americanos avancen? ¿Mucho, algo, poco, o nada?

4 Mucho

3 Algo

2 Poco

1 Nada

G4. Algunas personas han sugerido que los latinos o hispanos están en competencia con Afro-Americanos. Después que yo lea cada uno de los siguientes artículos, ¿podría decirme si usted cree que existe una competencia fuerte, una competencia débil, o que no hay competencia con Afro-Americanos? ¿Qué te parece . . .

G4.A en obtener trabajo?

   3 Competencia fuerte
   2 Competencia débil
   1 No hay competencia

G4.B en el tener acceso a la educación y las escuelas de calidad?

   3 Competencia fuerte
   2 Competencia débil
   1 No hay competencia

G4.C en obtener empleos con el gobierno de la ciudad o del estado?

   3 Competencia fuerte
   2 Competencia débil
   1 No hay competencia

G4.D en el tener representantes latinos en oficinas obtenidas por voto?

   3 Competencia fuerte
   2 Competencia débil
   1 No hay competencia

G5. ¿Qué tan importante es para los latinos . . . (READ ITEMS):

(ROTATE ITEMS)

G5.A Cambiar para integrarse a la sociedad norteamericana?

   3 Muy importante
   2 Algo importante
   1 Nada importante
   4 No sabe
   5 Rehusa

G5.B Mantener su distinta cultura?

   3 Muy importante
   2 Algo importante
   1 Nada importante
   4 No sabe
   5 Rehusa

G6. ¿Como describiría a sus amigos? Son ellos . . . (READ RESPONSE ITEMS)

   1 Mayormente latinos
   2 Mayormente blancos
   3 Mezcla de latinos y blancos
   4 Mayormente negros
   5 Mezcla de latinos y negros

   [FOR RESPONDENTS IN CA, TX, NY, IL ADD CATEGORIES OF:]

   6 Mayormente asiáticos
   7 Mezcla de Latino y asiáticos
   8 (NO LEA) Otro
   0 (NO LEA) Mezcla de todos los mencionados
   9 NS/NA

G7. ¿Como describiría a sus compañeros de trabajo? ¿Son ellos . . . ? (READ RESPONSE ITEMS)

1 Mayormente latinos
2 Mayormente blancos
3 Mezcla de latinos y blancos
4 Mayormente negros
5 Mezcla de latinos y negros
8 (NO LEA) Otro
0 (NO LEA) Mezcla de to todos mencionados
9 NS/NA

Section H. Gender

H1. La gente frecuentemente tiene opiniones diferentes en cuanto a la posición social de la mujer. Por favor dígame si usted está fuertemente de acuerdo, algo de acuerdo, algo en desacuerdo, fuertemente en desacuerdo, o si usted no tiene opinión acerca de las siguientes declaraciones:

H1.A "Los hombres y las mujeres deberían obtener igual paga cuando están en el mismo trabajo."

5 Fuertemente de acuerdo
4 Algo de acuerdo
3 No tiene opinión
2 Algo en desacuerdo
1 Fuertemente en desacuerdo
9 NA

H1.B "Las madres deberían de ser más responsables que los padres por el cuidado de sus niños."

5 Fuertemente de acuerdo
4 Algo de acuerdo
3 No tiene opinión
2 Algo en desacuerdo
1 Fuertemente en desacuerdo
9 NA

H1.C "Las mujeres deberían de tener acceso fácil a control de la natalidad/contraceptivos."

5 Fuertemente de acuerdo
4 Algo de acuerdo
3 No tiene opinión
2 Algo en desacuerdo
1 Fuertemente en desacuerdo
9 NA

H1.D "Los hombres están mejor calificados que las mujeres para ser líderes políticos."

5 Fuertemente de acuerdo
4 Algo de acuerdo
3 No tiene opinión
2 Algo en desacuerdo
1 Fuertemente en desacuerdo
9 NA

I1. ¿Está usted registrado(a) para votar en la actualidad en los EE.UU.?

1 Si
2 No
3 No sabe
4 NA

I2. ¿Aproximadamente, cuál era su edad cuando se registró por primera vez en los EE.UU.?
(RECORD EXACT AGE, DO NOT ACCEPT A RANGE, REFUSED = 99)

_____Edad cuando se registró

I7. Hablando con la gente acerca de las elecciones, a menudo hallamos que muchas personas no pudieron votar porque no estaban registradas, estaban enfermas, o simplemente no tenían tiempo. En cuanto a usted, ¿votó en las elecciones presidenciales del mes de noviembre pasado?

1 Si
2 No
3 NS/Rehusa

I3. En las elecciones del 2004, ¿alguien hizo contacto con usted para votar o contribuir dinero para un candidato o una campaña política?

1 Si
2 No (SKIP TO I5A)
3 No sabe

[PARA VOTATENTES]

I5a. ¿Por quién votó para presidente en estas últimas elecciones?

1 George W. Bush
2 John Kerry
3 Ralph Nader
4 Otro
8 NS

[PARA PERSONAS QUE NO VOTARON O QUE NO SON CIUDADANOS]:

I5b. ¿A quién favorecía o prefería para presidente en estas últimas elecciones?

1 George W. Bush
2 John Kerry
3 Ralph Nader
4 Otro
8 NS

I6. Si un partido o candidato estuviera tratando de hacer contacto con usted acerca de una elección, ¿a cuál de lo siguiente prestaría usted más atención?

1 Envío por correo o volante en su puerta
2 Llamada telefónica automatizada
3 Llamada telefónica de una persona real
4 E-mail (correo electrónico)
5 Visita personal
6 NS/Rehusa

(IF REGISTERED, SKIP TO I9)

ASK ONLY OF NON-VOTING REGISTERED US CITIZENS (FOR THOSE IN I1 THAT RESPONDED "NO" WOULD BE THE NON-REGISTERED CITIZENS)

I8. Mucha gente no pudo votar debido a una variedad de motivos. En cuanto a usted, ¿cuál fue el motivo principal por el cual no pudo votar en las elecciones del mes de noviembre pasado?

1 No tuvo tiempo/demasiado ocupado(a)
2 No está interesado(a) en las elecciones/la política
3 Emergencia familiar
4 No le gustaron los candidatos
5 Fuera de la ciudad

6   Se olvidó de las elecciones
7   No tenía medio de transporte
8   Líneas muy largas para votar
9   Trató de votar pero le dijeron que no era eligible
10 La elección parecía haber terminado en el momento en que yo estaba dispuesto a votar

11 Pensé que mi voto no importaba
12 Enfermo(a)
13 Demasiado complicado
14 Otro: (especifique)
15 NS/Rehusa

I9. ¿Está usted registrado como Republicano(a), Demócrata, Independiente o con algún otro partido?

1   Demócrata
2   Republicano(a)
3   Independiente
4   Algún otro partido
5   No era requerido en el estado
6   NS

I10. ¿Usted sabe cómo y dónde registrarse para votar?

1   Si
2   No
3   No está seguro(a)

J1. En términos generales, ¿usted se considera normalmente Demócrata, Republicano(a), Independiente, de algún otro partido, o algo diferente?

1   Demócrata
2   Republicano(a)
3   Independiente (SKIP TO J3)
4   No le interesa (SKIP TO J4)
5   No sabe/otro partido (SKIP TO J4)

IF DEMOCRAT OR REPUBLICAN:

J2. ¿Usted se considera ser fuertemente (Demócrata o Republicano(a)), o no muy fuertemente (Demócrata o Republicano(a))

1   Fuertemente Demócrata
2   Fuertemente Republicano(a)
3   No muy fuertemente Demócrata
4   No muy fuertemente Republicano(a)

IF INDEPENDENT:

J3. ¿Usted se considera más cerca del partido Republicano o del Demócrata?

1   Republicano
2   Demócrata
3   NS/ No está seguro(a)

IF OTHER:

J4. ¿Usted se considera más cerca del partido Republicano o del Demócrata?

1   Mas cerca del Republicano
2   Mas cerca del Demócrata
3   NS/Rehusa

J5.¿Cuál de los siguientes describen mejor como sus sentimientos acerca de los partidos han cambiado en los últimos años?

1   Me siento mucho más cerca a los Republicanos de lo que estaba antes
2   Me siento algo más cerca a los Republicanos de lo que estaba antes
3   Me siento mucho más cerca a los Demócratas de lo que estaba antes
4   Me siento algo más cerca a los Demócratas de lo que estaba antes
5   Mis sentimientos no han cambiado
6   No sabe/Otro

J6. En términos generales, en lo relacionado a política, ¿usted se considera ser conservador[a], centro izquierdo[a] /(o en los EE.UU dicen liberal), estar entre los dos, o usted no piensa de sí mismo(a) en estos términos?

1   Conservador(a)
2   Centro izquierdo(a) (o en los EE.UU dicen liberal) (SKIP TO J8)
3   Entre los dos (SKIP TO J9)
4   No piensa de sí mismo(a) en estos términos
5   No sabe

J7 ¿Usted se considera ser fuertemente o no muy fuertemente conservador(a)?

1   Fuertemente conservador(a)
2   No muy fuertemente conservador(a)
3   No sabe
4   No es aplicable

J8. ¿Usted se considera ser fuertemente o no muy fuertemente liberal?

1   Fuertemente liberal
2   No muy fuertemente liberal
3   No sabe
4   No es aplicable

J9. ¿Usted se considera ser más del centro izquierdo(a) (o en los EE.UU. dicen liberal), o más como un conservador, o verdaderamente está entre los dos?

1   Se inclina a conservativo(a)
2   Se inclina a centro izquierdo(a) (en los EE.UU. dicen liberal)
3   Firmemente entre los dos
4   No sabe
5   No es aplicable

J10. ¿Qué partido político, Demócrata o Republicano, tiene la mayoría en la Cámara de Representantes de EE.UU.?

1   Demócrata
2   Republicano
3   (NO LEA) NS

J11. En los EE.UU., las elecciones presidenciales son decididas estado-por-estado. Puede decirme, en las elecciones del 2004, ¿qué candidato, Bush o Kerry, ganó la mayoría de votos en (el estado en donde vive hoy)?

1   Bush
2   Kerry
3   NS
4   NA/Rehusa

J12. ¿Cuál de los partidos políticos es más conservador que el otro a nivel nacional, el Demócrata o el Republicano?

1 Demócrata
2 Republicano
3 NS/Rehusa

FOR RESIDENTS OF WASHINGTON STATE

J13. Algunos estados tienen programas de agencias estatales y universidades para aumentar las oportunidades específicamente enfocadas a mujeres y minorías, incluyendo latinos, mientras que otros estados prohíben estos programas. ¿Tiene el estado de Washington tales programas o se prohíben estas prácticas?

1 Hay una prohibición
2 Permite tales programas
3 NS/NA

FOR RESIDENTS OF IOWA STATE

J14. Muchos estados tienen leyes que limitan las actividades y servicios del gobierno al idioma inglés. ¿Tiene Iowa tal ley?

1 Si
2 No
3 No está seguro(a)/No sabe

FOR RESIDENTS OF COLORADO

K2b. En 2004, Ken Salazar y John Salazar fueron elegidos como miembros del Senado de EE.UU. y de la Cámara de Representantes de EE.UU., para Colorado. Qué efecto tiene esta elección en la representación de hispanos/latinos? Usted diría que los hispanos/latinos están ahora . . . ?

5 Mucho mejor representados
4 Un poco mejor representados
3 Representados casi igual que antes
2 No tan bien representados
1 Mucho menos representados

K2. La gente puede preferir a un candidato por una variedad de diferentes motivos. Qué tan importante es para usted que un candidato . . .

K2A. sea Latino?

3 Muy importante
2 Algo importante
1 Nada importante

K2.B hable español?

3 Muy importante
2 Algo importante
1 Nada importante

K2.C comparta sus posiciones y preocupaciones?

3 Muy importante
2 Algo importante
1 Nada importante

K3. La gente tiene diferentes ideas acerca del gobierno en los EE.UU. Por favor, ¿dígame qué tan fuertemente usted está de acuerdo o en desacuerdo con cada una de estas declaraciones?

K3A. "El gobierno está mayormente administrado por unos pocos grandes intereses que buscan su propio beneficio, y no para el beneficio de todo el pueblo." Está usted de acuerdo, ni de acuerdo ni en desacuerdo, o en desacuerdo con esta declaración?

4 Fuertemente de acuerdo
3 Algo de acuerdo
2 Algo en desacuerdo
1 Fuertemente en desacuerdo
9 NS/NA

K3B. "La gente como yo no tiene voz en lo que hace el gobierno. Una persona como yo no puede realmente entender lo que está sucediendo."

4 Fuertemente de acuerdo
3 Algo de acuerdo
2 Algo en desacuerdo
1 Fuertemente en desacuerdo
9 NS/NA

K3.C "A veces la política y el gobierno parecen ser tan complicados que una persona como yo no realmente no entiende lo que está pasando."

4 Fuertemente de acuerdo
3 Algo de acuerdo
2 Algo en desacuerdo
1 Fuertemente en desacuerdo
9 NS/NA

K3.D "Es mejor para la gente evitar el contacto con el gobierno."

4 Fuertemente de acuerdo
3 Algo de acuerdo
2 Algo en desacuerdo
1 Fuertemente en desacuerdo
9 NS/NA

K4. ¿Qué parte del tiempo usted confía en que el gobierno hará lo que es propio/debido? ¿Casi siempre, la mayoría del tiempo, parte del tiempo, o nunca?

4 Casi siempre
3 La mayoría del tiempo
2 Parte del tiempo
1 Nunca

K5. ¿Estaría usted fuertemente de acuerdo, algo de acuerdo, algo en desacuerdo, fuertemente en desacuerdo con las siguientes declaraciones, o usted no tiene una opinión?

K5.A "Sin interesar cuáles son las creencias políticas de una persona, tienen derecho a gozar de los mismos derechos y protecciones legales como cualquier otro."

4 De acuerdo
3 Algo de acuerdo
2 Algo en desacuerdo
1 Fuertemente en desacuerdo
5 NS/Rehusa

K5.B "La mayoría de la gente que no progresa no debería de culpar al sistema politico, solo tienen a sí mismos para culpar."

4   De acuerdo
3   Algo de acuerdo
2   Algo en desacuerdo
1   Fuertemente en desacuerdo
5   NS/Rehusa

K5.D "No es realmente un problema tan grande si algunas personas tienen más oportunidades que otras en la vida."

4   De acuerdo
3   Algo de acuerdo
2   Algo en desacuerdo
1   Fuertemente en desacuerdo
5   NS/Rehusa

K6. Ahora quisiera hacerle preguntas acerca de sus sentimientos hacia el Presidente Bush. Pensando en el tipo de persona que él es, ¿usted diría que lo ve muy favorablemente, algo favorablemente, algo desfavorablemente, muy desfavorablemente, o usted no tiene un sentimiento hacia él en un sentido u otro?

5   Muy favorablemente
4   Algo favorablemente
3   Algo desfavorablemente
2   Muy desfavorablemente
1   No tiene ningún sentimiento
6   NS/Rehusa

K7. Le voy a leer una lista de características acerca del Presidente Bush. De la siguiente lista, ¿cuáles son los motivos más importantes por los que usted lo ve a él favorablemente? (INTER-VIEWER: READ LIST).

1   En sus políticas publicas
2   Lo agradable que es
3   Su liderazgo
4   Su habilidad para hablar español
5   El hecho de que se identifica bien con los latinos
6   Su dedicación a su fe cristiana

K8. ¿Qué tan fuertemente usted aprueba o desaprueba cómo el Presidente Bush se está desempeñando como presidente? ¿Usted diría que aprueba fuertemente, aprueba un poco, desaprueba un poco, desaprueba fuertemente, o usted no tiene fuertes sentimientos acerca de eso?

4   Aprueba fuertemente
3   Aprueba un poco
2   Desaprueba un poco
1   Desaprueba fuertemente
5   No tiene fuertes sentimientos
6   NS/No responde

K10. Ahora, pensando acerca de la economía en el país en total, usted diría que a través del último año la economía de la nación ha mejorado, permanecido casi igual, o empeorado?

3 Mejorado
2 Permanecido casi igual
1 Empeorado
4 NS/Rehusa

K11. ¿Qué diría de su situación financiera personal? A través del último año, ¿ha mejorado, permanecido casi igual, o empeorado?

3 Mejorado
2 Permanecido casi igual
1 Empeorado
4 NS/Rehusa

K12. ¿Cuál es su estado actual en cuanto a empleo? Deténgame cuando yo lea su situación. Está usted . . . ? (READ ITEMS FROM LIST, STOP WHEN RESPONDENT INDICATES APPROPRIATE ANSWER)

1 Trabajando en empleo regular
2 Trabajando en más de un empleo
3 Trabajando a jornada parcial
4 Trabaja en empleos ocasionales o por el día
5 Actualmente desempleado
6 Es estudiante regular
7 Jubilado(a) o incapacitado(a) permanentemente
8 No está trabajando fuera de su hogar

K13. ¿Qué tipo de trabajo hace usted normalmente? Por ejemplo, ¿es usted principalmente carpintero, maestro, empleado de ventas, colocador de ladrillos, procesador de carne, hace labor de agricultura, etc.?

_____

K14. ¿Qué tipo de trabajo hace usted normalmente en los EE.UU.? Por ejemplo, ¿es usted principalmente carpintero, maestro, empleado de ventas, colocador de ladrillos, procesador de carne, hace labor de agricultura, etc.?

_____

K15. Es usted o alguien en su hogar miembro de un sindicato laboral?

1 Si
2 No
3 NS/Rehusa

K16. Donde usted vive actualmente, ¿le han pagado alguna vez menos de lo prometido, o no le han pagado, por un trabajo que usted completó?

1 Pagado menos
2 No le pagaron
3 Ambos
4 Ninguno de estos
5 NS
6 Rehusa/NA

K17. Es usted dueño(a) de su residencia en los EE.UU., o alquila?

1 Dueño(a)
2 Alquila

3 Otro

4 Rehusa

K18. ¿Por cuántos años ha vivido en su domicilio actual? (RECORD EXACT NUMBER OF YEARS, DO NOT ACCEPT A RANGE) (LESS THAN 1 YEAR = 0; REFUSED = 99)

_____años que ha vivido en su domicilio actual

FOR RESIDENTS OF WASHINGTON STATE

K18A1. Durante el último año, ¿ha usted considerado o dado algún paso para mudarse fuera de California?

1 Si

2 No

K18A2. ¿A qué estado(s) ha considerado mudarse?

_____

K18A3. ¿Cuál es el motivo principal por el que está considerando mudarse fuera del estado? (NO LEA LA LISTA)

1 Familiares o amigos se han ido

2 Oportunidades de trabajo limitadas en California

3 Salarios demasiado bajos

4 Malas escuelas

5 Malos barrios/vecindades

6 Alquileres o precio de las casas altos

7 Ambiente hóstil contra los latinos en el estado

8 Otro (ESPECIFIQUE)

K19. ¿Usted ha vivido en algún otro estado de los EE.UU. anteriormente?

1 Si

2 No

3 NS/Rehusa

K19b. ¿En qué estado?

_____

L1. Pensando en asuntos como oportunidades de trabajo, logros educacionales o ingreso monetario, ¿cuánto tiene usted en común con otros latinos/hispanos? ¿Diría que usted tiene mucho en común, algo en común, poco en común, o nada en común?

4 Mucho

3 Algo

2 Poco

1 Nada

5 NS/NA

L2. Ahora, pensando en asuntos como servicios y empleos del gobierno, poder político, y representación, ¿cuánto tiene usted en común con otros latinos/hispanos? ¿Diría que usted tiene mucho en común, algo en común, poco en común, o nada en común?

4 Mucho

3 Algo

2 Poco

1   Nada
5   NS/NA

L3. ¿En qué medida depende que usted avance de que otros latinos/hispanos también avancen? ¿Mucho, algo, poco, o nada?

4   Mucho
3   Algo
2   Poco
1   Nada
5   NS/NA

L4. Pensando en asuntos como oportunidades de empleo, educación o ingreso, ¿cuánto tiene en común con otros latinos/hispanos? ¿Diría que tiene mucho en común, algo en común, poco en común, o nada en común con otros latinos?

4   Mucho
3   Algo
2   Poco
1   Nada
5   NS/NA

L5. Ahora, pensando en asuntos como servicios y empleos del gobierno, poder político, y representación, ¿cuánto tiene en común con otros latinos/hispanos? ¿Diría que tiene mucho en común, algo en común, poco en común, o nada en común con otros latinos?

4   Mucho
3   Algo
2   Poco
1   Nada
5   NS/NA

L6. ¿En qué medida depende que los [Respuesta a pregunta B4] avancen de que otros latinos o hispanos también lo estén pasando bien? ¿Mucho, algo, poco, o nada?

4   Mucho
3   Algo
2   Poco
1   Nada
5   NS/NA

L6b. ¿En general, cómo evaluaría la actitud del público en \:SAMPLE: hacia los inmigrantes latinos? Usted diría que han sido muy bienvenidos, bienvenidos, muy poco bienvenidos, o nada bienvenidos?

4   Muy bienvenidos
3   Bienvenidos
2   No muy bienvenidos
1   Nada bienvenidos
9   NS/NR

L7. Algunas personas han sugerido que los Latinos/Hispanos están en competencia con otros latinos. Después que yo lea cada uno de los siguientes artículos, ¿podría decirme si usted cree que es una competencia fuerte, una competencia débil, o que no hay competencia con otros latinos?

L7.A En obtener trabajo.

3 Competencia fuerte
2 Competencia débil
1 No hay competencia

L7.B En tener acceso a la educación y a escuelas de calidad.

3 Competencia fuerte
2 Competencia débil
1 No hay competencia

L7.C Obteniendo empleos con el gobierno de la ciudad o del estado.

3 Competencia fuerte
2 Competencia débil
1 No hay competencia

L7.D En tener representativos latinos en puestos obtenidos por el voto de la gente.

3 Competencia fuerte
2 Competencia débil
1 No hay competencia

Le voy a leer una lista de rótulos que describen a la gente, y quisiera que me diga qué tan fuertemente usted se identifica con cada uno. El primero es . . .

(ROTATE THE ORDER OF THE NEXT THREE QUESTIONS)

L8. "Americano." [En general,] ¿Qué tan fuertemente usted piensa de sí mismo(a) como Americano(a)?

4 Muy fuertemente
3 Algo fuertemente
2 No muy fuertemente
1 Nada
5 NS/NA
6 Rehusa

L9. "(Respuesta para la pregunta B4)." [En general,] ¿Qué tan fuertemente usted piensa de sí mismo(a) como (Respuesta para la pregunta B4)?

4 Muy fuertemente
3 Algo fuertemente
2 No muy fuertemente
1 Nada
5 NS/NA
6 Rehusa

L10. Finalmente, [en general,] ¿Qué tan fuertemente usted piensa de sí mismo(a) como hispano(a)/ latino(a)?

4 Muy fuertemente
3 Algo fuertemente
2 No muy fuertemente
1 Nada
5 NS/NA
6 Rehusa

L11. De los tres términos anteriores, latino(a) o hispano(a), (Respuesta para la pregunta B4), o Americano(a), ¿cuál lo(a) describe mejor a usted?

1 Latino(a)/hispano(a)
2 Nacionalidad a su país de origen
3 Americano(a)
4 Ninguno de éstos
5 NS/NA
6 Rehusa

L12. Cuando usted piensa en lo que significa ser completamente Americano(a) en los ojos de la mayoría de los Americanos, usted piensa que es muy importante, algo importante, o nada importante . . .

L12.A haber nacido en los EE.UU.?

3 Muy importante
2 Algo importante
1 No importante

L12.B hablar bien en inglés?

3 Muy importante
2 Algo importante
1 No importante

L12.C ser blanco(a)?

3 Muy importante
2 Algo importante
1 No importante

L12.D ser Cristiano(a)?

3 Muy importante
2 Algo importante
1 No importante

L13. ¿Cuál piensa que es el problema más importante que el país est enfrentando ahora? (NO LEA LAS RESPUESTAS POSIBLES)

1	La economía	11	Inmigración ilegal
2	Desempleo / trabajos	12	Acción afirmativa
3	Educación / escuelas públicas	13	Asistencia Social ["Welfare"] / Reforma a la Asistencia Social
4	Crimen		
5	Drogas	14	Medio ambiente
6	Cuidado de la salud	15	Sistema político / corrupción /escándalo
7	Relaciones entre las razas	16	Política exterior / Preocupaciones
8	Valores / Valores de la familia / Moralidad	17	Aborto
		18	Guerra en Iraq
9	Déficit del presupuesto	19	Alguna otra cosa
10	Social Security / cuidado de gente mayor	20	NS/RF

L14. ¿Qué partido político usted piensa que tiene el mejor método para enfrentar a este problema? ¿Diría que es . . . el Republicano o el Demócrata, o ninguno de los partidos es mejor que el otro?

1 Republicano
2 Demócrata
3 Ninguno de los partidoses mejor que el otro
4 NS/RF

L15. ¿Cuál piensa que es el problema más importante que la comunidad latina está enfrentando hoy en dia? [NO LEA LAS RESPUESTAS POSIBLES]

OPEN ENDED RESPONSE

1 La economía	11 Inmigración ilegal
2 Desempleo / trabajos	12 Acción afirmativa
3 Educación / escuelas públicas	13 Asistencia Social ["Welfare"] / Reforma a la Asistencia Social
4 Crimen	
5 Drogas	14 Medio ambiente
6 Cuidado de la salud	15 Sistema político / corrupción /escándalo
7 Relaciones entre las razas	16 Política exterior / Preocupaciones
8 Valores / Valores de la familia / Moralidad	17 Aborto
	18 Guerra en Iraq
9 Déficit del presupuesto	19 Alguna otra cosa
10 Social Security / cuidado de gente mayor	20 NS/RF

L16. ¿Qué partido político usted piensa que tiene el mejor método para enfrentar al problema que usted ha identificado? ¿Diría que es . . .

1 Republicano
2 Demócrata
3 Ninguno de los partidos es mejor que el otro
4 NS/RF

L17. ¿Usted piensa que la policía en su comunidad trata imparcialmente a los latinos?

1 Si
2 No
3 No sabe

L18. ¿Ha sido usted alguna vez víctima de un crimen en este país?

1 Si
2 No
3 NS/Rehusa

L19. ¿Era la persona quién lo perpetró hispano, blanco (Anglo Americano), negro (Afro Americano), o no sabe?

1 Negra
2 Blanca
3 Hispana
4 Otra
5 No sabe

Social Ideology/Social Policy

L20. Le voy a hacer preguntas acerca de asuntos de la administración nacional. Por favor dígame, ¿qué tan fuertemente usted apoya o se opone a las siguientes políticas? Su respuesta puede ser: apoya fuertemente, apoya, se opone, o se opone fuertemente. Si usted no está seguro(a) de qué siente o si no sabe, por favor dígamelo. Comencemos con . . . (REPEAT RESPONSE CHOICES AS NEEDED)

L20.A Mantener a las tropas de EE.UU. en Irak por tanto tiempo como sea necesario para estabilizar su gobierno.

4 Apoya fuertemente

3   Apoya

2   Opone

1   Opone fuertemente

5   No está seguro(a) / NS

L20.B "El gobierno debería proporcionar apoyo monetario a quienes lo necesitan."

4   Apoya fuertemente

3   Apoya

2   Opone

1   Opone fuertemente

5   No está seguro(a) / NS

L20.C "El sistema actual de cuidado de la salud necesita la intervención del gobierno para mejorar el acceso y reducir costos."

4   Apoya fuertemente

3   Apoya

2   Opone

1   Opone fuertemente

5   No está seguro(a) / NS

L20.D "A los inmigrantes indocumentados que asisten a la universidad deberían cobrarles un matrícula más alta en los colegios y universidades del estado, aún si ellos crecieron y se graduaron de una escuela secundaria en el estado."

4   Apoya fuertemente

3   Apoya

2   Opone

1   Opone fuertemente

5   No está seguro(a) / NS

The remaining items (e) through (j) are split sample items in which one-half of the respondents are asked the questions.

L20.E "Uso de matrícula consular-como identificación producida por países extranjeros-como una forma aceptable de identificación para los inmigrantes en los EE.UU."

4   Apoya fuertemente

3   Apoya

2   Opone

1   Opone fuertemente

5   No está seguro(a) / NS

L20.F "Uso de exámenes estandarizados para determinar si un niño es promovido al próximo grado o si se gradúa de la escuela secundaria."

4   Apoya fuertemente

3   Apoya

2   Opone

1   Opone fuertemente

5   No está seguro(a) / NS

L20.G Split sample (NOTE: THIS SHOULD BE ASKED OF ALL IN TX)
"Asignar fondos a la educación pública para que todos los distritos escolares tengan casi la misma cantidad de dinero para gastar por cada estudiante."

4   Apoya fuertemente
3   Apoya
2   Opone
1   Opone fuertemente
5   No está seguro(a) / NS

L20.H "Proporcionar vales (o lo que se dice en inglés 'vouchers') para la escuela para pagar una porción del costo de enviar a niños a escuelas privadas."

4   Apoya fuertemente
3   Apoya
2   Opone
1   Opone fuertemente
5   No está seguro(a) / NS

L20.I "Reemplazar la instrucción bilingüe multi-anual en las escuelas con instrucción solo en inglés después de un año de instrucción."

4   Apoya fuertemente
3   Apoya
2   Opone
1   Opone fuertemente
5   No está seguro(a) / NS

L20.J "El gobierno debería proporcionar apoyo monetario a quienes tratan de mantenerse por sí mismos, pero no pueden hacerlo adecuadamente."

4   Apoya fuertemente
3   Apoya
2   Opone
1   Opone fuertemente
5   No está seguro(a) / NS

L21. Cuál es su percepción de parejas del mismo sexo? Debería serles permitido . . . ?

1   Casarse legalmente
2   Formar uniones civiles
3   No deben recibir reconocimiento legal
4   No tiene opinión/NA

L22. En términos generales, usted piensa que el aborto debería ser . . . ?

1   Legal en todas las circunstancias
2   Legal en la mayoría de las circunstancias
3   Legal solamente cuando es necesario para salvar la vida de la mujer o en casos de la violación o incesto.
4   Ilegal en todas las circunstancias
5   No está seguro(a)

L23. ¿Están los siguientes servicios del gobierno disponibles en español en su comunidad? Responda "si" o "no" para cada tipo de servicio.

L23.A Servicios sociales incluyendo clínicas u hospitales para la salud pública.

1   Si
2   No
3   NS
4   REF/NA

L23.B Policía o cumplimiento de la ley, cortes/representación legal.

1   Si
2   No
3   NS
4   REF/NA

L23.C Información en las escuelas públicas.

1   Si
2   No
3   NS
4   REF/NA

SPLIT SAMPLE A/B

L24A. Observando las condiciones en su barrio, ¿qué tan impactado está su barrio hoy por polución, desechos tóxicos, basurales?

4   Muy impactado
3   Algo impactado
2   No muy impactado
1   Nada impactado
5   NS/Reh

L24B. ¿Usted cree que es más probable, igualmente probable, o menos probable, que la polución, desechos tóxicos, etc. sean ubicados en barrios con minorías?

4   Muy impactado
3   Algo impactado
2   No muy impactado
1   Nada impactado
5   NS/Reh

L25. ¿Cuál de estas frases está más cerca a sus propias ideas?

1   Los inmigrantes hoy fortalecen nuestro país debido a su trabajo duro y talentos.
2   Los inmigrantes hoy son una carga en nuestro país porque toman nuestros trabajos, cubierta, y cuidado médico.

L26. ¿Cuál es su política preferida en cuanto a la inmigración ilegal o indocumentada? ¿Debería de haber . . . ? (READ RESPONSES)

1   Legalización inmediata de los inmigrantes indocumentados actuales
2   Un programa de trabajadores invitados encaminados eventualmente a la legalización
3   Un programa de trabajadores invitados que les permite a los inmigrantes estar en el país, pero solo temporariamente
4   Un esfuerzo para cerrar la frontera para detener la inmigración ilegal
5   Ninguno de éstos

L27. Cada vez más, los nuevos inmigrantes mexicanos se han radicado en Nuevo México. ¿Son las relaciones entre hispanos nacidos aquí y los inmigrantes generalmente . . . ? (LEE LA LISTA)

1   Positivas
2   Negativas
3   Ni positivas ni negativas
4   (AMBAS)

L28. ¿Apoya usted limitaciones al acceso de inmigrantes indocumentados a nuestros programas de servicio social del estado [por ejemplo clases educativas para adultos, matrícula universitaria en el estado y cuidado de niños con subsidio?]

    5   Apoya fuertemente
    4   Apoya un poco
    3   Ni apoya ni se opone
    2   Se opone un poco
    1   Se opone fuertemente

L29. Una enmienda constitucional propuesta para hacer que el inglés sea el idioma oficial para nuestro Estado estará en el boleto para votar en 2006.

    5   Apoya fuertemente
    4   Apoya un poco
    3   Ni apoya ni se opone
    2   Se opone un poco
    1   Se opone fuertemente

L30. Recientemente, varios grupos opuestos al número de inmigrantes indocumentados que vienen a los EE.UU. ha enviado gente a hacer patrullas en la frontera. ¿Cuál de lo siguientes se acerca más a lo que usted piensa? ¿Usted piensa que estas acciones . . . ? (RANDOMIZE ORDER OF OPTIONS)

    1   Ha mejorado el control de la frontera
    2   Ha hecho poca diferencia en el control de la frontera
    3   Ha creado más hostilidad hacia los inmigrantes
    4   Ha creado más hostilidad hacia todos los latinos
    5   No tiene opinión
    6   No le interesa

M1. ¿Qué tan seguido se pone usted en contacto con amigos y familiares en (Respuesta a la pregunta B4)?

    1   Una vez por semana o más
    2   Una vez por mes o más
    3   Una vez cada varios meses
    4   Nunca
    5   NS/NA

M2. Desde que usted vino a los EE.UU., ¿qué tan seguido ha regresado a (Respuesta a la pregunta B4)?

    1   Una vez por semana o más
    2   Una vez por mes o más
    3   Una vez cada varios meses
    4   Nunca
    5   NS/NA

M3. ¿Ha usted alguna vez regresado para vivir allí (en lugar de solo visitar) por una porcion de tiempo?

    1   Si
    2   No
    3   NS/NA

M5. ¿Por cuánto tiempo piensa que se quedará en los EE.UU.?

2   Menos de cinco años
3   Tanto como pueda
4   Hasta que me jubile
5   Toda mi vida
6   Otro

M6. ¿Es usted dueño(a) de tierra, una casa o un negocio en (Respuesta a la pregunta B4)?

1   Si, tierra
2   Si, casa
3   Si, negocio
4   No
5   NS/NA

M7. ¿Qué tan seguido va a visitar a (Respuesta a la pregunta B4)?

1   Más de una vez por año
2   Una vez por año
3   Una vez en los últimos tres años
4   Una vez en los últimos cinco años
5   Hace más de cinco años
6   Nunca
7   NS/NA

M8. ¿Usted tiene planes para regresar a (Respuesta a la pregunta B4) para vivir allí permanentemente?

1   Si
2   No
3   NS
4   NA

M9. ¿Qué tan seguido usted envía dinero a (Respuesta a la pregunta B4)?

1   Más de una vez por mes
2   Una vez por mes
3   Una vez cada unos pocos meses
4   Una vez por año
5   Menos de una vez por año
6   Nunca
7   NS/NA

M10. ¿Cuál es el monto promedio que usted envía cada vez? (RECORD EXACT DOLLAR AMOUNT OR BEST ESTIMATE) (DO NOT ACCEPT A RANGE, REFUSED = 99999)

_____monto promedio

M11. ¿Usted participa en las actividades de un club, asociación o federación conectada a la ciudad o provincia de donde su familia vino, en (Respuesta a la pregunta B4)?

1   Si
2   No
3   NS/NA

M12. ¿Cuánta atención usted diría que presta a la política en (Repuesta a la pregunta B4)? ¿Diría que presta mucha atención, algo de atención, poca atención, o nada?

1   Mucha
2   Algo
3   Poca
4   Nada
5   NS/NA

M13. Antes de venir a los EE.UU., ¿votó alguna vez en elecciones en (Respuesta a la pregunta B4)?

1   Si
2   No
3   No sabe
4   NA

M14. ¿Ha votado alguna vez en elecciones de (Respuesta a la pregunta B4) desde que ha estado en los EE.UU.?

1   Si
2   No
3   No sabe
4   NA

M15. ¿Usted votó desde los EE.UU., o en (Respuesta a la pregunta B4)?

1   Desde los EE.UU.
2   EN (Respuesta a la pregunta B4)

M16. Desde que vino a los EE.UU., ¿ha contribuido dinero a un candidato o partido en su país de origen?

1   Si
2   No
3   NS/Rehusa

M17. Antes de venir a los EE.UU., ¿qué tan activo(a) estaba usted en un partido político, una organización política, o en cualquier otros tipos de organizaciones tal como sindicatos laborales, organizaciones estudiantiles u organizaciones de paramilitares?

5   Muy activo(a)
4   Algo activo(a)
3   Un(a) miembro pero no activo(a)
2   Nada activo(a)
1   Nunca se unió
6   Rehusa

M19. Algunas personas creen que es apropiado que los (Respuesta a la pregunta B4C) que viven en los EE.UU. puedan votar en elecciones nacionales de (Respuesta a la pregunta B4) desde los EE.UU. ¿Usted estaría fuertemente de acuerdo, algo de acuerdo, algo en desacuerdo, o fuertemente en desacuerdo, o no ha pensado mucho acerca de eso?

5   Fuertemente de acuerdo
4   Algo de acuerdo
3   NS/ no ha pensado acerca de eso
2   Algo en desacuerdo
1   Fuertemente en desacuerdo

N1. Para las siguientes preguntas, por favor indique cuánto usted está de acuerdo con cada frase:

N1.A ¿La gente pobre puede avanzar en los EE.UU. si trabajan duro?

4   Fuertemente de acuerdo
3   Algo de acuerdo
2   Algo en desacuerdo
1   Fuertemente en desacuerdo
5   NS

N1.B ¿Los latinos pueden avanzar en los EE.UU. si trabajan duro?

4   Fuertemente de acuerdo
3   Algo de acuerdo
2   Algo en desacuerdo
1   Fuertemente en desacuerdo
5   NS

N2. En las siguientes preguntas estamos interesados en saber lo que usted cree acerca del modo en que otra gente lo(a) ha tratado a usted [IF FOREIGN BORN ADD THE INTRODUCTION: EN LOS EE.UU.] ¿Alguna vez ha usted . . .

N2.A sido despedido(a) de su trabajo o negado un trabajo o promoción injustamente?

1   Si
2   No
3   NS/NA

N2.B sido tratado injustamente por la policía?

1   Si
2   No
3   NS/NA

N2.C sido injustamente prevenido de mudarse a una vecindad o barrio porque el administrador o el agente de inmuebles rehusaba venderle o alquilarle una casa o apartamento?

1   Si
2   No
3   NS/NA

N2.D sido tratado(a) injustamente o malamente en restaurantes o tiendas?

1   Si
2   No
3   NS/NA

N3. Hay muchos motivos posibles por los que la gente podría ser tratada injustamente. ¿Cuál piensa usted que fue el motivo principal para su(s) experiencia(s)? ¿Diría que fue por . . . ? (LEE LA LISTA):

1   Ser latino
2   Ser un inmigrante
3   Su país de origen
4   Su idioma o acento
5   El color de su piel
6   Su sexo
7   Su edad
8   Otro
9   NS/NA

N4. En el incidente más reciente que usted experimentó, ¿cuál era la raza o etnicidad de la(s) persona(s) que lo(a) trataron injustamente?

1 Blanco
2 Negro
3 Asiático
4 Latino
5 NS/NA

FOR RESIDENTS OF FLORIDA

IF RESPONSE TO QUESTION B4 IS 6 (CUBA) CONTINUE

N4b. ¿Estaría usted de acuerdo con que los EE.UU. re-establezcan relaciones diplomáticas con Cuba bajo una de las siguientes condiciones?

1 Si, bajo las circunstancias actuales
2 Si, cuando Fidel se haya ido, pero el régimen persiste
3 Si, solo despues de que el comunismo se haya ido
4 No tiene opinión
5 No sabe

N4c. ¿Que diría si Cuba cambiara a una forma de gobierno democrático? ¿Qué probabilidad habría de que usted regrese a Cuba para vivir? ¿Diría que es muy probable, algo probable, no muy probable, o nada probable?

4 Muy probable
3 Algo probable
2 No muy probable
1 Nada probable

ASK ONLY OF CUBANS IN FLORIDA (DO NOT ASK NON-CUBANS IN THIS STATE)

N4d. ¿Qué piensa acerca de los recientes cambios en las políticas federales que limitan los viajes y los envíos a miembros de la familia en Cuba?

5 Fuertemente de acuerdo
4 Ligeramente de acuerdo
3 Ni de acuerdo ni en desacuerdo
2 Ligeramente en desacuerdo
1 Fuertemente en desacuerdo

N5. ¿Cuál de lo siguientes describe mejor el ingreso total ganado por todos los miembros de su hogar durante el año 2004?

1 Menos de $15,000
2 $15,000 - 24,999
3 $25,000 - 34,999
4 $35,000 - 44,999
5 $45,000 - 54,999
6 $55,000 - 64,999
7 $65,000 o más
8 Rehusa

N6. ¿Cuántas personas trabajan para contribuir a este ingreso combinado? (RECORD EXACT NUMBER OF PEOPLE, REFUSED = 99)

_____ Número de personas

N7. ¿Cuántas personas son actualmente mantenidas por este ingreso combinado? (RECORD EXACT NUMBER OF PEOPLE, REFUSED = 99)

_____ Número de personas mantenidas por este ingreso combinado

N8. ¿Usted recibe ahora o ha recibido alguna vez algún tipo de asistencia del gobierno?

   1   Recibe ahora
   2   Recibió en el pasado
   3   Nunca recibió
   4   NA/NS

FIN

About the Contributors

Tony Affigne is Professor of Political Science and Black Studies at Providence College and was previously Visiting Professor of American Studies at Brown University. He holds a doctorate from Brown University and a master's in public administration from the University of Rhode Island. In 1995, he was cofounder of the American Political Science Association (APSA) research section on Race, Ethnicity, and Politics (REP), in 1998 helped found the Latino Caucus in Political Science / El Sector Latino de Ciencia Política, and served for three years as chair of APSA's Fund for Latino Scholarship. He serves on the board of the Rhode Island Latino Political Action Committee (RILPAC) and in 1992 founded the Green Party of Rhode Island / Partido Verde de Rhode Island. He currently serves as the party's state committee chair.

Manny Avalos is Professor of Political Science in the Department of Public and International Affairs at the University of North Carolina Wilmington (UNCW). He received his Ph.D. in political science from the University of New Mexico and did postdoctoral work at the Center for Mexican American Studies at the University of Texas at Austin. His publications have appeared in *Sociological Perspectives*, *Harvard Journal of Hispanic Policy*, and *Policy Studies Journal* and as chapters in several edited volumes by Rodolfo de la Garza and Louis DeSipio examining the impact of the Latino vote on presidential elections.

Matt A. Barreto is Associate Professor of Political Science at the University of Washington, Seattle, and the director of the Washington Institute for the Study of Ethnicity and Race. Barreto is a founding principal of Latino Decisions. He received his Ph.D. in political science from the University of California, Irvine, in 2005. His research has been published in the *American Political Science Review*, *Political Research Quarterly*, *Social Science Quarterly*, *Public Opinion Quarterly*, and other peer-reviewed journals. He is the author of the book *Ethnic Cues: The Role of Shared Ethnicity in Latino Political Behavior* (2010) and has just finished a book manuscript coauthored with Christopher Parker, *Change We Can't Believe In: Exploring the Sources and Consequences of Tea Party Support* (2012).

Regina Branton is Associate Professor of Political Science at the University of North Texas. She holds a Ph.D. in political science from the University of Arizona, an M.A. in political science from the University of Wyoming, and a B.A. in political science from the University of South Carolina. She has published articles in the *Journal of Politics*, the *American Journal of Political Science*, *Political Research Quarterly*, and other journals. She is currently a member of the editorial board of the *Journal of Politics*, a member of the State Politics and Policy section for APSA, the WPSA executive council, and the president of the MPSA Latino Caucus.

Ana Franco is a first-year doctoral student in the Political Science Department at Stanford University, where she is also a graduate fellow at the Center for Comparative Studies in Race and Ethnicity. She holds a bachelor of arts in political science and a bachelor of science in psychology from the University of Texas–Pan American. As a research associate at the Center for Survey Research at UTPA, she worked on projects examining the role of acculturation and descriptive representation in shaping Latino public opinion and trust, the impact of ethnic context and intergroup contact on immigration attitudes, and media influence on student identity and mobilization. Her current research interests are in racial and ethnic politics, the psychology of political behavior, and political methodology.

Katrina Gamble, Ph.D., is Political Director for the Leadership Center for the Common Good, a national organization that provides training and support to grassroots organizations in seventeen states. Prior to arriving at Common Good, she was Assistant Professor of Political Science at Brown University, where she worked with the Center for Study of Race and Ethnicity in America and served on the Gender and Sexuality Studies Concentration Board. Her work on race and political representation can be found in journals such as *Polity*, *Legislative Studies Quarterly*, and *PS: Political Science and Politics*.

John A. García is Research Professor and Director of Community Outreach at the Inter-university Consortium for Political (Institute for Social Research–ISR at the University of Michigan), as well as Faculty Associate in the Center for Political Studies. In addition, he directs the Resource Center for Minority Data (ICPSR). Dr. García has held a professorship in the School of Government and Public Policy at the University of Arizona for thirty-seven years. He received his Ph.D. in government at Florida State University (1971). He has published eleven books and over sixty articles and book chapters.

Sarah Allen Gershon is Assistant Professor in the Political Science Department at Georgia State University. She received her Ph.D. from Arizona State University in 2008. She has published articles in the *Journal of Politics*, *Political Research Quarterly*, *Political Communication*, the *Journal of Women, Politics & Policy*, *Social Science Quarterly*, the *Journal of Ethnic and Migration Studies*, and the *International Journal of Press/Politics*. She has also contributed chapters to the edited volumes *Latinas/os in the United States: Changing the Face of América* and *The Promise of Welfare Reform: Political Rhetoric and the Reality of Poverty in the Twenty-First Century*.

Evelyn Hu-DeHart is Professor of History, Ethnic Studies, and American Studies and was previously Director of the Center for the Study of Race and Ethnicity in America at Brown University. She joined Brown from the University of Colorado at Boulder, where she was Chair of the Department of Ethnic Studies and Director of the Center for Studies of Ethnicity and Race in America. At Brown University and previously at the University of Colorado at Boulder, Hu-DeHart has been most prominently associated with the development of the academic field of ethnic studies, of which Latino studies is an important component. Trained as a historian of Latin America and the Caribbean, her own research focuses on Asians in the Americas, including the construction of Asian-Latinos.

Jessica Lavariega Monforti is Associate Professor of Political Science and Senior Faculty Research Associate at the Center for Survey Research at the University of Texas–Pan American. Her recent publications include articles in *Social Science Quarterly*, the *Social Science Journal*, *PS: Political Science*, the *Latino/a Research Review*, *Camino Real*, and the *Journal of Women, Politics & Policy*. She also edited a book with William E. Nelson, Jr., titled *Black and Latino/a Politics: Issues in Political Development in the United States*.

Melissa R. Michelson is Professor of Political Science at Menlo College. She received her B.A. in political science from Columbia University in 1990 and her Ph.D. from Yale University in 1994. She is coauthor with Lisa García Bedolla of *Mobilizing Inclusion: Redefining Citizenship through Get-Out-the-Vote Campaigns* (2012). She has published thirty articles in peer-reviewed academic journals and a dozen chapters in edited volumes, including recent pieces in the *Election Law Journal*, the *Quarterly Journal of Political Science*, and *Political Behavior*.

Domingo Morel is a Ph.D. candidate in the Department of Political Science at Brown University. His research interests are in the fields of American politics and political theory with a focus on race and ethnic, urban, and education politics. His dissertation focuses on state takeovers of local school districts to examine how state intervention affects Black and Latino political empowerment. Morel is cofounder and cochair of the Latino Policy Institute at Roger Williams University and previously served as an adjunct faculty member in the Africana Studies Department at the University of Rhode Island.

Marion Orr is the Frederick Lippitt Professor of Public Policy, Professor of Political Science and Urban Studies, and Director of the Taubman Center for Public Policy at Brown University. He is the author and editor of five books including *Black Social Capital: The Politics of School Reform in Baltimore*. He is the editor of *Transforming the City: Community Organizing and the Challenge of Political Change*. Professor Orr has held a number of fellowships, including an appointment as Research Fellow at the Brookings Institution, a Presidential Fellowship from the University of California, Berkeley, and a fellowship from the Ford Foundation.

Adrian D. Pantoja is Professor in Political Studies and Chicano Studies at Pitzer College, a member of the Claremont Colleges. He is also a Senior Analyst with Latino Decisions, a political polling firm surveying and analyzing the Latino electorate. He received his B.A. from the University of San Francisco and Ph.D. in political science from the Claremont Graduate University in 2001. His research has appeared in numerous books and academic journals, including *Political Research Quarterly*, *Political Behavior*, and *Social Science*. He has offered expert commentary on Latino politics to various media outlets, including the *New York Times*, the *Washington Times*, the *Christian Science Monitor*, the *Arizona Republic*, and *La Opinion*.

Gabriel R. Sanchez is Associate Professor of Political Science at the University of New Mexico and Interim Executive Director of the Robert Wood Johnson Foundation Center for Health Policy at the University of New Mexico. He is Director of Research for Latino Decisions. Sanchez received his Ph.D. in political science from the University of Arizona. His work has been published in a wide range of journals, including *Political Research Quarterly*, *Social Science Quarterly*, *American Politics Research*, and other peer-reviewed outlets. Professor Sanchez is also a coauthor of *Hispanics and the U.S. Political System* (2008) and editor of *The Latino Vote in the 2012 Election* (2013).

Heather Silber Mohamed is Assistant Professor of Political Science at Clark University. She received her Ph.D. and M.A. from Brown University, where she also worked as a Visiting Lecturer. She holds an M.Sc. from the London School of Economics and a B.A. from Tufts University. Before completing her Ph.D., she worked for six years as a legislative aide in the U.S. Congress, including three years for the late Senator Edward M. Kennedy (D-MA). Most recently, her work on identity and the 2006 immigration protests was published in *American Politics Research* and featured in the *Boston Globe*.

Atiya Kai Stokes-Brown is Associate Professor in the Department of Political Science at Bucknell University. She received her Ph.D. in political science from the University of Maryland, College Park, in 2004. She is the author of *The Politics of Race in Latino Communities: Walking the Color Line* (2012), and her work has appeared in numerous journals including the *Journal of Politics*, *American Politics Research*, *Politics and Policy*, and *Social Science Quarterly*.

Robert Wrinkle is Professor of Political Science and Director of the Center for Survey Research at the University of Texas–Pan American. He holds a Ph.D. from the University of Arizona. He is the coauthor of *Electoral Structure and Urban Policy* and *American Government, Policy, and Non-decisions*. He has published in the *American Journal of Political Science*, the *Journal of Politics*, and *Political Research Quarterly*, as well as in a number of other journals.

Index